Immigration

CQ's Vital Issues Series

Immigration

Ann Chih Lin, editor

Nicole W. Green, author

CQ PRESS

A Division of Congressional Quarterly Inc.

WASHINGTON, D.C.

CQ Press
1255 22nd St. N.W., Suite 400
Washington, D.C. 20037

(202) 729-1900; toll-free, 1-866-4CQ-PRESS (1-866-427-7737)

www.cqpress.com

Printed in the United States of America
06 05 04 03 02   5 4 3 2 1

Grateful acknowledgment is made to the following for granting permission to reprint material: CQ Press, *The CQ Researcher* (July 14, 2000): "Debate Over Immigration," by David Masci.

Cover design: Debra Naylor

♾ The paper used in this publication meets the minimum requirements of the
American National Standard for Information Sciences—Permanence of Paper for
Printed Library Materials, ANSI Z39.48-1992.

Library of Congress Cataloging-in-Publication Data

Lin, Ann Chih
  Immigration / Ann Chih Lin, editor; Nicole W. Green, author.
    p.   cm. -- (CQ's vital issues series)
  Includes bibliographical references and index.
    ISBN 1-56802-662-5 (cloth : alk. paper) -- ISBN 1-56802-661-7 (pbk. :
alk. paper)
    1. United States—Emigration and immigration —Government policy. 2.
United States —Emigration and immigration—History.   3.
Terrorism—Prevention.   I. Green, Nicole W., II. Title. III.
Series.
JV6483 .L56 2002
325.73—dc21
                                                                    2002008175

Contents

Preface   VII

Introduction   IX

1. **Issues, Viewpoints, and Trends** / *The CQ Researcher* Immigration Update   **1**

The Issues   1

Background   17

Outlook   23

Notes   28

Bibliography   29

2. **Politics and Policy**   **37**

Who Comes to the United States?:

    The Characteristics of American Immigration   40

Closed Door, Open Door: The IIRIRA and Immigration Enforcement   58

Immigration: Understanding and Evaluating

    Its Impact on the United States   76

The Response to Terrorism: Changing Immigration Policy   100

Conclusion   111

Notes   112

3. **Agencies, Organizations, and Individuals**   **122**

Important Governmental Agencies and Actors   123

Nongovernmental Actors   128

International Organizations   149

Notes   154

4. International Implications   155

Comparing Countries of Immigration: United States and Canada   156

Mexico–U.S. Relations   164

Converging Policy Models: A Comparative Analysis of
U.S. and European Immigration Policies   180

The U.S. Role in International Refugee Law and Policy   187

Notes   193

Appendix   199

Further Research and Chronology   201

Bibliography of Book Sources   201

Bibliography of Journal and Report Sources   203

Bibliography of News Sources   206

Bibliography of Internet Sources   210

Chronology   212

Primary Documents   216

Convention Relating to the Status of Refugees (1951)   216

Protocol Relating to the Status of Refugees (1967)   230

Immigration and Nationality Act of 1952   234

Illegal Immigration Reform and Immigrant Responsibility Act of 1996
(Public Law 104-208)   242

Treaty on European Union (1993)   247

California Proposition 187 (1994)   250

North American Free Trade Agreement (1994)   255

AFL-CIO Executive Council Actions (2000)   260

U.S.–Mexico Migration: Joint Communiqué (2001)   263

Supreme Court Decision in *Zadvydas v. Davis* (2001)   268

The Smart Border Declaration and Action Plan (2001)   272

Index   279

Preface

CQ Press is pleased to present CQ's Vital Issues Series, a new reference collection that provides unparalleled, unbiased analyses of controversial topics debated at local, state, and federal levels. The series covers all sides of issues equally, delving into the topics that dominate the media, shape election-year politics, and confront the American public. Each book includes portions from *The CQ Researcher* that introduce the subject; in-depth explanations of relevant politics, policy, and political actors; analyses of major for-profit and nonprofit business interests; and discussion of international reaction to how the United States handles the issue. In addition, each volume features extensive appendixes to aid in further research. Titles in the series include *Welfare Reform, Capital Punishment,* and *Immigration.* We believe CQ's Vital Issues Series is an exceptional research tool, and we would like your feedback. Please send your comments to VIfeedback@cqpress.com.

Introduction

This volume in CQ's Vital Issues Series exemplifies our commitment to combine the timely analysis of policy developments with the background information that helps to put recent events in context. After the tragedies of September 11, 2001, it was clear that immigration policy was about to undergo dramatic change. Unlike the terrorism of the 1995 Oklahoma City bombing, the destruction and loss of lives at the World Trade Center and the Pentagon were linked to foreign nationals, many of whom had entered the country legally. Although technically the bombers were not "immigrants," or permanent migrants to the United States, the Immigration and Naturalization Service (INS) came under intense scrutiny. Long-time critics of the agency took center stage with their proposals for reorganizing the INS. Meanwhile, policies ranging from the management of U.S. borders to procedures for screening immigrants were reexamined.

This volume was slated for publication in fall 2001. But all who were involved in the book agreed that we were committed to updating it to reflect the rapidly changing policy environment. As a result, this book contains information as recent as May 2002. The proposed reorganization of the INS, the changes in border security, the shift in the immigration debate from economic to security concerns, and the apprehension that many immigrants felt after September 11 are but some of the many important developments added to this text. In addition, everything from the organizational profiles in Chapter 3 to the discussion of ebbs and flows in immigration policy now reflects the impact of recent events.

At the same time, we are proud of the fact that this book, as with other titles in the Vital Issues Series, provides careful thought and thorough knowledge as well as up-to-date coverage. The constant motor of U.S. immigration policy has been the economy, and even today's security-conscious policy-makers have not forgotten this. Thus this volume discusses the economic, social, and political implications of immigration; provides a comprehensive look at the politics and policy developments of the last decade; describes the most important business, nonprofit, and political actors that influence the debate; and places U.S. policy in an international context. For those new to the subject, a Vital Issues book provides all the necessary background in a readable and accessible format. For those already acquainted with the topic, a Vital Issues volume is a reference for the facts on different aspects of the issues, for analyses of how those aspects fit together, and for further sources of information.

Each of the three books in the series so far—*Capital Punishment, Welfare Reform,* and this volume, *Immigration*—follows a format designed to make research and understanding as easy as possible. The first chapter of each book, "Issues, Viewpoints, and Trends," is a lively, succinct, and balanced account of the current policy debate. Reprinted from portions of *The CQ Researcher,* this section of the book is a primer for the novice. The second chapter, "Politics and Policy," presents a thorough look at policymaking and implementation. What have been the major developments of the past decade? How have debates at the level of policy formulation been translated into policy on the ground? This section of the book pays particular attention to variations at the state and local levels: a Vital Issues book gives the reader not only the story from Washington, D.C., but also an account of innovations around the country and a summary, when appropriate, of what each state's experience has been.

The third chapter, "Agencies, Organizations, and Individuals," explains the specific role that business, nonprofit, and political actors play in shaping—and continuing to shape—policy developments. Sketches of important organizations and their contributions are included, along with contact information and Web site references to allow the reader to do further research. The final chapter, "International Implications," draws attention to the international context of our policy debates. Often Americans forget that our policies affect and are affected by events and policies in other countries and ignore the experience of other nations in struggling with similar problems. One of the distinctive contributions of the Vital Issues Series is that it summarizes this international context, reporting accurately but simply on the major worldwide trends, comparisons, and reactions that Americans need to know to make good policy at home.

As the United States continues to adjust to the new and sobering realities of the world we live in, we may find ourselves, more self-consciously than before, speaking both as interested individuals with differing points of view and as citizens with a responsibility to our common life. It is our hope that CQ's Vital Issues Series will provide the information and perspective necessary to have these conversations. Whether you are a student educating yourself for a class or an activity, a journalist explaining the news to your readers, an activist looking for background about your cause, or a citizen concerned about the policies of your country, this series is for you. Let us know if we have been successful.

Ann Chih Lin
University of Michigan

1 | Issues, Viewpoints, and Trends

The CQ Researcher Immigration Update

More than one million immigrants enter the United States, legally and illegally, each year. Many experts credit the new arrivals with helping to create and sustain the nation's current economic prosperity. But others argue that although immigration gives employers access to a cheap and plentiful labor force, American workers suffer because the newcomers take jobs and suppress wage levels. Critics of the current policies call for stricter limits on immigration and a crackdown on U.S. employers who knowingly hire undocumented workers. But supporters of liberal immigration policies warn that severely limiting legal immigration will hurt the economy and that, in any event, employer sanctions are not effective.

The Issues

Hail a taxi, drop off dry cleaning, buy a lottery ticket at the local 7-Eleven. Chances are good that an immigrant from Ghana, South Korea, Mexico, or some other far-away nation served you. Indeed, there is a good chance programmers from India or China wrote some of the software in your computer.

Across the country, in towns and cities alike, the United States, more than ever before, is a nation of immigrants.

"It's amazing how things have changed since the 1970s, how many people there now are in this country who were not born here," says Steven Moore, an economist at the Cato Institute, a libertarian think tank.

This article was written by David Masci for *The CQ Researcher* (July 14, 2000): 569–592.

In the last thirty years the United States has absorbed the biggest wave of immigrants since the turn of the century, when millions arrived at Ellis Island in search of a better life. Today, more than twenty-five million Americans are foreign born—nearly 10 percent of the population.[1]

And that is good for the economy, according to Federal Reserve Chairman Alan Greenspan, who says the pools of skilled and unskilled workers created by high levels of immigration have greatly contributed to the nation's prosperity.

"As we are creating an ever more complex, sophisticated, accelerating economy, the necessity to have the ability to bring in . . . people from abroad to keep it functioning in the most effective manner increasingly strikes me as [sound] policy," he told lawmakers on Capitol Hill in February 2000.[2]

Greenspan's comments were just the latest salvo in the continuing debate over immigration, a debate that is older than the country itself. More than 200 years ago, for instance, Benjamin Franklin pronounced recent arrivals from Germany as "the most stupid in the nation. Few of their children speak English, and through their indiscretion or ours, or both, great disorders may one day arise among us."[3]

But to immigration boosters such as Greenspan, immigrants' work ethic and motivation make them cornerstones of America's economic prosperity.

"We're getting a lot of the best and brightest from other countries, and of course these people benefit the U.S. economy because they are driven to improve their lots," says Bronwyn Lance, a senior fellow at the Alexis de Tocqueville Institution, which works to increase understanding of the cultural and economic benefits of legal immigration. Lance and others say immigrants are more likely to start businesses—from corner grocery stores to giant computer companies—than native-born Americans are. Even newcomers with little education aid the economy, immigration boosters say, taking undesirable jobs that employers cannot fill with native-born Americans.

Opponents of expanded immigration counter that the United States does not need a million newcomers each year to ensure a strong economy. Most immigrants are not well-educated entrepreneurs but "poorly educated people who take low-skilled jobs for little money," says Dan Stein, executive director of the Federation for American Immigration Reform (FAIR), which opposes high immigration levels. In Stein's view, immigration largely benefits employers by providing a cheap and plentiful labor force. Moreover, he says, the newcomers take Americans' jobs and suppress wage levels.

Flow of Immigrants Steadily Increased

From 1990 to 1999, about ten million immigrants were legally admitted into the United States, more than in any previous decade since the 1940s and nearly double the number in the 1980s. The total reflects the higher cap on immigrants set by the 1990 Immigration Act and the admittance of large numbers of refugees.

Immigrants Admitted to United States

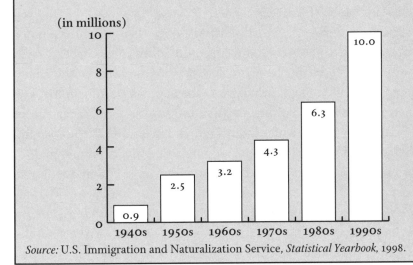

(in millions)

Source: U.S. Immigration and Naturalization Service, *Statistical Yearbook*, 1998.

Immigration opponents also reject the argument that immigrants are willing to do the jobs that most Americans will not do. In parts of the country with few immigrants, low-wage jobs still get done, and by native-born people, says Mark Krikorian, executive director of the Center for Immigration Studies.

"Employers could find Americans to do these jobs if they wanted to, but they'd have to provide training and raise wages to do so," Krikorian says. Immigrants are simply an easier and cheaper alternative for businesses, he and others maintain.

Finally, opponents point out, high immigration levels are overcrowding the United States, especially in urban areas, and preventing immigrants already here from assimilating into American society.

"The way we're going now we won't turn these people into Americans, and without assimilation we will increasingly be beset by ethnic conflicts," says John O'Sullivan, editor-at-large at the conservative *National Review* magazine and a noted expert on immigration.

Still, immigration supporters argue, today's newcomers, such as those who sailed into New York Harbor in the past, come because they want to be Americans.

"We've always been afraid that new immigrants aren't assimilating and becoming American," Moore says. But immigrants are attracted to the United States for more than job opportunities. "America is more than a country, it's an idea with concepts like freedom," he says. "Most new immigrants buy into this idea. That's one of the reasons they want to be here."

Not all immigrants, of course, are here legally. Although there is wide disagreement about how many newcomers the nation should admit, most experts favor taking at least some steps to block the estimated 300,000 or more illegal immigrants who come to the United States annually. Many support beefing up the U.S. Border Patrol, the enforcement arm of the Immigration and Naturalization Service (INS), and some call for greater use of a rarely enforced provision of the 1986 immigration law that punishes employers who knowingly hire illegal immigrants.[4]

Proponents of employer sanctions argue that some form of "internal enforcement" is necessary to catch the thousands who slip by border police. "The way things are right now we're sending a message to illegal aliens that once they get into the country they don't have to worry about getting caught," Krikorian says. This encourages more people to try to enter the U.S. illegally, he says.

Opponents of employer sanctions argue, however, that instead of discouraging illegal aliens, sanctions merely force them to take jobs with employers who are more likely to exploit them.

"In many cases, all we do is push people to take jobs for less pay and with unsafe working conditions," says Cecilia Muñoz, vice president for policy at the National Council of La Raza, the nation's largest Latino advocacy group. Moreover, Muñoz adds, if employer sanctions did work, many businesses, especially in the service sector, would find themselves without workers.

"Many industries rely on [undocumented] labor," she says, pointing out that illegal aliens are ubiquitous on farms and construction sites and other sectors of the economy that depend on low-skilled workers willing to do grimy, often backbreaking labor.

America's Changing Demographics

Fifty years ago, the population of the United States was 89 percent white and 10 percent black. Latinos, Asians, and other minority groups constituted a mere sliver of the demographic pie. Thanks to immigration, everything has changed.

Today, more than one-quarter of Americans are not white—more than double the percentage in 1950. Hispanics now account for 12 percent of the population and are about to surpass African Americans as the nation's largest minority. Asians, although only making up 4 percent of the U.S. population, are the nation's fastest-growing minority group.

Fifty years from now, America will look even more different. According to the U.S. Census Bureau, slightly more than half of the anticipated 400 million residents will be white. Fully one-fourth of the nation will be of Latin American descent. And there will be almost as many Asians as there are African Americans.

Some immigration experts warn, however, that census projections can be misleading. "There are a lot of assumptions built into the data that may not be correct," says Jeff Passel, a demographer for the Urban Institute, a social policy think tank in Washington, D.C. "It's really impossible to know these numbers."

The numbers can get tricky because, for instance, no one knows how many new immigrants will enter the United States in the future. In addition, it is difficult to predict what the birth rates will be among various immigrant groups.

More important, Passel says, the Census Bureau's projections assume that today's racial categories will remain the same. "One hundred years ago," he says, "Americans didn't think of Italians, Jews, and other immigrants from Southern and Eastern Europe as white. Now, obviously they do." Future racial categories may be much broader, incorporating Hispanics and Asians into the same racial group, for instance. "In fifty years people may not make distinctions between, say, Hispanics and whites, just like they don't between Italians and whites today," Passel says.

The blurring of racial distinctions may be nudged along by high rates of intermarriage between new immigrant groups and other Americans. Third-generation Asian Americans marry outside their race more than 40 percent of the time, according to the National Immigration Forum. Similarly, third-generation Latinos marry non-Hispanics about one-third of the time.

"All of this mixing across racial lines is going to make these categories very fuzzy," Passel says, adding that fuzziness will allow these new groups to more easily integrate into American society, just as newcomers a century ago have done today.

But other experts are much more concerned about coming demographic changes. "Our ethnic component is part of what makes the United States what it is, and that's going to be radically altered," says Peter Brimelow, a *Forbes* magazine editor and author of *Alien Nation*, a 1996 book that makes a case against allowing high levels of immigration.

It is foolish, Brimelow contends, to assume that a society that is no longer dominated by one racial group—whites, in the case of the United States—will be able to avoid tremendous tensions. "I don't think multiracial societies work—period," he says. "Our differences are irrepressible."

He fears that a United States with large racial blocks could undergo the same ethnic tensions that have troubled countries like the former Yugoslavia. Some pockets of the country, he says, could diverge so greatly that they will become de facto independent states. "I think parts of the country are going to be as different as different parts of the world are today," Brimelow says.

But many immigration experts say such concerns are unfounded. They believe that new immigrants will do much as their predecessors did—work very hard to become part of American society while retaining pride in their heritage.

"People think that cities like [Los Angeles] are going to be so Mexican that they'll secede from the union," says Frank Sharry, executive director of the National Immigration Forum. "But L.A. is going to be Mexican in the same way that Boston is Irish or Milwaukee is German."

But immigrants are not just an important source of low-skill, low-wage labor. Skilled workers from abroad are also in demand, mainly in the high-technology sector, and controversy is raging over how many should be issued so-called H-1B visas and admitted on a temporary basis. The law in July 2000 permitted up to 115,000 H-1B workers, which employers said was not enough.[5]

Those who favor expanding the H-1B program argue that it is needed to offset the drastic labor shortage facing high-tech companies. They see the importation of highly educated and skilled workers from overseas as an unfortunate but necessary step in their efforts to stay competitive in a fast-changing and cutthroat industry. "Our colleges and universities are gearing up to turn out more people qualified to do this kind of work, and so we don't see [H-1B visas] as a long-term solution," says Harris Miller, president of the Information Technology Association of America (ITAA). "But right now, we simply don't have enough people to fill all of the jobs available."

Norman Matloff, a professor of computer science at the University of California at Davis, challenges that claim. "There are plenty of people right here for these jobs," he says, contending that high-tech firms would rather import well-educated workers from overseas at lower salaries than go to the trouble of recruiting and training Americans.

As the United States enters a new millennium, here are some of the questions being asked in the debate over how many newcomers the United States should admit.

Does the United States admit too many immigrants?

During the 1990s, the United States took in nearly ten million foreigners, almost double the number that came during the 1980s and more than in any previous decade.[6]

For many Americans the large number of newcomers and the prospect of millions more is disquieting. "We've already got gridlock from sea to shining sea," says FAIR's Stein. "So, of course, people are asking themselves how many new people does this country really need?"

But for the Cato Institute's Moore, the surge in immigration has largely been a blessing, one he hopes will continue. "Over the last twenty years, we've let in more than fifteen million people, and it's been a stunning success story," he says.

In fact, Moore and other immigration proponents credit immigrants with playing a key role in the American economy's stellar performance in the past decade. "If we want to keep this phenomenal economic growth rate up," the de Tocqueville Institution's Lance says, "then we'd better keep letting in immigrants because they are helping this economy."

Immigrants aid the economy, Lance and other experts say, because they tend, almost by definition, to be highly motivated and hard working. "This is a self-selected group of people," Moore says, "because the very act of leaving your home country and taking a risk to come here means that you're probably ambitious and likely to succeed."

Indeed, proponents say, studies show that immigrants start more small businesses than the native population. Although many are modest "mom and pop" operations, others are at the leading edge of the new economy. For instance, one out of every four new businesses in Silicon Valley is founded by an entrepreneur of Indian or Chinese origin.[7]

In addition, immigration proponents argue, immigrants are stoking the economic flames by taking hard-to-fill jobs. "Immigrants offer us a ready supply of hard-working people to fill niches in the labor market in vital ways, be it picking crops or making our food, driving taxis, caring for our children or building our buildings," Moore says.

La Raza's Muñoz agrees, adding: "I don't think people realize how many important jobs are done by immigrants and what would happen if they all went away."

What would happen, Muñoz, Moore, and others contend, is that many industries, especially in the growing service sector, would grind to a halt as the people who washed the dishes or cleaned the offices disappeared. "So many important parts of the economy have become very dependent on immigrants," Moore says.

But Stein says there is a downside to importing workers who are mainly poorly educated with few or no skills. "All we're doing is importing a huge pool of cheap labor, which helps employers but keeps wages low for Americans," he says.

The great need, Stein notes, is for people with a lot of education and skills. "Our future lies in improving productivity by providing our own people with training and education, not importing low-wage labor," he says.

Moreover, says the Center for Immigration Studies' Krikorian, immigrants are not irreplaceable in certain segments of the economy. "Anyone who imagines that the fruit won't get picked or that the dishes won't get washed without immigrants has a fundamental misunderstanding of market economics," he says. "All of this service work gets done in the parts of the country where there are few immigrants," he says, "and it's done by Americans. The question isn't whether the work is going to be done, but who's going to do it?"

Krikorian and others say that instead of importing workers to fill vacancies, the United States should be focusing on training the unemployed here. "If we lost immigration as a source of workers, employers would seek to increase the labor pool by increasing wages," he says. "They would also look to communities with higher unemployment rates—more marginal elements of the population—like those on public assistance, ex-convicts or the handicapped."

But opposition to immigration extends beyond its economic impact. Many argue that the nation's population is already too high and that admitting close to one million people annually is going to cause intolerable crowding in some areas. Indeed, the Census Bureau predicts the nation's population will rise from the current level of 270 million to more than 400 million by 2050.

"More than 70 percent of this growth is going to come from immigration," says Tom McKenna, president of Population-Environment Balance, a grassroots organization that advocates population stabilization to protect the environment. "Think

Crackdown Increased Arrests Along Border

The flow of undocumented immigrants across the 2,000-mile U.S.-Mexico border has persisted despite Operation Gatekeeper, a renewed Border Patrol enforcement effort that began in 1994. Apprehensions increased at traditional entry points, such as San Diego and El Paso. But officials say the crackdown has pushed more people to sneak across the border in remote areas.

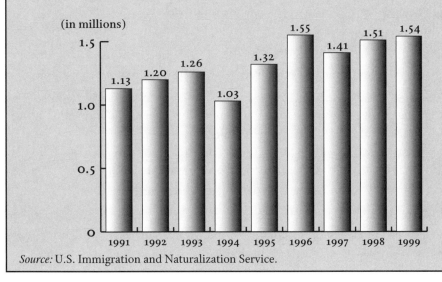

Apprehensions of Undocumented Immigrants

Source: U.S. Immigration and Naturalization Service.

about how crowded our cities are now, and then think about what it will be like with twice the number of people."

Immigration opponents also claim that the nation needs to reduce current immigration levels to allow the nation to absorb the tens of millions of newcomers who are already here. In particular, they say, a steady stream of immigrants will overwhelm efforts to turn recent arrivals into Americans. "When you have these high numbers of people coming in year after year, you can't assimilate them so easily," says the *National Review*'s O'Sullivan.

O'Sullivan contends that a lull in immigration would allow schools and governing institutions to teach immigrants English and give them an appreciation for American history and values. "We are a transnational society, and in order to work together effectively we must maximize our common cultural sympathies," he says.

"If every ethnic group retains its own cultural sympathies, it will be hard for us to work together as one people."

But immigration supporters say that concerns about assimilation are as old as the Republic and just as overblown now as they were in the eighteenth century. "People who come here want to be American," Lance says. "Very few would run the gauntlet to get here unless they wanted to become part of this country."

Lance and others point out that—just as with previous groups—today's immigrants are quickly integrating into American society and losing their ties to their country of origin. "Look at the Hispanic kids who grow up here," she says. "They don't speak Spanish or don't speak it well. They're American now."[8]

In addition, proponents doubt that continued immigration is going to turn the United States into an overcrowded country such as China or India. "The numbers [McKenna] uses assume that the birth rate among immigrants will stay constant for succeeding generations," Muñoz says, noting that recent arrivals have more children than native-born Americans. "But data show that the children of immigrants have far fewer children than their parents."

Should the Immigration and Naturalization Service crack down on employers who knowingly hire illegal immigrants?

Not long ago, the INS conducted a series of raids against undocumented aliens working in the onion fields of Vidalia, Georgia. Within days of the action, five members of the state's congressional delegation—including both U.S. senators—had fired off a letter to Attorney General Janet Reno complaining that the agency she supervises had shown a "lack of regard for the farmers."[9] The letter had the desired effect. The INS stopped arresting undocumented pickers, and the onion crop made it to market.

Similarly, in other parts of the country complaints from local and national politicians have prompted the INS to back off. "This is very ironic," Krikorian says. "Congress passed [the Immigration Reform and Control Act of 1986] making it illegal to employ illegal aliens and then basically told the INS not to enforce it."

The law, which made it a crime to knowingly employ undocumented workers, imposed fines on employers caught using illegal aliens and even authorized jail time for repeat offenders.[10]

But the employment-related provisions of the 1986 act have not worked. According to the INS, there are five million illegal aliens in the United States, an estimate that many immigration experts believe to be low. In addition, at least 300,000 are believed to enter the country each year. Many industries in the United States rely heavily on undocumented workers, from the meatpacking plants of the Midwest to the restaurants and garment factories of New York City. "It's very clear to me that we're not sufficiently enforcing the law at all," says Rep. Lamar Smith, R-Texas, chairman of the House Judiciary Subcommittee on Immigration.

In some places, the local economy is largely supported by the labor of illegal aliens. Thomas Fischer, who until recently headed the INS in Georgia and three other southeastern states, estimates that one out of every three businesses in Atlanta employs undocumented workers. "I'm talking about everything from your *Fortune* 500 companies down to your mom-and-pop businesses," he says.

For supporters of tough controls on illegal immigration, the presence of so many undocumented workers in so many industries represents a major failure in immigration policy. "The INS is making no effort whatsoever to fight the ever-increasing presence of illegal immigrants in this country," says Peter Brimelow, author of *Alien Nation,* a best-selling 1995 book that argues for stricter controls on immigration. According to Brimelow, a senior editor at *Forbes* and *National Review,* the INS's abrogation of duty has led to "the development of a huge illegal economy that is growing."

The solution, Brimelow and others say, is stricter enforcement of the sanctions already on the books. "They're absolutely necessary, because without them many employers feel free to hire illegal immigrants," Krikorian says.

Giving employers a green light to bring in undocumented workers has a snowball effect that leads to even more illegal immigration, Krikorian claims. "As long as people in other countries know that they can get jobs easily here, regardless of their status, they will keep coming," he argues. "Once they get in, there is little to fear since employment laws are basically ignored."

Moreover, Stein says, "Once someone hires illegal aliens they have a competitive advantage because their labor costs have dropped." That forces competitors to follow suit, leading to an even greater demand for illegal immigrants and fewer jobs for citizens or legal residents. "It's a vicious cycle."

But opponents of employer sanctions argue that they are not being enforced for a good reason: they do not work. "When they've tried to enforce employer sanctions in one area or another, they haven't reduced illegal immigration," says Frank Sharry, executive director of the National Immigration Forum, a think tank that favors increased immigration.

Sharry argues that sanctions only drive immigrants further into the underground economy. "The only thing employer sanctions do is push illegal immigrants from decent employers into the hands of unscrupulous employers," he says. "They push them down into the shadier parts of the economy, but not out of it."

Opponents of sanctions also argue that sanctions are unfair to employers, many of whom do not know they have hired illegal aliens. "Many illegal immigrants are hired unwittingly, because they forged the right documents," says Lance of the de Tocqueville Institution. "Only a minority of employers knowingly hire illegal immigrants, so imposing sanctions would get many of them in trouble for a good-faith mistake."

Cato's Moore agrees, adding: "Businesses should not be responsible for being immigration policemen." Such a system "would lead to great discrimination against foreigners—regardless of their status—because businesses would automatically wonder whether a foreign worker was illegal and worth the risk of hiring."

Moore and Muñoz are among those who say that illegal immigration should be controlled at the border, not at the office or factory. "We need to put more people and resources at the border," Muñoz says. "It can work if we put our minds to it."

But supporters of sanctions say that relying on the Border Patrol to stem the flow of illegal immigration is close to meaningless without "internal enforcement" since, by its own estimate, the patrol only catches one in three people trying to cross into the United States. *(See box, p. 13.)*

Moreover, 40 percent of all illegal immigrants initially enter the United States legally but stay longer than the time allowed on their visa. "There's no way to stop visa overstays because they came in a perfectly legal manner," Krikorian says.

Should the number of H-1B visas be increased?

Michael Worry has a problem. The CEO of Nuvation Labs, a thirty-person Silicon Valley software-engineering firm, said he is constantly grappling with a shortage of employees. "We've had positions go unfilled for months at a time," he said in April 2000.[11]

So Worry has done what many others in similar positions have done—hired workers from abroad, many admitted only on a temporary basis. In fact, one-third of his workers are temporary foreign employees.

For years, Worry and others in the information-technology industry have complained of an almost crippling shortage of skilled workers. "The number of jobs in

Armed Ranchers Aid Agents in Patrolling Porous U.S. Border

Every day, thousands of Mexicans, Central Americans, and others illegally cross into the United States along its southern border. The U.S. Border Patrol in 2000 apprehended more than 1.5 million undocumented immigrants.

Still, for each one caught entering illegally, at least two others sneak through. "It's clear that we're not doing nearly enough to secure our borders," said Gregory Rodriguez, a fellow at the New America Foundation, a think tank in Washington, D.C.

A major reason the border is so porous, Rodriguez and others contend, is that the Border Patrol is woefully understaffed. More than 9,000 agents guard the country's northern and southern borders. That is roughly double the number of personnel as in 1993. Still, said Mark Krikorian, executive director of the Center for Immigration Studies, the Border Patrol could easily use another 10,000 people in the field.

A recent University of Texas at Austin study estimates that the Immigration and Naturalization Service's enforcement arm needs 16,000 agents to effectively guard the 2,000-mile border with Mexico.[1] Agency officials have tried to add 1,000 personnel per year, as mandated by Congress in a 1996 law. (*See "Background," p. 17*)

But the Border Patrol's efforts to boost its size have been slowed by the lure of other opportunities. "They've been training a lot of people, but there's been a lot of turnover as well," Krikorian says. "They've lost a lot of people to organizations like the Houston Police Department because Border Patrol agents are a good catch since they have the most rigorous training of anyone in the federal government.

Indeed, as of last year, 40 percent of all Border Patrol agents had been on the job two years or less.[2] "A lot of the people on the border right now are young and inexperienced," says Tamar Adler, a policy analyst at the American Friends Service Committee.

SOLDIERS AND RANCHERS

For many who live along the southern border, the Border Patrol's current force is simply not enough. For example, in a recent poll, 89 percent of Arizona residents indicated that they favor using the military to help patrol the border.[3]

Some border residents have even taken matters into their own hands, policing their property and arresting undocumented immigrants caught trespassing. Over the last two years, Arizona ranchers Roger and Donald Barnett have captured about 3,000 illegal aliens and turned them over to the Border Patrol.

Some have accused the Barnetts, who use rifles and dogs for their property searches, and other ranchers of "hunting" human beings. "It's illegal for citizens to detain other people—

regardless of their status—unless they are breaching the peace," Adler says. "This is vigilante activity, plain and simple."

But the Barnett brothers defend their actions. "They're on my land, they're trespassing and I have a right to protect my property," said fifty-seven-year-old Roger Barnett, who owns a 22,000-acre ranch along the Mexican border near Douglas, Arizona.[4]

Others say neither military nor civilian action is the solution. Krikorian and others advocate giving the Border Patrol more of the tools it needs to adequately do the job. In addition to more agents, Krikorian favors erecting more physical barriers in areas where the flow of illegal aliens is heavy.

He also believes that those apprehended repeatedly should be imprisoned as a deterrent for them and those who would follow in their footsteps. "Right now, you have to be caught ten or fifteen times before you face prosecution," Krikorian says. "As things stand, everyone just gets an air-conditioned ride back to Mexico and a chance to try again."

And try again, they do. Many undocumented immigrants are willing to cross long stretches of desert and other rough terrain in order to enter the United States. Such determination has put some aliens at terrible risk. During a nine-month period in 2000, the Border Patrol found 217 undocumented aliens dead near the border. Most had either drowned or died of thirst in the desert. Agents rescued more than 1,000 others in imminent danger during the same period.

To reduce the number of deaths, the Border Patrol has stepped up its efforts to train agents in lifesaving techniques. The agency also is putting up warning signs along those parts of the border considered the most dangerous to cross—either because of long stretches of desert or dangerous waterways.

The high number of deaths along the border is "unacceptable," said Doris Meissner, commissioner of the Immigration and Naturalization Service, which oversees the Border Patrol. "We want to reduce the number of deaths and increase safety on both sides of the border," she said at a press conference in June 2000.[5]

1. William Branigin, "Border Patrol Being Pushed to Continue Fast Growth," *Washington Post*, May 13, 1999.
2. *Ibid.*
3. Tim McGirk, "Border Clash," *Time*, June 6, 2000.
4. Quoted in William Booth, "Emotions on the Edge," *Washington Post*, June 21, 2000.
5. Quoted in Michael A. Fletcher, "Lifesaving on the Border," *Washington Post*, June 27, 2000.

our industry has grown so fast that our colleges and universities just can't keep up with demand," says ITAA's Miller. "We have no choice but to look abroad."

Miller says there is already a huge gap between the number of jobs and qualified workers in the information-technology industry. Industry estimates of the shortage run as high as 800,000.[12] In addition, according to a recent Cato report, the demand for skilled high-tech jobs is expected to grow 150,000 per year during the next five years.[13]

Similar to many high-tech companies, Nuvation tries to bring in qualified workers from abroad using H-1B visas, which require applicants to have a bachelor's degree and allow a stay of up to six years.

But firms that fill vacancies with H-1B visa holders complain that the program is much too limited to fill their needs. "The demand for high-tech workers is clearly outpacing the number of people that can currently be brought in" under the H-1B program, says Rep. Smith.

In recent years high-tech companies and others have vigorously lobbied Congress to substantially increase the number of H-1B visas. But opponents of increasing H-1B visas—including many labor unions and some Democrats in Congress— argue that they are unnecessary and harmful to American workers. They say that companies clamoring for more temporary foreign workers are not taking advantage of the domestic labor force.

"Just call any employer of programmers in any city—large or small—and they'll tell you that they reject the overwhelming majority of job applicants without even giving them an interview," the University of California's Matloff says. For instance, he says, Microsoft rejects all but 2 percent of the applicants for technology jobs. "Now, how can they do this when they claim they're so desperate for workers?" he asks.

The real reason employers want more H-1Bs is they don't want to find and train skilled U.S. workers, Matloff says, although there are many highly qualified Americans who only need to have their skills updated. "These companies don't want to take the time and spend the money it takes to hire and train domestic workers," he says. "I think many of them are afraid that they'll lose someone after they've trained them."

In addition, opponents say, temporary visas allow companies to keep industry wages low. "If there were a labor shortage in one industry or another, wages would naturally rise and workers would shift into this area," says David A. Smith, director of public policy at the AFL-CIO. "But H-1B visas distort the market by bringing in outside workers, and that holds down wages."

Matloff points out that 79 percent of H-1B visa holders make less than $50,000 per year. Although such a pay level is above the national average, it is considered low for skilled high-technology workers. "This is the kind of industry where if you're any good, you make at least $100,000 a year," he says.

Finally, opponents argue, H-1B visas give employers too much leverage over these temporary workers, because many are desperate to get permanent work status and need the company's assistance to do so. According to the *National Review*'s O'Sullivan, "employers say that they will help them get a green card, but in the meantime, 'you belong to us.'" Since the process can take up to five years, O'Sullivan and others argue, an H-1B visa can often lead to a form of indentured servitude. "This whole aspect of the system is open to terrible abuse," he claims.

Instead of expanding the H-1B program, critics say business and the government should focus on training and hiring domestic workers for high-tech jobs. "H-1B visas prevent us from doing what we need to generate a long-term supply of skilled labor that we're eventually going to need in this industry," the AFL-CIO's Smith says.

But H-1B supporters counter that high-tech companies really are facing a skilled labor shortage. They note that the unemployment rate within the information-technology industry is generally much lower than the national rate. "Look, our colleges and universities simply can't keep up with demand," Miller says.

Moore agrees. "It's vital that we have access to these highly skilled workers in order to maintain our competitive edge," he says. "We're getting the cream of the crop from developing countries like India. It's sort of a form of reverse foreign aid, a gift from the rest of the world to the U.S."

In addition, supporters say, the information-technology industry is already doing much to train new and existing employees to keep up with industry changes. "We're already the leader in spending on worker training," Miller says. "We spend 60 percent more than the financial-services industry or more than $1,000 per year, per employee."

H-1B supporters also dispute the notion that they are trying to bring in temporary workers to permanently replace domestic talent in order to drive down wages. "The law requires that we pay these people the prevailing wage, so they are well compensated for what they do," Miller says.

Background

The Latest Wave

The foundation of the current immigration system dates back to 1965, when Congress overhauled the rules governing who could and could not enter the United States. Since 1920, immigration quotas had largely favored northern Europeans over people from other parts of the world. The quotas, coupled with the impact of the Great Depression and World War II, markedly reduced immigration into the country.

From 1930 to 1950, fewer than four million newcomers arrived in the United States, less than half the number in the first decade of the twentieth century. The heated debates that had accompanied the great waves of immigration in the late nineteenth and early twentieth centuries faded, replaced by smaller questions, such as whether to allow refugees from Europe to emigrate after World War II. "Immigration didn't even really exist as a big issue until 1965, because we just weren't letting that many people in," author Brimelow says.

In 1965 the landscape changed. The quota system was replaced by one that gave preference to immigrants with close relatives already living in the United States and to those with special skills needed by American industry. The law, which took effect in 1968, set an overall annual cap of 290,000 immigrants—170,000 from the Eastern Hemisphere and 120,000 from the Western Hemisphere.

The 1965 law dramatically changed the face of immigration. Until the late 1960s, most immigrants came from Europe. Thereafter, the majority of newcomers hailed from the developing world—nearly half from Latin America. Initially, the country took in many refugees escaping communist regimes in Cuba and Indochina. In the late 1970s and 1980s, a large group of immigrants came from Central America, where a number of brutal wars were raging.[14] But the largest number of newcomers—fully 20 percent of all immigrants between 1968 and 1993—came from impoverished Mexico.[15]

In the wake of the 1965 law, the United States also began grappling with illegal immigrants, also mainly from Mexico. The number of undocumented aliens entering the United States increased dramatically from the mid-1960s to the mid-1980s, in spite of beefed-up Border Patrol efforts. The number of illegal aliens apprehended at the border reflects the increase. In 1965 fewer than 100,000 undocumented aliens were stopped, but by 1985 the number had exceeded 1.2 million.[16]

Many of the illegal aliens had for decades been accustomed to crossing the southern border for agricultural work and then returning to Mexico at the end of

Chronology

1920–1964   *After decades during which tens of millions of people emigrated to the United States, a new, restrictive immigration policy substantially limits the number of newcomers who can settle in the country.*

1921   Congress passes the Quota Act, which establishes a new system of national-origin quotas favoring northern Europeans over immigrants from southern Europe and elsewhere.

1924   Congress passes the Johnson-Reed Act, which stiffens the national-origin quotas established three years earlier. The law also creates the U.S. Border Patrol to combat illegal immigration.

1930   The coming decade will see immigration drop to roughly 500,000, down substantially from the more than eight million who emigrated to the United States during the first decade of the twentieth century.

1942   Workers from Mexico and other nations are admitted to work temporarily in the United States, mainly in California's agricultural industry, under an initiative later called the Bracero Program.

1952   The McCarran-Walter Act retains the national-origins quota system.

1954   The U.S. government institutes "Operation Wetback" to stem the increase in illegal immigration. The program is successful.

1964   The Bracero Program ends.

1965–1980   *The civil rights movement prompts Congress to end racially restrictive immigration quotas. The new law leads to a large influx of immigrants from Latin America and Asia.*

1965   Congress passes the Immigration and Nationality Act Amendments, which remove racial quotas and substantially increases the number of immigrants allowed entry into the United States each year.

1968   Immigrants from the Western Hemisphere, previously admitted freely into the United States, are subjected to quotas, largely in response to a surge in illegal immigration after the 1964 expiration of the Bracero program.

1980   The annual number of legal immigrants entering the country surpasses a half-million.

1981–2000s *An increase in legal and illegal immigration prompts Congress to change the system.*

1986 The Immigration Reform and Control Act makes many illegal aliens eligible for permanent residence and establishes sanctions against employers who hire illegal workers.

1990 Congress passes the Immigration Act, which raises the immigration ceiling to 700,000 a year and grants preferences to relatives of U.S. residents or citizens and to aliens with high-demand work skills.

1992 Patrick J. Buchanan makes curtailing legal and illegal immigration one of the cornerstones of his bid for the Republican presidential nomination.

1993 Some 880,000 legal immigrants arrive in the United States.

1994 Californians pass Proposition 187, which denies social services to illegal aliens. The initiative is later struck down in the courts.

1996 Congress passes the Illegal Immigration Reform and Immigrant Responsibility Act, which toughens border enforcement and streamlines deportation procedures.

1998 Immigrant voters, particularly Latinos, prove crucial in a host of congressional and gubernatorial elections.

2000 GOP presidential candidate George W. Bush proposes splitting the Immigration and Naturalization Service into two separate agencies—one to guard the border and the other to process legal immigrants.

the picking season. In fact, for more than two decades the United States had allowed migrant pickers into the country legally. But the so-called Bracero Program was discontinued in 1964, prompting many to begin crossing the border illegally.

In 1986 Congress moved to stem illegal immigration by passing the Immigration Reform and Control Act (IRCA). IRCA attacked the problem by using a carrot-and-stick approach. On one hand, the act granted a general amnesty to all undocumented aliens who could prove that they had been in the United States before 1982. But it also imposed monetary sanctions against employers who knowingly hired undocumented workers. Repeat offenders risked prison.

Four years later Congress moved to overhaul the system governing legal immigration, passing the Immigration Act of 1990. The new law increased the number

Table 1-1 Top Countries of Origin for U.S. Immigrants, 1998

More legal immigrants came from Mexico in 1998 than any other country, in part because U.S. immigration law grants preference to relatives of recent immigrants, a policy known as "family reunification." Although no individual African country made the top fifteen, the United States admitted more than 40,000 Africans in 1998.

Rank	Country	Number Entering United States Legally
1.	Mexico	131,575
2.	China	36,884
3.	India	36,482
4.	Philippines	34,466
5.	Former Soviet Union	30,163
6.	Dominican Republic	20,387
7.	Vietnam	17,649
8.	Cuba	17,375
9.	Jamaica	15,146
10.	El Salvador	14,590
11.	South Korea	14,268
12.	Haiti	13,449
13.	Pakistan	13,094
14.	Colombia	11,836
15.	Canada	10,190

Source: U.S. Immigration and Naturalization Service.

of aliens allowed to enter from roughly 500,000 each year to 700,000. It also set new country-based quotas in an effort to alter the impact of the 1965 law, which had heavily favored immigrants from Latin America and Asia. Newcomers from other countries, especially from Europe, received a greater share of the entry visas. In addition, more visas were set aside for workers with special skills.[17]

The decade that followed the 1990 act saw the largest influx of immigrants in U.S. history, with nearly ten million newcomers arriving on America's shores. Most still came from Latin America (particularly Mexico) and Asia. But a substantial number came from eastern Europe in the wake of the Soviet Union's collapse and the breakup of Yugoslavia.

Foreign-Born Americans on the Rise

The percentage of the U.S. population made up of foreign-born adults and their children is expected to surpass 25 percent by the middle of the century. That nearly equals the level attained during the late 1800s following a massive influx of Germans and Irish.

Immigrants and Their Children in the United States

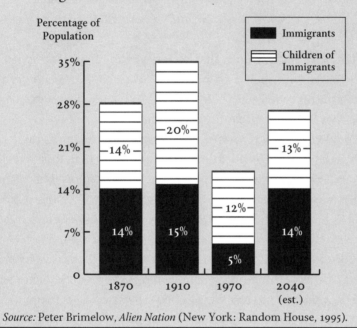

Percentage of Population

Legend: ■ Immigrants ▤ Children of Immigrants

35% —
28% —
21% — 14% ... 20% ... 13%
14% —
7% — 14% ... 15% ... 12% ... 14%
0 — 5%

1870   1910   1970   2040 (est.)

Source: Peter Brimelow, *Alien Nation* (New York: Random House, 1995).

Congress took one more stab at reforming the rules governing legal and illegal immigration in 1996. But efforts to lower levels of legal immigration stalled after running into tough opposition from business groups and others. Instead, the new law focused on curbing illegal entry into the United States by beefing up the Border Patrol and streamlining deportation procedures.[18]

Family Reunification

The rules governing legal immigration are often criticized for being everything from misguided to contradictory. "It's actually worse than the tax code because there's absolutely no real rationale behind it," Brimelow says. "It's just a collection of accidents."

But others say the current system actually works quite well, especially given the number of people who emigrate to the United States each year. "We have a very well-regulated immigration system," La Raza's Muñoz says. "It actually does work."

The cornerstone of the current system revolves around family reunification. Roughly two-thirds of all immigrants who enter the United States legally each year are sponsored by a close relative. Of these, around 75 percent are either the sponsor's spouse or child.

The idea behind family reunification is that people already living in the United States should be able to live with their close relatives. "Doesn't your neighbor José have the right to live with his wife Maria?" Muñoz asks. "That's the question people need to ask when they think about family reunification."

Few Americans would answer "no" to Muñoz's question. But many immigration experts say that although family reunification is an important goal, it is given too much weight in the current immigration system in the United States. For his part, Brimelow says family reunification takes legal immigration "out of the realm of public policy and turns it into a civil rights issue, giving certain people a right to immigrate."

Brimelow and others would like to see a much greater share of visas issued to necessary and skilled workers. "An employment-based system would benefit this country much more than one that stresses family ties," he says.

Even the National Immigration Forum's Sharry, who favors the current high levels of family-based immigration, supports an increase in employment-related visas. "Employers need to be able to sponsor a greater number of people each year," he says. "The existing numbers are much too low."

Currently, the INS can issue up to 140,000 employment-related visas—known as green cards—per year. Unlike H-1B and other temporary work visas, a green card gives an immigrant permanent status. The rules allow no more than 9,800 work visas to be given to people from any one country, to ensure a certain amount of ethnic diversity. The INS also issues an additional 50,000 green cards each year by lottery, attracting 7 million applicants.[19]

The low number of permanent work visas makes it difficult for employers to sponsor workers from abroad. According to Sharry and others, this leads many businesses to turn to illegal immigration. "If you're a restaurant owner and you need people and can't sponsor someone, of course you're going to turn to undocumented workers," he says.

There are other ways for immigrants to enter the United States. For instance, the country can take in tens of thousands of refugees per year. The number, 78,000 in fiscal year 2000, is determined each year by the president and Congress.[20]

Of course, many foreigners also enter or remain in the country illegally. The INS estimates that around 300,000 people per year move to the United States without proper documentation. Few are ever detected and fewer still deported.

"The dirty little secret of our system in this country is that once you get here you can stay if you want to," Moore says. "It's like lawyers say: possession is nine-tenths of the law."

Outlook

Focus on the Economy

There is a commonly held belief among immigration opponents and boosters alike that when the economic growth slows or stops, so will support for letting immigrants into the United States. "Immigration is always driven by the economy—is always a big issue when the economy is poor and a nonissue when it's doing well," says Cato's Moore, who favors continued high levels of immigration.

"Only when this economy goes south and your job is threatened will an atmosphere of fear and insecurity take over," he says. "When it's José who is competing with you, most people will say, 'Things would be fine if only we could keep José and his kind out of the country.' "

Immigration opponent Stein of the Federation for American Immigration Reform agrees that the last decade of high economic growth has left the immigration debate withering on the vine. But unlike Moore, Stein approaches the prospect of an economic downturn with anticipation, not worry.

"In the current heady, narcotic trance this country's in, there's a detachment from reality about immigration," he says. "But when the economy comes down to Earth, this issue will come to the fore, and there will be a backlash."

Stein believes that when the American people actually turn their attention to immigration, they will demand substantial reductions in the number of people allowed entry each year. "I think the public really wants a breather for at least twenty if not thirty or forty years," he says.

Should illegal immigrants be permitted to remain in the United States if they have been here for several years?

YES

Frank Sharry
Executive director, National Immigration Forum
Written for *CQ Researcher*, July 2000

"Vicente" and his wife are from Latin America and graduated from U.S. colleges in the early 1980s. They stayed on and led exemplary lives. He works in customer service for a technology company; she does marketing for a direct-mail firm. Their three U.S.-born children are all-star Little League players. There's only one hitch: Mom and Dad are in the United States illegally. They missed the 1982 cutoff for the previous legalization program.

Then there is "Blanca." She graduated from high school with top honors but found her hopes of attending college dashed because she does not have proper immigration papers. Her family fled persecution and civil war in El Salvador, but inequitable treatment under successive administrations has kept her parents in legal limbo.

Three legalization measures pending before Congress would enable some 750,000 people in situations like these to live and work in the United States legally. The proposed bills, all of which enjoy bipartisan support, would

- Update an immigration law provision that allows undocumented immigrants of good moral character who have resided and worked in America since before 1986 to remain permanently;

- Correct for past unequal treatment among groups of similarly situated Central American and Haitian refugees; and

- Restore Section 245(i) of the immigration code to allow those on the verge of gaining permanent status to remain in the United States to complete the paperwork process.

Enactment of the three measures is both the right thing and the smart thing to do. It will correct past mistakes that have unfairly kept immigrant families in bureaucratic limbo, stabilize our workforce at a time of growing labor shortages, and keep families together.

As President Ronald Reagan said when he signed the legalization provisions of the 1986 Immigration Reform and Control Act, offering permanent legal status to those already rooted in our communities "will go far to improve the lives of a class of individuals who now must hide in the shadows, without many of the benefits of a free and open society. Very soon many of these men and women will be able to step into the sunlight and, ultimately, if they choose, become Americans."

It is time to revive our great heritage as a nation of immigrants and reward those who have already proven to be valued and positive members of our country by enacting these targeted measures this year.

Should illegal immigrants be permitted to remain in the United States if they have been here for several years?

NO

Dan Stein
Executive director, Federation for
American Immigration Reform
Written for *CQ Researcher*, July 2000

Politicians perpetually talk about the need to control illegal immigration. But because the talk is rarely backed with action, about six million illegal aliens now reside in the United States. Now, some in Congress are suggesting illegal immigration once again be rewarded by granting amnesty to millions of brazen law violators.

What sort of signal does this send? It tells people we will do little to stop them and even less to deport them if they decide to bypass the legal immigration process. It tells them we will grant them legal status if they have the fortitude to stick it out for a few years. Is it any wonder the illegal immigrant population equals the population of Massachusetts?

The last amnesty in 1986—which Congress pledged would never be repeated—legalized some three million people and cost taxpayers an estimated $78 billion.

Today, immigration enforcement has virtually collapsed. And despite the fact that financial institutions manage to run millions of electronic verifications every day, the government has yet to develop a system that can even authenticate a job applicant's right to work and live in the United States. Consequently, the availability of jobs and generous social services continues to attract illegal immigrants.

Another amnesty would tell the world that the United States literally is unable to control its borders. Such an admission inevitably would force a reappraisal of the validity and purposes of the meaningless immigration quotas now on the books.

Illegal immigration also inflicts economic injury on Americans in the lower half of the wage structure. Numerous studies show that immigration, especially illegal immigration, results in wage loss for Americans who must compete against illegal immigrants.

While amnesty proponents argue that legalization will give illegal aliens more bargaining leverage, even this questionable merit is likely to be short-lived. Another amnesty is guaranteed to set off an even greater influx of illegal immigration as people perceive this to be our way to deal with the problem periodically.

Amnesty is not the answer. The only way to stop illegal immigration is to link aliens' ability to immigrate with their willingness to play by our rules. Encourage those here illegally to return to their home countries through incentives and get control of our borders—only then would any discussion of an amnesty and reward program be responsible.

The *National Review*'s O'Sullivan concurs, arguing that Americans "will come to see that we need to reduce it at least for a while, so that we can absorb the people we already have." O'Sullivan doesn't "see us closing the doors, but bringing it down to the level it was in the 1950s, when we let a quarter of a million people in each year."

Others also predict a backlash when the economy slows, but not against continued high levels of immigration. "Instead of doing something about immigration, we'll stick it to the immigrants themselves when things slow down," Krikorian says. "That's what we've done in the past."

Krikorian sees the potential for another Proposition 187—the 1994 California ballot initiative that denied social services to illegal immigrants. "The reason Proposition 187 passed wasn't because people really favored it. They were pissed off at our immigration policy, and it was the only way they could register their opposition."

"Sticking it to the foreigners" is the easy way for policy-makers to assuage the public's concern about immigration without actually doing anything about it, he says. "We'll continue to propose these anti-immigrant measures instead of sensible restrictions on immigration because too many powerful groups have an interest in keeping things as they are," he says.

Krikorian and others blame both major political parties for wanting to preserve the immigration status quo. GOP support parallels that of big business, which favors high levels of immigration in order to maintain a steady supply of both unskilled and skilled labor. Democratic support for immigration stems from its connection to various ethnic groups—largely Asian and Hispanic—that favor higher levels.

But others say a backlash, in any form, is unlikely for a number of different reasons. According to the de Tocqueville Institution's Lance, newcomers will continue to be welcome because the American people have come to accept high immigration levels as almost a permanent condition.

"If you look at the past ten years, it seems that the pendulum has really swung in favor of immigration," she says. "Sure, we may have moments—especially during recessions—when there is a fear of foreigners, but unless there is a major catastrophe, like a war or a depression, I don't think the American people will seriously question" current immigration policies.

Sharry agrees. "I think the premise is that immigration is a good thing and will increasingly be viewed as a crucial part of our economy," he says. Besides, Sharry

For More Information

Alexis de Tocqueville Institution, 1611 N. Kent St., Suite 901, Arlington, VA 22209; (703) 351-0090; www.adti.net. The institution works to increase public understanding of the cultural and economic benefits of immigration.

Center for Immigration Studies, 1522 K St., NW, Suite 820, Washington, DC 20005; (202) 466-8185; www.cis.org. The center conducts research on the impact of immigration.

Federation for American Immigration Reform (FAIR), 1666 Connecticut Ave., NW, Suite 400, Washington, DC 20009; (202) 328-7004; www.fairus.org. FAIR lobbies in favor of strict limits on immigration.

National Council of La Raza, 1111 19th St., NW, Suite 1000, Washington, DC 20036; (202) 785-1670; www.nclr.org. La Raza monitors legislation and lobbies on behalf of Latinos in the United States.

National Immigration Forum, 220 I St., NE, Washington, DC 20002; (202) 544-0004; www.immigrationforum.org. The forum advocates and builds public support for proimmigration policies.

U.S. Immigration and Naturalization Service, 425 I St., NW, Suite 7100, Washington, DC 20536; (202) 514-1900; www.ins.usdoj.gov. The Immigration and Naturalization Service (INS), part of the Department of Justice, administers and enforces U.S. immigration and naturalization laws.

says, the economy is unlikely to take the kind of nose-dive that would actually prompt people to rethink immigration policy.

"I think the economy's going to stay relatively strong for the foreseeable future," he predicts, "and this will lead not only to a preservation of the current system but to an expansion of it."

Notes

1. Data provided by the U.S. Census Bureau. For background, see Charles S. Clark, "The New Immigrants," *CQ Researcher*, January 24, 1997, 49–72.

2. Greenspan testified before the Senate Committee on Banking, Housing and Urban Affairs on February 24, 2000.

3. Quoted in John Micklethwait, "The New Americans," *Economist*, March 11, 2000.

4. For background, see Kenneth Jost, "Cracking Down on Immigration," *CQ Researcher*, February 3, 1995, 97–120.

5. For background, see Kathy Koch, "High-Tech Labor Shortage," *CQ Researcher*, April 24, 1998, 361–384.

6. Figures provided by the Immigration and Naturalization Service.

7. Micklethwait, "New Americans."

8. For background, see David Masci, "Hispanic Americans' New Clout," *CQ Researcher*, September 18, 1998, 809–832.

9. Quoted from Douglas Holt, "INS Is Scaling Back Its Workplace Raids," *Chicago Tribune*, January 17, 1999.

10. Mary W. Cohn, ed., *Congressional Quarterly Almanac* (Washington, D.C.: Congressional Quarterly, 1986), 61.

11. Quoted in Karen Cheney, "Foreign Aid: Hiring Abroad Can Ease Your Labor Woes," *Business Week*, April 24, 2000.

12. Micklethwait, "New Americans."

13. Suzette Brooks Masters and Ted Ruthizer, "The H-1B Straitjacket," CATO Institute, March 3, 2000.

14. For background, see David Masci, "Assisting Refugees," *CQ Researcher*, February 7, 1997, 97–120.

15. For background, see David Masci, "Mexico's Future," *CQ Researcher*, September 19, 1997, 817–840.

16. Figures cited in Peter Brimelow, *Alien Nation* (New York: Random House, 1995), 34.

17. Kenneth Jost, ed., *Congressional Quarterly Almanac* (Washington, D.C.: Congressional Quarterly, 1990), 482.

18. Jan Austin, ed., *Congressional Quarterly Almanac* (Washington, D.C.: Congressional Quarterly, 1996), 5–3.

19. Micklethwait, "New Americans."

20. Mary H. Cooper, "Global Refugee Crisis," *CQ Researcher*, July 9, 1999, 569–592.

Bibliography

Books

Brimelow, Peter. *Alien Nation: Common Sense About America's Immigration Disaster*. New York: Random House, 1995.

Brimelow, a *Forbes* magazine senior editor, makes what many consider a strong case for a restrictive immigration policy. He argues that unless the flood of newcomers to America's shores is halted or at least curtailed, the United States will become a nation of ethnic fiefdoms, each pulling in a different direction. If present trends continue, Brimelow writes, "Americans themselves will become alien to each other."

Smith, James P., and Barry Edmonston, eds. *The Immigration Debate*. Washington, D.C.: National Academy Press, 1998.

This collection of essays by immigration experts examines the fiscal, economic, and demographic effects of the recent wave of newcomers to the United States. In particular, the book discusses whether immigrants add to or detract from the economy.

Articles

Cheney, Karen. "Foreign Aid: Hiring Abroad Can Ease Your Labor Woes." *Business Week*, April 24, 2000.

Cheney examines the current debate over H-1B visas, which allow high-skilled workers to enter the United States on a temporary basis.

Cooper, Mary H. "Immigration Reform." *CQ Researcher*, September 23, 1993.

A slightly dated but valuable overview of immigration-related debates that still are relevant today. Particularly valuable is Cooper's examination of the economic impact of immigration.

Kempner, Matt. "The Big Wink: Undocumented Latino Workers Are So Vital to Georgia's Economy That Those in Charge Look the Other Way." *Atlanta Journal*, January 23, 2000.

Kempner examines the impact of illegal immigration in Georgia and finds that many industries are heavily dependent on undocumented workers.

Koch, Kathy. "High Tech Labor Shortage." *CQ Researcher*, April 24, 1998.

Koch examines the debate surrounding the perceived shortage of workers in the high-technology industry and details the drive to allow businesses to bring in more high-skilled foreign workers on a temporary basis.

Micklethwait, John. "The New Americans." *Economist*, March 11, 2000.

This superb series of articles explores the economic, political, and cultural impact of the most recent wave of immigration on the United States. Micklethwait acknowledges the many challenges associated with absorbing millions of foreigners, many of whom are poor and speak little or no English. Still, he argues that immigrants, with their energy and drive, will make the United States a more prosperous nation.

Samuelson, Robert J. "Ignoring Immigration." *Washington Post,* May 3, 2000.

Samuelson, a columnist for *Washington Post,* advocates dramatically changing the nation's policy on legal immigration. He proposes admitting better-educated immigrants instead of the low-skilled people who make up the lion's share of newcomers each year.

Stern, Marcus. "A Semi-Tough Policy on Illegal Workers; Congress Looks Out for Employers." *Washington Post,* July 5, 1998.

Stern argues that even though Congress has shown a great willingness to pass laws aimed at curtailing illegal immigration, many lawmakers defend businesses in their districts that use undocumented workers.

Reports and Studies

Lance, Bronwyn, Margalit Edelman, and Peter Mountford. "There Goes the Neighborhood—Up: A Look at Property Values and Immigration in Washington, D.C." Alexis de Tocqueville Institution, January 2000.

Evidence in this report counters the commonly held belief that property values fall when large numbers of immigrants move into an area. Indeed, the de Tocqueville researchers found that property values actually rise.

Masters, Suzette Brooks, and Ted Ruthizer. "The H-1B Straitjacket: Why Congress Should Repeal the Cap on Foreign-Born Highly Skilled Workers." Cato Institute, March 3, 2000.

The authors, both attorneys, make the case for expanding the H-1B temporary work visa program. They argue that the current shortage of skilled foreign workers is forcing high-tech companies to move their operations overseas.

THE NEXT STEP: ADDITIONAL INFORMATION

Immigration

"Illegal Immigration: A Lucrative Business and a Global Concern." UPI News, June 22, 2000

Illegal immigration is a growing concern worldwide. The collapse of the Soviet Union and the disappearance of the Iron Curtain have opened the gates to a massive flow of population movements, perhaps the largest since World War II. Tens of thousands of eastern Europeans in search of better economies have been arriving in droves in western Europe every day.

"New Immigration Bill Breaks Stalemate on High-Tech Workers." UPI News, April 11, 2000.

Breaking a stalemate over immigration, a key House chairman introduced new legislation to eliminate the existing caps on temporary visas for foreign workers taking high-tech jobs in the United States. The bill marked a dramatic turn in a long-simmering dispute over how to fill hundreds of thousands of high-tech jobs that are available in the United States. The legislation proposed by Rep. Lamar Smith, R-Texas, would eliminate the cap on the number of visas available to foreign workers but would require U.S. industries to prove that their hiring and pay of U.S. workers does not drop off with the rise in foreign workers.

"U.S., Citing Elian Case, Opts to Review Immigration Policy." *Los Angeles Times*, June 30, 2000, A8.

U.S. Attorney General Janet Reno, reflecting on the end of the Elian Gonzalez saga, said that federal officials will undertake a review of immigration policies to determine whether any changes are needed in light of the seven-month ordeal. The Immigration and Naturalization Service, which is part of the Justice Department, took a pounding along the way in the lengthy debate, drawing criticism from some activists who believe that U.S. policy is riddled with inconsistencies.

Branigin, William. "Colombians Fleeing Homeland; U.S. Officials Worry About Tide of Immigration Flowing North." *Washington Post*, July 28, 1999, A14.

Driven by worsening economic conditions and political violence, growing numbers of Colombians are fleeing their country in an exodus that U.S. officials fear may turn into an immigration crisis. Activists are urging the federal government to help the fleeing Colombians by offering temporary refuge to those who reach the United States and by softening the criteria for granting political asylum.

Branigin, William. "Immigration Rules to Be Eased for Salvadorans, Guatemalans." *Washington Post*, May 20, 1999, A27.

The Clinton administration has announced long-awaited regulations that will make it easier for nearly a quarter-million Salvadorans and Guatemalans to obtain legal status in the United States. The regulations, in the works at the Immigration and Naturalization Service for the past year and a half, will allow illegal immigrants from El Salvador and Guatemala who are covered by a previous class-action lawsuit to apply to remain in this country through a new, simplified procedure outside a courtroom.

Branigin, William. "Trouble Getting Out of Africa; Immigration Effort Hits 5-Year Mark." *Washington Post,* **June 22, 2000, V1.**

They first caught each other's eye at a teacher-training session in a suburb of Harare, the capital of Zimbabwe. It was late 1993. He was a newly arrived Peace Corps volunteer, she a Zimbabwean student-teacher on her way to a rural school. With Mark Forror's two-year tour nearing an end, they got engaged and made plans to marry in the United States. Forror, an Alexandria, Virginia, resident, applied for a visa for his bride-to-be, a process he expected would take a few months. Instead, five years have passed, with the couple separated not only by an ocean but by what the thirty-eight-year-old Forror describes as a bureaucratic morass worthy of Kafka.

DeYoung, Karen. "U.S., Cuba Discuss Immigration Pact; Washington and Havana at Odds on Smuggling, Return of Illegal Migrants." *Washington Post,* **December 13, 1999, A19.**

Cuba says the United States promotes the smuggling of illegal immigrants by sea to Florida even as it professes to want to stop the practice. Washington says Havana impedes the legal emigration of Cuban physicians and other medical personnel to the United States in violation of existing agreements. To make immigration more orderly, Washington has agreed to admit at least 20,000 Cubans a year, many of them chosen by lottery, and Cuba has agreed to facilitate their departure.

DeYoung, Karen, and Eric Pianin. "Cuba Delays Talks on Immigration, Citing Elian Case." *Washington Post,* **June 20, 2000, A8.**

Cuba has indefinitely postponed an upcoming round of biannual migration talks with the United States, citing its "preoccupation with the return of Elian Gonzalez as the reason," the State Department said. The talks, held twice yearly under agreements signed by Havana and Washington in 1994 and 1995 to regularize the flow of Cuban immigrants to this country, were due to begin in New York on June 27, 2000.

Escobar, Gabriel. "Immigration Transforms a Community; Influx of Latino Workers Creates Culture Clash in Delaware Town." *Washington Post,* **November 29, 1999, A1.**

Celbin DeLeon is a pioneer. He is among the first Guatemalans to buy a house in Georgetown, Delaware, setting roots in a community that has not warmed to the arrival of Latinos drawn by the poultry industry's voracious need for workers. Until the wave of immigrants this decade, the quiet seat of Sussex County had not changed much in generations. By 1995, a sudden and large influx of Guatemalans turned this into a modern-day company town.

Greenhouse, Steven. "Coalition Urges Easing of Immigration Laws." *New York Times,* **May 16, 2000, A16.**

Jack Kemp, the former Republican candidate for vice president, and Henry G. Cisneros, the former secretary of Housing and Urban Development, are leading an unusual coalition of conservatives and liberals that is beginning a major campaign to persuade Congress to ease the nation's immigration laws. Kemp and Cisneros are scheduled to announce an initiative in conjunction with immigrant groups and the nation's Roman Catholic bishops that calls for admitting more immigrants into the United States and granting amnesty to hundreds of thousands of illegal immigrants.

Krueger, Alan B. "Economic Scene; Work Visas Are Allowing Washington to Sidestep Immigration Reform." *New York Times,* **May 25, 2000, A2.**

The inscription on the Statue of Liberty is quietly being rewritten: "Give me your tired, your poor, your huddled masses yearning to breathe free; I'll also take your skilled employees under the temporary visa program, H-1B." The H-1B visa was established in 1990 to permit foreigners with a college degree or higher to work in the United States for a renewable three-year term for employers who petition on their behalf. In 1998 the program was expanded to allow 115,000 workers, up from 65,000, to enter the United States in fiscal years 1999 and 2000. President Clinton and many members of Congress would like to increase the limit to 200,000 a year the next three years.

Montgomery, Paul L. "Immigration: All Decry System of Illegal Workers, While All Use It." *Los Angeles Times,* **June 25, 2000, M1.**

The questions surrounding immigration, in both Europe and the United States, are as full of contradictions as any in politics. The United States, in its mythology "a nation of immigrants," in fact gave preference in its immigration policy through much of the twentieth century to white people from northern Europe, with southern European people allowed some access and the rest of the world subjected to strict quotas. The Justice Department estimates there are five million illegal immigrants in the United States now, attracted by jobs that are low-paying to U.S. workers.

Pae, Peter, and Mary Jordan. "Hands—and Hopes—Across the Sea; Tough U.S. Immigration Policy Keeps Asian Families Apart." *Washington Post,* **February 1, 1999, A1.**

Fairly or unfairly in a land built by and for immigrants, U.S. immigration policy results in the rending of millions of families, with some members in America and some in their homelands.

Pan, Phillip P. "Demonstration Presses for Immigration Rule Change; 5,000 Urge Congress to Grant New Amnesty." *Washington Post,* **October 17, 1999, C5.**

More than 5,000 protesters from across the country, including illegal immigrants from four continents, marched through Washington and staged a noisy demonstration in Lafayette Square urging Congress to grant a new amnesty for all illegal immigrant workers. It has been thirteen years since Congress passed the Immigration Reform and Control Act, which granted amnesty to nearly three million illegal immigrants in the United States. Now, according to government estimates, there are more than five million illegal immigrants living in the United States, with an additional quarter-million arriving every year.

Pan, Philip P. "Protesters Demand Immigration Amnesty." *Washington Post,* **June 25, 1999, B2.**

Hundreds of Central American immigrants staged a colorful demonstration to urge the U.S. government to grant all refugees who fled civil war and poverty in the region the same amnesty given to Cuban and Nicaraguan immigrants two years ago. The Clinton administration issued regulations making it easier for as many as 50,000 Salvadorans and Guatemalans to become permanent residents, including many who had been in legal limbo for as long as fifteen years.

Pressley, Sue Anne. "Hispanic Immigration Boom Rattles South; Rapid Influx to Some Areas Raises Tensions," *Washington Post,* **March 6, 2000, A3.**

As the 2000 census is sure to confirm, the Hispanic population in America is exploding, from 22.4 million in 1990 to an estimated 30.3 million in 1998. Once the census is completed, many believe the latest estimates will prove shockingly low. In small towns and large cities, particularly across the South, the influx of Hispanic immigrants, mostly illegal, is straining schools and social services, forcing police departments and other agencies to rethink their ways of dealing with citizens and changing forever the old idea of what a southerner is.

Sengupta, Somini. "The Immigration Debate; Full Employment Opens the Door." *New York Times,* **June 18, 2000, A4.**

Just a few years ago, lawmakers were in full cry about the supposed dangers of immigration—from crime to welfare cheats to lost jobs. Yet now Congress is poised to pass a bill that would grant visas to tens of thousands more temporary high-tech workers from abroad. And an unlikely coalition of business and immigrants rights groups is pushing to fling the door open wider: to unskilled workers who could fill shortages in hotels and on farms, and even to roll back an array of restrictive measures passed with great fanfare in 1996.

Tulsky, Fredric, N. "Abused Woman Is Denied Asylum; Immigration Ruling Reflects Split Over Gender Persecution." *Washington Post,* June 20, 1999, A1.

A foreign woman fleeing a violently abusive spouse cannot gain asylum in the United States even if she faces a direct and serious threat of harm in her home country, a federal immigration panel has ruled in a case that is drawing protests from asylum advocates and women's groups. The decision by a sharply divided Board of Immigration Appeals, the Justice Department panel that sets and interprets U.S. immigration policy, reflects a growing philosophical tension over how to treat women's claims of gender persecution.

Immigration and the Courts

"Court Rules Against Immigration Statute; Law Applies to Out-of-Wedlock Births." *Washington Post,* September 5, 1999, A18.

A long-standing immigration law making it easier for a child born out of wedlock overseas to become a U.S. citizen if the child's mother is a citizen is unconstitutional sex discrimination, a federal appeals court has ruled. The law relies on "outdated stereotypes . . . the generalization that mothers are more likely to have close ties to and care for their children than are fathers," the court said.

"Court Upholds Civil Fines in Immigration Cases." *Los Angeles Times,* June 10, 1999, A29.

A hearing officer who works for the Justice Department and is not a judge can impose fines for the use of forged immigration documents, a federal appeals court ruled. In a 2–1 decision, the 9th U.S. Circuit Court of Appeals said the fines were civil penalties, not criminal punishment, and did not have to be imposed by a federal judge with life tenure. Federal immigration law since 1924 has made it a crime to forge immigration documents or to knowingly possess or use forged documents. A 1990 law added civil penalties of between $250 and $2,000 for each forged document that was used to evade the ban on employment of illegal immigrants.

MacGregor, Hilary E. "Judge Bans Indefinite Jailing by INS; Ruling Affects Noncitizens Who Are Ordered Deported but Can't Go Back to Home Countries." *Los Angeles Times,* January 29, 2000, A1.

A U.S. District Court judge in Los Angeles has ruled that the federal government may not indefinitely jail noncitizens who have been ordered deported because of crimes, but whose home countries will not take them back. The issue of how to handle people whom the Immigration and Naturalization Service (INS) terms "criminal aliens" has been a recurring one nationwide. The INS currently holds about 3,800 such "lifers" across the country, ranging from petty thieves to murderers.

Savage, David G. "Justices Uphold Broad Deportation Power for U.S. Immigration; Supreme Court Rules That Crimes Committed in Homeland Can Be Grounds for Expulsion." *Los Angeles Times,* **May 4, 1999, A3.**

The U.S. Supreme Court made it harder for those fleeing political persecution to win asylum in the United States, ruling that the government is free to deport an illegal immigrant who committed a serious crime in his homeland. The 9–0 ruling upholds the government's broad power over immigration matters, a consistent theme of the court's recent rulings.

Immigration and Naturalization Service

"INS Reports Progress in Naturalization: Immigration Agency Says It Has Greatly Reduced Its Backlog of Citizenship Applications; Critics Say It Has Sacrificed Other Responsibilities." *Los Angeles Times,* **October 29, 1999, A23.**

The U.S. Immigration and Naturalization Service announced it slashed the nation's immense backlog in citizenship applications by nearly a quarter last year and said applicants can now expect to wait about twelve months to become citizens, down from twenty-eight months a year ago. But critics questioned the INS statistics and complained the agency had fallen behind in other work—such as issuing green cards. The backlog reached a high of 1.8 million applications last year, with immigrants in some cities facing waits as long as three or four years after submitting their paperwork.

Branigin, William. "INS Shifts 'Interior' Strategy to Target Criminal Aliens; Critics Say Plan to Curtail Work-Site Raids Will Hurt Immigration Compliance." *Washington Post,* **March 15, 1999, A3.**

In what it calls a "major shift" in strategy, the Immigration and Naturalization Service is moving away from its traditional raids on job sites to round up illegal immigrants, emphasizing instead operations against foreign criminals, alien-smuggling rings, and document fraud. The new "interior enforcement strategy" affords a measure of relief to the estimated 5.5 million illegal immigrants living in the United States and the thousands of businesses that employ them.

Mittelstadt, Michelle. "Legal Immigration at 10-Year Low; Congressional Action Blamed." *Washington Post,* **August 12, 1999, A6.**

The United States granted permanent residence to 660,477 foreigners last year, marking the lowest level of legal immigration in a decade as the federal immigration service struggled to deal with a growing backlog of green card applications. The figures for fiscal 1998, announced by the Immigration and Naturalization Service, reflected a 17 percent drop from 1997 and a 28 percent drop from the year before that.

2 Politics and Policy

In 2000, 28.4 million U.S. residents, representing approximately 10 percent of the total population, were foreign-born.[1] Foreign-born persons are those who are not U.S. citizens at birth but who live in the country as naturalized citizens, legal or illegal immigrants. The proportion of foreign-born residents in the nation's population is at its second highest in U.S. history: the foreign-born represented 15 percent of the population at the turn of the twentieth century (1890).[2] These residents reflect the cumulative effects of immigration over time. Immigration reached an all-time high in 1991, when more than 1.5 million immigrants were admitted to the United States. According to the U.S. Census Bureau: "Among the foreign born in 2000, 39.5 percent entered the United States in the 1990s, another 28.3 percent came in the 1980s, 16.2 percent entered in the 1970s, and the remaining 16.0 percent arrived before 1970."[3] Today, the yearly flow of immigrants has been substantially reduced: in 1998 only 660,477 immigrants entered the United States legally. Moreover, just under half of these had already been living in the United States and simply adjusted their status.[4] New arrivals, therefore, make up only a fraction of the foreign-born.

U.S. immigration policy responds to fundamental questions about the nature of American society. Who should be members of U.S. society? Should the nation admit newcomers? If so, how many? Whom should the nation admit? What role should immigrants play once they arrive? For the greater part of U.S. history, policy-makers have assumed that the United States is a destination for more people than Americans are prepared to accept. Often, it appears that newcomers will arrive regardless of efforts to keep them out. So new questions arise: How can policy manage immigration flows? How does immigration benefit the United States and how it does cost American society? How can the nation ensure that newcomers will be productive members of the community?

Domestic conditions often influence the way policy-makers respond to these questions, particularly questions of how many immigrants to admit and what role they should play once they arrive. The most common metaphor for immigration policy is a door through which immigrants must pass to enter the United States. The door swings open when liberal immigration policies take effect and closes when restrictive policies prevail. Although immigration is sometimes spoken of as a human rights issue or, more recently, a security threat, the strongest determinant of the direction in which the door swings has always been the U.S. economy. When times are good, the door swings open; when times are bad, the door closes. As the U.S. Commission on Immigration Reform stated: "Recession and economic depression in the United States is often the underlying stimulus for a response of immigrant exclusion."[5]

During the 1990s, U.S. immigration policies followed trends in economic conditions. In the first half of the decade, policy-makers introduced a host of restrictive immigration measures following the nationwide recession of 1991–1992. Restrictive policies culminated with passage of the Illegal Immigration Reform and Immigrant Responsibility Act of 1996. However, as the economy boomed in the latter half of the 1990s, achieving unprecedented growth and unemployment rates, policy-makers began to undo some of their most restrictive immigration measures, and the door began to open again.

While the size of the immigrant population expands and contracts in response to economic conditions, the recruitment of immigrants who meet specific economic needs has always been an important, but secondary, policy tool. Instead, U.S. immigration policy has been regulated by other concerns. From 1921 to 1965, immigration quotas were based on nationality, and countries received quotas based on the proportion of Americans originally from that country. The Immigration Act of 1965 eliminated these quotas, replacing them with categories based on family ties, occupational skills, and humanitarian concerns. Today, the United States admits roughly 70 percent of immigrants based on family preferences, while 12 percent of immigrants are admitted through employment categories, and 8 percent through refugee or other humanitarian considerations. The remainder is admitted through what is known as the "Diversity Visa Lottery," which selects at random up to 55,000 applicants annually from countries with low rates of immigration to the United States.[6]

The Immigration and Naturalization Service (INS) oversees the administration of immigrant visas according to these broad categories and enforces laws against

Figure 2-1 U.S. Immigration Admissions, 1990–1999

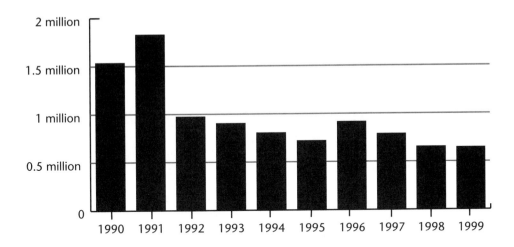

Source: U.S. Immigration and Naturalization Service, *Statistical Yearbook of the Immigration and Naturalization Service, 1999* (Washington, D.C.: Government Printing Office, 2001).

unauthorized immigrants. The agency defines "immigrants" as persons who legally obtain permission—often known as the "green card"—for permanent residence in the United States. Persons who have only temporary authorization to reside in the United States are called "nonimmigrants," including those who enter with temporary work visas or foreign student visas. Most immigrants and nonimmigrants must be sponsored by a family member who is a legal U.S. resident or by a U.S. employer to qualify for a visa. Often, persons with a nonimmigrant visa may "adjust" their status by applying for permanent residence. Immediate relatives of U.S. citizens—defined as spouses, minor unmarried children, or parents of a citizen who is over twenty-one—and U.S. permanent residents who are returning from a year or more abroad enjoy unlimited entry to the United States. All others may be subject to limits on certain admissions categories and must wait to be admitted based on a system of preferences and priorities.

This chapter is divided into four main sections. First, it presents a general discussion of three major categories of immigrants and nonimmigrants: legal permanent residents, unauthorized migrants, and temporary foreign workers. Then, it examines the Illegal Immigration Reform and Immigrant Responsibility Act of 1996 (IIRIRA) and explains the changes in illegal immigration policy, the treatment of criminal aliens, and INS enforcement that both predated and followed the IIRIRA. Next the chapter considers the effect of immigration on American society. In particular, it examines the economic costs and benefits of immigration, the challenges of cultural integration, and the involvement of immigrants in political activity. The chapter concludes with a look at how the terrorist attacks of September 11, 2001, have brought about changes in U.S. immigration policy.

Who Comes to the United States?: The Characteristics of American Immigration

Legal Permanent Residents

There is no typical immigrant to the United States. Immigrants come from countries across the globe, representing many different languages, cultures, education levels, occupations, and income levels. Immigrants are a diverse group that does not lend itself easily to stereotypes. Nevertheless, some demographic patterns among immigrants are clear, particularly in comparison to the native population.

Immigrants come from virtually every country in the world, although in 2000 the majority (51 percent) were born in Latin America: Central America, the Caribbean, and South America. Mexico is the single largest source of immigration, accounting for approximately 20 percent of the immigrant population.[7] Another quarter of the foreign-born population is from Asia. The remainder is from Europe (15.3 percent), Canada, Australia, Africa, and other regions (8.1 percent).[8] These proportions reflect a gradual expansion of immigration from Latin America and Asia beginning in the 1960s. Immigration from traditional sources such as Europe and Canada has declined steadily over this period.

Once they arrive in the United States, immigrants tend to concentrate in a handful of states, and nearly all immigrants live in metropolitan areas. INS statistics from 1998 report that two-thirds of all immigrants intended to reside in six states—California, New York, Florida, Texas, New Jersey, and Illinois—a trend borne out since the 1970s.[9] Even within these states, immigrants exhibit extreme geographic concentration compared with the native population. Almost 95 percent of foreign-born residents live in a metropolitan area, leaving only 5 percent in rural areas. In contrast, less than 80 percent of native-born residents live in urban areas. The difference is even more pronounced in central cities, where nearly half of the foreign-born population resides, yet where a little more than one-quarter of the native population lives.[10] INS data shows that more than 20 percent of immigrants intended to reside in Los Angeles or New York City.[11] At the same time, recent data shows surprising growth in the immigrant population of nontraditional states. According to a study by the Urban Institute, the immigrant populations of North Carolina and Nevada increased 73 and 60 percent, respectively, from 1995 to 1999.[12]

In general, the foreign-born are more likely to be of working age than native-born Americans. U.S. Census figures show that, in 2000 "79.0 percent of the foreign born were 18 to 64 years of age, whereas 59.7 percent of natives were in this age group."[13] New immigrants are especially likely to be young adults, although this long-term trend in age distribution "has gradually shifted toward both children and older immigrants," as U.S. policy has made it easier for both the minor children and the parents of current residents to immigrate.[14]

The emphasis on family unification also contributed to a shift toward a more equal balance of men and women among immigrants to the United States. Historically, the overwhelming proportion of immigrants was male, especially within the working-age population. However, since the 1930s—and throughout the 1990s—the gender balance has remained fairly steady. In 1995, for example, women accounted for 54 percent of all legal immigrants—a ratio that is close to that of the native-born.

If there is one stereotype of immigrants in America, it should be that they are family-oriented. The foreign-born—particularly new immigrants—are more likely than natives of the same age to be married, and more likely to live in a household with five or more people. Again, the emphasis on family unification in U.S. immigration policy helps explain immigrants' high marriage rates. It is also more common among immigrant households to find a male head with no wife present, a situation that often occurs when immigrants live with their siblings, cousins, grandchildren, or other relatives in their extended families.[15]

Overall, immigrants' educational attainment has improved in absolute terms since the 1970s but has been declining relative to the native-born population. In 2000 the proportion of foreign-born residents with a bachelor's degree or more education (25.8 percent) was roughly equal to that of natives (25.6 percent). At the same time, immigrants are far more likely than natives to be high school dropouts, or to have even lower levels of schooling. While 86.6 percent of natives age twenty-five and over had at least a high school education in 2000, only 67.0 percent of foreign-born residents of the same age had earned their high school diploma.[16] These differences reflect both changes in U.S. society as well as changes in the types of immigrants who come. Education levels among native-born Americans are rising, which would cause the gap between native-born and immigrant educational attainment to increase even if nothing in the immigrant population had changed. But as was mentioned above, the fact that younger children and older adults make up a larger proportion of new immigrants should also affect education levels: children have not yet finished their education, and older adults are likely to have less education than the younger relatives who sponsor their entry into the United States.

Educational attainment also varies with immigrants' legal status and country of origin. New immigrants are likely to have less education than naturalized citizens. While immigrants from Asia, Europe, and other regions have high school graduation rates similar to those of the native-born (83.8 percent, 81.3 percent, and 86.6 percent, respectively), Latin American immigrants are much less likely to have graduated from high school (49.6 percent). Even among Latin American immigrants, education levels vary significantly. Central American immigrants are the least likely to have completed high school (37.3 percent), while the large majority of immigrants from South America and the Caribbean have done so (68.1 percent and 79.6 percent, respectively).

Finally, immigrants work in many different occupations and earn a range of incomes. Just as immigrants' educational status tends to be concentrated at relatively extreme levels, they tend to hold jobs that reflect either a great deal of skill and training—such as college teaching, science, or health care—or that require little skill, such as housekeeping, farm labor, or taxicab driving. As a result, immigrants are concentrated at the top and the bottom of the earnings distribution. However, since the majority of new immigrants have less education than native workers, they also earn less, are more likely to be unemployed, and are more likely to live in poverty than native workers.[17] With the bulk of immigrants in low-skill occupations, their overall socioeconomic status falls below that of native workers. In 2000 foreign-born workers were more likely than natives to be in service occupations and less likely to hold managerial or professional occupations. Immigrants were also less likely than natives to earn $50,000 or more annually (19.1 percent and 24.6 percent, respectively), and more likely to live below the poverty line (16.8 percent compared with 11.2 percent of natives). Foreign-born residents without U.S. citizenship were more than twice as likely as naturalized citizens to live in poverty.[18]

Looking at the big picture, these data show that immigrants are a heterogeneous group, representing many different countries of origin, age groups, family structures, education levels, occupations, and income levels. Clear patterns emerge from these statistics—such as being born in Latin America, living with large families, and working in low-skill occupations—that lend themselves easily to immigrant stereotypes. But this is a narrow perspective that does not encompass the complexity of the immigrant population. In some cases, U.S. immigration policies such as the emphasis on family reunification explain certain demographic trends. In other cases, outside factors such as culture, natural disaster, or war influence immigrant characteristics. In every instance, although demographic data are compelling, it is important to remember that immigration happens one person at a time.

Illegal Immigrants

In 1993 President Bill Clinton's nominee for attorney general, Zoë Baird, found herself under intense congressional and public scrutiny for hiring an immigrant without work authorization to provide child care in her home. The fact that Baird employed an illegal immigrant effectively blocked her appointment to become head of the Justice Department, which oversees the INS. In 2001 President George W. Bush's nominee for secretary of labor, Linda Chavez, met a similar fate when she admitted to paying an undocumented immigrant to do household chores.

The strong national response to these incidents reveals Americans' ambivalence—both political and personal—toward illegal immigrants. On one hand is the conviction that people should obey the laws and the fear that hordes of immigrants will arrive unchecked. But these viewpoints are balanced by the dependence of important sectors of the economy on the labor of illegal immigrants and the humanitarian claims their situations so often pose. During the past decade illegal immigrants have often been viewed as unwelcome guests who take jobs away from Americans and overburden public schools, hospitals, and other social services. At the same time, illegal immigrants may be drawn to the U.S. by family ties to legal residents, recruited by U.S. employers, or fleeing violence in their home countries. Complicating matters further is the integration of illegal immigrants into communities of legal residents and citizens. Efforts to "weed out" illegal residents of immigrant communities often lead to infringements on legal residents' civil rights, particularly through discrimination and ethnic or racial profiling.

Figure 2-2 Average Annual Number of Immigrants, 1825–1995

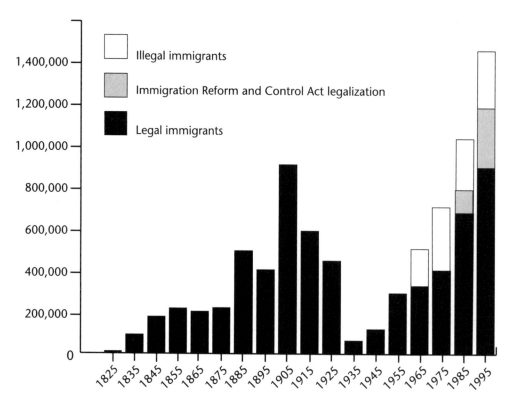

Source: James P. Smith and Barry Edmonston, eds., *The New Americans: Economic, Demographic, and Fiscal Effects of Immigration* (Washington, DC: National Academy Press, 1997), 51.

For some, this ambivalence leads to contradictory policies: "We are encouraging hypocrisy," said Sen. Pete Domenici, R-N.M. "At the border we arrest, but once they get here everyone opens their arms and says we've got a job for you." Others suggest that current policies are overly restrictive in light of public sentiment. Chavez wrote in 1994 that, "So long as they stay out of trouble once they're here, most Americans ignore illegal aliens." Frank Sharry of the National Immigration Forum also noted the disconnect between politics and public perceptions: "If illegal immigrants are so scary, why do America's mothers turn our children over to them every day?"[19]

Most experts believe that the United States is now experiencing its first great wave of illegal immigration. It is not surprising, therefore, that restrictive immigration policies have gained unprecedented support during the past decade. In October 1996 the INS estimated that 4.6 to 5.4 million undocumented immigrants were residing in the United States—about 1.9 percent of the total U.S. population. It projected that the number of undocumented immigrants would grow constantly by approximately 275,000 each year. By these estimates, the rate of growth of the undocumented immigrant population had declined since 1988. The 2000 census revised these figures upward, estimating that the illegal immigrant population ranges from 7.1 to 9 million. According to these new estimates, more than one-quarter of the foreign-born population is in the country illegally.[20]

The 1996 estimates showed that the vast majority of illegal immigrants—80 percent—come from the Western Hemisphere. The top five countries of origin for illegal immigrants are geographic neighbors to the United States: Mexico, El Salvador, Guatemala, Canada, and Haiti. Only two of the top fifteen countries of origin—the Philippines and Poland—are outside the Western Hemisphere. Mexico is the leading country of origin, accounting for 54 percent of, or 2.7 million, illegal immigrants. The average annual growth of the undocumented population of Mexican immigrants was approximately 150,000 between 1988 and 1996, according to INS estimates.

Approximately 60 percent of illegal immigrants enter the United States by crossing the border between official ports of entry. Officially designated "entry without inspection" (EWI), those who enter the United States this way—mostly Mexican and other Central American immigrants—receive the most public attention. But roughly 40 percent of illegal immigrants actually enter the United States legally, by obtaining a temporary visa for tourism, work, or study. They then remain in the United States illegally, by staying beyond the specified period of admission. These immigrants, who represent many nationalities, are known as "nonimmigrant overstays."[21]

As with all immigrants, once they arrive in the country, most illegal immigrants are concentrated in a handful of states. Eighty-three percent of illegal aliens lived in seven states in 1996, according to the INS. California was the leading state of residence, with approximately 2 million or 40 percent of undocumented aliens, followed by Texas (700,000), New York (540,000), Florida (350,000), Illinois (290,000), New Jersey (135,000), and Arizona (115,000). By comparison, 76 percent of all immigrants (legal and illegal) arriving in the United States during the 1980s resided in these same states, with the exception of Arizona. However, this trend appears to be changing, as 2000 census figures reveal significant new immigrant enclaves in Georgia and West Virginia, for example.[22]

Overall, the accuracy of these figures is limited, because of a variety of uncertain factors. Illegal immigrants are, statistically speaking, a hidden population. In simple terms, the illegal immigrant population is estimated by subtracting the number of legal immigrants (obtained through INS data) and naturalized citizens (obtained through Census data) from the total foreign-born population (also obtained through Census data). But this number assumes that illegal immigrants are counted in the Census, which is likely inaccurate for many immigrants because illegal residents actively avoid contact with federal officials. In addition, information about the long-term undocumented immigrant population, the net number of nonimmigrant overstays, the number of EWI immigrants, the mortality rate of the undocumented resident population, and the amount of emigration from the U.S. by undocumented immigrants can only be estimates.

As uncertain as these numbers are, however, most Americans "greatly overestimate the proportion of immigrants who are in the United States illegally."[23] Although even revised INS figures show that only one-quarter of the foreign-born population is here illegally, two-thirds of respondents in a 1993 poll believed that the majority of recent immigrants were undocumented. Beliefs such as these can have an important political impact, as the section below on the 1996 immigration reforms shows. These beliefs have also, however, spurred a search for other solutions to the problem of unauthorized immigration. One such solution is the establishment of programs for temporary foreign workers.

Temporary Foreign Workers

The Immigration Act of 1990 created a variety of visa categories for the temporary admission of foreign workers. Since then, congressional debates over frequent proposals to increase the number of temporary foreign workers have pitted powerful coalitions of business groups and industry lobbyists against labor unions and other workers' advocates. As the 1990s drew to a close, immigration analyst Demetrios G. Papademetriou noted that, "The essential, and not yet answered, question is how to promote U.S. competitive interests by facilitating access to key foreign-born personnel without unnecessary procedures while simultaneously not undermining the broader social policy goal of advancing the interests of U.S. workers overall."[24]

The admission of temporary workers to the United States is particularly interesting because it parallels conflicts over the admission of other immigrants. As with the population of legal immigrants, temporary workers cluster at the two ends of the skill ladder: in the technology sector, where highly educated immigrants are sought, and in agriculture, where low-skilled labor is the norm. In each case, the same debate arises: Are immigrants filling jobs that native-born Americans cannot or will not take, or are they providing cheap labor for corporations that refuse to pay the wages necessary to maintain an American workforce? Questions about what the United States owes temporary workers are equally pressing: Should workers have a chance to "adjust" their status to legal permanent residence after some years of employment in the United States, and if so, how can employers be prevented from taking advantage of their role in sponsoring immigrants?

However, the debate over how to manage highly skilled temporary workers diverges from the debate over low-skilled workers, because each is influenced differently by tensions over other issues. Chief among these issues is illegal immigration. The use of illegal migrants in place of temporary foreign workers is common in U.S. agriculture, and thus policy on temporary agricultural workers and policy on illegal immigration must be coordinated. By contrast, the substitution of illegal migrants for temporary foreign workers is less prevalent in the high-tech industry. However, technology jobs can be exported overseas with much greater ease than agricultural jobs, and debates over the need for temporary high-tech workers often become debates over the quality of American science and technology education. Thus, arguments over education policy and American economic competitiveness often form a subtext to debates on how to provide temporary worker visas to skilled foreign workers.

TEMPORARY FOREIGN AGRICULTURAL WORKERS AND THE H-2A DEBATE The first U.S. government-sponsored recruitment of Mexican workers occurred in 1917, when the Department of Labor suspended head taxes and literacy tests for Mexicans coming to work for American farmers. During the 1930s the Depression created a surplus of farmworkers, especially in California, and Mexican workers either left of their own accord or were forcibly returned to Mexico. But by 1942 World War II had drawn American farmworkers to the battlefields abroad. California farmers predicted labor shortages and called for the importation of between 40,000 and 100,000 Mexican farmworkers for the coming harvest. That year, the U.S. and Mexican governments created what came to be known as the Bracero Program—a "farm labor supply agreement" that allowed Mexican workers (*braceros*) to do farm work in the United States on an emergency basis when U.S. workers were not available. The

Table 2-1 Nonimmigrant Visa Categories

There are many different categories of nonimmigrant visas—so many, in fact, that the system can seem like an alphabet soup to applicants and analysts trying to navigate it. The chart below briefly describes each category.

Visa Category	Description
A	An ambassador, public minister, or career diplomatic or consular officer and family/personal employees.
B	A temporary visitor for business or pleasure.
C	A person in transit through the United States, or foreign official in transit to and from the United Nations Headquarters.
D	Crewmembers of sea or aircraft temporarily embarking at U.S. ports.
E	A treaty trader or investor and family.
F	A student at an established college, university, seminary, conservatory, academic high school, elementary school, or language training program and family.
G	A representative of a foreign government or international organization, officials and staff members of such an organization and family.
H	(1B) Temporary skilled workers in specialty occupations, such as technology and scientific research; (2A) Temporary agricultural workers; (2B) Temporary workers in nonagricultural, often low-skill occupations, such as hotel and restaurant industries.
I	A representative of foreign press, radio, film, or other information media and family.
J	An exchange visitor, such as a teacher or professor, for the purpose of teaching, conducting research or receiving training, and family. This category includes students receiving graduate medical training.
K	A fiancé(e) or child of the fiancé(e) of a U.S. citizen.
L	An intracompany transferee and family.
M	A student at an established vocational or other nonacademic institution, and family.
N	A spouse or child of certain retired employees of international organizations.

Table 2-1 *continued*

Visa Category	Description
O	A person who "has demonstrated extraordinary ability in the sciences, arts, education, business, or athletics . . . or, with regard to motion picture and television productions a demonstrated record of extraordinary achievement," assistants and family.
P	An internationally recognized athlete, artist, or entertainer and family.
Q	A participant in an international cultural exchange program and family.
R	A person in a religious occupation and family.
S	An informant who possesses "critical reliable information concerning a terrorist organization, enterprise, or operation," and family.
T	A victim of human trafficking and family.
U	A victim who has suffered substantial physical or mental abuse as a result of criminal activity on U.S. territory in violation of U.S. laws, such as rape, torture, incest, domestic violence, female genital mutilation, being held hostage, slave trade, extortion, murder or conspiracy, and family.
V	A person whose petition for legal immigration status was filed before the enactment of the Legal Immigration Family Equity (LIFE) Act and remains pending.

Sources: Demetrios G. Papademetriou and Stephen Yale-Loehr, *Balancing Interests: Rethinking U.S. Selection of Skilled Immigrants* (Washington, D.C.: Carnegie Endowment for International Peace, 1996), 71; the Immigration and Nationality Act, Section 101(a). Quotations are from the act.

program required U.S. farmers to provide contracts that included payment of roundtrip transportation and wages equal to those of American farmworkers.[25]

During the war years foreign workers under the Bracero Program peaked at less than 2 percent of the nation's 4 million hired workers. After World War II, however, the situation changed. Although the U.S. and Mexican governments had hoped the Bracero Program would divert the illegal flow of Mexican workers into legal channels, the program actually appeared to stimulate illegal immigration in the postwar years. Despite recommendations by the President's Commission on

Migrant Farmworkers

There are currently over 1.8 million seasonal farmworkers in the United States, laborers whose employment shifts with the changing demands of planting, tending, and harvesting our nation's crops. These workers have over 3 million dependents, most of whom are children, bringing the nation's total population of seasonal farmworkers and their families to over 4.8 million. Migrant farmworkers are those seasonal farm laborers who travel from one place to another to earn a living in agriculture. There are 900,000 migrant farmworkers in the United States, who are accompanied by 300,000 children and 150,000 adult dependents, bringing the country's total population of migrant farmworkers and their families to over 1.3 million.

Migrant farmworkers have special needs related to their continual movement, dislocation, and status as outsiders in the communities where they work. When arriving in a new community, migrant workers must find temporary housing, either in labor camps provided by their employers or in short-term rental housing. If they don't have their own vehicles, migrants need to find ways of getting to stores, and from one harvest to another. Since migrant farmworkers have limited resources and few contacts in the communities they pass through, they rely upon intermediaries and informal networks in order to survive. In this way, migrant workers are socially invisible; they play a crucial role in the local economies where they labor, yet their struggles are generally hidden from view.

Seasonal farmworkers are the poorest laborers in the United States, earning an average of $7,500 each year. Farmworkers who migrate are poorer than settled seasonal laborers, with over half of all migrants earning less than $5,000 per year. The most vulnerable migrant workers, such as those laboring for farm labor contractors in eastern states, earn average wages as low as $3,500. Although migrant families commonly pool the wages of several workers, over two-thirds of our nation's migrant households and 80 percent of migrant children live below the poverty line.

Farmworkers' life expectancies are lower than that of most Americans, and infant mortality among farmworker children is double the national average. Physicians treating farmworkers generally compare their health to that of residents in the developing world. Farmworkers suffer from chronic infections, advanced untreated diseases, and numerous problems resulting from limited access to medical care. Farmwork is the second most dangerous job in the nation. Workplace accidents, many of which involve children, are common, and farm labor has the nation's highest incidence of workplace fatalities and disabling injuries.

Most farmworkers are men, although many women also labor in the fields. The average age of farmworkers is 31, with over half under 29. Nearly 90,000 farmworkers are between the ages of 14 and 17. Farmworker families often work together, with children laboring beside their parents and eventually becoming key contributors to the family's survival. Forty percent of migrant children work in the fields. Farmworker families often have difficulty balancing the economic demands of farm labor with the children's education. In general, farmworker children do poorly in school. Fifty percent of migrant children fall below national scholastic averages as early as the first grade and the majority never graduate high school.

Seasonal farm labor draws workers from a variety of backgrounds and ethnic groups. Currently, two out of every ten seasonal farmworkers were born in the United States, a diverse mix of Latinos, African Americans, whites, and Native Americans. The remaining 80 percent of the nation's farmworkers are immigrants, over 90 percent of whom are from Mexico. Other immigrants come from Central America, particularly Guatemala or El Salvador, or Caribbean nations such as Haiti or Jamaica. A small percentage of farmworkers are from Asian countries such as the Philippines, Laos, and Vietnam.

Farmworkers born in the United States generally hold more stable, higher-wage positions, while the less-appealing jobs are filled with recent immigrants, who are virtually all minorities. These immigrants generally have low levels of formal education and often speak little to no English. Nationally, about half of all farmworkers are undocumented. The percentage of farm laborers who lack working papers has been steadily increasing over the last decade.

Source: Excerpted from Daniel Rothenberg, *With These Hands: The Hidden World of Migrant Farmworkers Today,* Los Angeles: University of California Press, 1998, 6–7.

Migratory Labor to end the program in 1951 because of its adverse effects on wages and labor standards, the Bracero Program continued until 1964. By this time, significant migratory patterns had been established between Mexico and U.S. farms, including entrenched channels of illegal immigration.

Today, U.S. growers acknowledge that the bulk of their labor supply is composed of illegal immigrants. In 1998 the U.S. Department of Agriculture reported that there were 1.45 million hired farmworkers; at the same time, the Department of Labor's National Agricultural Workers Survey found that "52 percent of hired farmworkers lacked work authorization."[26] The primary effort to address this problem under immigration policy is the H-2A visa category for seasonal farmworkers, created by the Immigration Act of 1990. Employers who apply for H-2A visas on behalf of their workers must attest that they have exhausted efforts to recruit U.S. laborers and will provide contracts to foreign laborers guaranteeing payment of prevailing wages and adequate housing facilities. Yet in 1998 the Department of Labor only certified the need for 34,898 H-2A workers.[27] These numbers show that H-2A workers make up only a small fraction of the seasonal agricultural workforce, particularly compared with the large proportion of undocumented workers.

Farm employers say that the H-2A program is underused because its requirements are "inflexible." By 1995 the National Council of Agricultural Employers had released a proposal calling for a new temporary agricultural worker program. Growers proposed increasing admissions under the H-2A category. They also suggested shifting a portion of currently undocumented farmworkers into legalized status, a process commonly known as "amnesty," which they argued would help stabilize the industry's labor supply. Their legalization program would allow foreign workers who remain in agriculture for five years, working 180 days each year, to be eligible for green cards. That year, the House and Senate began hearings on farmers' requests for an alternative to the H-2A program, hearings that would be repeated in subsequent years. During the latter half of the 1990s, the House and Senate frequently debated migrant farmworker policy and even produced proposals for pilot programs that passed in committee, but no relevant legislation passed the full Congress.[28]

This active stalemate over temporary agricultural worker policy reflects the comparable strength yet divergent aims of the opposing coalitions in the debate. As one commentator put it, "Despite widespread agreement that the status quo is not acceptable, there is no agreement about what should be done. . . ."[29] Generally, farm business advocates, such as the American Farm Bureau and Republican members of Congress, have pushed for higher numbers of admissions and greater employer flexibility on recruitment, wage, and housing requirements. They argue that lower labor costs are essential to maintaining global competitiveness and agriculture's leading role among the nation's exports. Indeed, economic figures show that the overall value of U.S. fruit, vegetable, and horticultural production in 1997 was more than $35 billion, while U.S. farm commodities registered a trade surplus of nearly $20 billion.[30] Jon Wunsch of the Michigan Farm Bureau told the Senate Subcommittee on Immigration in May 2000 that "the thriving U.S. economy has put farm employers in competition for a limited pool of labor with employers in other industries who can offer longer-term, often year-round employment and better compensation and benefits. . . . But even where changing public policy and economic conditions have not contributed to new shortages of workers, chronic shortages prevail and are unlikely to dissipate."[31]

Farmworker advocates, including labor unions and Latino groups, oppose both the current H-2A program and the agricultural industry's proposals for reform. They object that both versions of the program fail to protect workers' economic and social rights. The United Farm Workers have referred to the program as a form of "indentured servitude,"[32] because even documented workers have limited recourse against employers' violations of minimum wage rules and other labor standards. Although migrant workers earn far more on U.S. farms than they would at home, they remain in poverty because of a combination of chronic underemployment and low wages. During the 2000 fruit tree harvest in Washington, pruners earned from $6.50 an hour, the state minimum wage, to $7.25 an hour. "But even in a good year—working through the high-season harvest months and doing sporadic pruning and thinning jobs in the winter and early spring," the typical farmworker makes only $10,000 to $12,000.[33]

Farmworker advocates charge that the current program does not effectively enforce existing labor laws, particularly rules on minimum wages and benefits. About one-fifth of employers flout hourly minimum wage rules, using instead a piece-rate system that produces even lower earnings.[34] Although migrant workers send some of these earnings home to their families, they often pay for food, rent, and utilities despite the H-2A law. Some farmworkers find at the end of the season that the foreman's records show that their expenses exceed their earnings, forcing them to continue working. "[T]he status quo is indeed untenable, not because of over-regulation of labor standards in agriculture but because of a complete lack of enforcement of the few labor standards that actually apply to farm work,"[35] said Cecilia Munoz of the National Council of La Raza (NCLR), in testimony before the Senate Subcommittee on Immigration in May 2000.

Figures from the National Agricultural Workers Survey (NAWS) support this argument. "Over the period of the 1990's [sic], with a strong economy and greater, increasingly widespread prosperity, farm worker wages have lost ground relative to those of workers in the private, nonfarm sector. . . . Consequently, farm workers have lost 11 percent of their purchasing power over the last decade."[36] Farmworker advocates also cite the NAWS to counter industry claims of labor shortages; they say that farmworkers' chronic underemployment provides evidence of an oversupply of labor.

According to NCLR, part of this oversupply of labor is because of an overrepresentation of undocumented workers as a result of competition among labor contractors to provide growers with the cheapest available workers. Because illegal immigrants are usually the most vulnerable to exploitation, NCLR has proposed a legalization program based on past farm work, unlike the proposal of the agricultural industry that would require work in the future. The NCLR plan would "allow workers who have already contributed to the U.S. economy through their sweat and labor an opportunity to become legal residents, without any conditions that would further subject workers to more exploitation."[37]

Noticeably absent from the debate thus far have been consumer groups, who benefit from lower fruit and vegetable prices that reflect the agricultural industry's cheap labor supply. According to one study, "Americans spend 8.4 percent of their income on the consumption of food and alcohol—about 25 percent less than in 1970."[38] Some reform advocates believe that a public awareness campaign that educates Americans about the conditions under which their food is produced would improve consumer tolerance for higher food prices, similar to students' campaigns against sweatshops.

The political momentum behind proposals to expand guest worker programs received a boost with the 2000 elections of U.S. president George W. Bush and Mexican president Vicente Fox. Since taking office President Fox has made it clear that he would like to increase the number of Mexicans allowed to work legally in the United States. In April 2001 Fox visited California, where he "told hundreds of farmworkers that he would press the United States to enact laws to give a blanket legal status to illegal immigrants working on farms here."[39] President Fox continued this campaign during his three-day state visit to Washington in early September 2001, urging President Bush and the U.S. Congress to finalize recommendations for overhauling immigration policies by the end of the year. President Bush voiced agreement with Fox's proposals without embracing any timetable for action, calling Mexican immigration "an incredibly complex issue."[40] Support in the U.S. Congress has been ambiguous. Labor leaders and several American growers' associations supported a proposal by Rep. Howard L. Berman, D-Calif., and Sen. Gordon H. Smith, R-Ore., that would increase the numbers of guest workers to 150,000 in five years, eliminate many requirements on employers to demonstrate a genuine labor shortage before they hire foreign workers, and allow migrants with several years of agricultural service to apply for legal residency.[41] But many Republicans expressed skepticism of such proposals, even as they applauded Fox's leadership. However, the national security crisis and scrutiny of U.S. immigration policy that resulted from the terrorist attacks of September 11, 2001, ground to a halt negotiations on migration policy with Mexico and moved the issue to a back burner. For now, the future of the Fox and Bush administrations' joint "migration working group" remains uncertain.

TEMPORARY FOREIGN HIGH-TECH WORKERS AND THE H-1B DEBATE In the late 1980s the National Science Foundation (NSF)—in an unpublished report that was nonetheless widely circulated and roundly criticized—predicted imminent shortages of scientists and engineers. The 1990 Hudson Institute's "Workforce 2000" report seemed to bolster the NSF prediction. Congress cited both studies when it amended immigration law in 1990, substantially increasing the number of skilled workers allowed to immigrate to the United States each year.[42] This legislation created the H-1B visa category that granted work authorization to professionals and highly skilled individuals in specialty occupations. H-1B workers must be sponsored by their employers, "who must attest that they will fulfill a number of wage and working conditions designed to protect U.S. workers."[43] The 1990 law capped annual H-1B admissions at 65,000.

Immediately thereafter, the Soviet Union broke up, defense spending was slashed, and the aerospace and other industries were aggressively downsized. Not surprisingly, the job market for scientists and engineers collapsed. Still, from 1990 to 1993, the United States produced 50 percent more bachelors' degrees in computer science, math, and engineering than it needed. Despite the oversupply of domestic engineers and scientists, more than 314,000 foreign scientists and engineers entered the country on a variety of temporary visas between 1991 and 1995, said immigration researcher and former Labor Department official David S. North. In 1993 and 1994 the TV news shows *60 Minutes* and *48 Hours* revealed that labor contractors had brought in hundreds of programmers on H-1B visas to replace Americans being laid off. The Labor Department said that because of loopholes in the H-1B law, companies were increasingly using it to bring in lower-end programmers en masse. In 1995 Labor Secretary Robert Reich told the Senate Judiciary Committee that many employers hire H-1B workers through job contractors, sometimes known as "body shops," whose "workforce [is] composed predominantly, and even entirely, of H-1B workers." INS figures showed that in 1998 the largest importer of H-1B workers was Mastech, a Pittsburgh, Pa., labor contractor who imported 672 workers and whose clients included AT&T, Citibank, the Department of Defense, and the Federal Aviation Administration.[44]

Some opponents of H-1B visas argue that the push to lift the cap on H-1B visas is simply an effort by business to exploit cheap foreign labor at the expense of native professionals. Norman Matloff, a computer science professor at the University of California Davis, charges in an online report that, "Access to cheap labor is the 'hidden agenda' behind the campaign of the Information Technology Association of America (ITAA) to develop an image of a software labor shortage in the public consciousness."[45] The Federation for American Immigration Reform (FAIR), one of the strongest opponents of increasing the number of H-1B visa admissions, argues that the program allows employers to exploit foreign workers because most need their employers to sponsor them for permanent visas when their H-1Bs expire.[46]

Most opponents and proponents of the H-1B program seem to agree, however, that the rapid technology boom of the late 1990s created a labor shortage in the technology industry, and that its roots lie in education. Although labor advocates blame the technology industry for inadequate investment in training and worker education programs, the industry points to the failure of America's education system, whose students ranked poorly in the Third International Mathematics and Science Study (TIMSS). One high-tech recruiter noted that engineers from Ireland, Scotland, India, and China are "better trained" than their American counterparts.[47] Hans Meeder, former executive director of the 21st Century Workforce Commission, a panel chartered by Congress, said, "What exists right now seems to be a disconnect between what employers need and what local schools are offering . . . and hence, we aren't getting enough students in the pipeline to fill new-economy jobs down the road."[48]

The solutions offered for this shortage, however, are very different. The ITAA has been one of the most forceful proponents of increasing H-1B admissions. ITAA president Harris N. Miller has argued that the shortage of information technology professionals "threatens the growth of the entire U.S. economy, our global competitiveness and the wage stability that is the bedrock of this country's low inflation." Business executives have testified before Congress that shortages of qualified American workers could force U.S. firms to locate future factories abroad, taking thousands of U.S. jobs with them. The Hudson Institute predicts that if left unaddressed, the labor shortage could result in a 5 percent drop in economic growth—$200 billion in lost output. "We are in the midst of the most far-reaching technology revolution we have ever known," said then-Secretary of Commerce William H. Daley.

"There is a very real threat that technology could overwhelm us—that it could move faster than our ability to train our people to manage it."[49]

On the other side, labor unions such as the AFL-CIO attribute the labor shortage to the technology industry's poor human resource practices. The union has charged that the industry's tight labor situation is "self-inflicted" largely because of insufficient training and education programs, and discrimination against older workers. It also cites flaws in legislation that allow fraud and abuse, such as "manipulation of the system by employers who seek to gain entrance for a family member"[50] and concerns that the program depresses American wages. Other opponents argue that a better way to address labor shortages would be to admit more immigrants as permanent residents. In May 2000 the Immigration Reform Coalition "published an open letter in *Roll Call* calling on Congress to begin replacing H-1B visas with 'conditional green cards' that would allow foreign workers to qualify for citizenship like other immigrants." The letter was signed by Paul Donnelly, who worked on the Immigration Act of 1990 and served on the Commission on Immigration Reform. Other supporters included representatives of the Institute of Electronics and Electrical Engineers (IEEE), Linus Torvalds, inventor of the Linux operating system and himself a beneficiary of an H-1B visa, and Steven Wozniack, cofounder of Apple Computer.[51]

Lobbied heavily by the technology industry, Sen. Spencer Abraham, R-Mich., led congressional initiatives to raise the cap on H-1B visas in the late 1990s. His initial efforts were thwarted in 1996, when chair of the Senate Subcommittee on Immigration, Alan K. Simpson, R-Wyo., joined attempts by Sen. Edward M. Kennedy, D-Mass., Labor Secretary Reich, and the Clinton administration to make it harder for employers to import foreign workers. However, in 1998, with growing pressure from high-tech companies back home, Simpson retired from Congress, and Reich no longer Labor secretary, Kennedy teamed with Sen. Dianne Feinstein, D-Calif., whose constituency includes Silicon Valley, to offer an alternative to Abraham's proposal. This alternative, eventually rejected, would have increased H-1B admissions modestly while including enforcement provisions that would require employers to first try to recruit Americans. It would have also made it illegal to lay off Americans and hire foreigners.

Instead, Democrats and Republicans agreed on compromise legislation, signed by President Clinton in 1998, that increased the number of six-year H-1B visas available for three years, from 65,000 to 115,000 before returning to 65,000 in 2002. It included layoff and recruitment requirements for H-1B dependent businesses—those that had a certain percentage of H-1B workers—and those that planned to hire workers who did not have master's degrees and who would be paid less than $60,000 a year. The compromise also assessed a $500 fee on employers for every visa application and renewal, raising about $75 million a year that would go to college scholarships and job training for low-income students studying math, engineering, or computer science.[52]

Even these increases, however, were not enough. Companies continued to fill the H-1B admissions quota months before the end of the fiscal year. A report published by the National Academy of Sciences in October 2000 found that companies in the United States employed about five million information technology workers—a number that was projected to grow by about 7 percent annually until the year 2008—while 800,000 jobs in the industry remained unfilled.[53] Phil Bond, senior vice president of the Information Technology Industry Council, which represents thirty-one of the nation's largest high-tech companies, noted that many technology companies are committed to investments in education and training, and view the H-1B program "as only a Band-Aid solution" to labor shortages. Despite testimony from labor advocates arguing that not enough time had passed to evaluate the effectiveness of protections included in the 1998 legislation,[54] Congress approved a further increase in H-1B admissions on October 3, 2000, that lifted the annual cap to 195,000 through fiscal year 2003.

However, by spring 2001, the technology bubble had burst, sending the economy into its first recession in a decade, and leading to massive layoffs among high-tech firms. Again, a debate emerged over whether ailing firms would be inclined to lay off temporary foreign workers before Americans, or to retain foreign workers who may be paid less than American workers. What is certain is that, for the first time in years, firms' demand for temporary foreign workers did not surpass the annual cap. Although the H-1B visa cap remained at 195,000 for fiscal year 2001, only 163,000 visas were approved as the fiscal year ended, with 29,000 petitions pending.[55]

Closed Door, Open Door:
The IIRIRA and Immigration Enforcement

The coalitions of business, ethnic, and religious groups that lobby to increase or decrease the admission of legal immigrants confound many of the partisan assumptions behind American politics. "Conservative" figures such as business leaders and "liberal" groups such as ethnic organizations rarely make common cause on other issues, but immigration routinely creates strange political bedfellows. The same is true for the opposition to increased immigration. In the middle of the 1990s, a bipartisan coalition formed to pass the Illegal Immigration Reform and Immigrant Responsibility Act (IIRIRA), called "the most sweeping overhaul of American immigration policy in 30 years—and the sharpest immigration crack-down and restriction since the 1920s."[56]

As early as 1993 the new Clinton administration had embarked on a series of "tough on crime" policies to counter the perception that Democrats were "soft on crime." Policies against illegal immigration were one way to make this case. Introducing his immigration policy in July, President Clinton announced, "We will make it tougher for illegal aliens to get into our country. We will treat organizing a crime syndicate to smuggle aliens as a serious crime. And we will increase the number of Border Patrol personnel, equipping and training them to be first-class law enforcement officers." Attorney General Janet Reno announced specific initiatives to prevent illegal entry, to remove and deport illegal aliens and criminal aliens expeditiously, and to strengthen criminal penalties and investigative authorities.

The following year, the so-called "Save Our State" initiative, listed on California ballots as Proposition 187, drastically cut public assistance and services to illegal immigrants. It received national attention as it quickly became a symbol for the debate over immigrants' (both legal and illegal) role in American communities. When Proposition 187 was approved by California voters in November 1994, it signaled a consensus that illegal immigrants drain public resources to which they are not entitled. "People should not expect to come to this country with their hands out to receive benefits paid for by taxpaying Americans," said chair of the House Ways and Means Committee, Rep. Bill Archer, R-Texas, in February 1995.[57] Support of Proposition 187 also had boosted Republican California Gov. Pete Wilson's successful reelection campaign in 1994.

By early 1996 the immigration debate had reached the presidential election campaigns. Republican primary candidate Bob Dole told the Senate, "Wherever you go, illegal immigration is a big, big issue."[58] As the outcry over illegal aliens grew louder, issues of legal and illegal immigration became increasingly confounded. Pat Buchanan, a Republican primary candidate, made anti-immigration rhetoric a feature of his campaign, suggesting that immigrants represent a "foreign invasion." "Within six months I'd stop immigration across the border cold. . . . I would supply a security fence along those areas where huge amounts of illegal immigrants run into this country at will," he said during a speech in Tucson, Arizona.[59]

Immigration Policy at the State Level: California's Proposition 187

The nation's most populous state, California, is also the state with the highest concentration of immigrants—legal and illegal—and hence becomes a frequent focal point for immigration policy debates. The 1994 uproar over Proposition 187, a statewide referendum that barred illegal immigrants and their children from receiving government services, illuminated the debate over immigration's fiscal effects and had important political repercussions at national, state, and local levels.

The referendum, stimulated by a nongovernmental organization known as the "Save Our State" (SOS) initiative, included provisions that prevented illegal immigrants from attending public schools and receiving social services and health care. It also required that local police, school administrators, and social and medical workers turn in suspected illegal immigrants to federal and state immigration authorities and established state criminal penalties for creating, using, and selling fraudulent documents to conceal a person's illegal immigration status.[1]

Republican Gov. Pete Wilson's support of Proposition 187 during his reelection campaign "became a national symbol of anger over illegal immigration."[2] Political advertisements depicted immigrants illegally crossing the border from Mexico and aimed to convince California voters that they were straining the state's budget and economy. SOS cochairman Ron Prince argued that the state's two million illegal immigrants (a higher figure than the official INS estimate of 1.4 million) imposed serious costs on the state government. One state study estimated that state and local governments spent $2.95 billion on illegal aliens and their U.S.-born children in fiscal 1993 for primary and secondary education, corrections, Medicaid, and Aid to Families with Dependent Children (AFDC). Supporters also contended that it was only natural to deny government services to people who had no lawful right to be in the United States.[3]

The measure passed by 1.4 million votes—nearly 60 percent of California voters. However, the referendum's passage galvanized its opponents. Seventy-seven percent of California Hispanics had voted against it. The vote led to one of the largest protests in state history, as 70,000 people gathered in Los Angeles.[4] On the day after the election, lawyers for a coalition of immigrants' rights groups led by the American Civil Liberties Union filed a lawsuit in federal court in Los Angeles on behalf of eight undocumented aliens seeking to block implementation of Proposition 187. They argued that the measure was inconsistent with federal immigration law and violated immigrants' equal-protection rights. The court found much of the measure unconstitutional, but the Wilson administration appealed the decision.

Opponents also disputed estimates of large fiscal costs imposed by illegal immigrants and stressed instead that denying education and health services to immigrants would ultimately harm society as a whole. "Denying anyone treatment for an infectious disease, denying anyone immunizations—that poses a public health threat to everyone," said

Thomas Saenz, an attorney with the Mexican American Legal Defense and Educational Fund (MALDEF) in Los Angeles.[5]

The anti-immigrant backlash epitomized by Proposition 187 also spurred legal immigrants across the country to naturalize, thereby increasing their political participation. Arturo Vargas, executive director of the National Association of Latino Elected and Appointed Officials (NALEO) noted that the increasing interest in naturalization "is a reaction, in fact, to Proposition 187 in California," as immigrants realized the power of the vote in keeping public benefits and fighting discrimination.[6] Many consider Proposition 187 to be responsible for voter turnout in 1998 that elected Gray Davis, the state's first Democratic governor in sixteen years, along with a Hispanic lieutenant governor and speaker of the state assembly. Davis had campaigned as an opponent of Proposition 187 and promised not to enforce many of its provisions. Once in office, Davis betrayed this promise by pursuing the state's appeal to reverse the federal court decision nullifying Proposition 187. But Hispanic voters claimed victory again when Davis, under intense political pressure, agreed to drop the appeal in 1999.

---

1. Evelyn Nieves, "California Calls Off Effort to Carry Out Immigrant Measure," *New York Times*, July 30, 1999.
2. Ibid.
3. "Cracking Down on Immigration," *CQ Researcher*, February 3, 1995.
4. Nieves, "California Calls Off Effort."
5. "Cracking Down on Immigration."
6. Arturo Vargas, "Latino Voters: The New Political Landscape," *Vital Speeches of the Day*, January 1, 2000.

Thus given credibility by the leaders of both parties, the issue of illegal immigration became one on which the Republican Congress and the Democratic president could reach agreement. Signed by President Clinton on September 30, 1996, IIRIRA included provisions which, though directed against illegal immigration, inevitably affected legal immigrants as well. It included funding for border enforcement, penalties against alien smuggling and document fraud, deportation and exclusion provisions, employer sanctions, welfare eligibility restrictions, and refugee and asylum procedures.

Notably absent in the 1996 immigration law were improved or additional sanctions against employers who hire illegal immigrants. The Commission on Immigration Reform had concluded in 1994 that "the centerpiece of any effort to stop illegal entrants should be to turn off the jobs magnet that attracts them."[60] The late chair of the commission, Rep. Barbara Jordan, D-Texas, had recommended a national database of Social Security numbers that would allow employers to check the legal status of every job applicant. The Clinton administration, however, rejected the idea because of concerns for protecting civil liberties. Business groups also pressured Congress to limit employers' responsibility. In the end, IIRIRA contained only three pilot programs to test the effectiveness of electronic workplace verification systems, all of which are voluntary for employers.

This section of the chapter follows the aftermath of IIRIRA into the beginning of the Bush administration in 2001. The first part examines the ways in which IIRIRA's benefit reductions to illegal immigrants were followed by a restoration of some benefits and a revival of the pro-amnesty movement. The next part looks at the criminal alien provisions of IIRIRA, their impact on the criminal justice system, and the eventual success of legal challenges to many of them. Finally, the last part turns its attention to the changes that IIRIRA brought to the way that the INS enforces laws against illegal immigration, both at the border (exterior enforcement) and within the country (interior enforcement).

Benefits, Amnesty, and the Return of the Pro-Expansion Coalition

Perhaps the most controversial provisions in IIRIRA were those that drastically curtailed illegal immigrants' access to benefits. IIRIRA echoed not only the sentiments of Proposition 187 but also those enshrined in welfare reform. The Personal Responsibility and Work Opportunity Reconciliation Act had placed new restrictions on benefits for legal immigrants. IIRIRA did the same for illegal aliens, barring them from receiving any federal, state, or local public benefit, including retirement, welfare, health or disability benefits, public or assisted housing, postsecondary education, food assistance, and unemployment benefits. Even legal aliens were denied eligibility for these benefits for a period of five years after entering the country. Only a brief list of benefits remained available to illegal and new immigrants: emergency medical assistance, in-kind emergency disaster relief, free school lunches (under the National School Lunch Act and the Child Nutrition Act), and public health assistance for immunizations and the testing and treatment of communicable diseases.[61]

As IIRIRA took effect, it quickly became apparent that restrictions on immigrants' eligibility for government-sponsored benefits shifted a huge burden onto private, nonprofit organizations. Churches, community centers, and other charitable organizations suddenly became the only source of food and housing assistance, education, and health care for new and illegal immigrants. Immigrant aid groups also faced a surge of people seeking advice about the naturalization process: legal immigrants hoped to become citizens to remain eligible for welfare benefits, and illegal immigrants hoped to secure legal status to avoid tougher deportation procedures. For instance, on the busiest days, one could see people lined up out the door, down the block and around the corner at organizations such as the Northern Manhattan Coalition for Immigrant Rights.[62]

IIRIRA was the crest of a wave of anti-immigrant backlash that blurred the distinction between legal and illegal immigrants. But in its wake, pro-immigrant groups, fueled by a growing economy, began to mobilize in defense of immigrant rights. By 1998 a coalition of immigrant advocates started a campaign seeking amnesty for undocumented immigrants. "It's a labor and human rights issue," said Raynald Laforest, director of Haitian Constituency USA Inc., a member of a coalition based in Queens, New York.[63] This call for amnesty was not new. The Immigration Reform and Control Act of 1986 legalized the status of undocumented aliens who could prove their long-term residence in the United States. The 1986 amnesty provision temporarily reduced the size of the illegal immigrant population. But by 1996 the population had returned to preamnesty levels.

Renewed calls for amnesty gained force by 2000, when two unlikely supporters joined the campaign. First, labor unions, which had traditionally accused immigrant workers of depressing wages and breaking strikes, changed their policies and supported amnesty as a way to enable immigrant workers to stand up against exploitation by employers. The American Federation of Labor and Congress of Industrial Organizations (AFL-CIO) called for a blanket amnesty "because employer sanctions had failed to stem the tide of immigration and because immigrants represented such a large part of the workforce in dozens of industries," according to union officials. "We, the labor movement, have to put ourselves in a leadership position in immigrant rights," said president of the United Farm Workers, Arturo Rodriguez.[64] At the same time, the AFL-CIO resolution called on the federal government to toughen sanctions on employers who recruit or encourage illegal immigrants to work in the United States, and to maintain efforts to keep illegal immigrants from entering the country.

A second coalition made up of conservative politicians, business executives, and religious leaders joined amnesty advocates in May 2000. Jack Kemp, a former Republican candidate for vice president, Americans for Tax Reform, the United States

Catholic Conference, and the National Retail Federation joined pro-immigrant groups such as the Arab-American Institute, the National Asian Pacific American Legal Consortium, and the National Coalition for Haitian Rights in a broad effort to persuade Congress to ease immigration restrictions. While business groups favored the amnesty to gain access to more workers in a tight economy, religious leaders cited the preservation of family ties as an important reason to grant amnesty. "The bishops strongly believe that the groups involved have lived in this country for several years, established ties and built equities and thus are deserving an opportunity to remain in our country on a permanent basis," said Kevin Applebee, director of migration and refugee policy for the U.S. Catholic Conference.[65]

Opponents of the amnesty proposal argued that it would reward people who break the law and encourage more immigrants to try to enter the country illegally. Dan Stein, executive director of the Federation for American Immigration Reform (FAIR), argued that granting amnesty to illegal immigrants would tell them they can bypass the immigration process and "we will grant them legal status if they have the fortitude to stick it out for a few years."[66] He argued further that, "Another illegal amnesty will only trigger an even greater wave of illegal immigration in the expectation that violating U.S. immigration laws eventually leads to a *de jure* acceptance of their presence here."[67]

In December 2000 Congress granted limited amnesty by restoring section 245(i) of the Legal Immigration Family Equity (LIFE) Act, which had been in effect between October 1994 and September 1997.[68] Under this provision, immigrants already living in the United States with family or employer sponsors were given a four-month window to apply for a new type of visa without returning to their homeland. The visa, which cost $1,000, would allow them to adjust their immigration status until they became permanent residents. The provision represented a rare opportunity for illegal immigrants to gain legal status, since ordinarily they would have to return to their home countries to apply for a visa and most would not risk leaving the United States with no sure prospect of legal reentry. The government promised it would not arrest illegal immigrants for deportation on the basis of their 245(i) applications.

The INS estimated that about 540,000 immigrants would be eligible under the act. But the act did not cover or benefit many immigrants who were seeking to normalize their status. Many employers refused to sponsor applicants because they worried that INS officials might sanction them for acknowledging that they had hired undocumented workers. Because family sponsorship was limited to close relatives of green card holders or U.S. citizens, thousands of immigrants were not eligible. In Detroit, for example, only 10 percent of 1,000 immigrants who packed an informational session were eligible.[69] Yet as the April 30, 2001, filing deadline approached, immigrant marriages increased and crowds of immigrants and their sponsors filled INS offices around the country. INS spokesperson William Strassberger said that "couples were being married every 15 minutes" at courthouses in Montgomery, Maryland, to enable immigrants to beat the midnight deadline. On April 30, 2,600 applicants were camped outside the Los Angeles, California, immigration office by 6 a.m. The measure received such praise from proimmigrant and human rights groups that President George W. Bush agreed to support a bipartisan bill to extend the program by as much as one year.[70]

Criminal Aliens and IIRIRA

In addition to stepping up border enforcement and curtailing immigrants' access to public services, the 1996 immigration law toughened penalties for criminal aliens: noncitizens, both legal permanent residents and illegal aliens, who have been convicted of crimes subject to deportation. The idea that criminal aliens should be deported became law in the 1986 Immigration Reform and Control Act, which identified "aggravated felonies" by aliens as crimes warranting removal. However, the 1986 law did not result in significant increases in the number of deportations. Because courts and immigration officials did not systematically share records, many immigrants who had committed crimes served their sentences and returned to normal lives in American society. Criminal aliens who did face removal proceedings could be granted relief by immigration judges who considered their family ties to U.S. citizens and permanent residents. The law also contained a provision for the federal government to reimburse states for criminal justice costs attributable to illegal aliens.

But along with increasing levels of immigration in the early 1990s came increasing numbers of criminal aliens. They became the target of many lawmakers' ire. In 1992 Sen. Alfonse D'Amato, R-N.Y., proposed that the federal government imprison criminal aliens, even after they had served their sentences, until they were deported. According to D'Amato, the legislation would have saved his state millions of dollars a year. The Bureau of Prison facilities estimates that more than 25 percent of the federal prison population is foreign-born,[71] while alien inmates make up nearly 8 percent of state and local prison populations.[72] The U.S. Sentencing Commission reports that 11 percent of criminals sentenced in federal district courts in 1995 were illegal aliens.

Overall, these figures represent a nearly tenfold increase in the number of criminal aliens under law enforcement supervision since 1980. With the costs of incarceration in mind, many politicians viewed the deportation of criminal aliens as an opportunity to reduce a fiscal burden. The primary architect of IIRIRA, Representative Lamar Smith, R-Texas, argued that "U.S. taxpayers are unwilling to spend money incarcerating the prison inmates who are foreign-born; it would be better to have them deported."[73]

The resulting IIRIRA provisions expanded the category of criminal aliens subject to expedited removal, mandated detention pending removal, and barred judicial review of most removal orders.[74] First, IIRIRA expanded the list of crimes that would qualify an alien for deportation. No longer did the list include only "aggravated felonies" such as drug trafficking and assault. Instead, "crimes of moral turpitude," which, depending on state statutes, could be as serious as rape or as minor as shoplifting, could also subject an immigrant to deportation. In the same year, the Antiterrorism and Effective Death Penalty Act made immigrants who had committed a broad range of offenses ineligible to seek a waiver of deportation and restricted judicial review for immigrants in custody. Moreover, IIRIRA could be applied retroactively, so that immigrants with a criminal record were subject to detention and removal if immigration and law enforcement authorities were alerted to their history. Immigrants who committed a crime in the past and now attempt to naturalize, adjust their immigration status, reenter the country after traveling, or defend themselves against another crime, may trigger an INS review of their FBI file and find themselves in deportation proceedings.

IIRIRA also increased the categories of immigrants subject to mandatory detention, so that virtually all aliens convicted of "aggravated felonies" must remain in prison after serving their sentences to await deportation. It eliminated immigration officers' and judges' discretion to release detained immigrants on humanitarian or other grounds. Finally, it limited federal judges' ability to review decisions regarding detention and removal. Unsurprisingly, deportations soared. INS Commissioner Doris Meissner testified before Congress in February 1999 that deportations of criminal aliens had nearly doubled from 28,600 in fiscal year 1993 to 56,100 in fiscal year 1998.[75]

Supporters of the new law argued that immigrants should not and do not have the same rights as citizens. "Immigration to the United States is not a right, it's a privilege and Congress has said that those individuals who have been granted that privilege are expected to meet the highest standards," said INS spokesperson Russell A. Bergeron.[76] Supporters of the law contend that immigrants who commit crimes are costly to society—both in terms of their criminal activities and in government spending on police, prosecution and jail space—and therefore do not deserve the right to remain.

But the impact of the law also provoked strong proposals for reform from immigrant rights advocates. As the new deportation numbers were being announced in February 1999, policy analysts, embassy officials, and immigrant rights groups gathered for a conference at the Carnegie Endowment for International Peace in Washington, D.C., to discuss the local and international repercussions of the law:

> The consequences have been severe both in the United States and abroad. In the United States, families have been divided, with immigrants removed at great emotional and financial cost to their United States citizen children and spouses. Immigrants have been returned to countries in which they have few family, economic, or even linguistic ties—countries, in effect, to which they no longer belong. Returning nationals have often proven disruptive, difficult to assimilate, destabilizing, and even dangerous.[77]

Many advocates called on the government to restore judicial discretion in removal and detention decisions. "We should remember that crime is part of the fabric of our society, as much as we may not like it," said Bishop Nicholas DiMarzio, chair of the U.S. Bishops' Committee on Migration. "Many long-term permanent residents who have lived here since childhood learned crime here, not in their home countries." The American Immigration Lawyers' Association called for the restoration of judicial discretion and review, and for the prohibition of retroactivity, "because it is unfair to change the rules in the middle of the game."[78]

Foreign consular officials also noted the harshness of the law, as their nationals faced removal from the United States and returned home. Caribbean countries received one-quarter of the 36,909 criminal aliens deported in 1996 and voiced dismay at both the criminal activities imported by returning nationals and at their cultural estrangement. "The exchange rate is one hundred forty to one U.S. dollar," said Brentnold Evans, the Guyanese counsel general in New York. "These guys who are deported are leaving a society where you're accustomed to certain luxuries. When you return to Guyana, they're in for quite a drastic change."[79]

Another problem emerged as the number of criminal aliens in custody skyrocketed: a lack of detention space. Even as it rented space in state and local prisons, the INS lacked the huge number of beds needed to accommodate detained aliens, and the media reported deteriorating conditions as the facilities grew more crowded. In response to this problem, a series of court decisions allowed the INS to revise its mandatory detention rule to release "noncitizens with criminal records who are not believed to pose a danger to the community or a flight risk in advance of their final deportation hearing."[80] Still, even this improvement in INS discretion could not solve the second detention problem: criminal aliens who are deportable to countries that refuse to accept them, such as Cuba and Vietnam. Numbering nearly 3,500 in 1998, these "lifers" face indefinite detention in U.S. prisons for even the most minor crimes—a predicament that some advocates charged was unconstitutional.

The Supreme Court made two decisions in June 2001 that addressed the problems in the 1996 laws regarding criminal aliens. First, the Court heard arguments in the case of a Haitian native, Enrico St. Cyr, who entered the United States as a lawful permanent resident in 1986 and pleaded guilty to a charge of drug trafficking just before the 1996 laws took effect. When INS officials began proceedings to deport him in 1997, the new laws denied St. Cyr's request for a waiver of deportation. In *INS v. St. Cyr*, the Court ruled five to four against the laws' retroactive application and preclusion of judicial review, allowing St. Cyr to seek a waiver of deportation. Writing for the majority (which included Justices Anthony M. Kennedy, David H. Souter, Ruth Bader Ginsburg, and Stephen G. Breyer), Justice John Paul Stevens argued that to "entirely preclude review of a pure question of law by any court would give rise to substantial constitutional questions. . . . Congress must articulate specific and unambiguous statutory directives to effect a repeal."[81]

Second, the Court took up the question of "lifers": Should the government be able to detain deportable aliens indefinitely simply for lack of a country willing to accept them? The Court's decision, *Reno v. Kim Ho Ma* and *Zadvydas v. Davis*, applied to two cases. The first case concerned a Cambodian man admitted to the United States as a refugee when he was a child and later convicted of a gang-related killing. The man, Kim Ho Ma, had already served a state prison sentence for the killing but remained in detention indefinitely awaiting deportation since Cambodia has no repatriation agreement with the United States. The Court combined this case with an appeal by Kestutis Zadvydas, a man without citizenship who had been admitted to the United States as a child and later acquired a long criminal record.

Although he was ordered deported in 1994, no state had accepted responsibility for him. Again, the Court ruled five to four in favor of immigrants' rights. Justice Stephen G. Breyer wrote for the majority: "In our view, the statute, read in light of the Constitution's demands, limits an alien's post–removal-period detention to a period reasonably necessary to bring about that alien's removal from the United States. It does not permit indefinite detention."[82] Justice Breyer observed further that in the Constitution, "the Due Process Clause applied to all 'persons' within the United States, including aliens, whether their presence here is lawful, unlawful, temporary or permanent."[83]

Enforcement

Among IIRIRA's most visible provisions was an increase in federal spending to hire at least 1,000 full-time, active-duty border patrol agents and 300 support personnel each year until 2001. It also authorized the hiring of 900 additional INS investigators to track alien smuggling and employer sanctions violations, and 300 additional investigators to detect visa overstayers.[84]

The INS prevents illegal entry into the United States in two ways: by inspecting people who arrive at legal ports-of-entry, and by guarding border areas between those ports-of-entry. In the past decade, screening at airports, sea ports, and land border checkpoints has focused on keeping specific categories of people out of the country: terrorists, drug traffickers, and other illegal aliens. Meanwhile, the bulk of INS efforts to deter illegal entry have been placed along the border. Particularly along the southwestern land border, the INS has mounted several operations to intercept and deter illegal immigrants from Mexico and Central America.

The INS also enforces immigration laws in the U.S. interior, by attempting to locate, punish, and remove people who have entered the United States illegally, or who have helped others to enter. This category includes undocumented workers and aliens who commit violent crimes, as well as employers who knowingly hire unauthorized workers, produce counterfeit documents, or traffic in human beings. INS investigations have established a link between alien smuggling operations and the employers of unauthorized workers. Consequently, interior enforcement focuses on employer audits and surveys, sanctions, and employment site raids.

Since 1994, U.S. immigration enforcement strategies have emphasized the prevention and deterrence of illegal immigration—"border enforcement"—over the pursuit of illegal aliens already inside U.S. borders—"interior enforcement."

Interior enforcement has waxed and waned with the nation's economy. In the late 1990s, the booming economy's tight labor market increased tolerance for undocumented workers. However, as *The New York Times* noted, "A downturn in the booming economy and any resulting uptick in unemployment could lead the INS to revive its pursuit of illegal immigrants at work."[85] More recently, the terrorist attacks on the World Trade Center and Pentagon in September 2001 revived policy-makers' interest in interior immigration enforcement, because several of the terrorists had entered the country legally but then overstayed their visas. Attention has focused on coordinating intelligence on suspected terrorists between immigration officials, the FBI, CIA, and state and local law enforcement organizations so that visa overstayers and unauthorized immigrants may be easier to intercept in the country's interior.

BORDER ENFORCEMENT In October 1993 the INS launched a pilot program to prevent illegal border crossings in El Paso, Texas, called Operation Hold the Line. INS field managers deployed 400 agents along the border, stationing them within sight of each other to literally form a line through downtown El Paso. The strategy also included repairing fences and introducing technology such as infrared scopes, night vision goggles, underground sensors, and an automated fingerprint identification system. This concentration of resources and technology on a high-volume crossing point effectively created a blockade along the fifteen-mile border stretch. By June 1994 apprehensions for illegal entry along the El Paso border had dropped from a former daily level of 800 to 1,000 to a much lower 150.[86] Over its entire duration, Operation Hold the Line produced a 50 percent decline in apprehensions.

Policy-makers deemed Operation Hold the Line a success. Barbara Jordan, then-chair of the U.S. Commission on Immigration Reform, testified before the Senate that this prevention strategy was "more cost-effective than apprehension and removal, it eliminates the cycle of voluntary return and reentry that has characterized unlawful border crossings, and it reduces potentially violent confrontations between Border Patrol officers and those believed to be seeking illegal entry."[87]

With such positive initial results, Attorney General Reno and INS Commissioner Meissner announced a "National Border Patrol Strategy" calling for "prevention through deterrence." The multiyear strategy sought to strengthen land border enforcement by increasing the number of border patrol agents, improving equipment and infrastructure technology, and targeting areas considered vulnerable to illegal entries. During the next four years the INS launched a series of border operations. In October 1994, Operation Gatekeeper focused initially on a five-mile stretch of land in Imperial Beach, California, "that accounted for nearly 25 percent of all illegal border crossings" in the country. As illegal crossings declined in that area, Operation Gatekeeper expanded to cover more territory, eventually covering most of California's border with Mexico. In 1995 Operation Safeguard was launched in Arizona with the aim of dispersing illegal border crossers away from urban areas near the Nogales port-of-entry. And in August 1997, the INS launched Operation Rio Grande "to gain control of the border in the Rio Grande Valley" and eventually coordinate coverage of territory in Texas and New Mexico with Operation Hold the Line.

The plan to expand Border Patrol resources found ready support among politicians eager to crack down on illegal immigration. By 1995 some lawmakers proposed more than doubling the number of Border Patrol agents—from 4,500 to 10,000.[88] In May, President Clinton submitted the "Immigration Enforcement Improvement Act of 1995" to Congress, authorizing dramatic increases in Border Patrol agents and staff during the next three years. Congress codified these commitments in 1996 legislation, requiring the Border Patrol to hire as many as 1,000 new agents per year for five years beginning in 1997, and authorizing $877 million in funding.[89]

Advocates of this buildup at the border point to a number of indicators of its success. In addition to the decline in apprehensions of illegal entrants, they observe falling crime rates in border communities (such as Laredo and Brownsville, Texas), an increase in alien smugglers' fees, and a shift in the flow of illegal immigrant traffic to other crossing corridors. However, human rights activists are alarmed at the "militarization" of the border.[90] In response to tighter enforcement, migrants increasingly turned to smugglers or were diverted away from heavily trafficked crossing points to remote areas. Both create hazardous conditions for illegal crossers. As the INS notes, "A clear indication of the initiative's deterrent effect is that alien smugglers have raised their fees from $250 per person to as much as $1,500." Smugglers, known as "coyotes," often pack illegal immigrants into vans or trucks, or force them to walk for miles without food or water through less-patrolled border areas, such as desert or mountain terrain. When problems arise, such as a broken-down vehicle or a fear of apprehension, smugglers often abandon the immigrants. During a heat wave in August 1998, twenty deaths occurred under the auspices of Operation Gatekeeper in California's Imperial Valley. Despite the

Border Patrol's poster and radio campaigns to warn would-be immigrants of the dangerous heat and treacherous terrain, Imperial Valley saw a substantial increase in apprehensions.[91] In 2000 more than 360 illegal aliens died along the frontier between the United States and Mexico—a significant increase from years past.[92] When fourteen migrants crossing the Arizona desert died in 115 degree heat in May 2001, activists' outrage over the increasing number of migrant deaths along the U.S.-Mexico border prompted the countries' leaders to design a joint effort to improve border safety. As one measure, the nations agreed to increase the sharing of intelligence on suspected smugglers.

The INS also increased the number of inspectors and modernized its identification techniques at ports of entry. These changes are supposed to facilitate legitimate passenger traffic and trade but make it easier to intercept illegal aliens, terrorists, drugs, and contraband at the same time. The Port Passenger Accelerated Service System (PortPASS) identifies preapproved, frequent border crossers: for instance, SENTRI (Secure Electronic Network for Travelers Rapid Inspection) admits preenrolled participants who frequently drive across the U.S. border using dedicated commuter lanes. Similarly, the Outlying Area Reporting System (OARS) allows people operating recreational boats between the United States and Canada to use videophones at public marinas to report their entry and exit after a single, seasonal inspection. At the Mexican border, the INS and the Customs Service have launched a five-year plan to improve inspections along the Mexican border, particularly targeting narcotics and alien smuggling. The two agencies also operate the Remote Video Inspection Service (RVIS) to inspect travelers at remote ports of entry along the U.S.-Canadian border.

However, the diverse conditions between ports of entry—not only between the Mexican and Canadian frontiers but even between localities along the same border—have challenged federal policies. While ports of entry along the Mexican border are predominantly land crossings, the Canadian border includes several bridge crossings and very remote crossing points in rural areas. A further geographic distinction is that 90 percent of Canadians live within 100 miles of the U.S. border, while the American and Mexican populations are more evenly distributed throughout their respective countries.

The economic development of the United States' neighbors also plays a significant role in cross-border movement. In 1997 more than $1 billion in goods and services crossed the U.S.-Canadian border daily; the Ambassador Bridge between Detroit, Michigan, and Windsor, Ontario, accommodated the largest commercial exchange in the entire United States (almost 11 million vehicles, including more than 2.5 million trucks). On the passenger side, in recent years, more than 30 million people went through the Detroit ports-of-entry each year, followed by almost 30 million crossings in the Buffalo district, and more than 20 million in the Seattle district.[93] In contrast, Laredo, Texas, hosts the largest volume of trade across the Mexican border, with 2.8 million pedestrian crossings and 1.2 million truck crossings in 1997.[94]

The challenge that immigration inspections and trade can pose to each other was made obvious in the 1996 IIRIRA and again following the terrorist attacks of 2001. Section 110 of the IIRIRA would have required the INS to create an automated system to track the entry and exit of all noncitizens by 2001. The system would identify criminal suspects as well as immigrants who had overstayed their visas. However, Section 110 confronted two major obstacles. On a national level, constituents and policy-makers protested the implicit trend toward a national identification system. More convincingly, residents of Canadian border regions protested the burden the provision would impose on cross-border traffic facilitation. With more than 10,000 daily crossings in Detroit alone, Sen. Spencer Abraham, R-Mich., predicted that the provision would effectively shut down the border by causing major backups as traffic slowed through inspection booths. Congress successfully repealed the provision in 1998, approving Abraham's bill to block such inspections at land borders while requiring tighter checks at airports.[95] However, the terrorist attacks of September 2001 would lead many lawmakers to regret this decision. Due to the lack of an entry-exit system, the INS had few ways to intercept visa overstayers: immigrants could enter the country with a legal visa, stay beyond the visa's expiration date, leave the country, and later return with new visas—without ever alerting the INS that they had violated the terms of their original visa. Several of the September 11 hijackers exploited this loophole in order to pursue terrorist activities, leading lawmakers to revive mandates for an entry-exit tracking system. The USA Patriot Act of 2001 mandated the Departments of Justice, State, Commerce, and Treasury and the Office of Homeland Security to establish an Integrated Entry and Exit Data System Task Force, required the system to use biometric technology and tamper-resistant documents and ordered the implementation of such a system at all U.S. ports-of-entry "with all deliberate speed and as expeditiously as practicable."[96]

INTERIOR ENFORCEMENT The INS Investigations unit has two major responsibilities: the reduction of immigrant trafficking and work site inspection and enforcement.

The INS Investigations unit's efforts to counter immigrant trafficking are coordinated with the Border Patrol's operations, as well as through strategies to combat document fraud and apprehend criminal aliens. Work site enforcement forms the second major responsibility of INS Investigations. Although traditionally distinct from antismuggling efforts, work site enforcement now must also deal with the organized provision of illegal labor to particular employers.

The INS focuses its countertrafficking measures on organized smuggling rings, rather than illegal entry assisted by friends or relatives for personal reasons. These rings typically generate profits for their leaders by charging immigrants for the cost of transportation or forcing smuggled persons into indentured servitude or prostitution. Smaller rings smuggle mostly Mexican nationals, while larger groups have extensive international networks and charge substantially higher fees. A November 1999 Intelligence Assessment by the INS found that the major organized smuggling operations in the United States are based in Russia, China, and Mexico, with other organized criminal groups coming from Colombia, Nigeria, and Albania.

Operation Seek and Keep, a year-long INS investigation in 1998, dismantled the largest smuggling cartel to date. Smuggling as many as 300 aliens per month to employers across thirty-eight states, the organization transported primarily "Indian nationals through Moscow, Russia, to Havana, Cuba, by air and then to the Bahamas, Quito, Ecuador or other South America transit countries." Employers usually paid the alien's smuggling fee of $20,000; the alien then worked for the employer until the fee was paid off. Enlisting the cooperation of multiple law enforcement agencies, the INS relied on money-laundering statutes and help from the governments of Panama and the Bahamas to break the cartel's infrastructure and seize the smugglers' assets.

The following year Congress authorized a spending increase specifically for antismuggling efforts in eleven interior states. With these new funds, the INS deployed 200 agents in forty-five rapid-response teams in Arkansas, Colorado, Georgia, Iowa, Kentucky, Missouri, Nebraska, North Carolina, South Carolina, Tennessee, and Utah.[97] These teams are strategically located in smuggling corridors and use community relations to detect and disrupt immigrant smuggling operations, document fraud, and other criminal alien activities.

Document fraud—including the manufacture, distribution, or use of counterfeit immigration or identity documents, such as Social Security cards, passports, and visas—is frequently tied to organized criminal alien activity. INS Investigations emphasize prosecution of large-scale schemes rather than individual cases of document fraud: "In one raid on a warehouse [in November 1998] in Los Angeles, the immigration service found boxes with two million fake identification documents."[98]

Work site enforcement has also targeted businesses involved in immigrant smuggling, many of which commit human rights abuses. This focus on employers is part of a larger policy shift to remove "magnets" of illegal immigration. But for both technical and political reasons, sanctions against the employers of illegal immigrants have often proved ineffective. The 1986 Immigration Reform and Control Act made it illegal to hire undocumented aliens, imposing employer sanctions such as civil fines and even imprisonment. The law requires employers to check workers' documentation but does not require employers to verify the documents' authenticity. Employers who suspect their workers of using fraudulent documents are expected to alert INS investigators. Many employers, however, are able to feign ignorance. For instance, an audit of an IBP meatpacking plant in Gibbon, Nebraska, identified questionable documentation for 68 percent of the plant's 471 workers.[99]

During the early 1990s, employer sanctions came under fire particularly from Sens. Orrin Hatch, R-Utah, and Kennedy, D-Mass., following claims that the law encouraged job discrimination against workers who looked "foreign."[100] Immigrant advocates protested that employers often preemptively fire suspected illegal workers for fear of INS sanctions. These controversies kept enforcement of employer sanctions weak. Meanwhile, the INS continued to conduct "raids" on work sites where undocumented aliens could be identified and ultimately deported. In 1995 President Clinton announced a policy shift to strengthen enforcement of employer sanctions, saying, "we will be able to crack down on employers who knowingly hire illegal immigrants. If we turn off the employment stream for illegal workers, far, far fewer of them will risk the difficult journey here."[101] The effects of this policy appeared prominently in 1999, when the INS began "auditing workers' documentation in industries across the country, from the farmlands and fruit-packing plants . . . in the Northwest to beef-packing plants in the Midwest to hotels of South Florida." Rather than initiating cumbersome deportation proceedings against undocumented workers, the INS fines the employer and orders the workers' dismissal. In the spring of 1999, for example, the agency told the owner of a small fruit-packing house in Wapato, Washington, to fire nine of his forty-five workers.[102]

According to INS Commissioner Meissner, the policy's intent was to "change the dynamics, change the climate, and change the decision-making process of these migrants." However, the worker dismissals have appeared to disrupt immigrants' lives without significantly affecting their decisions to return to their countries of origin or hurting companies' production. Many dismissed workers choose to remain in the United States, look for a new job, and risk being caught again. Employers have not experienced labor shortages. Migrant advocates, workers, and employers alike have expressed resentment at the immigration agency for imposing hardship on immigrant families, many of which have been settled in the United States for years and include children who are U.S. citizens.

The Equal Employment Opportunity Commission (EEOC) attempted to address some of these criticisms when, in October 1999, it extended broad antidiscrimination rights to illegal immigrants for the first time. Promising that it would not ask immigrants to produce employment authorization if they filed discrimination charges, the EEOC's new policy ensures that illegal immigrants who are fired or discriminated against because of their race, sex, age, or religion will enjoy the same remedies as legal workers, including back pay, punitive damages, and—if they have legal work documents—reinstatement.[103]

In the end, the greatest relief for undocumented immigrant workers may have come from the economy's unprecedented strength in the late 1990s. An unemployment rate of only 4 percent helped soften INS work site enforcement measures. Arrests for the purpose of deportation fell to 8,600 in 1999 from 22,000 in 1997, according to the INS.[104] Although the agency continues to fine employers for knowingly hiring illegal workers, the demand for labor has drawn both employers and unions to protect undocumented workers. In fall 1999 a major union in Chicago's commercial laundry industry, UNITE, negotiated contracts that require employers to bar an INS raid unless the agents have a search warrant. Employers of highly skilled immigrants have also pressured the INS to soften its enforcement tactics.

Immigration: Understanding and Evaluating Its Impact on the United States

The effects of immigration on the United States are multifaceted. As the preceding discussion has shown, the primary determinant of immigration expansion or contraction has been the country's economic condition and business needs. Standard evaluations of the benefits and costs of immigration, therefore, focus on the economic contribution of immigrants to the economy and the costs they impose through the use of social services.

Immigration policy, however, is also influenced by humanitarian, social, and political reasons. If economic costs or benefits were the only motivation for admitting immigrants to the United States, immigrants would be admitted based on the match between their vocational skills and the U.S.'s economic needs. But as discussed earlier in this chapter, family preferences are, in fact, the way in which most immigrants gain admission to the United States. This policy is based on social as well as humanitarian grounds: the federal government not only holds that citizens should have a right to bring close family members to the country but also recognizes that new immigrants with family ties are likely to have more success in resettling than immigrants without these kinds of social networks. Family preferences also make sense politically. Citizens who would not derive any direct economic benefit from the entry of immigrants might not support an expansion of skills-based immigration. But if their relatives are able to come to the United States, they may be more willing to support an expansion of immigration that benefits business as well.

Another type of immigration policy that serves primarily humanitarian and political needs is refugee policy. Technically, refugees and immigrants are two different categories of entrants to the United States. Refugees are subject to different quotas and a different entry process. They are eligible for different kinds of benefits and assistance after entry. They face different restrictions and requirements for becoming permanent residents or citizens. Many of the problems of resettlement that they also face are specific to their refugee status or to the situations that caused them to flee. On the other hand, once in the United States, it is often difficult to tell the difference between a refugee and an immigrant, and many of the social and economic issues they both face are the same.

Immigration's effects are also more wide-ranging than a calculation of economic costs and benefits might show. Immigrants change American culture and society, and they are also changed by it. Issues immigrants make salient, such as language use and bilingualism, have a significant effect on public institutions such as schools and government offices, on quasi-public organizations such as the media, and on private businesses and nonprofit organizations. When immigrants become voting citizens, they also influence the distribution of political power. As illustrated with the passage of Proposition 187 and IIRIRA, political groups and politicians may come to power based on their opposition to certain types of immigrants or immigration policy.

This section examines these issues in more detail. The first part explains the way that the economic benefits and costs of immigration are calculated. The next part looks at refugee policy as a particular type of immigration policy, one usually not considered on economic grounds. The discussion then turns to a brief examination of the cultural and social impact of immigration, in particular on bilingual education and the English-only movement. The last part looks at the growing political presence of immigrants in the United States.

The Economic Benefits and Costs of Immigration

As immigrants' share of the U.S. population has increased during the past decade, and the immigration debate has intensified, a number of studies have sought to discover whether immigration benefits or harms the U.S. economy and society. Presumably, if the net effect of immigration is positive, then policy-makers should increase admissions, and if the net effect is negative, admissions should decrease. However, the solution is not so simple; the studies' authors frequently disagree about both methods of analysis and their conclusions. This section highlights areas of consensus and dispute, in an effort to provide a solid framework for thinking about immigration's benefits and costs.

The first question—one that is often overlooked—is: Who bears the costs or benefits of immigration? The first assumption is that immigration generally benefits immigrants, whether through economic gain, political freedom, or reunion with their families. As one study phrased it: "If they had not felt that they would gain, they were free not to immigrate."[105] Immigration also affects the communities left behind. In some cases, emigrants' departure costs home communities by reducing the supply of workers. In other cases, that cost is outweighed by remittances—money sent home from earnings abroad. U.S. immigration policy-makers and analysts focus on immigration's costs and benefits to American society, particularly to native-born residents, and assess these effects specifically in terms of economic outcomes.

Immigrants' characteristics are the starting point for this investigation. For example, immigrants' geographic concentration in a handful of states and metropolitan areas implies that they will have an acute impact on those communities. Immigrants' age distribution makes them less prone to demand social programs; with more working-age adults and fewer elderly, "immigrants are more likely than the native-born to be paying into the Social Security System and less likely to be receiving benefits,[106] such as Supplemental Security Income or Medicare. At the same time, it is possible that immigrants' lower skill and income levels and higher poverty rate increase their use of welfare programs.

At a theoretical level, analysts agree on immigration's effects on the labor market. Immigrants may work as substitutes or complements to domestic workers, depending on their skill level. For example, imagine a factory in which there are production workers (unskilled) and supervisors (skilled). Immigrants who are production workers compete for the same jobs as domestic production workers; they have the same skills, so they can "substitute" for them. This has two effects on domestic unskilled workers: some workers may lose their jobs to immigrants, and all workers will be paid less because the increased supply of workers means that wages will decrease. At the same time, as the number of production workers rises, the demand for supervisors increases. This raises the wages of skilled domestic workers. In this scenario, unskilled immigrants complement skilled domestic workers. On the whole, immigration leads to higher incomes for skilled domestic workers who complement unskilled immigrants, but lower incomes for unskilled domestic workers who compete with unskilled immigrants.

The competition that immigrants create in the labor market has both positive and negative outcomes. On the negative side, immigrants who act as substitutes for domestic workers may depress wages and even cause displacement, as one analyst hypothesized:

> perhaps one of the citizen laborers is out sick, or meditating in the woods on unpaid leave, at the moment the immigrant arrives. The immigrant latches onto that citizen's job. When the previous occupant of the job gets back, he cannot immediately find another job and classifies himself as unemployed. Another possibility: the immigrant arrives, goes to the nearest business and says: "I'll work harder and cheaper than the laborer you now employ." And the owner promptly fires the citizen and hires the immigrant.[107]

Labor unions traditionally cited these effects as their strongest argument against immigration. They found little consolation in the fact that immigration also increases incomes for domestic workers who complement immigrants' skills, as discussed above. This redistribution of wealth exacerbates income inequality. Although the net effect on domestic workers' wages remains ambiguous, increasing income inequality is generally considered costly to society because it increases political tensions and strains social institutions.

On the positive side, competition because of immigration increases production efficiency and therefore improves national output. Immigration expands consumer markets and spurs innovation in business practices—both of which give the United States an advantage in international markets. The increase in gross domestic product (GDP) that results as a consequence of immigration clearly benefits the American economy.

Yet the question remains: How do these costs and benefits balance out? Does immigration make native-born Americans better- or worse-off? Immigration analysts often disagree on the answer to this question, because they use different analytical methods to calculate the magnitude of immigration's benefits and costs. Most disagreements occur over measuring immigrants' fiscal impact—weighing their contributions in tax dollars against the resources required to support the public services they consume.

For example, most studies account for use of social services, health care, and schools, but others also consider services such as libraries, highways, community colleges, and parks. Similarly, most count immigrant payments to income taxes and often sales taxes, but others also include contributions to excise taxes, motor vehicle fees, even lottery tickets.[108]

Some scholars point out that immigrants present a windfall for government tax revenue, because their age distribution suggests that they contribute payroll taxes equal to or greater than those of domestic workers but are less likely to collect public benefits. Others dispute this argument, noting that immigrants' lack of education compared with native-born workers, and the corresponding decline in relative wages, may have increased the fiscal costs of immigration. Although immigrants were less likely than natives to receive public assistance in 1970, by 1990 immigrant households' welfare participation rate had risen to 1.7 percentage points higher than that of native households.[109] One pair of studies calculated that immigrants pose an annual fiscal burden of $229 per native household in New Jersey, and $1,174 per native household in California.[110] Others argue that immigrants' consumption of public assistance actually decreases the marginal costs of providing it through economies of scale, so that the net fiscal impact is positive.[111]

Nearly all of these discussions of immigration's costs and benefits rest on an economic premise: "[I]mmigration policy should increase the national income of natives . . . [therefore, government should] maximize the immigration surplus net of the fiscal burden imposed by immigrants on native taxpayers." But the pursuit of economic interests is not the government's sole objective in setting immigration policy. U.S. immigration policy also pursues social and humanitarian objectives by incorporating family reunification visa categories, and international human rights protection by admitting refugees and asylum seekers. These objectives present their own set of benefits and costs, which prove more difficult to measure quantitatively. For instance, although analysts might easily discern that refugees pose a cost to native-born taxpayers—15 percent were on welfare in 1996—their presence may serve domestic political interests (as in programs for refugees from Cuba), help meet America's responsibilities to its allies (as in the resettlement of refugees from South Vietnam), or simply help mitigate the effects of an international crisis (as in the admission of refugees from Kosovo). Many of these effects are impossible to estimate quantitatively, but they are important considerations nonetheless.

Refugee and Asylum Policy

U.S. refugee policy has long posed a struggle between international laws and principles of human rights and domestic political interests. On the one hand, the United States has presented itself to the world as a beacon of freedom from persecution. On the other hand, it is reluctant to open its doors to masses of refugees, for the same reasons that many Americans oppose immigration in general.

Refugees occupy a very distinct area of U.S. immigration policy; some refugee advocates even argue that refugee policy should be entirely separate from immigration policy. Since U.S. refugee policy is based on humanitarian rather than economic considerations, persons admitted to the United States as refugees enjoy a full range of benefits and become eligible for permanent legal status after one year of residency. The Department of Health and Human Services' Office of Refugee Resettlement provides refugees, often through contracted private agencies, with services to help them begin their new lives in the United States, including English classes, job training, and housing assistance. As a party to the 1951 Convention Relating to the Status of Refugees and Additional Protocol of 1967, the United States is obligated under international law to grant certain rights to persons who meet the refugee definitions, including the right to wage-earning employment, housing, and public education. Most fundamental, however, is the right to *nonrefoulement,* meaning that the United States must not expel or return refugees to any country where their lives or freedom would be threatened.

Interdicting Haitian Boat People

U.S. policy toward Haitian boat people highlights the primacy of domestic political interests in formulating refugee policy. In the early 1990s, the threat of mass influxes of refugees from America's tiny, impoverished Caribbean neighbor prompted U.S. policy-makers to press for U.N.-sponsored sanctions and eventually to invade Haiti.

After decades of authoritarian rule under the Duvalier regime, Haitians democratically elected President Jean-Bertrand Aristide in 1990, only to see him ousted in a military coup in September 1991. Although small groups from a variety of countries had set out across the Caribbean in search of better lives for many years, the number of Haitian boat people attempting to reach U.S. shores increased dramatically following Aristide's overthrow. If they reached U.S. shores, the boat people would be able to enter the country illegally or file an application for asylum. Yet many Haitians took to the rough waters in unseaworthy boats, making the passage extremely dangerous and often deadly.

The U.S. Coast Guard routinely rescued Haitians from hazardous boats and brought them to the U.S. Naval Base at Guantanamo Bay, Cuba, where they received humanitarian assistance and had the opportunity to file a claim of asylum. However, as the population at Guantanamo Bay reached 13,000 and thousands more continued to take to the sea in 1992, the Bush administration deemed this policy unsustainable, as it provided a magnet for those seeking entry to the United States. In a controversial move, President Bush ordered the Coast Guard to return Haitians picked up at sea directly to Haiti. Within less than one month, the Coast Guard had forcibly returned 2,887 Haitians.[1]

Democrats in Congress, the Congressional Black Caucus, the U.N. High Commissioner for Refugees, and other refugee advocates objected vehemently to this policy, asserting that it violated the United States' international commitment to *nonrefoulement* stipulated in the 1951 Refugee Convention. The Bush Administration argued in response that "most of those fleeing Haiti were economic, not political refugees and would not qualify for asylum," and that an important goal of the policy was to save lives.[2]

Critics also contended that the policy posed a stark inequality between treatment of Haitians and treatment of Cubans. Cubans had also boarded thousands of rickety boats in recent years to flee both economic and political oppression under President Fidel Castro's Communist regime. *(See box on page 96)* U.S. refugee policy accepts up to 20,000 Cubans annually according to a special agreement with the Cuban government; yet, no such policy exists for Haitians. As the policy toward Haiti took effect in 1992, U.S. deputy assistant secretary for refugee programs, Brunson McKinley, defended the policy, saying, "the anomaly lies in the preferential status accorded Cubans not in discrimination against Haitians. Cuban asylum seekers picked up by the Coast Guard are brought to the United States because they are fleeing a repressive, totalitarian regime. This is longstanding U.S. policy for which we believe there is bipartisan congressional support. Otherwise, our policy of interdicting illegal immigrants is not discriminatory; it applies to other Caribbean nationalities besides Haitians." [3]

Although he had criticized the Bush administration's policy during his election campaign, once in office President Bill Clinton continued the policy of repatriating Haitian refugees. In June 1993, the Supreme Court upheld the policy, ruling 8-1 in the case of *McNary v. Haitian Centers Council* that America's international "obligation extends only to refugees who reach U.S. soil or territorial waters." [4]

Still, the spectre of an influx of Haitian refugees persisted as the country's military dictators retained power. The Clinton administration first pressed the United Nations to impose economic sanctions on the already impoverished nation. Then, in 1994, the president fostered support in Congress for a U.S. military invasion to restore Aristide to power. In an address to the nation, Clinton justified the use of force: "the United States must protect our interests—to stop the brutal atrocities that threaten tens of thousands of Haitians, to secure our borders and to preserve stability and promote democracy in our hemisphere. . . ." [5]

In this case, the use of force to shield U.S. borders from masses of refugees epitomized the primacy of domestic political interests over international legal and humanitarian commitments.

---

1. "U.S. Policy on Haitian Refugees," U.S. Department of State Dispatch, Washington, D.C., June 15, 1992.

2. Pamela Fessler, "Foreign Policy: Members Decry Haiti Policy, Vow to Seek Changes," *CQ Weekly*, May 30, 1992, 1547.

3. "U.S. Policy on Haitian Refugees," U.S. Department of State Dispatch, Washington, D.C., June 15, 1992.

4. Holly Idelson, "Supreme Court: Haitian Policy Sanctioned; Refugee Groups Object," *CQ Weekly*, June 26, 1993, 1666.

5. "Clinton Offers Justification for Invasion of Haiti," *CQ Weekly*, September 17, 1994, 2605.

The U.S. definition of a refugee, found in Section 101(a)(42) of the Immigration and Nationality Act, is based on, though not identical to the 1951 convention definition; it states:

> The term 'refugee' means: (A) any person who is outside any country of such person's nationality or, in the case of a person having no nationality, is outside any country in which such person last habitually resided, and who is unable or

unwilling to return to, and is unable or unwilling to avail himself or herself of the protection of, that country because of persecution or a well-founded fear of persecution on account of race, religion, nationality, membership in a particular social group, or political opinion, or (B) in such circumstances as the President after appropriate consultation . . . may specify, any person who is within the country in which such person is habitually residing and who is persecuted or who has a well-founded fear of persecution on account of race, religion, nationality, membership in a particular social group, or political opinion.

This definition strays from the 1951 convention definition by including persons who are not outside their country of origin (clause B). It lays out two main classes of admission in U.S. refugee policy: refugees and asylum seekers. Refugees are persons living abroad who apply for protected status through overseas processing programs. Asylum seekers file claims for protection after they have reached the United States. Overseas resettlement programs allow the United States more control over refugee admissions by designating home governments that offer inadequate protection, providing secure travel for persons in flight, and mitigating "the difficulty of dealing with unpredicted flows."[112]

Traditionally, the cold war significantly shaped U.S. refugee policy. Refugee admissions were somewhat *ad hoc,* and largely reserved for persons fleeing communism, particularly from the Soviet Union, Vietnam, and Cuba. The Refugee Act of 1980 created a more formal system for refugee admissions, requiring the president to consult with Congress each year to determine the number of refugees to be admitted, and to allocate portions of this number by region. The end of the cold war in the early 1990s posed two major challenges to U.S. refugee policy. First, the break-up of the Soviet bloc disrupted political and economic ties among former communist countries, provoking civil wars and ethnic conflicts that vastly inflated the number of refugees worldwide. Second, the "new world disorder" meant that many refugees from nontraditional source countries now sought protection in the United States.

Trends in U.S. refugee and asylum admissions roughly mirror trends in the number of refugees and asylum seekers worldwide during the past decade. As the global population of refugees peaked in 1992, so did U.S. admissions. That year, the number of refugees and asylum seekers worldwide reached 17,600,000,[113] while the United States authorized more than 127,000 refugee and asylum admissions.[114] As the global population of refugees and asylum seekers declined during the remain-

Table 2-2 U.S. Refugee Allocations, 1995–2000

	Fiscal Year 1995	*Fiscal Year 2000*
Europe		
(including the former Soviet Union)	48,000	47,000
East Asia	39,000	8,000
Africa	7,000	18,000
Latin America	8,000	3,000
Near East	5,000	8,000
Unallocated Reserve	4,000	6,000
Total	111,000	90,000

Sources: For fiscal year 1995: U.S. Immigration and Naturalization Service, *Statistical Yearbook of the Immigration and Naturalization Service, 1998* (Washington, D.C.: Government Printing Office, 2000), 96; for fiscal year 2000: U.S. Department of State, Bureau of Population, Refugees, and Migration, "Fact Sheet: U.S. Refugee Admissions and Resettlement Program," January 2000.

der of the decade, so did U.S. admissions. By 1998 the worldwide population of refugees and asylum seekers had fallen to 13.5 million,[115] and the United States authorized just under 96,000 admissions.[116]

About 80 percent of admitted refugees come from overseas processing programs.[117] The INS maintains in-country refugee processing programs in Havana, Cuba, Ho Chi Minh City, Vietnam, and Moscow, Russia, where persons seeking refugee status in the United States may file an application, be interviewed, and learn if their claim has been granted or denied. Overseas processing also occurs in INS district offices, in Bangkok, Thailand, Mexico City, Mexico, and Rome, Italy, and through referrals by the United Nations High Commissioner for Refugees or private nonprofit organizations under contract with the State Department (known as joint voluntary agencies, or JVAs).

The regional allocation of overseas admissions consistently favors refugees from eastern Europe and the former Soviet Union. The Immigration Act of 1990 included a provision authored by Sen. Frank Lautenberg, D-N.J., that identified specific groups vulnerable to persecution in the former Soviet Union for special consideration for U.S. protection. The Lautenberg Amendment, as it is called, targets Jews, Evangelical Christians, and certain members of the Ukrainian Catholic and Orthodox Churches for admission as refugees, the vast majority of whom have family ties to the United States. In fiscal year 1999, nearly 20 percent of refugees resettled in the United States were from the former Soviet Union. At the same time, roughly 43 percent of resettled refugees came from the war-torn former Yugoslavia, namely Bosnia and the province of Kosovo.[118] Vietnamese represented the next largest group resettled in the United States in 1999, at nearly 12 percent.

Critics contend that this system of regional allotment for overseas refugee admissions is inflexible, biased, and outmoded. "We're doing it for domestic reasons [to satisfy] ethnic politics and because we still have a cold war mentality," said Georgetown University professor Charles Keeley. He and others argue that refugee admissions should be dictated more by circumstances than politics. Mark Krikorian, executive director of the Center for Immigration Studies, suggested that regional ceilings should be eliminated and replaced with a system based on need alone. "We need to restrict refugee resettlement to those people who have no other options," he said.[119] Another argument asserts that attention to numbers is misguided because refugee flows are "notoriously difficult to predict," and that the U.S. refugee program requires flexibility in order to respond to humanitarian needs and U.S. foreign policy interests. [120]

Legislators may have anticipated these charges of cold war bias and inflexibility when they created a provision for "temporary protected status" (TPS) in the 1990 Immigration Act. Under this provision, the U.S. attorney general may designate a formal visa status to foreign nationals already living in the United States when conditions in their home country (such as war or natural disaster) prompt a need for temporary protection. The 1990 law was designed specifically for nationals of El Salvador, "whose asylum claims had been systematically rejected despite their claims of fear of persecution by the country's military junta."[121] In general, however, "[t]emporary protection is appropriate for outflows relating to armed conflict or severe internal crises in which individual status determination is initially *impractical*, because of the numbers involved, and *unhelpful*, in that people who do not meet strict refugee criteria nonetheless should not be sent home to conditions of grave danger." [122]

In accordance with UNHCR guidelines, U.S. law allows individuals granted TPS to eventually apply for formal status through the asylum system. However, those who are not granted asylum must return to their home country when the attorney general deems conditions there to be safe again and ends temporary protection. For example, on January 5, 1999, the attorney general granted TPS for eighteen months to nationals of Honduras and Nicaragua already in the United States because of the devastation caused by Hurricane Mitch. By the end of 1999, TPS was also in effect for nationals of Kosovo, Bosnia, Montserrat, Guinea-Bissau, Somalia, Sierra Leone, Sudan, and Burundi.

In comparison to refugees who apply for entrance to the United States from overseas processing programs, the asylum system admits a far smaller number of people each year. There is no limit to the number of people who can be granted asylum; however, the chances of making a successful claim are low. Any person who arrives at the U.S. border, legally or illegally, may request asylum. The 1996 immigration law requires that asylum seekers file an application with the INS within one year of arriving in the United States, and that undocumented asylum seekers be detained until their claims are decided. Both of these provisions are meant to prevent fraudulent claimants from escaping into anonymity. INS asylum officers— who under 1995 regulations, must rule on an asylum request within six months[123]—interview each applicant to determine if the person can demonstrate a well-founded fear of being persecuted at home for reasons of race, religion, nationality, political opinion, or membership in a particular social group. If INS officers have doubts about the asylum seeker's claim, they refer the case to an immigration judge, who makes the final decision.

In 1999 the United States approved 38.2 percent of requests for asylum, representing an increase from approval rates of 23.0 percent in 1998 and 18.7 in 1997. However, these figures disguise the fact that the number of asylum applications filed has fallen dramatically since 1996. Admissions through the asylum program peaked at 18,556 in 1996 and since have declined sharply as IIRIRA's asylum provisions took effect. "Asylum applications in 1999 represented a 25 percent decrease from the 54,952 applications filed in 1998 and a 48 percent decrease from the 84,839 applications filed in 1997."[124]

This decline in the number of asylum requests may be a result of restrictive measures in the 1996 law, which provided for expedited procedures at points of entry in an effort to quickly reject and send back those without a solid claim.[125] Wary of the threat of mass influxes of asylum seekers and the potential for fraudulent claims, lawmakers allowed INS officers at ports of entry to place an alien in "expedited removal" proceedings if the officer determines that the claim is not credible. Refugee advocates charge that "expedited removal" denies asylum seekers due process, particularly those who do not speak English, come from different cultural backgrounds, or may suffer psychological stress due to the trauma of being persecuted.

Table 2-3 Asylum Applications and Approval Rates by Nationality, 1999

Largest Number of Asylum Requests	Highest Asylum Approval Rate
China	Afghanistan
Somalia	Cuba
Haiti	Ethiopia
El Salvador	Sudan
Guatemala	Somalia
Mexico	Myanmar (Burma)

Source: U.S. Committee for Refugees, "Country Reports: United States," *Worldwide Refugee Information.* Accessible at http://www.refugees.org/world/countryrpt/amer_carib/us.htm.

Refugee advocates have also pushed to expand the number of categories for refugee status to include people suffering from discrimination based on their gender, sexual orientation, or resistance to coercive population-control methods. In a landmark case in 1996, the Board of Immigration Appeals granted asylum to a woman from Togo who had fled to avoid genital mutilation, a common practice throughout much of Africa. On the other hand, in June 1999, the court overturned a grant of asylum to a Guatemalan woman fleeing violent domestic abuse by her husband.

Cultural Assimilation and the Politics of Language

The rapid growth of the country's immigrant population during the past decade has led to a proliferation of academic research and an intensified public debate about how immigrants are transforming American society in an age of increasing diversity. These questions focus more on changes in cultural assimilation and identity than economic or fiscal impacts because of immigration. How will immigrants shape the character of their communities and the nation over time? And how will they be transformed to become the newest Americans? What will be the legacy of the new immigration to the United States?

Some analysts examine homeownership as an indicator of attachment to American life. According to one scholar, "If immigration is the story of uprooting one-

U.S. Asylum Law and China's One-Child Policy

The U.S. reaction to China's one-child campaign is reflected primarily in asylum law, which has been affected by the U.S. abortion debate. The current law, however, has a rocky history. In the 1989 *Matter of Chang* decision, the Board of Immigration Appeals (BIA) held that a Chinese national did not qualify for asylum based on his and his wife's desire to have more than one child. The BIA said that even forced sterilization would not constitute persecution in this context, given China's extraordinary population problems and the fact that the policy is one of general applicability (the Changs were not treated differently than anyone else). The BIA added that the one-child policy could be persecutory if it was being selectively applied against members of a particular religious group, or was being used to punish individuals for their political opinion.

Despite arguments that involuntary sterilization is a violation of both international human rights and the U.S. Constitution, the BIA said that fact itself would not mean that a person subject to such measures was persecuted on account of one of the five grounds in the refugee definition. The BIA concluded:

> The issue before us is not whether China's population control policies, in whole or in part, should be encouraged or discouraged to the fullest extent possible by the United States and the world community. This issue is whether the respondent demonstrates persecution or a well-founded fear of persecution. . . . Whether these policies are such that the immigration laws should be amended to provide temporary or permanent relief from deportation to all individuals who face the possibility of forced sterilization as part of a country's population control program is a matter for Congress to resolve legislatively.

Congress did not wait long to respond. In November 1989, it passed a bill in response to the Tiananmen Square massacre, primarily focusing on the situation of Chinese students in the United States. The bill included an amendment to provide asylum to people fleeing the one-child policy. The wording required the INS to give "careful consideration" to asylum applicants from the People's Republic of China (PRC) who expressed a fear of persecution related to the policy. It also provided that if the applicant establishes that he or she "has refused to abort or be sterilized, such applicant shall be considered to have established a well founded fear of persecution, if returned to China, on the basis of political opinion."

President Bush vetoed the legislation for diplomatic reasons. However, he ordered implementation of all of the bill's provisions by executive action. With regard to the one-child policy, Bush directed that "enhanced consideration be provided under the immigration laws for individuals from any country who express a fear of persecution upon return to their country related to that country's policy of forced abortion or coerced sterilization."

A subsequent increase in asylum applications from China, including the highly publicized 1993 grounding of the *Golden Venture* ship near Long Island, forced the courts to hear more Chinese cases, although they often reached conflicting decisions. Meanwhile, the Clinton administration became more concerned about international smuggling.

As a result, in August 1994 the Administration instructed asylum officers to follow *Chang* but said a form of "extraordinary humanitarian relief" would be available outside the asylum context. Specifically, INS district directors were to consider granting a stay of deportation and work authorization in cases where a PRC national: (1) faced imminent danger of forced abortion or involuntary sterilization upon return to China; (2) suffered or would suffer severe harm for refusing to submit to such procedures, or (3) suffered or would suffer severe harm because he violated other unreasonable family planning restrictions.

The Justice Department made clear, however, that implementing officers should carefully evaluate the applicant's credibility. "This is not an open gate. . . . Relief will be provided only in very extraordinary and credible cases," the Justice Department said.

The matter stood until September 1996, with the enactment of the Illegal Immigration Reform and Immigrant Responsibility Act (IIRIRA). IIRIRA amended the Immigration and Nationality Act's (INA) definition of a refugee to provide that a person fleeing forced abortion or sterilization "shall be deemed" to have been persecuted, or to have a well-founded fear of persecution, on account of political opinion.

The amendment's chief sponsor was Rep. Christopher Smith (R-N.J.), a longtime critic of China's human rights practices and one of Congress's most vocal pro-life members. To address concerns about overwhelming numbers of asylum seekers, the amendment specified that in any fiscal year no more than 1,000 persons may be admitted as refugees or granted asylum on the basis of resistance to coercive population control methods. Although the 1,000 ceiling has not been reached in any fiscal year (partly because Chinese nationals are not currently admitted as refugees from overseas), the Justice Department has said that if the ceiling is reached they will hold approved applications for final grants of asylum in the next fiscal year.

Source: Excerpted from: U.S. Committee for Refugees, "Worldwide Refugee Information." Accessible at http://www.refugees.org/world/articles/women2_rr99_8.htm.

self, then assimilation is the story of putting down roots in one's country of choice. . . . [O]wning a home signifies that an immigrant family has attached its well-being to the fate of the country."[126] This research notes that immigrants who have lived in the United States for twenty-five years or more buy their own homes at a faster rate than the native-born population, suggesting a great commitment to American life.

Others look at intermarriage as an indicator of societal integration, noting that immigrants' grandchildren have high rates of intermarriage with members of other ethnic groups. Still others point to naturalization rates as indicators of immigrants' loyalty to the United States.

The crux of the debate, however, revolves around questions of cultural assimilation. Although academics define assimilation simply as "the manner in which immigrants blend into larger societies," they also acknowledge that, "[i]n a normative sense, assimilation is linked to an expectation that foreigners will shed, or at least contain, their native cultures while embracing the mores and languages of the host country."[127]

This expectation derives largely from Americans' last experience with a major wave of immigration during the early twentieth century, when the children of European immigrants proved eager to adopt an "American identity" and reject the ethnic cultures and identities of their parents. Under the "straight-line" assimilation model, immigrant groups become more similar to mainstream Americans and more economically successful with each succeeding generation.[128] At the same time, native-born Americans aggressively promoted an extreme form of assimilation, known as "Americanization." Under this scheme, "Immigrants would be welcome as full members of the American family if they agreed to abide by three simple precepts: (1) They had to accept English as the national language; (2) They were expected to take pride in their American identity and believe in America's liberal democratic and egalitarian principles; and (3) They were expected to live by what is commonly referred to as the Protestant ethic—to be self-reliant, hardworking and morally upright."[129]

This historical experience has meant that, during the current wave of immigration, all eyes have been on immigrant children and U.S.-born children of immigrants (the "second generation"), to examine their language acquisition, ethnic identification, academic achievement, and career ambition. Researchers are finding that, unlike their European-origin predecessors who followed a "straight-line" assimilation model, today's children of immigrants from Latin America, the Caribbean, and Asia face racial discrimination and limited opportunities for advancement in the working class. This leads to "segmented assimilation." In this new model, "different groups experience either traditional assimilation and upward mobility, downward mobility by unsuccessfully competing in the mainstream economy, or upward mobility by living and working in ethnically homogeneous immigrant communities."[130]

In other words, children of immigrants today may still follow the path of "Americanization" to survive and prosper in the United States. But many children of immigrants face barriers to success in the form of racial discrimination, so that their choice of ethnic identification plays a role in their ambition and achievement. For example, one study found that, "The children of black immigrants in the United States face a choice about whether to identify as black American or whether to maintain an ethnic identity reflecting their parents' national origins."[131] For some, identity by national origin serves as a hedge against racial identity in order to maintain mobility when threatened with racial discrimination. Immigrants who identify themselves by national or ethnic origin tend to stress cultural values of hard work and ambition that are consistent with American middle-class values. On the other hand, children of immigrants who identify with black Americans reject ethnic identity as "acting white," and embrace alternatives to mainstream American culture.

This emergence of segmented assimilation has convinced some people that immigrants' emphasis on diversity and ethnicity threatens the traditional "melting pot" of American society. As the *Washington Post* reported, "There is a sense that, especially as immigrant populations reach a critical mass in many communities, it is no longer the melting pot that is transforming them, but they who are transforming American society."[132] Indeed, some immigration advocacy and ethnic groups view "assimilation" as a dirty word, and prefer metaphors such as "salad bowl" and "mosaic" to describe the sense of separate identities within one nation.

Immigrants' concentration in urban enclaves tends to reinforce perceptions of segregation, particularly because most immigrants today are people of color. These perceptions are based on the assumption that integration facilitates assimilation. New immigrants frequently live near other immigrants who can provide a network of support as they adapt to their new environment. Because many analysts believe that integration facilitates assimilation, immigrant enclaves sometimes become symbols of a rejection of assimilation and a defiance of "mainstream American culture." University of Michigan demographer William Frey's study of migration patterns within the United States drew much attention as it identified a pattern of "demographic balkanization": "Under this scenario, areas where immigrants account for most of the demographic change will become increasingly multicultural, younger, and more bifurcated in their race and class structures. Other parts of the country, whose growth is more dependent on internal migration flows, will become far less multicultural in their demographic makeup and will differ as well in other social, demographic, and political dimensions."[133] This study and others affirmed recent theories of "white flight" from immigrant-heavy, metropolitan areas, presenting a serious challenge to proponents of ethnic and racial integration.

The confluence of cultures in immigrant enclaves produces many social issues. One of the most controversial of these during the past decade has been education. It is commonly held that the longer immigrants live in the United States, the more assimilated they will become; or, if individuals do not fully assimilate, then their children and certainly their grandchildren will join the mainstream society. Thus, the children of immigrants (often referred to as the second and third generations) are frequently the subject of studies on immigrant assimilation. Debates over bilingual education focus on children's principal social setting—school—and distinguishing cultural characteristic—language. The issue is particularly important considering that immigrant children and U.S.-born children of immigrants account for nearly 20 percent of all American children today.[134]

Opponents of bilingual education argue that "a common culture is what holds a nation together, and that a common language is needed to convey and preserve that culture. Consequently, they want bilingual education programs to focus on teaching English, and programs that reinforce newcomers' native languages to be reformed or abolished. [Many advocate making English the official language of the United States.] Bilingual-education advocates argue that cultural and language diversity are national strengths that should be nurtured. They view official English as unnecessary, and probably unconstitutional, and [have opposed] legislation designed to make English the national language and, in one case, to abolish bilingual education outright."[135]

Congress passed the Bilingual Education Act in 1968 to help stem the high school drop out rate among Hispanics. The National Center for Educational Statistics reported that in 1995 the school drop out rate for Hispanics born in the United States was 17.9 percent, while that of Hispanic immigrants was 46.2 percent. In contrast, the drop out rates of blacks and whites were 12.2 percent and 8.6 percent, respectively.[136] However, opposition to bilingual education grew with the general anti-immigrant atmosphere of the mid-1990s. In 1995 "Congress cut $38.5 million from the $195.2 million fiscal 1995 bilingual-education budget." In 1996 "at least two official-English bills before Congress propose[d] eliminating the Department of Education's Office of Bilingual Education and Minority Language Affairs"—a move that would have left "bilingual education to state and local governments and rob[bed] bilingualism of the federal commitment proponents say it should have."[137] By 1996 twenty-two states had passed laws or constitutional amendments making English their official language.

The controversy peaked in 1998 with a referendum in California that sought to eliminate most bilingual education programs in the state and replace them with a one-year program of intensive English instruction for nonnative speakers. Proposition 227 was "the work of a white Republican Silicon Valley millionaire named Ronald K. Unz," yet was supported by at least half of the state's Hispanic voters, according to opinion polls. Many supporters of the initiative felt that bilingual education actually prevented nonnative speakers from succeeding. "I kept seeing kids doing poorly in the upper grades after they had gone through bilingual education," said Virginia Martinez, a former bilingual education teacher in Santa Ana, California. "There was no transition to English. I felt that bilingual education was holding them back." However, opponents feared that without bilingual education programs, nonnative speaking parents would not be able to participate in their children's education and the children themselves would miss basic instruction in other subjects as they struggled to understand English. On June 2, 1998, California voters approved Proposition 227. Most other states continue to permit bilingual education, and it is mandated in ten states.

Nevertheless, most studies suggest that "the children of immigrants outperform the native-born, work harder at schooling, are more engaged and motivated, and value education more." Despite perceptions of isolated foreign language enclaves, the vast majority of the children of immigrants "not only come to speak, read, and write English with fluency, but prefer it overwhelmingly to their parents' native tongue." "The findings suggest that the linguistic outcomes for the third generation—the grandchildren of the present wave of immigrants—will be little different than what has been the age-old pattern in American immigration history. The grandchildren may learn a few foreign words and phrases as a quaint vestige of their ancestry, but they will most likely grow up speaking English only."[138]

Immigrants in U.S. Politics

Immigrants play an awkward role in America's political landscape, in part because most are not U.S. citizens and therefore are not eligible to vote, and in part because their diversity tends to prevent the formation of a single voting bloc or agenda. For this reason, immigrants' political interests are traditionally represented by ethnic constituent groups such as the NCLR, the National Asian Pacific American Legal Consortium, and the Arab American Institute. During the past decade naturalization has become a key factor in understanding immigrants' political participation.

Historically, immigrants are more likely to naturalize the longer they have lived in the United States. Among the foreign-born population in 2000, 80.4 percent of those who had entered the country before 1970 were citizens, whereas only 8.9 percent of those who had entered after 1990 had naturalized.[139] Overall, the percentage of foreign-born residents who are U.S. citizens has declined from close to 70 percent in 1970 to approximately 40 percent in 1990—a fact that researchers attribute to several reasons. First, the growing proportion of new immigrants means that relatively fewer of the foreign-born have accumulated the number of years of residence required to naturalize. Second, Mexican immigrants have dominated recent immigration but tend to be sojourners, meaning they intend to return to Mexico, and hence have a low rate of naturalization. Finally, U.S. immigration policy now admits a greater number of "nonimmigrants," such as temporary workers, who are not eligible to naturalize.

However, the number of naturalization applications skyrocketed in the 1990s in response to political threats to deny immigrants' public benefits. "[S]trong messages were sent to immigrants starting in the early '90s that they should become citizens because, as noncitizens, they were vulnerable," says Josh Bernstein, policy analyst for the National Immigration Law Center, a Los Angeles-based organization that represents low-income immigrants. The success of Proposition 187 in California, federal immigration and welfare reforms in 1996, and laws that increased the threat of deportation for criminal aliens pushed many immigrants to safeguard their rights by naturalizing. "People are realizing that there is a different standard for rights protections for citizens and noncitizens," says Sasha Khokha, a spokesperson for the National Network for Immigrant and Refugee Rights. "They may have had a green card for 30 years. They may have children who are citizens and are very rooted in their communities, but they're still subject to these laws if they are not naturalized citizens."[140] Adding to the push were ethnic advocacy groups, who encouraged immigrants to naturalize by holding workshops to explain the process and help fill out applications. In 1997 alone 1,412,712 petitions for naturalization were filed, according to the INS.[141] As the applications poured in, the INS drew criticism for its growing backlog, which had already reached 800,000 by 1995. Telling Congress that, "one of my primary goals as Commissioner has

The Elián González Episode

How did a six-year-old boy become the focus of a national immigration debate that reverberated around the world? Elián González, whose story saturated the American media for months, became both a symbol of the Cuban refugee experience and a lightning rod for political arguments over U.S. policy toward Cuba.

Similar to tens of thousands of Cubans who attempt to flee the last Communist nation in the western hemisphere, Elizabet Brotons and her son, Elián, set out on a perilous ninety-mile journey across the Florida Straits with ten others from the Cuban town of Cardenas. The refugees' seventeen-foot-long aluminum boat fared poorly in the rough seas. On Thanksgiving Day 1999, a Miami fisherman plucked Elián from the waters near Fort Lauderdale, Florida. The small boy had clung to an inner tube for two days after the others aboard the boat, including his mother, drowned.

According to the 1994 U.S.-Cuban Migration Agreement, Elián became eligible for legal immigration status when he set foot on a Florida beach, officially entering U.S. territory. This policy resulted when Fidel Castro announced he would no longer block Cubans attempting to leave for the United States by boat, and thousands of refugees threatened to flood U.S. shores. After intercepting 21,000 refugees at sea in the fall of 1994 and detaining them at the Guantanamo Bay Naval Station, President Clinton agreed to issue at least 20,000 visas each year to Cubans for legal immigration to the United States, including any who reach U.S. territory, and to return to Cuba those refugees intercepted at sea by the U.S. Coast Guard.[1]

Aware of his immigration status, Elián's Miami relatives assumed custody of him, but the boy's father, who remained in Cuba, demanded his return. For more than six months, the battle over Elián raged. Some called it the latest struggle in a nearly forty-year cold war between the United States and Fidel Castro. In January 2000, U.S. Attorney General Janet Reno ordered that the boy be returned to Cuba to be reunited with his father. His Miami relatives refused and sued in American courts to gain permanent custody of the boy. Elián's father arrived in the United States prepared to bring his son home.

Elain's plight drew worldwide attention, as television cameras followed the boy. In a presidential election year, the dispute over Elián's immigration and family status became a hot political issue. Both presidential candidates Vice President Al Gore and Texas Gov. George Bush endorsed granting the boy permanent residency.[2] Several members of Congress introduced bills to grant Elián citizenship. A House subcommittee issued a subpoena compelling the six-year-old child to testify before Congress. One representative even brought the boy a puppy.

As Attorney General Reno tried to convince Elián's Miami relatives to release the boy, crowds of protestors demonstrated outside his residence. Some complained that the plight of Haitian refugees and others from Latin America and Africa merited equal attention. Others viewed Elián's return to Cuba as an assault on his human rights. "God brought him to us. He wasn't touched in the sea for days. God brought him to us for the hope of Cuba," said Jimmy Farfan, a twenty-one-year-old Cuban exile who stood outside the house every night until 2 a.m. for weeks awaiting federal agents.[3]

In the early morning of April 22, 2000, armed immigration officers removed a sobbing Elián González from his relatives' house and reunited him with his father at an Air Force base outside Washington. Two months later, after the U.S. Supreme Court refused to intervene, Elián and his father returned to Cuba.

---

1. Steven Greenhouse, "U.S. Will Return Refugees to Cuba in Policy Switch," *New York Times,* May 3, 1995, A1. See also Kathleen Newland, *U.S. Refugee Policy: Dilemmas and Directions,* Washington, D.C.: Carnegie Endowment for International Peace, 1995, 10–11 (see footnotes).
2. Katharine Q. Seelye, "Gore Supporting Residency for Cuban Child," *New York Times,* March 31, 2000, A1.
3. Lizette Alvarez, "Lawyers for Boy's Miami Relatives Rule Out Directly Releasing Him to His Father," *New York Times,* April 1, 2000, A9.

been . . . to put the 'N' back into INS," agency head Meissner launched Citizenship USA, an initiative designed to reduce the backlog and improve processing times. As part of the initiative, INS hired an additional 900 employees, opened nine new offices, and automated certain parts of the process."[142] Still, the backlog grew; by 1999 1.8 million immigrants were waiting to become U.S. citizens.[143]

The backlash against anti-immigrant sentiments also mobilized immigrant voter turnout in 1996 and subsequent elections. Empirical studies show that "naturalized citizens are less likely to register and to vote than native-born citizens";[144] yet exit polling in 1996 showed that "traditionally Democratic groups such as Mexican-Americans turned out in record numbers."[145] Republican sponsorship of immigration restrictions led most of these new immigrant voters to support Democratic candidates. According to Arturo Vargas, executive director of the National Association of Latino Elected and Appointed Officials (NALEO), "the political hostility toward immigrants and Latinos contributed to the increase of legal permanent residents applying for U.S. citizenship and participating in voting, which set the stage for an overwhelming support for Democrats from Latinos from 1994 through 1998."[146] In the 1996 election, President Clinton improved 16 points from

Table 2-4 Partisan Sentiments

Ethnic Group	Strong Democrat	Democrat	Independent	Republican	Strong Republican
Mexican	31.0 %	35.8%	11.5%	17.1%	4.4
Cuban	14.4	11.1	5.7	21.0	47.8
Chinese	2.3	26.9	27.7	27.7	9.9
Filipino	8.3	35.8	22.5	23.3	8.3
Vietnamese	1.8	35.5	19.1	24.5	19.7

Source: Table excerpted from Carnegie Endowment for International Peace, "New American Co-Ethnic Voting," *Research Perspectives on Migration*, 1(3), March/April 1997, 7.

his 1992 performance among Latino voters to earn 71 percent of their vote. He also won a majority of the Asian American vote, usually a "swing" constituency, and nearly doubled his showing among Cuban Americans, who traditionally vote Republican. Most remarkably, Clinton captured more than 80 percent of the vote among newly naturalized citizens.[147]

Some analysts predict that immigrants' political influence will remain strong even as their feeling of vulnerability fades. They point out first that the continuing growth of the foreign-born population will raise immigrants' importance not only as voters but also as members of communities that are increasingly important to their well-being, whether as relatives, business patrons, or other service providers. They also expect that immigrants' geographic concentration will continue to have a pronounced impact on congressional, state, and local elections. In New York, for example, Dominican Americans now dominate politics in the neighborhood of Washington Heights, one of the most concentrated immigrant enclaves.[148] Similarly, the 2001 Los Angeles mayoral race between James Hahn and Antonio Villaraigosa revealed the increasing influence of Latino voters, many of whom were newly registered in the wake of anti-immigrant measures. According to the *Los Angeles Times*, "Latinos represented slightly more than a fifth of the electorate [on voting day], casting about three times the number of votes that they did in the 1993 mayor's race. . . . Latinos voted for Villaraigosa by a margin of 4 to 1."[149] Villaraigosa, the son of an immigrant father and former labor organizer, was poised to become the city's first Hispanic mayor since 1872. Sherry Bebitch Jeffe, senior scholar at the University of Southern California's School of Policy, Planning and

Development, characterized the candidates: "It is Jim Hahn who represents the civic establishment of Los Angeles, versus Antonio Villaraigosa, who represents the face of the future of Los Angeles."[150] Although Villaraigosa lost the election, many expressed confidence that Latinos' political power would continue to grow. Former mayor of San Antonio and U.S. Secretary of Housing and Urban Development under President Clinton, Henry Cisneros predicted on election night that, "Even if [Villaraigosa] doesn't ride the crest tonight, someone else will." Harry Pachon, president of the Tomas Rivera Policy Institute, compared the rise of Hispanic mayors in the nation's big cities, in the late 1990s to the rise of black mayors in the late 1960s.[151]

By the 2000 elections Republicans had already gotten the message loud and clear: anti-immigrant measures alienate many Hispanics, who form an increasingly important part of the electorate. As his presidential campaign entered its final days, George W. Bush told a group of Latinos in Anaheim Hills, California, about his plans for immigration reform:

> Family values don't stop at the Rio Grande River. People are coming to America because they're moms and dads trying to feed their children. These new Americans should be treated with respect by the U.S. government. Sometimes the INS sends a different message. My administration will reform the INS, and make it worthy of a nation of immigrants. It should be divided into two separate agencies: enforcement, to secure the border; and immigration, to welcome and serve new Americans. All people—citizens, future citizens, aspiring citizens—deserve to be treated with dignity and respect. We're going to allow husbands, wives, and children of permanent residents to visit while the INS is handling their residency applications. There is no reason to keep family members from seeing each other while they wait for the papers to come through. And every INS application should be fully processed within six months of submission. Legal immigrants are the future and the changing face of America, and we should welcome them. And we should say to all new Americans, *El sueno Americano es parta ti.* Immigration is a sign of our success as a great and hopeful nation.

Still, immigrants face internal challenges to their political influence: "They are so diverse that their impact on the power structure is fractured."[152] A major problem is that "few immigrants think of themselves in pan-ethnic terms" so that "feelings of solidarity extend [only] to those of their own national-origin."[153] In Flushing, New York, for example, Asian Americans make up the majority of the population, but come from China, Korea, India, Bangladesh, and Pakistan, making it difficult for political candidates to appeal to a unified immigrant constituency. Kam Kuwata, a spokesperson for the Hahn campaign in Los Angeles told reporters: "Give voters some credit. Are there Latinos who are going to vote for [Villaraigosa] just because he's a Latino? Yes. But everybody I've met is going to vote for somebody because they think he's the best candidate."[154]

The Response to Terrorism: Changing Immigration Policy

Similar to many other policies, U.S. immigration policy came under intense scrutiny following the terrorist attacks of September 11, 2001. The Federal Bureau of Investigation (FBI) identified all nineteen hijackers aboard the four planes that crashed into the World Trade Center, Pentagon, and rural Pennsylvania to be foreigners of Middle Eastern origin, at least two of whom were in the country illegally after overstaying temporary visas. The terrorists' complete immigration status and the extent of fraudulent documentation used by them remain to be determined; however, it appears that the terrorists entered the United States lawfully, and in some cases repeatedly over several years, to carry out the plot of their international terrorist network, Al Qaeda. These facts exposed weaknesses in U.S. immigration policy that made the country vulnerable to attack, prompting lawmakers, enforcement agents, and other officials to demand urgent reform of the immigration system.

These calls for immigration reform signal a rare shift in underlying policy assumptions. Before September 11, the predominant assumption among immigration policy-makers was that immigrants—both legal and illegal—seek entry to the United States for economic gain. Other reasons to immigrate included family reunification and protection from persecution—assumptions that are reflected in the major admissions categories. Considering these ideas together, it is clear that the overriding assumption was that immigrants arrive in this country with good intentions, even if policy-makers do not agree about immigrants' actual impact on the U.S. economy, communities, politics, and culture. The terrorist attacks prompted policy-makers to seriously question this assumption. At a minimum, the attacks forced policy-makers to acknowledge that some immigrants wish to harm the United States. More broadly speaking, the attacks shifted the focus of immigration policy from economic considerations to national security concerns.[155]

The major weaknesses in immigration policy identified as a result of the September 11 attacks are related to border security and immigration intelligence. Ironically, these areas of immigration policy had received significant attention and resources before the terrorist attacks, and variations of the post–September 11 reform proposals also had been put forth earlier; yet, antiterrorism had not been a priority, so the proposals were scuttled.

Border Security

Within hours of the attacks, immigration officials took emergency actions to close virtually all U.S. borders. Flights around the country were grounded, airports closed, ships were diverted from sea ports, and immigration inspectors and border patrol agents closed ports-of-entry along U.S. land borders with Mexico and Canada. These extreme measures blocked transportation in an effort to prevent other potential terrorists from entering the country and carrying out their deadly mission. However, the costs of sealing the borders were staggering; there were not only operational costs of deploying additional enforcement agents with proper equipment and overtime pay, but also great costs in trade and industry, disrupting more than $1 billion in trade per day with Canada alone. As the immediate threat of further attacks passed, this emergency policy became unsustainable.

During the next few days, ports-of-entry reopened under tight security, with agents checking every passenger and vehicle entering the country. Still, slower border crossings with enormous traffic backups posed formidable costs to trade and industry. The challenge of balancing facilitation and security objectives at the border never seemed so relevant, igniting debates among policy analysts about the role of border control in fighting terrorism.

Steven Camarota of the Center for Immigration Studies portrayed the border as an essential element of national security, telling the Senate: "The simple fact is that if the terrorists can't enter the country, they won't be able to commit an attack on American soil."[156] On the other side of the debate, Stephen Flynn, a senior fellow at the Council on Foreign Relations and former U.S. Coast Guard commander, argued:

> By closing airports and restricting access through land borders on and after September 11, the U.S. accomplished the historical feat of embargoing itself. Such a drastic response was necessary because the U.S. had no established way to address a threat like the one that presented itself in September. In light of the economic consequences of the move, the U.S. should reconsider its security strategy at all of its borders and ask questions such as whether certain functions can be accomplished only at the border or what the costs and benefits of doing them elsewhere might be.[157]

While this debate continues, most agree that increased coordination of border enforcement activities is necessary, along with the notion that more "seamless" border management will eliminate the "cracks" through which potential terrorists and other unwanted immigrants may slip. Specifically, two proposals for government reorganization—both offered before September 11 by separate commissions devoted to antiterrorism policy—came to the forefront of the antiterrorism agenda. These proposals agreed that the threat of terrorism required a significant reorganization of government functions, but disagreed on the nature of this reorganization.

The Advisory Panel to Assess Domestic Response Capabilities for Terrorism Involving Weapons of Mass Destruction (commonly known as the Gilmore Commission after its chair, former Virginia governor James S. Gilmore III) proposed the creation of a National Office for Combating Terrorism in the Executive Office of the President, which would coordinate federal, state, and local antiterrorism efforts, including those related to immigration. The Commission on National Security/21st Century (commonly known as the Hart-Rudman Commission after its chairs, former senators Gary Hart and Warren Rudman) proposed the creation of a new federal homeland security agency that would merge the Federal Emergency Management Agency (FEMA), Customs Service, Coast Guard, and Border Patrol.

In a nod to the Gilmore Commission's proposal, President Bush created an Office of Homeland Security in the White House and appointed Pennsylvania governor Tom Ridge as director. However, support for the Hart-Rudman proposal remained strong, with Sen. Joseph I. Lieberman, D-Conn., leading the debate in Congress. Once in office, Homeland Security Director Ridge considered a variation on the Hart-Rudman proposal: creating a border security agency, presumably by merging components of the Customs Service, Coast Guard, and Border Patrol. "I may very well come up and ask them to reconfigure some of these agencies so there are more direct lines of accountability," said Ridge.[158]

This focus on border security compelled Immigration and Naturalization Service (INS) enforcement functions to bolster their operations and reexamine border strategies. Since 1994, the Border Patrol's national strategy had emphasized disruption of illegal immigration activities along the Southwest border with Mexico, devoting higher levels of resources and staffing to what were perceived to be high-risk areas for criminal activity, particularly migrant smuggling. The terrorist attacks of September 11 changed perceptions of risk, making the northern border with Canada appear extremely vulnerable. Members of Congress seized on the fact that, before September 11, the Border Patrol had more than 9,000 agents stationed along the Southwest border, but only 334 stationed along the northern border, which is more than twice as long.[159] The INS faced similar staffing challenges in inspections: roughly half of the northern border's 126 official crossings were guarded only by an orange cone in the road at night. In the wake of the terrorist attacks, the Border Patrol added roughly 300 agents to the northern border,[160] the National Guard was deployed in many states to protect border infrastructure, and Congress quickly passed the USA Patriot Act (Public Law No. 107-56), which authorized funding to triple border staffing levels, among other immigration-related provisions.

Still, the challenge of securing the northern border remains daunting, and many policy-makers oppose the "militarization" of what had been dubbed the world's longest undefended land border. This predicament has given new impetus to calls for regional coordination of North American borders, sometimes referred to as "perimeter defense." One of the strongest proponents of a North American perimeter has been U.S. Ambassador to Canada, Paul Cellucci. "Closing the borders is not the answer," said Cellucci, former governor of Massachusetts. "We all recognize that if this border becomes an impediment [to trade], that's one more way for the terrorists to win."[161]

The Bush administration took a step in this direction when the United States and Canada signed an agreement to further integrate border management on December 12, 2001. Known as the "Smart Border Declaration," the agreement set out an action plan to secure the flow of people and goods, secure infrastructure at key crossing points, and coordinate and share law enforcement information. Under these broad objectives, the plan laid out thirty specific points for joint action, including the development of biometric identifiers, preclearance cooperation, expanded Integrated Border and Marine Enforcement Teams, binational threat assessments, and coordination of refugee and asylum policies.

Immigration Intelligence

The terrorist attacks also exposed a need to improve coordination among American intelligence systems, including immigration intelligence. Government officials pointed out a number of deficiencies in immigration intelligence. First, the lack of intelligence sharing among the FBI, CIA, State Department, INS, and state and local law enforcement agencies meant that immigration enforcement officers could not always identify and therefore intercept criminals or suspected terrorists cross-ing U.S. borders. Second, poor reporting mechanisms between U.S. universities and the INS allowed foreigners admitted on student visas to skip school or even fail to enroll while pursuing other endeavors. This loophole was highlighted by the dis-covery that one of the hijackers, Hani Hanjour, had been admitted on a student visa to attend a language course but never showed up to class. And third, poor intelli-gence sharing combined with weaknesses in consular staffing had led to inade-quate background checks for visa applicants overseas.

Congress immediately sought to address these deficiencies through legislation amending the Immigration and Nationality Act. The USA Patriot Act of 2001 re-quired the INS and FBI to enhance their fingerprint identification systems, and to share files from the National Crime Information Center with the State Depart-ment, so that consular officers could access criminal history records and create an automated visa lookout database. The Patriot Act also mandated the INS and De-partment of State to fully implement and expand the foreign student monitoring program that had been established by the Illegal Immigration Reform and Immi-grant Responsibility Act of 1996.

The severity of the situation led several senators to seek immigration reforms beyond the provisions of the Patriot Act. Sens. Feinstein (D-Calif.) and Jon Kyl (R-Ariz.) began to prepare legislation that would deny student visas to applicants from nations on the State Department's list of countries sponsoring terrorism. The Feinstein-Kyl bill also required the CIA, FBI, State Department, and other agencies to share information to create a "comprehensive lookout database" available to consular officers who issue visas.[162] Sens. Kennedy (D-Mass.) and Sam Brownback (R-Kan.) joined together to prepare competing legislation. Their bill simply required special scrutiny of applicants for student visas from countries on the State Department list, and mandated studies on improvements in identification tech-nology. The four senators eventually reached a compromise and introduced legisla-tion in December 2001. The bipartisan bill mandates more extensive background checks on nonimmigrant visa applicants, allowing visas to be issued to citizens of countries on the State Department list only after "it has been determined that such alien does not pose a threat to the safety or national security of the United States."[163] The bill also stipulates reporting requirements between the INS and ed-ucational institutions. The INS is required to notify the institutions when foreign-ers enter the United States on student visas, and colleges must then report whether the student has arrived for classes. Universities must also provide information on the students' residence, academic major, and attendance.

Lobbyists for institutions of higher education historically had blocked such reporting and student monitoring requirements over practical objections to cost and bureaucracy and philosophical objections to associating students with criminal intent and intruding on their privacy. These objections proved no match against the security concerns posed by the terrorist attacks, and lobbyists expressed relief that the compromise bill was not as harsh as they had feared. "I think we're grateful that the amount of information that is specified that we give back to the Immigration and Naturalization Service is reasonable," said David Ward, president of the American Council on Education.[164]

The Investigation

Although U.S. immigration policy came under fire for the weaknesses exposed by the terrorist attacks, immigration law proved an important tool in the investigation of terrorist activities. As federal authorities rounded up potential suspects in the days and weeks following the attacks, immigration law provided a means to hold persons in custody despite the government's lack of evidence of terrorist activity. Gallup and other opinion polls showed strong public support of the Justice Department's use of immigration laws to track down suspected terrorists. However, many immigrant advocates and others assailed the policies as infringing on civil rights, particularly through racial or ethnic discrimination.

Beginning immediately after the attacks, the Justice Department took a series of steps to enforce immigration law in the name of national security. First, FBI agents and other Justice Department officials arrested at least 1,200 people during the first four months of the terrorist probe, of which more than 400 were later cleared and released.[165] The remainder (more than 725 people, predominately Middle Eastern men) were detained on immigration charges, including 460 who remained in custody through January 2002. The Justice Department charged a separate group of more than 100 foreign nationals with criminal offenses in connection with the attacks. Delays in processing caused by this large caseload combined with the secrecy surrounding cases potentially related to national security meant that, in many cases, the government held individuals for weeks before charging them with immigration violations and did not release their identities to the public.

INS Restructuring

As the nature and volume of immigration flows changed over the course of the 1990s, policy-makers grew increasingly dissatisfied with the ability of the Immigration and Naturalization Service (INS) to manage its responsibilities. Consensus emerged among lawmakers that the agency suffered from "mission overload" and needed dramatic restructuring, including greater distinction between enforcement and service functions. However, Republicans and Democrats disagreed over the extent of this divide. By the end of the decade, annual efforts to pass legislation that would mandate INS restructuring regularly died in committee. Ultimately, the terrorist attacks of September 2001 provided the driving force needed to make the restructuring happen.

Reports by the General Accounting Office and U.S. Commission on Immigration Reform in the early 1990s forged the perception that the INS needed fundamental restructuring to address the agency's mission overload, conflicting responsibilities, and poor performance. The Commission on Immigration Reform, for example, recommended a Bureau for Immigration Enforcement within the Justice Department for border and interior enforcement; an Undersecretary of State for Citizenship, Immigration, and Refugee Admissions within the State Department with responsibility for benefit adjudication; an Agency for Immigration Review for independent repeals of administrative decisions; and a transfer of immigration-related employment standards enforcement to the Labor Department.[1]

The legislative initiative emerged chiefly from Republican criticism that the INS was not effectively combating illegal immigration. Representative Harold Rogers, R-Ky., led the charge in 1998 through his position as chairman of the House Appropriations' Commerce, Justice, State and Judiciary Subcommittee, which funds the agency. In the fall of 1999, he sponsored a bill (HR 2528) that would disband the INS and separate immigration enforcement and service functions in two new agencies. At the same time, the subcommittee drafted fiscal 2000 spending measures that would devote two-thirds of immigration funding to enforcement.

The Clinton administration, congressional Democrats, and immigrant advocacy groups agreed with the GOP that the INS needed to be restructured to eliminate inefficiencies. However, they opposed GOP-sponsored legislation because they believed the new Bureau of Immigration Enforcement, which would oversee the Border Patrol and deportations, would receive a disproportionate allocation of resources: "Democrats say not enough would be spent on the new Bureau of Immigration Services, which would be in charge of applications for citizenship, 'green card' residency permits and legal benefits."[2] Instead, Democrats supported the proposal of INS Commissioner Doris Meissner, who testified before the House Subcommittee on Immigration and Claims in May 1998: "[Our restructuring plan] builds a strengthened law enforcement operation and a new service-oriented organization within one agency by splitting enforcement and service functions into two distinct chains of command." She emphasized that "these tasks are too interconnected to be handled by more than one agency."[3]

Efforts to pass INS restructuring legislation broke down in 1998, 1999, and 2000 before ever reaching the full Judiciary Committee in the House or Senate. However, the administration of George W. Bush began to push the issue in the summer of 2001. After promising to restructure INS during his election campaign, President Bush appointed James Ziglar to be commissioner of the INS and made agency restructuring a top priority. At the same time, two Republican representatives, James Sensenbrenner (R-Wis.) and George Gekas (R-Pa.) pushed a separate agenda for INS restructuring. The chair of the House Judiciary Committee and the chair of the Subcommittee on Immigration and Claims, respectively, Sensenbrenner and Gekas issued a statement linking their support for any Bush immigration reforms to a restructuring of the INS.

The weaknesses in the immigration system exposed by the terrorist attacks of September 11, 2001, added to already mounting pressure for INS restructuring. By mid-November, Ziglar and Attorney General John Ashcroft announced the administration's plan for agency restructuring, which created separate bureaus for immigration services and enforcement with distinct chains of command under unified policy leadership.

However, Sensenbrenner remained dissatisfied with the administration's plan and vowed to push his own plan through Congress. With a last-minute endorsement from the Bush administration, the House voted in May 2002 overwhelmingly in favor of Sensenbrenner's bill, which would abolish the INS and create separate services and enforcement bureaus under a new associate attorney general for immigration affairs in the Justice Department. Sens. Edward M. Kennedy (D-Mass.) and Sam Brownback (R-Kan.) prepared parallel legislation that would increase the authority and accountability of the new associate attorney general. House minority leader Richard A. Gephardt (D-Mo.) helped explain the rare bipartisanship: "We saw in the 9/11 incident some of the problems in the INS that many of us had seen before. It became clear, I think, to everybody in the country and in the Congress that we needed reform."[4]

---

1. T. Alexander Aleinikoff, Deborah Waller Meyers, and Demetrios G. Papademetriou, *Reorganizing the U.S. Immigration Function: Toward a New Framework for Accountability* (Washington, D.C.: Carnegie Endowment for International Peace, 1998), 58.

2. Karen Foerstel, "House Panel Approves INS Breakup," *CQ Weekly*, November 6, 1999.

3. Doris Meissner, Testimony before the U.S. House of Representatives Committee on the Judiciary Subcommittee on Immigration and Claims, "Alternative Proposals to Restructure the Immigration and Naturalization Service," May 21, 1998.

4. Eric Schmitt, "Vote in House Strongly Backs an End to I.N.S." *New York Times*, April 26, 2002, A1.

Immigration lawyers and civil liberties advocates vehemently objected that these actions violated the detainees' rights.[166]

Taking further steps, the Justice Department swiftly expanded its powers to detain immigrants. In late October 2001, Attorney General John Ashcroft signed a new rule that took effect within three days without public notice. The rule made it easier to detain immigrants by allowing the INS to set aside any release orders issued by immigration judges "to prevent the release of aliens who may pose a threat to national security."[167] To set aside an immigration judge's release order, the INS would file a form that says it plans to appeal the decision to the Board of Immigration Appeals (BIA). If the BIA orders the detainee released on appeal, the INS could also set aside that order, under the new regulation, by taking the case to the attorney general.

Immigrant advocates again criticized the Justice Department's expanded powers to detain aliens, particularly in light of the Supreme Court's June 2001 decision prohibiting such indefinite detention. "With this rule change, the government can lock someone up on very little or even no evidence and throw away the key until they decide to let them go," said David W. Leopold, an immigration lawyer in Cleveland representing eleven Israelis who continued to be detained after a judge had ordered them released. "In effect, it just takes immigration judges out of the mix, bypassing their role entirely." The immigration service defended the rule saying the system might have required the release of aliens who pose security threats before the agency could present its case to the appeals board, citing the heavy case load of the service.

The USA Patriot Act also greatly expanded the government's ability to detain immigrants indefinitely. Section 412 says that upon the attorney general's certification that he or she has "reasonable grounds to believe" that a noncitizen is engaged in terrorist activities or other activities that threaten the national security, a noncitizen may be detained for as long as seven days without being charged with either a criminal or immigration violation. If the noncitizen is charged with an immigration violation, he is subject to mandatory detention and is not eligible for release until he is removed or until the attorney general determines that he or she should no longer be judged a terrorist. While immigration proceedings are pending, the attorney general is required to review his certification once every six months.[168]

At the same time, Section 411 of the Patriot Act expands the types of criminal activities considered "terrorist," which also makes them grounds for deportation. It defines "terrorist activity" to encompass any crime that involves the use of a "weapon or dangerous device (other than for mere personal monetary gain)." The provision also revised a definition that had confined "terrorist organization" to organizations that have had their terrorist designations published in the *Federal Register,* thereby increasing the number of organizations potentially identified as "terrorist" by the attorney general.

The Justice Department's third major step to advance immigration enforcement expanded the government's ability to obtain evidence. The department announced in October 2001 that it would eavesdrop on conversations between detainees and their lawyers whenever the attorney general concluded that there was a "reasonable suspicion" to believe that these conversations were being used to facilitate terrorism.[169] Ashcroft defended the new rule as essential to protect national security and noted in testimony before Congress that the Justice Department was required to notify the attorney and the client in writing before that happened and that less than ten individuals were having their conversations monitored.

As a fourth component of its terrorism investigation, the government announced in November 2001 that it would seek voluntary interviews with more than 5,000 primarily Middle Eastern men aged eighteen to thirty-three who had entered the United States since January 1, 2000, on nonimmigrant student, tourist, or business visas. Some immigrant advocacy groups denounced the plan as harassment and counseled those who had received the letters not to respond. Others provided legal advice to young men who chose to respond. The vast majority of the men agreed to be interviewed by the FBI and local law enforcement officers. In most cases, the government said it would over look technical violations of immigration law—such as overstaying a temporary visa.

At the same time, federal investigators visited more than 200 U.S. college campuses and contacted administrators to collect information about students from Middle Eastern countries—such as their academic major, residence, and other activities. The investigators also paid unannounced visits on the students themselves, asking questions on topics ranging from their views on Al Qaeda leader Osama bin Laden to their educational plans.[170]

In a complementary move, the Justice Department offered S-visas—dubbed "snitch-visas" by some—to immigrants who provided material information about future terrorist attacks, and even offered the possibility of citizenship. "People who have the courage to make the right choice deserve to be welcomed as guests into our country and perhaps to one day become fellow citizens," said Ashcroft.[171]

As a final step, in December, the INS announced a plan to pursue immigrants who had failed to appear at their immigration hearings and were issued orders of removal in absentia. Termed "absconders," these immigrants essentially disappeared from immigration authorities, who could not easily track them down for deportation. The new INS plan designated funds to enter the names of 314,000 absconders into a national computer directory. In a controversial move, the agency said that in the near term it would focus on about 6,000 absconders mostly from Middle Eastern countries. "Terrorist attacks by Al Qaeda within the United States are a continuing threat to Americans. We will continue to focus investigative, intelligence-gathering and enforcement operations on individuals in the U.S. from countries with highly active Al Qaeda networks to protect Americans," the Justice Department said in a statement.[172]

Aside from legal objections, many of the Justice Department's actions explicitly targeted Arab immigrants, raising concerns about racial and ethnic discrimination and profiling. The American Civil Liberties Union (ACLU) and the American Arab Anti-Discrimination Committee called the expansion of government power unnecessary and discriminatory.[173] A poll of Arab Americans in southeast Michigan—the region with a large concentration of people of Arab background—found in October 2001 that: "Most Arab Americans . . . believe that profiling, or extra scrutiny of people with Middle Eastern features or accents by law enforcement officials, has escalated since the Sept. 11 terrorist attacks."[174] Yet the poll also found that a majority of Arab Americans (61 percent) believed such profiling was justified.

Fears also mounted that some discrimination might take the form of violent retaliation against Arabs living in the United States. The murder of a Yemeni convenience store owner in California just weeks after the terrorist attacks produced anxiety that hate crimes against Arab residents would rise.[175] The Justice Department said it was aggressively investigating hate crimes against Middle Easterners in the wake of the September 11 attacks, opening more than 250 investigations into incidents across the country and indicting more than a dozen. "The government is using the same vigilance, the same diligence in investigating attacks against Arab Americans and Muslims that it is in the main terrorism investigation . . . These attacks are un-American and will not be tolerated," said Ralph Boyd Jr., the assistant attorney general for civil rights.[176]

Still, many perceived anti-Arab sentiment giving way to anti-immigrant sentiment as the nation declared war on terrorism—or, at least, life for foreigners in the United States got harder. As the government prepared to make airport security workers federal employees, policy advisors questioned whether noncitizens currently working in airport security should be allowed to keep their jobs. Some states moved to close loopholes that had allowed illegal immigrants to obtain driver's licenses. Tight border controls forced many undocumented Mexican immigrants to decide to stay in the United States for the holidays, or to go home and not come back.

These policies and many others reflected a shift in assumptions about immigrants' role in U.S. society. This shift was as abrupt as the plane crashes that destroyed the World Trade Center. However, few immigration policy-makers abandoned long-standing views on immigration policy overall. If the terrorist attacks shifted the weight of different immigration variables, they did not change the basic equation. "Immigrants are not the problem," said Sen. Kennedy in November 2001. "Terrorists are the problem."

Conclusion

Perhaps the most important lesson to take from the past decade is that U.S. immigration policy is extremely dynamic. Or, as former INS Commissioner Meissner put it, "Immigration has been an area of policy especially given to wild swings."[177] In a general sense, these swings have accompanied national economic trends. After the U.S. economy fell into recession in the early 1990s, policies to restrict immigrant admissions and rights earned strong support, leading to a "crack down" in both law enforcement and benefits provisions with the IIRIRA in 1996. As the economy boomed in the latter half of the decade, advocates of immigration expansion and immigrants' rights led efforts to undo some of the harsh provisions of the 1996 law, and policy-makers began to view immigration as a boon to economic growth. By early 2002, with the economy in recession again and the deadly terrorist attacks on the World Trade Center and Pentagon still fresh in American minds, the course of immigration policy appeared to teeter on the edge of restrictionism: after swinging open, the immigration door looked as if it might slam shut, but it also left room for more moderate policies to take hold.

Still, the metaphor of the door does not convey the complexity of the immigrant population, their reasons for seeking entry to the United States, and the role they play in American communities once they have arrived. As this chapter has shown, immigrants are diverse; they come from many different countries, representing a vast array of ethnic backgrounds, and bringing a range of education and work skills, family structures, and values. Although the United States admits a majority of legal permanent residents for family reunification, many others seek entry through refugee and asylum claims, temporary visas, or illegal channels. It is difficult to determine immigrants' impact on American society—some argue that immigrants create a fiscal burden, while others extol immigrants' contributions to their communities. Many of the costs and benefits of immigration prove too abstract to quantify. Likewise, it is not easy to predict how immigrants will integrate into American culture and institutions across succeeding generations, or how they will influence American politics.

Immigration policies are as dynamic and multifaceted as immigrants themselves. They present challenges and opportunities for continual nation-building, while carrying important consequences for individuals' lives. After a decade that encompassed a range of immigration policies, Americans continue to confront the basic questions of "whom to admit?" and "how?"—perhaps because immigration continues to change the fabric of American society.

Notes

1. Lisa Lollock, "The Foreign-Born Population in the United States: March 2000," *Current Population Reports* (Washington, D.C: U.S. Census Bureau, 2001), 1.

2. James P. Smith and Barry Edmonston, eds., *The New Americans: Economic, Demographic, and Fiscal Effects of Immigration* (Washington, D.C.: National Academy Press, 1997), 35.

3. Lollock, "Foreign-Born Population," 3.

4. U.S. Immigration and Naturalization Service, *Statistical Yearbook of the Immigration and Naturalization Service, 1998* (Washington, D.C.: Government Printing Office, 2000), 14, 19.

5. Sidney Weintraub, Francisco Alba, Rafael Fernández de Castro, and Manuel García y Griego, "Responses to Migration Issues," in Mexican Ministry of Foreign Affairs and U.S. Commission on Immigration Reform, *Migration Between Mexico and the United States: Binational Study*, Vol. 1. (Austin, Texas: Morgan, 1998), 439.

6. See http://travel.state.gov/visa;immigrants.html.

7. U.S. Immigration and Naturalization Service, *Statistical Yearbook, 1998*, 12.

8. Lollock, "Foreign-Born Population," 1.

9. Smith and Edmonston, eds., *New Americans*, 59.

10. Lollock, "Foreign-Born Population," 2.

11. U.S. Immigration and Naturalization Service, *Statistical Yearbook, 1998*, 12.

12. Paulette Thomas, "In the Land of Bratwurst, a New Hispanic Boom—In a Big Population Shift, Latino Immigrants Flock to Towns in the Midwest," *Wall Street Journal,* March 16, 2000, B1.

13. Lollock, "Foreign-Born Population," 2.

14. U.S. Immigration and Naturalization Service, *Statistical Yearbook, 1998,* 54.

15. Smith and Edmonston, eds., *New Americans,* 56.

16. Lollock, "Foreign-Born Population," 4–5.

17. Smith and Edmonston, eds., *New Americans,* 209–219.

18. Lollock, "Foreign-Born Population," 2.

19. Eric Schmitt, "Americans (a)Love (b)Hate Immigrants," *New York Times,* January 14, 2001, Wk1.

20. Susan Sachs, "A Hue, and a Cry, in the Heartland," *New York Times,* April 8, 2001, WK5.

21. Smith and Edmonston, eds., *New Americans,* 52.

22. Sachs, "A Hue, and a Cry," WK5.

23. Smith and Edmonston, eds., *New Americans,* 393.

24. Demetrios G. Papademetriou, "Skilled Temporary Workers in the Global Economy: Creating a Balanced and Forward-Looking Selection Process," in B. Lindsay Lowell, ed., *Foreign Temporary Workers in America: Policies that Benefit the U.S. Economy* (Westport, Conn.: Quorum Books, 1999), 31.

25. Philip Martin, "Guest Workers: Past and Present," in Mexican Ministry of Foreign Affairs and the U.S. Commission on Immigration Reform, *Migration Between Mexico and the United States: Binational Study,* Vol. 3. (Austin, Texas: Morgan, 1998), 877–895.

26. U.S. Department of Labor, Office of the Assistant Secretary for Policy, Office of Program Economics, "Findings of the National Agricultural Workers Survey (NAWS) 1997–98," Research Report No. 8, March 2000.

27. Demetrios G. Papademetriou and Monica L. Heppel, *Balancing Acts: Toward a Fair Bargain on Seasonal Agricultural Workers.* Carnegie Endowment for International Peace, 1999, 12.

28. T. Alexander Aleinikoff, "The Green Card Solution," *American Prospect,* December 20, 1999.

29. Ibid., 36.

30. Papademetriou and Heppel, *Balancing Acts,* 7.

31. Josh Wunsch, Member, Board of Directors, Michigan Farm Bureau, Testimony before the Senate Committee on the Judiciary, Subcommittee on Immigration, May 4, 2000.

32. Peter W. Cohn, "Congress Casts Hopeful Eye on Mexico's Transition," *CQ Weekly,* November 18, 2000.

33. Lynda V. Mapes, " 'I Need the Work, They Need the Work Done,' Northwest Farmworker Says," *Seattle Times*, June 19, 2000, A1.

34. U.S. Department of Labor, "Findings of the National Agricultural Workers Survey."

35. Cecilia Munoz, Vice-President for the Office of Research, Advocacy and Legislation of the National Council of La Raza, Testimony before the Senate Committee on the Judiciary, Subcommittee on Immigration, May 4, 2000.

36. U.S. Department of Labor, "Findings of the National Agricultural Workers Survey."

37. Munoz, Testimony before the Senate, May 4, 2000.

38. Papademetriou and Heppel, *Balancing Acts*, 8.

39. Ginger Thompson and Steven Greenhouse, "Mexican 'Guest Workers': A Project Worth a Try?" *New York Times*, April 3, 2001, A4.

40. Ginger Thompson, "Fox Urges Congress to Grant Rights to Mexican Immigrants in U.S.," *New York Times*, September 7, 2001, A6.

41. Ginger Thompson, "U.S. and Mexico to Open Talks on Freer Migration for Workers," *New York Times*, February 16, 2001, A1.

42. Much of this section is excerpted from Kathy Koch, "High-Tech Labor Shortage," *CQ Researcher*, April 24, 1998, 372.

43. B. Lindsay Lowell, "Temporary Visas for Work, Study, and Cultural Exchange: Introduction and Summary," in Lowell, ed., *Foreign Temporary Workers*, 3.

44. Koch, "High-Tech Labor Shortage," 367, 372.

45. Ibid., 365.

46. Dan Carney, "Immigration Bill's Fine Print Sends Industry into High-Tech Turmoil," *CQ Weekly*, May 2, 1998.

47. Koch, "High-Tech Labor Shortage," 376.

48. Bara Vaida, "Wanted! U.S. Citizens for High-Tech Jobs," *National Journal*, November 18, 2000, 3682.

49. Koch, "High-Tech Labor Shortage," 363.

50. David A. Smith, Director of Policy of the AFL-CIO, Testimony Before the U.S. House Committee on the Judiciary, Subcommittee on Immigration and Claims, August 5, 1999.

51. John B. Judis, "Temporary Help," *New Republic*, June 19, 2000, 21

52. Mary Agnes Carey, "Compromise Revives Measure to Increase Visas For Highly Skilled Workers," *CQ Weekly*, October, 17, 1998.

53. Vaida, "Wanted! U.S. Citizens for High-Tech Jobs," 3682.

54. Smith, Testimony Before the House, August 5, 1999. See also John M. Miano, The Programmer's Guild, Testimony Before the U.S. House Committee on the Judiciary, Subcommittee on Immigration and Claims, August 5, 1999.

55. Melissa Solomon, "H-1B refugees," *Computer World*, December 3, 2001.

56. David Tell, "Republicans and Immigration," *Weekly Standard*, February 26, 1996.

57. "Cracking Down on Immigrants," *CQ Researcher*, February 3, 1995.

58. Steven V. Roberts and Anne Kate Smith, "Uncle Sam, Bar the Door," *U.S. News & World Report*, April 29, 1996, 28.

59. Susan Crabtree, "Clinton Says 'Me Too' as GOP Blasts Immigration," *Insight on the News*, March 18, 1996, 11.

60. Dan Carney, "Special Report—Presidential Issues: Can the U.S. Regain Control of its Borders?" *CQ Weekly*, October 5, 1996.

61. Ibid.

62. Dan Carney, "Republicans Feeling the Heat as Policy Becomes Reality," *CQ Weekly*, May 17, 1997.

63. Merle English, "In Queens, Push to Get Amnesty for Immigrants," *Newsday*, February 11, 1998, A41.

64. Steven Greenhouse, "Labor Urges Amnesty for Illegal Immigrants," *New York Times*, February 17, 2000, A26.

65. Steven Greenhouse, "Coalition Urges Easing of Immigration Laws," *New York Times*, May 16, 2000, A16.

66. Dan Stein, "Should Illegal Immigrants Be Permitted to Remain in the United States If They Have Been Here for Several Years?" in "Debate Over Immigration," *CQ Researcher*, July 14, 2000, 585.

67. Dan Stein, "Amnesty for Illegal Aliens Undermines the Law," *Record* (Bergen Country, N.J.), November 26, 1999, L7.

68. "INS: Border, 245, Asylum, Detention," *Migration News*, May 2001.

69. David Shepardson, "New Law Opens Citizenship: Metro Immigrants Apply as April 30 Deadline Nears," *Detroit News*, April 30, 2001, A1.

70. Michael Janofsky, "Undocumented Immigrants Scramble to Get Through a Small Window of Opportunity," *New York Times*, May 1, 2001, A12.

71. "D'Amato Proposes Bill for Criminal Aliens," *New York Times*, January 13, 1992, A5.

72. Peter H. Schuck, "Removing Criminal Aliens: The Pitfalls and Promises of Federalism," *Harvard Journal of Law and Public Policy*, Spring 1999.

73. Jim Wilson, staff of Rep. Lamar Smith, "Legislative Proposals: A View from the Hill," remarks at the conference, "Criminal Aliens and Immigration: Taking Stock and Looking Ahead," held at the Carnegie Endowment for International Peace, Washington, D.C., February 10, 1999.

74. Schuck, "Removing Criminal Aliens."

75. Doris Meissner, INS Commissioner, "Criminal Aliens and Border Patrol Funding," Testimony before the U.S. House Committee on the Judiciary, Subcommittee on Immigration and Claims, February 25, 1999.

76. Shirley E. Perlman, "Deported/The No. 1. Priority for State, INS: Criminal Aliens," *Newsday,* May 11, 1997, A5.

77. "Criminal Aliens and Immigration: Taking Stock and Looking Ahead," conference report of the Carnegie Endowment for International Peace, Washington, D.C., February 10, 1999.

78. Jeanne Butterfield, president of the American Immigration Lawyers' Association, "Legislative Proposals: A View from the Hill," remarks at the conference, "Criminal Aliens and Immigration: Taking Stock and Looking Ahead," held at the Carnegie Endowment for International Peace, Washington, D.C., February 10, 1999.

79. Perlman, "Deported," A5.

80. Michelle Mittelstadt, "INS changes its mandatory detention policy for criminal aliens," Associated Press Wire, July 13, 1999.

81. Linda Greenhouse, "The Supreme Court: Supreme Court Roundup; Justices Permit Immigrants to Challenge Deportations," *New York Times,* June 26, 2001, A1.

82. "The Supreme Court; Excerpts from Opinions in Ruling on the Detention of Immigrants-Criminals," *New York Times,* June 29, 2001, A20.

83. Greenhouse, "Supreme Court," A1.

84. Augustin T. Fragomen Jr., "The Illegal Immigration Reform and Immigrant Responsibility Act of 1996: An Overview," *International Migration Review,* Summer 1997.

85. Louis Uchitelle, "I.N.S. Is Looking the Other Way as Illegal Immigrants Fill Jobs," *New York Times,* March 9, 2000, A1.

86. "A Bold Proposal on Immigration," *Atlantic Monthly,* June 1994, 34.

87. See Testimony of Barbara Jordan, Chair, U.S. Commission on Immigration Reform, Before the U.S. Senate Committee on the Judiciary Subcommittee on Immigration and Refugee Affairs, August 3, 1994.

88. Holly Idelson, "Proposals Would Crack Down on Illegals and Tighten Rules for Legal Immigrants," *CQ Weekly,* April 15, 1995.

89. Marjorie Valbrun, "Beefed-up Border Patrol Encounters Growing Pains," *Wall Street Journal,* October 15, 1998, 1.

90. Maria Puente, "At the Border, Preventive Policing," *USA Today,* February 18, 1997, 3A.

91. Joshua Hammer, "Death in the Desert Heat," *Newsweek,* August 24, 1998, 29.

92. James F. Smith, "Border Deaths; Mexico Weighs Ideas to Reduce Migrant Deaths; Borders: Activists in Both Countries See Urgent Need for New Policies, as Illegal Crossings Are Pushed into Remote Desert Areas," *Los Angeles Times,* May 25, 2001, A5.

93. Demetrios Papademetriou and Deborah Waller Meyers, Testimony before the U.S. House of Representatives Committee on the Judiciary, Subcommittee on Immigration and Claims, April 14, 1999.

94. Nestor Rodriguez and Jacqueline Hagan, "Transborder Community Relations at the U.S.-Mexico Border: The Cases of Laredo/Nuevo Laredo and El Paso/Ciudad Juarez," Report Submitted to the International Migration Policy Program of the Carnegie Endowment for International Peace, Washington, D.C., July 7, 1999, 5.

95. "Panel Approves Bill to Weaken Immigration Law," *CQ Weekly*, April 25, 1998.

96. The "Uniting and Strengthening America by Providing Appropriate Tools Required to Intercept and Obstruct Terrorism" (USA PATRIOT) Act of 2001, Section 414, signed by President George W. Bush, October 26, 2001.

97. Paul Leavitt, "INS deploying agents to target smuggling," *USA Today*, March 31, 1999.

98. Sam Howe Verhovek, "Illegal Immigrant Workers Being Fired in I.N.S. Tactic," *New York Times*, April 2, 1999," A1.

99. Elliot Blair Smith, "INS Cracks Down on Meatpackers," *USA Today*, April 13, 1999, 3B.

100. Idelson, "Proposals Would Crack Down on Illegals."

101. Bill Clinton, "U.S. Efforts to Expand and Strengthen the Fight Against Illegal Immigration," U.S. Department of State Dispatch, February 13, 1995.

102. Verhovek, "Illegal Immigrant," A1.

103. Steven Greenhouse, "U.S. to Expand Anti-Discrimination Rights for Illegal Immigrants Working in This Country," *New York Times*, October 28, 1999.

104. Uchitelle, "I.N.S. Is Looking the Other Way."

105. Smith and Edmonston, eds., *New Americans*, 136.

106. Ibid., 54.

107. Julian L. Simon, *The Economic Consequences of Immigration* (Ann Arbor: University of Michigan Press, 1999), 4–5.

108. Thomas MaCurdy, Thomas Nechyba, and Jay Bhattacharya, "An Economic Framework for Assessing the Fiscal Impacts of Immigration," in *The Immigration Debate: Studies on the Economic, Demographic, and Fiscal Effects of Immigration*, eds. James P. Smith and Barry Edmonston (Washington, D.C.: National Academy Press, 1998), 13.

109. George Borjas, "The Economic Benefits from Immigration," *Journal of Economic Perspectives*, Spring 1995, 3–4.

110. See Deborah L. Garvey and Thomas J. Espenshade, "Fiscal Impacts of Immigrant and Native Households: A New Jersey Case Study," and Michael S. Clune, "The Fiscal Impacts of Immigrants: A California Case Study," in *Immigration Debate*, eds., Smith and Edmonston, 66–182.

111. MaCurdy, Nechyba, and Bhattacharya, "An Economic Framework," 31.

112. Kathleen Newland, *U.S. Refugee Policy: Dilemmas and Directions*, Washington, D.C.: Carnegie Endowment for International Peace, 1995, 17.

113. U.S. Committee for Refugees, *World Refugee Survey 1998*, Washington, D.C., 1998, 3.

114. This figure—more precisely 127,459—is the sum of authorized refugee admissions (123,500) plus the number of individuals granted asylum by INS district director and asylum officers (3,959), according to the U.S. Immigration and Naturalization Service, *Statistical Yearbook, 1998*, Tables 24, 28.

115. U.S. Committee for Refugees, *World Refugee Survey 2001*, Washington, D.C., 2001, 4.

116. This figure—more precisely 95,951—is the sum of authorized refugee admissions (83,000) plus the number of individuals granted asylum by INS district director and asylum officers (12,951), according to the U.S. Immigration and Naturalization Service, *Statistical Yearbook, 1998*, Tables 24, 28.

117. Ibid., 100.

118. These percentages were calculated using data from the U.S. Committee for Refugees' Web site, which said that, "The United States resettled 85,006 refugees in fiscal year 1999," including 22,697 refugees from Bosnia, 16,922 from the former Soviet Union, and 14,156 from Kosovo. See U.S. Committee for Refugees, Worldwide Refugee Information, "Country Report: United States," http://www.refugees.org/world/countryrpt/amer_carib/us.htm.

119. David Masci, "Assisting Refugees," *CQ Researcher*, February 7, 1997.

120. Newland, *U.S. Refugee Policy*, 20.

121. Mary H. Cooper, "Global Refugee Crisis," *CQ Researcher*, July 9, 1999.

122. Newland, *U.S. Refugee Policy*, 26.

123. A large backlog of asylum cases prompted this streamlining effort. In 1995 the backlog of cases had climbed to 464,000. By the end of 1999, 341,622 cases were pending with the INS. See U.S. Committee for Refugees, "Country Report: United States."

124. U.S. Committee for Refugees, "Country Report: United States."

125. Masci, "Assisting Refugees."

126. Gregory Rodriguez, "A Look at . . . Assimilation; It Only Takes a Generation or Three," *Washington Post*, July 4, 1999, B3.

127. M. Patricia Fernandez Kelly and Richard Schauffler, "Divided Fates: Immigrant Children and the New Assimilation," in Alejandro Portes, ed., *The New Second Generation* (New York: Russell Sage, 1996), 30.

128. Mary C. Waters, "Ethnic and Racial Identities of Second-Generation Black Immigrants in New York City," in Portes, ed., *New Second Generation*, 175.

129. Peter D. Salins, "From Many, One Nation; America Must Again Assimilate Its Immigrants," *Washington Post*, February 9, 1997, C1.

130. Lief Jensen and Yoshimi Chitose, "Today's Second Generation: Evidence from the 1990 Census," in Portes, ed., *New Second Generation,* 83.

131. Waters, "Ethnic and Racial Identities," 72.

132. William Branigin, "Immigrants Question Idea of Assimilation," *Washington Post,* May 25, 1998, A1.

133. William H. Frey, "Immigration, Domestic Migration, and Demographic Balkanization in America: New Evidence for the 1990s," *Population and Development Review,* December 1996, 742.

134. Rubén G. Rumbaut, "Coming of Age in Immigrant America," *Research Perspectives on Migration,* January/February 1998, 1.

135. Excerpted from Craig Donegan, "Debate over Bilingualism," *CQ Researcher,* January 19, 1996.

136. Ethan Bronner, "Bilingual Education Is Facing Push Toward Abandonment," *New York Times,* May 30, 1998, A1.

137. Excerpted from Donegan, "Debate over Bilingualism."

138. Rumbaut, "Coming of Age," 3, 7, 12.

139. Lollock, "Foreign-Born Population," 2.

140. Marjorie Valbrun, "Clamor for U.S. Citizenship Spurs Debate on Its Cause," *Wall Street Journal,* February 25, 1999, A20.

141. U.S. Immigration and Naturalization Service, *Statistical Yearbook of the Immigration and Naturalization Service, 1998,* U.S. Government Printing Office: Washington, D.C., 2000, 172.

142. U.S. Department of Justice, Immigration and Naturalization Service, *INS Communiqué,* May 1997, 2.

143. Marjorie Valbrun, "Clamor for U.S. Citizenship Spurs Debate on Its Cause," *Wall Street Journal,* February 25, 1999, A20.

144. Loretta E. Bass and Lynne M. Casper, "Are There Differences in Registration and Voting Behavior Between Naturalized and Native-Born Americans?" *Population Division Working Paper No. 28,* U.S. Bureau of the Census, Washington, D.C., February 1999.

145. Dan Carney, "GOP Casts a Kinder Eye on 'Huddled Masses,' " *CQ Weekly,* May 15, 1999.

146. Arturo Vargas, "Latino Voters: The New Political Landscape," *Vital Speeches of the Day,* New York, January 1, 2000.

147. Carnegie Endowment for International Peace, "New American Co-Ethnic Voting," *Research Perspectives on Migration,* March/April 1997, 3.

148. James Dao, "Immigrant Diversity Slows Traditional Political Climb," *New York Times,* December 28, 1999.

149. Hector Tobar, Nancy Cleeland, and Patrick McDonnell, "Election 2001; In the End, It Was a Crusade for Latinos and for the Future; Voting: They Turned Out in Record Numbers to Back Villaraigosa. Even with His Loss, Many Said, Their Movement Will Keep Growing," *Los Angeles Times*, June 6, 2001, A19.

150. John Rogers, "L.A. Mayor Election Offers Two Liberals; One Could Make History," *Associated Press*, June 4, 2001.

151. Bob Keefe, "Hispanic's Bid for L.A. Mayor Could Mark a National Trend," *Cox News Service*, June 1, 2001.

152. Susan Sachs, "Give Me Your Tired, Your Poor, Your Vote," *New York Times*, April 8, 2001, A37.

153. Carnegie Endowment for International Peace, "New American Co-Ethnic Voting," 6.

154. Keefe, "Hispanic's Bid for L.A. Mayor."

155. This is not the first shift in assumptions about immigration from an economic focus to national security concerns. According to former INS Commissioner Doris Meissner, "the fact that the INS is organizationally located within the Department of Justice is based on a security outlook. Before World War II, the INS was in the Department of Labor. Its relocation was part of mobilizing all aspects of government to defend the nation in wartime. The explicit purpose was to control aliens, who were seen as especially prone to engage in subversive activity." See Doris Meissner, "After the Attacks: Protecting Borders and Liberties," *Policy Brief No. 8*, Carnegie Endowment for International Peace, November 2001, 2.

156. Steven Camarota, "Immigration and Terrorism," Testimony before the U.S. Senate Committee on the Judiciary, Subcommittee on Technology, Terrorism and Government Information, October 12, 2001.

157. Stephen Flynn, remarks made during a briefing at the Migration Policy Institute, "North American Border Zones: Security and Integration," October 30, 2001.

158. David S. Broder and Eric Pianin, "Border Agencies May Be Merged, Ridge Says," *Washington Post*, November 14, 2001, A31.

159. Michael Grunwald, "Economic Crossroads on the Line; Security Fears Have U.S. and Canada Rethinking Life at 49th Parallel," *Washington Post*, December 26, 2001, A1.

160. David Shepardson, "U.S. Northern Border Gets 200 More Agents," *Detroit News*, January 9, 2002.

161. Grunwald, "Economic Crossroads on the Line," A1.

162. Adam Clymer, "A Nation Challenged: Immigration Law; Bills Require C.I.A. to Share Its Information on Foreigners," *New York Times*, November 2, 2001, B7.

163. Diana Jean Schemo, "A Nation Challenged: Immigration; Senate Bill Would Stiffen Some Controls Over Visas," *New York Times*, December 6, 2001, B7.

164. Ibid.

165. David Firestone, "Al Qaeda Link Seen in Only a Handful of 1,200 Detainees," *New York Times,* November 29, 2001, 1A.

166. Dan Eggen, "Delays Cited in Charging Detainees; with Legal Latitude, INS Sometimes Took Weeks," *Washington Post,* January 15, 2002, 1A.

167. David Firestone, "U.S. Makes it Easier to Detain Foreigners," *New York Times,* November 28, 2001, 7B.

168. Nancy Chang, "How Does USA Patriot Act Affect Bill of Rights?" *New York Law Journal,* December 6, 2001, 1.

169. Edna Selan Epstein, "Can They Listen? Ashcroft and the Attorney-Client Privilege," *Legal Times,* November 26, 2001, 35.

170. Matthew Purdy, "Bush's New Rules to Fight Terror Transform the Legal Landscape," *New York Times,* November 25, 2001, 1A.

171. Cassio Furtado, "Justice Dept. Offers Foreigners a Deal for Tips; The S Visa Permits Favorable Treatment for Those Who Cooperate with U.S. Law Officials," *Philadelphia Inquirer,* November 30, 2001, A23.

172. Neil A. Lewis, "INS to Focus on Muslims Who Evade Deportation," *New York Times,* January 9, 2002, A12.

173. David Shepardson, "Community Airs Hate Crime Fears at Forum: Justice Dept. Promises to Protect Civil Rights of Arab Americans," *Detroit News,* November 21, 2001, A3.

174. Dennis Niemiec and Shawn Windsor, "Arab Americans Expect Scrutiny, Feel Sting of Bias," *Detroit Free Press,* October 1, 2001.

175. Evelyn Nieves, "Slain Arab-American May Have Been Hate-Crime Victim," *New York Times,* October 6, 2001, A8.

176. Shepardson, "Community Airs Hate Crime Fears at Forum," A3.

177. Doris Meissner, "After the Attacks: Protecting Borders and Liberties," Policy Brief No. 8, Carnegie Endowment for International Peace, November 2001, 2.

3 Agencies, Organizations, and Individuals

Because immigration is a multidisciplinary subject—involving law, sociology, demography, international relations, economics, and community development—there are many organizations that influence immigration policy, with many different agendas. Within the U.S. government, most immigration responsibilities rest with the Immigration and Naturalization Service in the Department of Justice; yet, other agencies contain offices devoted to specific aspects of immigration policy or perform functions that significantly affect immigration policy, so that immigration policy making often requires interagency cooperation. U.S. immigration policy also offers an example of the government's system of checks and balances, as the president, Congress, and Supreme Court frequently question each other's decisions.

Nongovernmental organizations devoted to immigration policy are even more diffuse and varied. While some advocate broadly for the liberalization or restriction of immigration, others provide independent research on immigration trends, and still others represent the specific interests of ethnic groups, business coalitions, or refugees.

International organizations both influence and are influenced by U.S. immigration policy. The unique role of the United States in world politics makes it a strong player in international migration decisions. However, as a destination country, the United States also relies on collective international efforts to manage migration trends resulting from economic and natural disasters, armed conflict, and human rights abuses.

These many actors in U.S. immigration policy fuel the complex, often passionate debates that this book describes in Chapters 2 and 4. This chapter provides information about a comprehensive selection of actors. First, it reviews national governmental actors in each of the three branches of government. Then it considers a wide selection of nongovernmental organizations. The chapter concludes with a brief discussion of several international organizations involved in migration issues worldwide.

Important Governmental Agencies and Actors

U.S. DEPARTMENT OF JUSTICE, IMMIGRATION AND NATURALIZATION SERVICE. An agency within the Department of Justice, the Immigration and Naturalization Service (INS) "is responsible for enforcing the laws regulating the admission of foreign-born persons (i.e., aliens) to the United States and for administering various immigration benefits, including the naturalization of qualified applicants for U.S. citizenship." With more than 33,000 employees, the INS has become one of the largest federal departments, growing more than 67 percent in the past five years. It is responsible for policing the nation's 8,000 miles of borders and inspecting 525 million people a year who seek entry to the United States. Increasingly, the agency has focused on the prevention of illegal immigration. In 1999 alone the Border Patrol apprehended 1,537,000 illegal immigrants along the Southwest border. But it is also struggling to keep up with a massive influx of applications for citizenship and residency, totaling more than 19 million active immigration files. Its biggest challenge may be its own restructuring. In 2002 both Congress and the Bush administration proposed splitting the agency into two parts, with one focusing on enforcement and the other on services to immigrants. (See box on page 106) The INS commissioner reports to the U.S. Attorney General.

U.S. Immigration and Naturalization Service
425 I St., NW
Washington, DC 20536
Phone: (202) 514-4316
Web: www.ins.gov

Doris Meissner. Doris Meissner was appointed INS commissioner in 1993 by President Bill Clinton and served until 2000. Meissner, the child of German immigrants, grew up in Milwaukee. She was involved in immigration issues for much of her professional career, serving in the Department of Justice under presidents from both parties and briefly serving as acting INS commissioner in 1981. Just before her appointment she had served as the director of the International Migration Policy Program of the Carnegie Endowment for International Peace. In interviews before her confirmation, Meissner emphasized that immigration was not simply an issue of controlling the border. She said, "We can't deal with this only as an enforcement issue in the United States. We have to look at it worldwide and attack the conditions that create the desperation."[1]

James W. Ziglar. James W. Ziglar was appointed INS commissioner in 2001 by President George W. Bush. Ziglar is a long-time Republican and childhood friend of Senate Minority Leader Trent Lott, R-Miss. Before his appointment as INS commissioner, Ziglar served as the Senate sergeant-at-arms. He is the former management director for Paine Webber, Inc., and Drexel Burnham Lambert, Inc. Ziglar told senators at his confirmation hearing: "The constant infusion of new immigrant blood into our society tests and strengthens our nation. Immigration is a virtue, not a distraction or a danger." Of the INS, however, he said, "I am convinced that an overhaul is needed." He recognized criticisms of his lack of experience in immigration issues or immigration law but said that he hoped his public- and private-sector experience would enable him to "take on this very difficult task with a measure of wisdom and judgment."[2]

U.S. DEPARTMENT OF STATE, BUREAU OF POPULATION, REFUGEES, AND MIGRATION. The Bureau of Population, Refugees, and Migration (PRM) has primary responsibility for refugee assistance and international migration policy. It monitors and coordinates U.S. contributions to international and nongovernmental organizations for overseas refugee relief operations, playing a critical role in recent crises in Kosovo and Afghanistan. PRM also oversees the admission of refugees to the United States and works closely with the Immigration and Naturalization Service, Department of Health and Human Services, and state and local governmental agencies to permanently resettle refugees in American communities. The bureau addresses "root causes" of international migration through diplomacy and international population policies. PRM represents U.S. interests in international migration negotiations, such as the Regional Conference on Migration with Central American countries (known as the "Puebla Process"), and works closely with the U.S. Agency for International Development to administer international programs aimed at controlling population growth in developing countries.

U.S. Department of State
Bureau of Population, Refugees, and Migration
2201 C St., NW
Washington, DC 20520
Phone: (202) 647-4000
Web: www.state.gov/g/prm

U.S. DEPARTMENT OF LABOR, BUREAU OF INTERNATIONAL LABOR AFFAIRS, DIVISION OF IMMIGRATION POLICY & RESEARCH. The Bureau of International Labor Affairs (ILAB) carries out the Department of Labor's international responsibilities and assists in formulating international economic, trade, and immigration policies affecting American workers. ILAB's immigration-related work includes implementing the North American Agreement on Labor Cooperation (NAALC), the labor supplemental agreement to the North American Free Trade Agreement (NAFTA), and assisting the U.S. trade representative in international trade negotiations, including immigration-related issues. ILAB also undertakes research on the impact of international trade and immigration policies on U.S. workers.

U.S. Department of Labor
Bureau of International Labor Affairs, Room C-4327
Washington, DC 20210
Phone: (202) 693-4770
Web: www.dol.gov/dol/ilab/

U.S. DEPARTMENT OF HEALTH AND HUMAN SERVICES, OFFICE OF REFUGEE RESETTLEMENT. Since 1975, more than two million refugees have been resettled in the United States. The chief goal of the refugee resettlement program is to provide assistance to these refugees so that they can achieve economic self-sufficiency and social adjustment within the shortest time possible following their arrival in the United States. In 1996 about $417 million was budgeted to serve refugees through five different programs: cash and medical assistance, employment services, preventive health services, the voluntary agency matching grant program, and the targeted assistance grant program. The Office of Refugee Resettlement (ORR) contracts with state and local government agencies and nongovernmental organizations to administer these benefits and services to refugees in their new communities.

Office of Refugee Resettlement
Administration for Children and Families
Department of Health and Human Services
370 L'Enfant Promenade, 6th Floor
Washington, DC 20447
Phone: (202) 401-9246
Web: www.acf.dhhs.gov/programs/orr/

U.S. CONGRESS. The primary congressional committees responsible for immigration policy are the House and Senate Judiciary Committees and their respective subcommittees on immigration. It is in these subcommittees where immigration issues are first reviewed. The members of these subcommittees often play important roles once the debate has moved to the full committee, to the House or Senate floor, and even to the conference committee responsible for reconciling differences between the two chambers.

Both Senate and House Judiciary Committees tend to draw strong ideologues and have a history of being quite polarized politically. However, the relative "status" of the two committees is very different. A Senate Judiciary slot is much sought after because members of this committee play an important role in reviewing presidential appointments to the judiciary (most notably the Supreme Court) and to the Department of Justice (which includes the INS). The House Judiciary Committee has a lower status, although it plays a prominent role in impeachment proceedings, as demonstrated by President Clinton's impeachment in 1998.

In addition, there are other congressional committees that can influence immigration policy. The House and Senate Agriculture Committees have influenced immigration policy, especially with respect to migrant farmworkers. As with all policy areas, the Appropriations Committees are vitally important, because they fund the operations of the national government and can affect the level of funding available for the implementation of immigration policy.

U.S. COMMISSION ON IMMIGRATION REFORM. Congress authorized the creation of the U.S. Commission on Immigration Reform (CIR) in its 1990 immigration legislation. The commission was charged with the responsibility of studying immigration issues and forwarding its recommendations for reform to Congress. The authorization of the commission ran from 1990 through 1997. Former representative Barbara Jordan (D-Texas) chaired the commission until her death in 1996.

The commission issued two influential reports, one in 1994 and another in 1995, that helped shape the debate over immigration in the 104th Congress (1995–1997). The CIR made policy recommendations for both illegal and legal immigration reform. To combat illegal immigration, the CIR recommended the creation of a computerized Social Security database to enable better verification of employment eligibility and to remove employment as an incentive for illegal immigration. With respect to legal immigration, the CIR recommended cutting yearly immigration levels and changing the priorities for admission—most notably by eliminating all nonnuclear family preferences including the preference for siblings and adult children of legal residents. In making this recommendation, the CIR sought to address the backlog in visa applications from family members, nuclear and otherwise, of existing legal residents—including the large group that had been granted amnesty in 1986. The CIR also recommended that the admission of parents of legal residents should be conditioned on a legally enforceable commitment by those residents to financially support their parents.

The Clinton administration initially endorsed the CIR's recommendations (though it would later reverse course on the recommendation to restrict legal immigration), and many of the provisions were included in versions of immigration reform legislation considered by the 104th Congress. However, many recommendations proved extremely controversial (such as the verification system and changed priorities for admission) and did not survive the legislative process. The CIR issued its final report in 1997 and again reiterated its recommendation for restrictions on legal immigration. Records and reports of the commission's work are available at the Web site listed below.

U.S. Commission on Immigration Reform
Web: www.utexas.edu/lbj/uscir/

U.S. SUPREME COURT. Although it does not craft immigration policy in the way that the president and Congress do, the Supreme Court plays a significant role in interpreting complex immigration laws and determining the rights of noncitizens under the U.S. Constitution. During the last decade, the Court has decided several cases that have altered the course of U.S. immigration policy. In June 2001 the Supreme Court ruled on two important cases. In one of its most significant decisions regarding the rights of immigrants, *Immigration and Naturalization Service v. St. Cyr,* the Court held that legal immigrants convicted of many crimes were entitled to judicial review of their cases. This decision nullified provisions in the Antiterrorism and Effective Death Penalty Act of 1996 and the Illegal Immigration Reform and Immigrant Responsibility Act of 1996, which were aimed at speeding up deportations.

In a second case, *Zadvydas v. Davis,* the Court ruled that the government could not indefinitely incarcerate aliens who had been convicted of crimes and had served their sentences but could not be deported because their home countries refused to accept them. About 3,000 prisoners were affected by the ruling, including about 1,200 from Cuba, Laos, Cambodia, and Vietnam (countries with which the United States has no repatriation agreement). (See the primary documents section in the Appendix for the Court's majority opinion in this case)

U.S. Supreme Court
Washington, DC 20543
Phone: (202) 479-3211
Web: www.supremecourtus.gov

Nongovernmental Actors

In addition to these governmental actors, many nongovernmental actors are active in immigration and refugee policy. In the listings below, these organizations are divided into five major groupings. The first grouping, advocacy organizations, includes organizations that are traditionally associated with either liberal or restrictionist positions on immigration and refugee policy. A second grouping, think tanks, lists research organizations that are either devoted to immigration policy or have staff members that are prominent immigration specialists.

The third grouping, refugee resettlement organizations, includes organizations and coalitions of organizations who assist with refugee resettlement in the United States. Many of these organizations either directly advocate on behalf of refugees or are members of coalitions that conduct direct advocacy. Several are sponsored by particular religious denominations and have affiliated organizations that focus on overseas emergency assistance to regions of the world experiencing refugee crises.

A fourth category, ethnic advocacy organizations, includes organizations founded and sponsored by ethnic communities within the United States. Many of these organizations are concerned with immigration and refugee policy both out of a concern for immigrant rights and because of the impact immigration policies can have on established ethnic communities in the United States. Organizations in the fifth category, business and labor organizations, have become an increasingly important part of immigration debates—especially given the prominent debates over expansions of employment-based immigration preferences.

In the listings below, key contact information is given for each organization as well as a brief description of each organization's mission and, if possible, the positions each has taken on recent immigration policy debates.

Advocacy Organizations

ALEXIS DE TOCQUEVILLE INSTITUTION. The Alexis de Tocqueville Institution (AdTI) works to increase public understanding of the cultural and economic benefits of immigration to a democratic society and supports increases in legal immigration to the United States. AdTI has sponsored reports on the patents and inventions that immigrants have contributed to the U.S. economy, and a study of the impact of immigrants on U.S. cities. It has also been active in supporting guest worker programs.

Alexis de Tocqueville Institution
1611 North Kent St., Suite 901
Arlington, VA 22209
Phone: (703) 351-0090
E-mail: foss@adti.net
Web: www.adti.net

AMERICAN IMMIGRATION LAWYERS ASSOCIATION. The American Immigration Lawyers Association (AILA) represents more than 7,200 attorneys and law professors who practice and teach immigration law. Founded in 1946, AILA is a nonpartisan, nonprofit organization that provides lawyers with continuing legal education, information, and professional services through its thirty-five chapters and more than seventy-five national committees. Its Web site says, "American immigration policy fulfills our commitment to religious and political freedom. 'Give me your tired, your poor, your huddled masses yearning to breathe free,' is not rhetoric, it is America's pledge to ensure that those brave men and women who face the prospect of ethnic cleansing, religious oppression, torture, and even death have a haven. Because this country was founded in large part by those who fled various kinds of political and religious persecution, it has become our historical responsibility to serve as an advocate for human rights."

American Immigration Lawyers' Association
1400 I St., NW, Suite 1200
Washington, DC 20009
Phone: (202) 216-2400
Web: www.aila.org

FEDERATION FOR AMERICAN IMMIGRATION REFORM. The Federation for American Immigration Reform (FAIR) is the advocacy organization that most strongly opposes additional immigration, wishes to reduce the admission of refugees, and calls for stiffer measures to prevent illegal immigration. It advocates for setting immigrant admissions "at the lowest feasible level." It called President Bush's proposal to offer residency to some of the three to four million Mexicans living in the United States "a betrayal of the American public."

Federation for American Immigration Reform
1666 Connecticut Ave., NW, Suite 400
Washington, DC 20009
Phone: (202) 328-7004
Web: www.fairus.org

LAWYERS' COMMITTEE FOR HUMAN RIGHTS. Founded in 1978, the Lawyers' Committee for Human Rights (LCHR) works to ensure that all governments uphold the International Bill of Human Rights. With respect to refugees, the LCHR represents asylum seekers and challenges legal restrictions on the rights of refugees in the United States and around the world. In recent years the LCHR has focused particular attention on the plight of refugees in Africa and Kosovo. It has also spoken up against the expedited removal of asylum seekers in the United States since 1996, in particular changes to immigration law that have eliminated judicial review of decisions made by immigration inspectors to deport potential immigrants with invalid or fraudulent travel documents. Since the terrorist attacks on the World Trade Center and the Pentagon in 2001, the LCHR has advocated for the application of the

Geneva Convention to the detainees held in Guantanamo Bay, and for the revocation of the Bush Administration's decision to allow military tribunals.

Lawyers' Committee for Human Rights
333 Seventh Ave., 13th floor
New York, NY 10001
Phone: (212) 845-5200
E-mail: lchrbin@lchr.org
Web: www.lchr.org

NATIONAL IMMIGRATION FORUM. Founded in 1982, the National Immigration Forum says its purpose "is to embrace and uphold America's tradition as a nation of immigrants." The Forum supports increased immigration, the reunification of families, the rescue and resettlement of refugees fleeing persecution, and the equitable treatment of immigrants under the law. It encourages immigrants to become U.S. citizens and promotes cooperation and understanding between immigrants and other Americans.

National Immigration Forum
220 I St., NE
Washington, DC 20002
Phone: (202) 544-0004
Web: www.immigrationforum.org

NATIONAL IMMIGRATION LAW CENTER. The National Immigration Law Center (NILC) sponsors research and provides legal advocacy on the employment and public benefit rights of low-income immigrants. The NILC regularly conducts analyses of new and proposed laws, convenes biweekly conference calls and monthly meetings with coalition partners to monitor wage and welfare issues, and provides training and technical assistance to social service organizations, advocates, legislators, and government officials. It does not provide legal assistance to individuals, but its attorneys bring suit to ask for injunctions and challenge INS regulations, often in collaboration with other legal defense groups. In recent years the NILC has been active in restoring immigrant rights to benefits that were lost under the 1996 welfare reform law, and in protecting the rights of immigrants to due process.

National Immigration Law Center
3435 Wilshire Blvd., Suite 2850
Los Angeles, CA 90010
Phone: (213) 639-3900
E-mail: info@nilc.org
Web: www.nilc.org

NATIONAL NETWORK FOR IMMIGRANT AND REFUGEE RIGHTS. The National Network for Immigrant and Refugee Rights (NNIRR) was founded in 1986 to bring together national and local organizations and coalitions who were active on refugee issues and opposed to INS raids. They initially formed to mobilize opposition against certain provisions of the congressional legislation that eventually became the Immigration Reform and Control Act of 1986. According to their mission statement, NNIRR "was founded upon the principles of equality and justice, and seeks the enfranchisement of all immigrant and refugee communities in the United States through organizing and advocating for their full labor, environmental, civil and human rights." NNIRR board members include individuals from the Service Employees International Union, United Methodist Committee on Relief, Filipinos for Affirmative Action, Asian American Legal Defense and Education Fund, and the Guatemala Support Project, among others.

National Network for Immigrant and Refugee Rights
310 8th St., Suite 307
Oakland, CA 94607
Phone: (510) 465-1984
Web: www.nnirr.org

U.S. COMMITTEE FOR REFUGEES. The U.S. Committee for Refugees (USCR) is an affiliate of Immigration and Refugee Services of America. (See listing under "Refugee Resettlement Organizations") USCR advocates for refugee rights and provides information about the plight of refugees around the world. It is guided by three core principles: (1) that refugees have basic human rights, including the principle that "no persons with a well-founded fear of persecution should be forcibly returned (refouled) to his or her homeland;" (2) that "asylum seekers have the right to a fair and impartial hearing to determine their refugee status;" and (3) that "all uprooted victims of human conflict, regardless of whether they cross a border, have the right to humane treatment, as well as adequate protection and assistance."

U.S. Committee for Refugees
1717 Massachusetts Ave., NW, Suite 701
Washington, DC 20036
Phone: (202) 347-3507
Web: www.refugees.org

Think Tanks

CATO INSTITUTE. The Cato Institute is a public policy research organization devoted to an analysis of policy issues from a perspective that values limited government and open markets. It argues that immigrants benefit the U.S. economy because they are self-selected on motivation, risk-taking, and work ethic; they bring skills, complement existing workers (rather than competing with them), and come to the United States during their prime working years; and their children often reach high levels of achievement. Cato generally favors generous immigration policies and opposes efforts to place additional requirements on businesses to verify the immigration status of their employees. It has actively supported the expansion of the H1-B skilled worker visa program and due-process rights for asylum seekers.

Cato Institute
1000 Massachusetts Ave., NW
Washington, DC 20001-5403
Phone: (202) 842-0200
E-mail: cato@cato.org
Web: www.cato.org

CENTER FOR IMMIGRATION STUDIES. The Center for Immigration Studies (CIS) was founded in 1985 as an "independent, nonpartisan, nonprofit research organization" and bills itself as the only think tank devoted exclusively to research and policy analysis of the economic, social, demographic, fiscal, and other impacts of immigration on the United States. It takes restrictive immigration positions on a host of issues. Its core belief is an "immigration policy that gives first concern to the broad national interest and . . . a low-immigration vision which seeks fewer immigrants but a warmer welcome for those admitted." It is well known not only for its active advocacy but also for its listserves, which deliver immigration news and information about current immigration publications to a wide range of subscribers.

Center for Immigration Studies
1522 K St., NW, Suite 820
Washington, DC 20005
Phone: (202) 466-8185
E-mail: center@cis.org
Web: www.cis.org

MIGRATION POLICY INSTITUTE. Formerly the Carnegie Endowment for International Peace's International Migration Policy Program, the Migration Policy Institute (MPI) is "the only independent policy institute in North America dedicated to analyzing the movement of people worldwide." The basic objectives of the organization are "to bridge the spheres of research and policy-making in the migration field; to inject objective, informed, and independent policy ideas into the increasingly heated debates on migration and refugee policies in the United States and abroad; and to enhance public understanding of these issues." It has active working programs on migration management, refugee protection, North American migration issues, and immigrant settlement and integration.

Migration Policy Institute
1400 16th St., NW, Suite 300
Washington, DC 20036
Phone: (202) 266-1940
E-mail: aclaros@migrationpolicy.org
Web: www.migrationpolicy.org

URBAN INSTITUTE, POPULATION STUDIES CENTER. Established in 1968, the Urban Institute is a public policy research organization that is noted for its analysis and evaluation of economic and social policy and government programs in the United States. It is nonpartisan but is often considered a liberal organization. Through the work of its Population Studies Center, the Urban Institute prepares studies on the impact of immigration on the U.S. economy and U.S. society. It also prepares reports on efforts to integrate new immigrants into U.S. society and efforts to control illegal immigration.

Urban Institute, Population Studies Center
2100 M St., NW
Washington, DC 20037
Phone: (202) 833-7200
E-mail: paffairs@ui.urban.org
Web: www.urban.org/centers/psc.html

Refugee Assistance and Resettlement Organizations

AMERICAN FRIENDS SERVICE COMMITTEE. The American Friends Service Committee (AFSC), a Quaker organization, works to further the civil and human rights of immigrants, refugees, and asylum seekers in several ways. Its Washington office lobbies and informs national decision-makers on immigration and refugee issues. Its Houston-based Immigration Law Enforcement Monitoring Project monitors law enforcement on the U.S.- Mexico border for instances of abuse, violence, and violation of human and civil rights. Additional programs are run out of regional AFSC offices and include the Central America Political Asylum Project (Southeastern Region) and the Immigrant Rights Project (Central Region) among others.

American Friends Service Committee
1501 Cherry St.
Philadelphia, PA 19102
Phone: (215) 241-7000
E-mail: afscinfo@afsc.org
Web: www.afsc.org

CHURCH WORLD SERVICE/IMMIGRATION AND REFUGEE PROGRAM. Church World Service (CWS) is the relief, development, and refugee ministry of thirty-six Protestant, Orthodox, and Anglican denominations, including among others the National Baptist Convention of America, the African Methodist Episcopal Church, the Orthodox Church in America, the Greek Orthodox Archdiocese of North and South America, United Church of Christ, and the United Methodist Church. Among other activities, CWS has operated an office in Miami since 1960 to assist with refugees fleeing Cuba as well as later waves of refugees from nations such as Haiti. CWS provides aid overseas as well as resettlement assistance in the United States and advocacy on behalf of refugees and asylum seekers.

Church World Service/Immigration and Refugee Program
475 Riverside Dr., Room 652
New York, NY 10115
Phone: (212) 870-2132
Web: www.churchworldservice.org

COUNCIL OF JEWISH FEDERATIONS/UNITED JEWISH COMMUNITIES. Council of Jewish Federations (CJF) provides a variety of immigrant assistance and refugee resettlement programs through Jewish communities around the United States. CJF traditionally lobbies for generous immigration and refugee resettlement assistance programs. CJF also has opposed efforts to cap refugee admissions to the United States. Its immigration priorities in 2001 included convincing the INS to act on the severe backlog in naturalizing legal residents who have applied to become citizens, having Congress pass the Lautenberg amendment to allow Soviet Jews, Evangelicals, and South East Asian refugees to be considered for refugee status in light of their historic experience with persecution, reinstating immigrant access to public benefit programs, and repealing the aggravated felony provision of the 1996 Illegal Immigration and Immigrant Responsibility Act.

Council of Jewish Federations/United Jewish Communities
111 Eighth Ave., Suite 11E
New York, NY 10011-5201
Phone: (212) 284-6500
E-mail: info@ujc.org
Web: www.cjfny.org

HEBREW IMMIGRANT AID SOCIETY. Founded in 1881, the Hebrew Immigrant Aid Society's (HIAS) core mission is to aid in the rescue, reunion, and resettlement of Jews around the world. HIAS helped to resettle a million Jewish refugees in Israel and more than 300,000 former Soviet Jews in the United States. HIAS also provides services and assistance to other threatened and oppressed populations. HIAS advocates on behalf of migrants and refugees to national and international organizations. For example, HIAS is currently advocating the extension of Temporary Protected Status (which allows individuals to remain and work in the United States because of a violent conflict, natural disaster, or other temporary/extraordinary condition at home) to refugees from Colombia, both Jewish and non-Jewish. In immigration debates, HIAS supports generous immigration and refugee resettlement assistance programs and has opposed efforts to cap refugee admissions to the United States.

Hebrew Immigrant Aid Society
333 Seventh Ave.
New York, NY 10001-5004
Phone: (212) 967-4100
E-mail: info@hias.org
Web: www.hias.org.

IMMIGRATION AND REFUGEE SERVICES OF AMERICA. Immigration and Refugee Services of America (IRSA) operates education and assistance programs for refugees in the United States and reports that it resettles about 10 percent of the refugees entering the United States each year. IRSA began resettling refugees in 1975 and continues to work with a network of community agencies throughout the United States to facilitate the refugee resettlement process. It also runs medical programs at some of its local sites, helps set up job programs, and runs training programs for staff at local resettlement programs. In order to divert refugee flows from gateway cities such as Los Angeles, Miami, and New York, IRSA also works with smaller cities and rural areas to identify locations where refugees can resettle. IRSA is affiliated with the U.S. Committee for Refugees. (See listing under "Advocacy Organizations")

Immigration and Refugee Services of America
1717 Massachusetts Ave., NW, Suite 701
Washington, DC 20036
Phone: (202) 797-2105
E-mail: irsa@irsa-uscr.org
Web: www.irsa-uscr.org

INTERACTION. InterAction is a coalition of more than 165 nonprofit organizations, also known as the American Council for Voluntary International Action. InterAction's Committee on Migration and Refugee Affairs (CMRA) is made up of organizations that focus on "refugee protection, assistance, processing, resettlement and advocacy." The CMRA enables these groups to coordinate their programs and policies, work together to adopt common positions on refugee issues, and coordinate interactions with national and international refugee agencies. Member organizations include: the American Red Cross, the Church World Service, the Ethiopian Community Development Council, and the Hebrew Immigrant Aid Society among others. Their Web site includes issue briefs on their advocacy priorities, including funding for refugee resettlement and for the UN High Commission for Refugees, judicial review of asylum rejections, and improved naturalization procedures. InterAction has also taken a leading role in asking for expanded humanitarian and development assistance for Afghanistan.

InterAction (American Council for Voluntary International Action)
1717 Massachusetts Ave., NW, Suite 801
Washington, DC 20036
Phone: (202) 667-8227
E-mail: cmra@interaction.org
Web: www.interaction.org

INTERNATIONAL RESCUE COMMITTEE. The International Rescue Committee (IRC) was founded in 1933 at the request of Albert Einstein to assist opponents of Hitler. The IRC provides on-the-ground assistance during humanitarian crises, including medical and public health services, shelter, and food. It emphasizes the link between protection and assistance for refugees. After the fighting in Afghanistan following the events of September 11, the IRC opened refugee camps around Mazar-i-Sharif and in Pakistan. IRC also assists with refugee resettlement for those who are unable to return to their homelands and qualified to resettle in the United States. The IRC's current advocacy priorities include increasing the number of refugee admissions to the United States, raising awareness of refugee crises in Africa, and continuing to assist in Afghanistan.

International Rescue Committee
122 East 42nd St.

New York, NY 10168-1289
Phone: (212) 551-3000
E-mail: irc@theIRC.org
Web: www.theIRC.org

JESUIT REFUGEE SERVICE. The Jesuit Refugee Service (JRS) is an international Catholic organization active in more than forty countries. It collaborates with local organizations and the local Catholic Church in each of its sites to provide refugee services, with an emphasis on "accompaniment and pastoral presence." In the Unites States, for example, the JRS operates a detention assistance project for refugees detained in Los Angeles, El Paso, and Bucks County, Pennsylvania. At the U.S. detention sites, JRS provides refugees with pastoral, legal, educational, and re-settlement services. Internationally, it has been active on the issues of internal dis-placement, child soldiers, landmines, and asylum policies.

Jesuit Refugee Service
1616 P St., NW, Suite 400
Washington, DC 20036
Phone: (202) 462-0400
E-mail: united.states@jesref.org
Web: www.JesRef.org

LUTHERAN IMMIGRATION AND REFUGEE SERVICES. Founded in 1939, the mission of the Lutheran Immigration and Refugee Services (LIRS) is to assist in the resettlement of refugees in the United States. It has helped to resettle more than 280,000 refugees of all faiths. It is one of only two resettlement agencies authorized to find foster care for unaccompanied minor refugees (the other is the United States Catholic Conference). LIRS also advocates on behalf of migrants and refugees to national and international organizations. For example, it advocates that the United States set generous admissions levels for refugees and that all refugee/asylee deten-tion decisions be subject to judicial review. In its "Forgotten Refugees Campaign" LIRS seeks to educate community groups about asylum seekers who have been long held in INS detention centers in order to build support for a review of U.S. de-tention policies.

Lutheran Immigration and Refugee Services
700 Light St.
Baltimore, MD 21230
Phone: (410) 230-2700
E-mail: lirs@lirs.org
Web: www.lirs.org

UNITED STATES CATHOLIC CONFERENCE/MIGRATION AND REFUGEE SERVICES. The United States
Catholic Conference (USCC) works to assist in the resettlement of refugees in the
United States and to assist local communities in meeting the pastoral needs of new
refugees to the United States. USCC traditionally lobbies for generous immigration
and refugee resettlement assistance programs. The USCC position on immigration
reform was restated in a November 16, 2000, resolution of the U.S. Conference of
Catholic Bishops, which called for numerous changes to the nation's immigration
system. This included calls for federal policy-makers to legalize the status of undocumented agricultural workers who have been living and working in the United
States, to use humane policies to enforce the U.S.-Mexico border, to restore procedural due process rights to detained asylum seekers, to expand public benefits for
legal immigrants, and to create a more efficient entry system that ensures family
reunification.

United States Catholic Conference/Migration and Refugee Services
3211 4th St., NE
Washington, DC 20017
Phone: (202) 541-3352
E-mail: mrs@usccb.org
Web: www.nccbuscc.org/mrs

Ethnic Advocacy Groups

AMERICAN-ARAB ANTI-DISCRIMINATION COMMITTEE. Founded in 1980, the American-Arab
Anti-Discrimination Committee (ADC) is a civil rights organization "committed
to defending the rights of people of Arab descent and promoting their rich cultural
heritage." It is the largest grassroots Arab American organization in the United
States. The Legal Services division conducts selected impact litigation in the arena

of immigration policy. ADC has been very active in challenging the INS' use of secret evidence to indefinitely detain individuals of Arab descent who are suspected of supporting terrorist organizations, and in representing the cases of Arab Americans who have been harassed after the events of September 11. It also monitors media stereotyping and maintains e-mail lists for mobilizing responses to cases of discrimination.

American-Arab Anti-Discrimination Committee
4201 Connecticut Ave., NW, Suite 300
Washington, DC 20008
Phone: (202) 244-2990
E-mail: ADC@adc.org
Web: www.adc.org

ARAB-AMERICAN INSTITUTE. The Arab-American Institute's (AAI) primary mission is "to represent Arab American interests in government and politics." Founded in 1985, the nonprofit organization provides leadership training, policy analysis (including U.S. immigration policy), outreach to foreign governments, research on Arab American political activity and voting trends, and "a forum for consensus positions on pressing domestic and foreign policy matters." The affiliated Arab American Leadership Council provides a national network for Arab American elected and appointed officials, while the Arab American Leadership Political Action Committee raises money in support of candidates for elected office. Following the September 11 terrorist attacks, AAI teamed with the *Detroit Free Press* to conduct a poll that showed that 61 percent of Arab Americans in metro Detroit believed that extra questioning and even profiling of their ethnic group by law enforcement authorities was justified. AAI president James Zogby spoke out against profiling and discrimination against Arab Americans but also praised the Bush Administration for its response to complaints by the Arab American community.[3]

Arab-American Institute
1600 K St., NW, Suite 601
Washington, DC 20006
Phone: (202) 429-9210
E-mail: aai@aaiusa.org
Web: www.aaiusa.org

CUBAN AMERICAN NATIONAL FOUNDATION. Established in 1981, the Cuban American National Foundation's (CANF) mission is to promote freedom and democracy in Cuba. As part of this mission, CANF has assisted Cuban refugees in the United States and helped to reunite Cuban refugees in third countries with their families in the United States. Considered to be the most powerful representative of the Cuban exile community, it has sought to influence U.S. policy on Cuba and on Cuban refugees. CANF strongly opposed the Clinton administration's 1995 policy change, which ended three decades in which Cuban refugees were automatically admitted to the United States as refugees from Communism. In 2001 CANF went through a period of internal strife about the types of strategies it should use to promote a democratic Cuba.

Cuban American National Foundation
1312 SW 27th Ave.
Miami, FL 33145
Phone: (305) 592-7768
E-mail: hq@canf.org
Web: www.canf.org

MEXICAN AMERICAN LEGAL DEFENSE AND EDUCATION FUND. Founded in 1968 in San Antonio, Texas, the Mexican American Legal Defense Fund (MALDEF) is one of the major Latino civil rights organizations in the United States. Much of its work is done through litigation and through programs educating Latino citizens and immigrants about their civil rights. During 1996, MALDEF lobbied against restrictions on legal immigration and against the proposed employer verification system. In this position it was joined by the National Council of La Raza (NCLR) and by the League of United Latin American Citizens (LULAC). Through its Immigrants' Rights Program, MALDEF achieved an important success through the final settlement in *Gregorio T. v. Wilson*. Governor Gray Davis and the state of California agreed not to appeal this federal district court's decision to strike down the majority of Proposition 187's provisions.

Mexican American Legal Defense and Education Fund
National Headquarters
634 S. Spring St.
Los Angeles, CA 90014

Phone: (213) 629-2512

Web: www.maldef.org

NATIONAL ASIAN PACIFIC AMERICAN LEGAL CONSORTIUM. Founded in 1991, the National Asian Pacific American Legal Consortium (NAPALC) "works to advance the legal and civil rights of Asian Pacific Americans through litigation, public education and public policy." In 1995 NAPALC strongly advocated dropping legal immigration reform provisions from the bill that eventually became the 1996 Immigration Act. Those provisions would have reduced the number of legal immigrants entering the United States and would have curtailed the categories of family relations eligible to emigrate to the United States. NAPALC continues to monitor INS implementation of the 1996 act and has sought the repeal of provisions it considers to be restrictive—particularly provisions eliminating immigrant due-process procedures.

National Asian Pacific American Legal Consortium

1140 Connecticut Ave., NW, Suite 1200

Washington, DC 20036

Phone: (202) 296-2300

E-mail: sscanlon@napalc.org

Web: www.napalc.org

NATIONAL ASSOCIATION OF LATINO ELECTED AND APPOINTED OFFICIALS. The National Association of Latino Elected and Appointed Officials (NALEO) was founded in 1981 to "promote the participation of Latinos in the American political process, from citizenship to public service." It consists of more than 5,400 Latino elected and appointed officials. The NALEO sponsors an active naturalization program and promotes voter education and mobilization. It frequently takes positions on immigration policy, for example, opposing INS plans to increase fees for immigration services and supporting HR 1918, the Student Adjustment Act, during the 107th Congress. The bill, sponsored by Rep. Chris Cannon, (R-Utah) would provide immigrant students the opportunity to regularize their status and pay in-state tuition to attend college.

National Association of Latino Elected and Appointed Officials

5800 S. Eastern Ave., Ste. 365

Los Angeles, CA 90040

Phone: (323) 720-1932
E-mail: csanchez@naleo.org
Web: www.naleo.org

NATIONAL COALITION FOR HAITIAN RIGHTS. This coalition of religious, labor, and human rights organizations originally focused its public education and advocacy campaigns on the plight of Haitian refugees and, particularly, asylum seekers in the United States. What began in 1982 as the National Coalition for Haitian Refugees evolved to embrace a broader mission in 1995 as the National Coalition for Haitian Rights (NCHR). Today, the 400-member coalition continues to advocate on behalf of Haitian asylum seekers and immigrants in the United States, but also seeks "to increase the political effectiveness of the Haitian American community," and to organize international support for human rights in Haiti.[4] In this latter endeavor, NCHR has worked closely with other human rights organizations, international organizations, and U.S. government agencies to monitor, report, and provide consultation on human rights policy toward Haiti.

National Coalition for Haitian Rights
275 7th Ave., 17th Floor
New York, NY 10001
Phone: (212) 337-0005
E-mail: dpparks@nchr.org
Web: www.nchr.org

NATIONAL COUNCIL OF LA RAZA. Founded in 1968, the National Council of La Raza (NCLR) is one of the nation's major Latino civil rights organizations. It was founded to reduce poverty and discrimination affecting Latino communities and to improve the lives of Latinos in the United States. NCLR maintains an active presence on Capitol Hill, advocating on issues such as farmworkers' rights, welfare and Social Security, economic development, health care, civil rights, and immigration. During 1996 NCLR lobbied against restrictions on legal immigration and against the proposed employer verification system. According to their Web site, "Though most Latinos in the United States are not immigrants, immigration policy has an important impact on the civil rights of all Hispanics, many of whom are often mistaken for immigrants. NCLR conducts immigration policy analysis and advocacy activities in its role as a civil rights organization. The primary focus of these activities is to encourage immigration policies that are fair and nondiscriminatory and to encourage family reunification, while assuring effective and orderly border controls."

National Council of La Raza
1111 19th St., NW
Washington, DC 20036
Phone: (202) 785-1670
Web: www.nclr.org

Business and Labor Organizations

AMERICAN BUSINESS FOR LEGAL IMMIGRATION COALITION. The American Business for Legal Immigration Coalition (ABLI) was last activated in the 2001 debate over lifting the cap on H-1B visas for skilled high-tech workers. It brought together more than 300 companies, universities, and business organizations to push for legislation that would allow for more visas while minimizing reporting and regulatory requirements on employers. Companies such as Microsoft, Apple, Intel, Motorola, Sun Microsystems, and Texas Instruments were major backers of the coalition. ABLI is chaired and housed by the National Association of Manufacturers (NAM), the largest trade association in the United States. NAM pulls its more than 14,000 member companies together to advocate on issues important to particular sectors of the business community, or on issues of concern to its constituency as a whole. It also maintains an active media presence.

American Business for Legal Immigration Coalition
National Association of Manufacturers
1331 Pennsylvania Ave., NW
Washington, DC 20004-1790
Phone: (202) 637-3000
E-mail: sboyd@nam.org
Web: www.nam.org (search for "American Business for Legal Immigration")

AMERICAN ELECTRONICS ASSOCIATION. Founded in 1943, the American Electronics Association (AeA) is an association of more than 3,500 high-tech companies. In addition to providing member services, it has an active government affairs office focusing on international trade, tax, and workforce issues. It has been supportive of expanded employment-based immigration, including the H-1B visa program and counts among its priorities in 2002 the protection of this kind of immigration from possible restrictions.

American Electronics Association
601 Pennsylvania Ave., NW
North Building, Suite 600
Washington, DC 20004
Phone: (202) 682-9110
Web: www.aeanet.org

AMERICAN ENGINEERING ASSOCIATION. The American Engineering Association (AEA) is a membership organization of engineers and scientists from all technical disciplines. It argues that other engineering membership organizations are led by corporate interests who have an interest in creating an oversupply of technical workers in the United States, in order to hold down workforce costs. Thus AEA opposes expansion of the H-1B visa program as a direct threat to American workers and has also opposed the creation of an agricultural guest worker program or an amnesty for illegal foreign agricultural workers. Its Web site proclaims that its mission is "to promote American leadership in engineering, science and related technical fields" and to attain this goal, *"Qualified citizens must be given the right of first refusal for jobs created in the United States."* (emphasis in original). The AEA also advocates against age discrimination and supports a portable benefits package for workers.

American Engineering Association
P.O. Box 820473
Fort Worth, TX 76182-0473
Phone: (817) 280-8106
E-mail: webmaster@aea.org
Web: www.aea.org

AMERICAN FARM BUREAU. The American Farm Bureau (AFB) is the largest general farm organization in the United States. It has an extensive network of local chapters and activities, and its Washington office maintains an advocacy effort on behalf of agricultural policy, environmental and conservation issues, and trade and labor policy. In the immigration area, the AFB supports reform efforts that make it easier for agricultural employers to hire foreign agricultural workers through the existing H-2A visa program or new "guest worker" initiatives. It also supports efforts to regularize the status of current farmworkers by allowing current undocumented farmworkers to gain legal status after fulfilling an agricultural work requirement.

American Farm Bureau
600 Maryland Ave., SW, Suite 800
Washington, DC 20024
Phone: (202) 484-3600
Web: www.fb.org

AMERICAN FEDERATION OF LABOR-CONGRESS OF INDUSTRIAL ORGANIZATIONS. The American Federation of Labor-Congress of Industrial Organizations (AFL-CIO) is a federation of sixty-four labor unions in the United States, representing more than 13 million workers. It is generally considered to speak for the labor movement. Labor unions traditionally have opposed efforts to liberalize employment-based immigration and have argued for stricter sanctions on employers who use undocumented labor. However, in recent years union membership growth has increasingly come from the ranks of service employees, including many recent Latino immigrants.

Unions such as the Service Employees International Union (SEIU) have taken the lead in pressing the AFL-CIO to take a more active role in representing both documented and undocumented immigrant workers. In July 2001 this pressure resulted in a landmark decision by the AFL-CIO Executive Council to advocate for permanent legal status for undocumented workers, for an end to the expansion of guest worker programs and reforms of the current program, and for the resolution to the backlogs in family reunification visas. In addition, the AFL-CIO abandoned its support for employer sanctions, instead proposing criminal penalties for businesses that exploit workers and urging protection for workers who expose illegal business practices or organize unions.

American Federation of Labor-Congress of Industrial Organizations
815 16th St., NW
Washington, DC 20006

Phone: (202) 637-5000
Web: www.aflcio.org

CANADIAN/AMERICAN BORDER TRADE ALLIANCE. The Canadian/American Border Trade Alliance is a broad-based, grassroots organization made up of businesses, private- and public-sector organizations, and individuals involved in U.S./Canadian trade and tourism. Its stated mission is "to maximize global commercial activity and ensure continued growth of two-way cross border trade along the entire common U.S./Canadian border and assure efficient, productive border crossing capabilities." It seeks to be a resource on border issues and advocates for border crossing procedures that will not unduly burden legitimate businesses or travelers. In November 2001 it issued a report, "Rethinking Our Borders: Statement of Principles," that sought to address the national security issues posed after September 11 while protecting "low-risk" trade and transport across the U.S./Canadian border.

CAN/AM Border Trade Alliance
P.O. Box 929
Lewiston, NY 14092
Phone: (716) 754-8824
Web: www.canambta.org

INFORMATION TECHNOLOGY ASSOCIATION OF AMERICA. The Information Technology Association of America (ITAA), the trade group for the information technology industry, has been a supporter of expansions of the H-1B visa program, enabling U.S. employers to hire foreign workers. Although it views such employment-based immigration as only a short-term solution to staffing shortages, it has continued to support the maintenance of high levels of H-1B visas. The ITAA also sponsors an "Immigration Policy Group," which brings industry representatives and officials from the State Department, INS, and Department of Labor together regularly to monitor the implementation of the H-1B program and other similar workforce programs.

Information Technology Association of America (ITAA)
1616 North Fort Meyers Dr., Suite 1300
Arlington, VA 22209-3106
Phone: (703) 522-5055
Web: www.itaa.org

UNITED FARM WORKERS. Founded in 1966 by the activist Cesar Chavez, the United Farm Workers (UFW) organizes agricultural workers and works to improve the employment and living conditions faced by these workers. The UFW played an important role in bringing Chicano issues to national attention in the 1960's Civil Rights Movement and has continued to be active on civil rights issues. It has sought to legalize the status of undocumented farmworkers, to ensure that their civil rights are protected, and to provide services such as a credit union, medical plan, and pension plan. In recent years, it has been especially active in promoting legalization/amnesty legislation for undocumented farmworkers, and in opposing temporary guest worker programs.

United Farm Workers
Political/Legislative Office
1010 11th St., Suite 305
Sacramento, CA 95814
Phone: (916) 341-0612
E-mail: UFWofamer@aol.com
Web: www.ufw.org

International Organizations

Many international organizations also work on issues of immigration and refugee assistance. From its inception, the United Nations (UN) has been concerned with migration: one of its first acts was to establish the UN High Commissioner for Refugees (UNHCR) to deal with the problems of displaced persons after World War II. The Universal Declaration of Human Rights lists, in Articles 13 to 15, basic tenets of the freedom to migrate: everyone shall have the freedom of movement within their country, the right to leave one's country and return, the right to request and receive asylum from persecution, the right to a nationality and the freedom to change it.[5] Other international organizations of nation-states, including the International Organization for Migration (IOM); economic alliances, such as the Organization for Economic Cooperation and Development (OECD); and regional bodies, such as the OAS (Organization of American States), also take migration issues as a large part of their work. Multiple nongovernmental organizations, such as the International Committee for the Red Cross, are also active, especially in refugee assistance work.

Because many nongovernmental organizations have been mentioned in the section on refugee resettlement, this section will primarily focus on international coordinating organizations whose voting members are nation-states, which have been established by the United Nations, or which have intergovernmental or quasi-intergovernmental status. Many of these also have observers who are nongovernmental organizations.

INTERNATIONAL COMMITTEE FOR THE RED CROSS. The International Committee of the Red Cross (ICRC) focuses on protecting "the lives and dignity of victims of war and internal violence" and providing them with humanitarian assistance. It has a special status internationally because of the role given to it by the Geneva Conventions and the Additional Protocols. These conventions are a series of international treaties with nearly 200 signatory countries. They give the ICRC a mandate to protect civilians in war areas and prisoners of war, to ensure that combatants in international conflicts are obeying international humanitarian law, and to provide assistance to the population of occupied areas. ICRC monitors thus have a right to visit prisoners of war, to set up relief operations to wounded combatants and the civilian population, and to ensure that those it protects are treated in accordance with the law. It also handles the reunification of families, the tracing of missing persons, and the issuance of travel documents to displaced persons. In peacetime the ICRC supports the dissemination of international humanitarian law and organizes seminars and other educational efforts.

Although it is not an agency of the United Nations or any other intergovernmental body, the ICRC enjoys similar international legal status, including immunity from national legal processes. This allows it to maintain neutrality and independence. The ICRC is also the founding body of the Red Cross/Red Crescent Movement and certifies National Red Cross/Red Crescent Societies, which respond to natural or man-made disasters in their home countries. The national societies are part of the International Federation of Red Cross/Red Crescent Societies, which provides support for the national societies.

International Committee for the Red Cross
19 Avenue de la Paix
CH-1202 Geneva
Switzerland
Phone: 41 22 734 60 01
Web: www.icrc.org

INTERNATIONAL ORGANIZATION FOR MIGRATION. Reorganized in 1989, the International Organization for Migration (IOM) is the successor organization to the Intergovernmental Committee for European Migration (and then the Intergovernmental Committee for Migration). IOM has ninety-one nation members, as well as thirty-one additional states and sixty-two international governmental and nongovernmental organizations that are designated as observers. Its mission is to help the nations of the world responsibly and humanely address migration issues. As it explains: "Today's world is confronted with a major migration dilemma: how to restore respect for and use of orderly migration as a positive and constructive force? The challenge is to forge strategies that address current problems and their causes, through an international commitment to seek practical and humane solutions."

IOM works to address these challenges through four main programs. The Humanitarian Migration program provides concrete assistance to migrant populations. The Migration for Development program assists nations in part by encouraging the migration of individuals with special skills to nations needing that expertise—either on a permanent or temporary basis. The Technical Cooperation program provides advisory assistance to governments on migration issues. Finally, the Migration Debate, Research and Information program sponsors international seminars and educational programs on migration issues.

International Organization for Migration
17 route des Morillons, C.P. 71,
CH-1211 Geneva 19, Switzerland
Phone: 42 11 717 91 11
E-mail: info@iom.int
Web: www.iom.int

ORGANIZATION FOR ECONOMIC COOPERATION AND DEVELOPMENT. The Organization for Economic Cooperation and Development (OECD) is the successor organization to the Organization for European Economic Co-Operation, which was founded at the end of World War II to administer the Marshall Plan's assistance program for the rebuilding of Europe. The OECD now has a much broader focus, including "to build strong economies in its member countries, improve efficiency, hone market systems, expand free trade and contribute to development in industrialized as well as developing countries." It is also seeking to contribute its expertise to nations around the world who have market economies. In 2001 the OECD council identified international migration as a new priority, with particular attention to research on trends in international migration, on the link between migration and development, and on the economic impacts of migration. It has also produced reports on migration and the labor market in Asia and on the migration of highly skilled workers worldwide.

Organization for Economic Cooperation and Development
2, rue Andre Pascal
F-75775 Paris Cedex 16
France
Phone: 33 1 45 24 82 00
E-mail: els.contact@oecd.org
Web: www.oecd.org

REGIONAL CONFERENCE ON MIGRATION/REGIONAL NETWORK OF CIVIC ORGANIZATIONS FOR MIGRATION. Led by Mexico, in 1996 Belize, Canada, Costa Rica, El Salvador, Guatemala, Honduras, Mexico, Nicaragua, Panama, and the United States created an intergovernmental forum on the regional issues raised by migration in North and Central America. Now joined by the Dominican Republic, the countries in the Regional Conference on Migration (RCM), also known as the "Puebla Process" after the location of the first meeting in Puebla, Mexico, hold a vice-ministerial meeting yearly to develop an action plan, implemented during the following year through seminars, consultations, and research. The 2001 conference, for instance, dealt with issues such as trafficking in migrants; migration management and transborder cooperation; the concentration of immigrants in border communities; and the arrest, detention, deportation, and reception of migrants. A parallel group of nongovernmental organizations called the "Regional Network of Civic Organizations for Migration" (RNCOM) also meets during the annual conference and has some joint sessions with the RCM. They are empowered to bring issues to the RCM for attention and are often called on for assistance in research and implementation. Several South American countries and international organizations, including the International Organization for Migration and United Nations High Commissioner for Refugees have observer status with the RCM/RNCOM. The RCM's president pro-tempore and secretariat rotates annually among the member countries and is usually the responsibility of the country's foreign affairs ministry or cabinet department. In 2002 the president pro-tempore of the RCM was Guatemala.

Regional Conference on Migration
Web: www.rcmvs.org

UNITED NATIONS HIGH COMMISSIONER FOR REFUGEES. The United Nations High Commissioner for Refugees (UNHCR) was established in 1950 by the United Nations General Assembly to help in the resettlement of European refugees after World War II. Continuing world strife, however, made the UNHCR relevant after its initial mandate had passed. Today, the UNHCR takes a lead role in coordinating international action to protect refugees and to help them rebuild their lives. Its primary purpose is to protect the rights of refugees and ensure their well-being, either by helping them seek refuge or asylum in other countries or by enabling them to voluntarily return to their home countries. This includes the provision of material assistance—tents, food, emergency health care—legal advocacy, physical security, resettlement assistance, and the eventual creation of "quick impact projects," or short-term building projects for schools, roads, and wells. It also proposes international refugee agreements and monitors national compliance with international law and international conventions. In recent years UNHCR has turned more of its attention to "internally displaced persons," people who are not officially considered "refugees" because they fled to other parts of their own country rather than crossing international boundaries, and has helped to start an international discussion about more systematic ways of recognizing and coordinating aid to this group.

UNHCR cooperates with other UN agencies and also with a host of international organizations, both governmental and nongovernmental. Only a small portion of its funding comes from the UN; the rest originates from contributions from governments, international organizations, and private and individual sources. With its annual budget just under $1 billion, UNHCR aids 21.8 million people worldwide.

United Nations High Commissioner for Refugees
C.P. 2500
1211 Geneva 2
Switzerland
Phone: 41 22 739 8111
Web: www.unhcr.ch

Notes

1. Martin Tolchin, "Woman in the News; Immigration Expert Who Takes Broad Approach—Doris Marie Meissner," *New York Times,* June 20, 1993, A26.

2. Statement of James W. Ziglar before the Committee on the Judiciary, United States Senate, July 18, 2001. Available at www.ins.gov/graphics/071801testimony.htm

3. Peter Slevin, "FBI Courting Arab, Muslim Communities; With Meetings, Agency Seeks Information, Easing of Tensions," *Washington Post,* September 19, 2001, A14.

4. See www.nchr.org/mnd/nc02000.htm

5. United Nations, Universal Declaration of Human Rights, December 10, 1948. Available at www.un.org/Overview/rights.html

4 International Implications

While U.S. immigration policy is hotly debated at home, it is often influenced by events around the world. War, economic depression, political changes, or natural disasters in other countries affect the number of people who decide to leave their homes. Other countries' immigration policies can cause migrants to prefer other destinations to the United States, or vice versa. Pressure from international organizations or the foreign policy agenda can affect asylum and refugee policy; pressure from international trade can create, or reduce, migration.

At the same time, U.S. immigration policy can also change governments and societies around the world. An expansive U.S. immigration policy can help to address unemployment in other countries. On the other hand, it can lead to a "brain drain" if the "best and brightest" leave for better opportunities. Migrants send money, ideas, and sometimes votes back to their countries of origin; their presence can change the diplomatic relationship between the sending and receiving countries. Immigration policy thus affects the U.S. role in international relations.

This chapter looks at immigration within the international context. It begins with a comparison of Canada and the United States, two "countries of immigration" that nevertheless have adopted different approaches to immigration policy. Next, the chapter examines the relationship between the United States and Mexico, focusing on ways in which the large Mexican migration to the United States has changed Mexico's government and economy. The chapter then discusses the developed countries of the European Union to understand how political and economic instability abroad can change U.S. domestic immigration policy. The chapter closes with a discussion of the U.S. role in international refugee law and policy.

Comparing Countries of Immigration: United States and Canada

The United States, Canada, and Australia attract exceptionally large immigrant populations and are described as "countries of immigration." In all three countries, settlers, primarily from Great Britain, displaced indigenous populations during the seventeenth and eighteenth centuries. The countries' vast territories contained valuable natural resources, facilitating development and industrialization. These led, in turn, to a great demand for foreign workers during the Industrial Revolution. Most of these workers came from less-developed countries in Europe, where the Industrial Revolution had not yet taken root, rather than from countries in Africa, Asia, or South America.

This migration pattern accords well with both neoclassical economic theory, which predicts that nationals of less-developed countries should migrate to countries where the need for labor is greater, and with world systems theory, which suggests that countries with economic ties to the receiving country will be more likely to send immigrants than countries without such ties. *(See box on page 174)* In keeping with economic theory, all three countries also severely limited immigration when economic conditions took a turn for the worse during the Great Depression. But political factors also played a role: non-European immigrants faced substantial immigration restrictions in all of these countries. It was not until the reform movements of the 1960s that nationals of countries in Asia, Latin America, Africa, and the Caribbean began to emigrate to the United States, Canada, and Australia in large numbers. Since the 1960s these immigrants from the new "periphery" have had an important role in shaping the economies of all three countries.

As the United States's neighbor and number one trading partner, Canada offers a notable opportunity to compare immigration policies. In general, the United States and Canada consider many of the same factors when formulating immigration policy, including economic conditions, a commitment to nondiscrimination, foreign policy considerations, and lobbying by various interest groups.[1] With more than one billion U.S. dollars in trade crossing the border with Canada each day, the Canadian and U.S. economies are closely tied to one another. To the extent that labor markets affect economic conditions, the countries share many similar concerns over labor migration, such as the importation of temporary agricultural workers. The two countries also share many cultural traits and political attitudes toward diversity and discrimination. Each is home to an array of ethnic interest groups, immigrant advocacy networks, immigration restrictionist organ-

Policy Differences on Immigration

David M. Reimers and Harold Troper summed up the key differences between U.S. and Canadian approaches to immigration policy:

> Economic issues have been far more important to Canadians than to Americans. The former have consciously used immigration as a way to promote economic and population growth. In the United States some Americans use the positive argument for more immigration, but the advocates of increased immigration usually argue that immigrants do not hurt American workers and that the American economy can absorb additional newcomers. But for the most part, in the United States other issues dominate.[1]

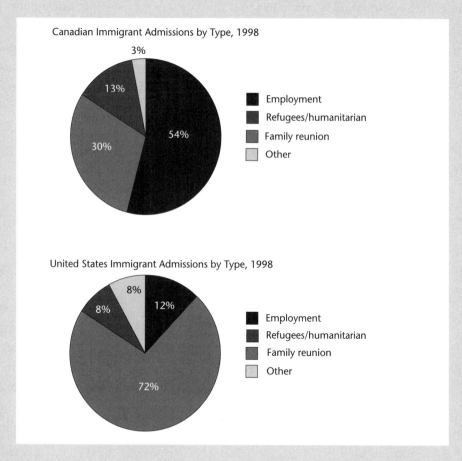

Canadian Immigrant Admissions by Type, 1998

- Employment
- Refugees/humanitarian
- Family reunion
- Other

United States Immigrant Admissions by Type, 1998

- Employment
- Refugees/humanitarian
- Family reunion
- Other

---

1. David M. Reimers and Harold Troper, "Canadian and American Immigration Policy since 1945," in Barry R. Chiswick, ed., *Immigration, Language, and Ethnicity: Canada and the United States* (Washington, D.C.: AEI Press, 1992), 15.

izations, and social service agencies, all of which play a role in formulating immigration policy.

Despite these similarities, Canada's immigration policy differs from its U.S. counterpart in two fundamental ways. First, Canada's overall population is significantly smaller than that of the United States, yet its territory and natural resources are of comparable size. In 1996 Canada's total population was 28.5 million, including 18 percent foreign-born.[2] In contrast, the total U.S. population in 1996 was 265.2 million, including roughly 9 percent foreign-born.[3] The historic difference in Canada's population size means that despite an already-high proportion of foreigners in the population, Canada has traditionally sought to attract immigrants as a means of fueling its economy. Canada's immigration agency, Citizenship and Immigration Canada (CIC), had expected to attract at least 200,000 immigrants in 1998, but the actual number of permanent residence permits issued reached only 174,100.[4] The United States, in contrast, often views immigrants as a strain on its economy, yet faces a seemingly unending "clamor at the gates."[5] The U.S. Immigration and Naturalization Service (INS) faces a substantial backlog of applications for immigrant status (809,000), despite issuing 660,500 permanent residency permits in 1998.[6]

Canada's demand for immigration—which sometimes goes so far as to involve recruiting or marketing schemes in selected countries abroad—leads to a second fundamental difference from U.S. immigration policy. Canada gives priority to economic immigration over family reunion, refugee and asylum, or other classifications. More than half of permanent immigrants to Canada enter as skilled workers, business immigrants, or their accompanying dependents. Roughly one-third of permanent immigrants enter on the basis of family reunion, while about 15 percent enter as refugees.[7] In contrast, the United States gives priority to admissions based on family reunification, followed by employment, refugees, and other categories.

These policies help explain the different composition of national origin among immigrants to Canada and the United States. A majority of immigrants to Canada come from Asian countries, while most immigrants to the United States come from Latin America. Other explanations include the notion that the United States acts as a "buffer" for Latin American migrants heading north, and the long-term establishment of migrant networks between the United States and Latin America.

Under the Immigration Act of 1976, Canada's prime minister consults with the provincial governments and then announces, each fall, the total number of immigrants to be admitted over the next year. In theory, Canada's admissions regulations give priority to family and refugee class immigrants. Family class immigrants must be sponsored by their Canadian relatives, who must attest that they will support the immigrants financially if necessary. According to its international treaty obligations and humanitarian traditions, Canada also admits 20,000 to 30,000 refugees and displaced persons each year. Technically, immigrants who do not fall into one of these two categories cannot enter until the demand in these first two categories has been satisfied. In reality, however, the majority of Canada's immigrants are neither close relatives of Canadian citizens nor refugees, and they enter through the "point system."[8]

The point system, introduced in 1967, assigns numerical values to general characteristics such as age, education, and language proficiency (in English or French), as well as targeted economic characteristics such as whether the applicant's occupation is in high demand in Canada, or whether he or she already has a job arranged. Applicants must obtain at least 70 out of a possible 100 points to qualify for admission. If the applicant fits into the "assisted relative class," meaning he or she is a distant relative of a Canadian citizen (such as a sibling, parent still active in the labor force, or child of majority age), he or she may be awarded 15 bonus points in order to pass the minimum threshold.[9] Applicants who obtain the requisite 70 points are admitted on a first-come, first-served basis.

The point system is "a potentially powerful tool for steering the composition of the [immigrant] inflow toward those occupations and skills believed to be in high demand in Canada."[10] Although it does not direct immigrants toward specific occupations, the point system effectively shifts the distribution of immigrant skills in favor of professional occupations rather than low-skilled jobs. The more immigrants are assessed through the point system, the higher the skill-level of inflow overall. The more admissions are based on family relations or humanitarian concerns, the greater the reduction in skill-level. The point system thus responds to arguments that immigrants displace low-skilled domestic workers by selecting high-skilled workers who are presumably demanded by the Canadian economy.

Immigrants to Canada come from many of the same countries as those in the United States, with one major exception: Canada does not have a significant Mexican immigrant population. Although Canada does have a formal program to import temporary agricultural workers from Mexico, the number of Mexicans admitted under this program is relatively small (about 2,000).[11] Because its only land border adjoins the United States, Canada does not face the challenge of illegal immigration from Central America that has preoccupied American officials.

Figure 4-1. U.S. and Canadian Immigrant Populations

Canada: Immigrant Population by Region of Birth, 1996

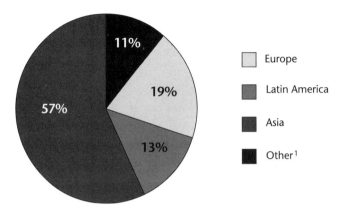

1. Includes United States, Africa, Oceania.

Source: Statistics Canada, 1996 Census; http://statcan.ca/english/Pgdb/People/Population/demo

United States: Immigrant Population by Region of Birth, 1997

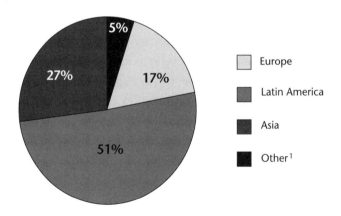

1. Includes Canada, Africa, Oceania.

Source: A. Dianne Schmidley and Campbell Givson, U.S. Census Bureau, *Current Population Reports,* Series P23-195, Profile of the Foreign-Born Population in the United States: 1997 (Washington, D.C.: Government Printing Office, 1999).

Instead, one of the most contentious issues in Canadian immigration policy during the past two decades has been the large number of asylum claims. In 1998 nearly half of the 22,650 refugees admitted to Canada claimed asylum on arrival in Canada rather than applying through overseas selection programs.[12] Although this number is roughly the same for the United States, proportionately it is large relative to Canada's refugee intake and total population. At the same time, rejected asylum seekers accounted for 63 percent of all removals from Canada. This rise in the number of deportations followed two policy changes in 1997. First, the government abolished a regulation that allowed rejected asylum seekers "who had been under removal orders for more than three years, but who had established themselves in Canada and had been employed for at least six months" to apply for permanent residency through the Deferred Removal Orders Class.[13] A similar measure streamlined the class of Post-Determination Refugee Claimants in Canada (PDRCC), so that rejected asylum claimants no longer received an automatic review of their cases with consideration for permanent residency. The regulation limited eligibility for the PDRCC class, subjecting more rejected asylum seekers to removal.

This increasing association of asylum seekers with illegal immigration and deportation contributes to a growing global perception of asylum as a back door to immigration that warrants restriction. For example, Palestinian refugee Abu Mezer was caught three times trying to cross into the United States from Canada before he was arrested in 1997 for plotting an attack on the New York subway system.[14] In December 1999 American inspectors in the Seattle district noticed that ferry passenger Ahmed Ressam appeared nervous, so they detained him before he could flee the landing area. Inside his car, they found bomb materials and evidence linking him to an Algerian terrorist ring, the Armed Islamic Group.[15]

Citing incidents such as this one, analysts in both countries have charged that Canada's liberal immigration and refugee policies make it a haven for criminals and terrorists targeting the United States. In December 2000 the White House released an interagency report saying that "Canada had become a North American port of entry and haven for Asian gang leaders" whose criminal activities impact the United States.[16] The terrorist attacks on the World Trade Center and Pentagon further exposed the abuse of Canada's refugee and asylum systems by members of "sleeper" terrorist cells. Shortly following the September 11 attacks, suspicions arose that the terrorist hijackers may have entered the United States from Canada by crossing the border at a remote point or low-volume port-of-entry. Although American officials publicly acknowledged that investigations showed none of the hijackers had entered from Canada, intelligence analysts in both countries reported that about fifty terrorist groups were operating in Canada. In response, U.S. and Canadian officials have committed to even greater cooperation than in the past, working together on the terrorist investigation, border security, and refugee and asylum policies. "We have to counter the image that Canada is the weak link in terms of North American security," said one senior official of Canada's Foreign Ministry.[17]

The Smart Border Declaration, signed by the United States and Canada on December 12, 2001, advances an agenda of cooperation between the two countries that had begun decades earlier. *(See Appendix for document)* The agreement moves the nations toward the creation of a North American perimeter, harmonized visa and refugee policies, joint border enforcement, and greater intelligence sharing. In this sense, it is not a departure from previous trends in U.S.-Canada relations, but instead a major boost in the same direction.

Before the terrorist attacks of September 11, wariness of Canada as a haven for criminals was the exception rather than the rule in U.S.-Canada relations. For the most part, immigration between the United States and Canada had run so smoothly that it rarely caught the attention of U.S. policy-makers. Citizens of both countries crossed the border with relative ease, many commuting daily to work or making regular trips to visit friends and family members. The economic integration and ensuing labor migration between the two countries is well-advanced, having developed from the 1965 Auto Pact to the 1989 U.S.-Canada Free Trade Agreement, the 1994 North American Free Trade Agreement (NAFTA), and the 1995 Shared Border Accord. With this integration, standards of living in the United States and Canada have converged, including similar trends in consumer culture.

In this context, many Americans view Canada as less foreign and expect large volumes of movement between the countries. Canadians, on the other hand, historically paid slightly greater attention to migration issues with the United States, in large part because they are more concentrated along the U.S. border (90 percent of Canadians live within 100 miles of the U.S. border). Although some Canadians voice concerns over the "invasion" of American culture, the preservation of a distinct Canadian identity, and the "brain drain" of talented Canadians to better paid jobs in the United States, relations between Canada and the United States remain extremely friendly and approaches to migration issues have been characterized by cooperation.

Since the terrorist attacks, policy-makers have sought to preserve the ease of movement between the United States and Canada while increasing border secu-

The North American Free Trade Agreement

The North American Free Trade Agreement (NAFTA), which took effect between the United States, Canada, and Mexico on January 1, 1994, is remarkable in terms of migration issues in two significant ways. First, unlike the series of treaties that created the European Union, NAFTA contains no major provisions addressing immigration policy.[1] Although the agreement liberalized trade in goods and services and contained key provisions on labor and environmental standards, it did not significantly promote freer flows of labor between the three countries. This absence may be the result of political pressure from labor activists and other NAFTA opponents in the United States during treaty negotiations. While Mexico and Canada approached the trade negotiations with enthusiasm as they began in 1991, the AFL-CIO, members of the U.S. Congress and others strongly opposed American participation in the proposed free trade zone. Presidential candidate H. Ross Perot told television viewers in 1992 that NAFTA would create "a giant sucking sound" as U.S. companies rushed to Mexico for a cheaper labor supply, taking jobs away from American workers in the process.[2] Only Chapter 16 of NAFTA addresses the movement of professionals between the United States, Canada, and Mexico. According to this aspect of the agreement, NAFTA-related migration to the United States occurs through special temporary employment visa categories, such as intracompany transferees, NAFTA workers, and their spouses and children.[3]

A second important feature of NAFTA in terms of migration policy is that the agreement is based on a principle of equal participation, yet vast differences exist between the countries' economies, populations, political systems, and cultures.[4] Almost all of the migration theories (described in the box on page 174) could be used to predict an increase in migration to the United States, especially from Mexico, as a result of NAFTA. Migrant laborers would be attracted to the capital-intensive U.S. economy, links because of increased trade would further establish migration institutions and systems, and migratory networks would flourish. Analysts could therefore anticipate a dramatic increase in immigration in the short term. However, over the long term, "one of the assumptions behind NAFTA was that it would facilitate Mexican economic growth and thus indirectly deter Mexican emigration."[5] This short-term surge and long-term decline in immigration to the United States has been dubbed "the migration hump."[6] At the same time, migration would act as a force of economic and cultural convergence under NAFTA. Nevertheless, in light of the vast differences between the U.S. and Mexican economies, the migration provisions contained in Chapter 16 limit the number of professional visas for Mexicans for the first ten years of NAFTA's operation while allowing Canadian professionals visa-free access.

1. Sidney Weintraub, Francisco Alba, Rafael Fernández de Castro, and Manuel García y Griego, "Responses to Migration Issues," in Mexican Ministry of Foreign Affairs and U.S. Commission on Immigration Reform, *Migration Between Mexico and the United States: Binational Study*, Vol. 1 (Austin, Texas: Morgan, 1998), 450.

2. B. Drummon Ayres, Jr., "Accepting a Dare to Debate, Perot Retakes the Spotlight," *New York Times*, November 6, 1993, A10.

3. Office of the United States Trade Representative, "Fact Sheet: Summary of Principal Provisions of NAFTA," *U.S. Department of State Dispatch*, 4(35), August 30, 1993.

4. Clint E. Smith, *Inevitable Partnership: Understanding Mexico-U.S. Relations* (London: Lynne Rienner, 2000), 193. See also U.S.-Mexico Migration Panel, *Mexico-U.S. Migration: A Shared Responsibility*, convened by the Carnegie Endowment for International Peace (International Migration Policy Program) and the Instituto Tecnológico Autónomo de México (Faculty of International Relations), 2001, 3.

5. Weintraub et al., "Responses to Migration Issues," 449.

6. Philip Martin, "Mexican-U.S. Migration: Policies and Economic Impacts," *Challenge*, March 1995. See also Wayne A. Cornelius and Philip L. Martin, "The Uncertain Connection: Free Trade and Rural Mexican Migration to the United States," *International Migration Review*, 27(3).

rity, illustrating a classic tension in border management between facilitation and control. Few want to sacrifice the countries' economic integration in order to prevent future terrorist attacks, making security a collective good despite concerns for sovereignty. "Anything that helps U.S. security helps Canada," said Canada's solicitor general, Laurence MacAulay, who oversees the country's law enforcement agencies.[18] The Smart Border Declaration adds security measures to the list of economic integration efforts that was developed from the 1965 Auto Pact through the North American Free Trade Agreement and 1995 Shared Border Accord. Over the longer term, U.S. and Canadian policy-makers face a choice between diminishing the role of the border or bolstering it.

Mexico–U.S. Relations

Mexico–U.S. relations can be characterized by increasing cooperation over the course of the 1990s following a more contentious relationship in the past. During this period, migration has been a focal point of discussions between Mexican and

U.S. policy-makers, with NAFTA as the single most important event of the decade. As the treaty took effect in 1994, Mexican deputy foreign minister Andrés Rozental predicted that, "[I]mmigration is going to be the number one issue between the United States and Mexico for the next several years."[19] From the U.S. perspective, priorities include illegal immigration, trafficking in migrants, and links to drug trafficking and trade in illegal narcotics. From the Mexican perspective, attention to the protection of migrants' rights is paramount; other Mexican objectives are to maintain stable migratory conditions by influencing U.S. immigration policy, and to gain recognition for the economic and social contributions Mexican migrants have made to the United States.[20]

The Causes of Mexican Migration

Like Canada, Mexico shares a long history with the United States. However, unlike Canada, relations between the United States and Mexico have been rocky since the Mexican-American War of the 1840s. As recently as the 1980s, the two countries disagreed over policies toward Nicaragua, Iran, and other cold war conflicts. At the same time, the migration relationship could be characterized as "nonengagement." The Mexican government for many years viewed migration as a largely inevitable result of the country's socioeconomic situation, so that any policies it might pursue to reduce emigration were unlikely to succeed in the face of U.S. demand. This "no-policy" migration policy kept Mexico disengaged from migration dialogues with the United States, which was then free to implement migration policies unilaterally.[21]

The shift in Mexico's position from disengagement to increasing cooperation with the United States has occurred over the 1990s with the liberalization of the Mexican economy. The *Mexico-U.S. Binational Study on Migration* notes that during the 1989–1993 period, "For the first time in the history of the bilateral relationship, both federal governments began to foster and facilitate economic integration instead of repressing it. For Mexico, this represented a departure from the traditional defensive attitude, and the recognition of economic interdependence; and for the United States it represented a less confrontational stance with its southern neighbor."[22]

The initiation of trade negotiations leading up to NAFTA in 1991 by U.S. President George Bush and Mexican President Carlos Salinas began a process of creating institutions and consultative mechanisms that made linkages between the federal governments stronger and more direct. This increased dialogue has touched on migration issues, particularly in the latter half of the decade. Created in 1987 as a condition of the U.S.-Mexico Bilateral Framework Agreement on Trade and Investment (a precursor to NAFTA), the Working Group on Migration and Consular Affairs began to meet independently of its parent entity, the Binational Commission, in 1992 and increased the frequency of its meetings after NAFTA's implementation in 1994. This group involves the highest-level officials dealing with migration affairs in both governments, including the INS commissioner, the assistant secretary for Inter-American affairs at the State Department, and the Mexican undersecretaries of migration at the Interior Ministry and bilateral affairs at the Foreign Ministry, among others.[23] Other formal bilateral institutions introduced through NAFTA negotiations are the Border Liaison Mechanisms, including the Citizen's Advisory Panel and the Mechanism of Consultation on the Activities of the INS and Consular Protection.

This shift toward cooperation on migration issues between Mexico and the United States became a practical necessity, given the profound effect NAFTA has had on the Mexican economy and rural sending communities. Both Mexican and U.S. analysts have argued that NAFTA will "diminish migratory pressures over time." The U.S. Commission for the Study of International Migration and Economic Development predicted a "migration hump" resulting from economic development that, once passed, would lead to lower levels of migration. Mexican President Salinas bluntly stated that, faced with the choice of exporting its people or its products, Mexico would prefer to export tomatoes rather than tomato pickers.[24] With both governments assuming that Mexican migration is inevitable at least in the short term, they expected that NAFTA would mostly affect the timing of the migration flow.

Trade liberalization under NAFTA has significantly affected the structure of the Mexican economy, particularly the agricultural and manufacturing sectors, and thus changed the labor conditions in which migration decisions are made. First, in order to compete with large-scale, capital-rich agricultural industries in the United States and Canada, many Mexican farms had to be consolidated. As one study noted, "Iowa alone produces twice as much corn as Mexico."[25] Economic models estimate that changes in Mexican farm policies and freer trade in agricultural products because of NAFTA would displace roughly 1.4 million Mexican workers, who would migrate both internally and externally. Trade liberalization also channeled new investment into Mexico's manufacturing industry, generating an increase in the number of *maquiladoras* (factories in Mexico that are subcontracted by U.S. firms). This restructuring of the labor market uprooted workers and increased their propensity to migrate, creating a surge in immigration from Mexico until the labor market regained stability. According to official statistics, roughly one million Mexicans left the country in 1998; however, this figure does not account for undocumented migrants.[26] Analysts expect this short-term, NAFTA-related migration adjustment to last about fifteen years[27] before reaching the other side of the "migration hump."

In addition to NAFTA, issues of population growth, democratic governance, and currency devaluation have influenced migration conditions in Mexico during the 1990s. Throughout the decade, nearly one million new workers entered the labor force in Mexico each year, creating labor surpluses in many areas and depressing wages. Not surprisingly, most of the major migrant sending communities are in areas where there is a large amount of surplus labor.[28]

Political and economic instability also played a role in migration decisions, particularly during the 1994 presidential election campaign. Accusations of election fraud in the 1988 Mexican presidential election, the Zapatista rebellion in Chiapas, and the assassination of Luis Donaldo Colosio (the chosen candidate of the ruling party, the Partido Revolucionario Institucional (PRI)), all shattered public confidence and began a decline in Mexico's economy. In this climate, the United States sent an official delegation to Mexico including Secretary of State Warren Christopher and Attorney General Janet Reno, who forcefully advocated democratic reforms and warned against election fraud.[29] For the United States, combating public corruption in Mexico is also tied to the effort to limit trafficking in migrants and particularly drugs across U.S. borders.

Poor economic conditions were exacerbated in late 1994, when the Mexican government undertook a 40 percent devaluation of the peso, and received a significant bailout package from the United States. INS Commissioner Doris Meissner and professor Ed Taylor of the University of California at Davis predicted that the peso devaluation would widen the wage gap between the United States and Mexico and therefore increase migration pressure. According to Taylor's village economic model, a 30 percent devaluation would increase exits from Mexican villages by 25 percent.[30]

Protecting the Rights of Mexican Migrants

As Mexicans continue to leave their country for the United States, and U.S. immigration policies have become more restrictive, there has been a growing concern in Mexico for migrants' rights. The approval in California of Proposition 187 proved to be a rallying cause for Mexicans from all parts of society. The executive branch of government, legislators, academics and intellectuals, religious organizations, and business communities all condemned the measure and called for a strong defense of the human rights of migrants. Both the Salinas administration and the administration of President Ernesto Zedillo, which followed it, viewed Proposition 187 as racist and xenophobic. Mexican academics and intellectuals "argued that failure to include the free mobility of labor between the signatory countries of NAFTA led to the discriminatory treatment of illegal workers."[31] The Catholic Church demanded greater dialogue between the U.S. and Mexican governments, proposed the creation of a "Free Labor Agreement," and urged the Mexican government to change conditions that compelled citizens to cross the border illegally. Similarly, 1996 television coverage of undocumented Mexican immigrants in California being beaten after a high-speed chase by Riverside County police provoked an outburst in Mexico over the violation of the rights of its nationals. Shortly after this incident, a public opinion poll taken of residents of Mexico City by the political and economic journal *Este País* showed that 85 percent of respondents believed that Mexicans do little or nothing to help their nationals abroad, while only 15 percent said they were aware of institutions to defend them.[32]

In addition to Proposition 187, dangerous conditions for undocumented migrants crossing the U.S.-Mexico border have worsened because of recent U.S. border enforcement policies and intensified the long-standing objections of migrants' rights advocates. As Operation Gatekeeper and other U.S. Border Patrol policies deterred undocumented migration from major ports of entry and surrounding areas, immigrants seeking unauthorized entry to the United States—often through smuggling operations—increasingly have attempted to cross in remote border areas. Their long treks in the desert heat expose them to risks such as dehydration and heat stroke. The Organization for Economic Cooperation and Development (OECD) reports that "between 1994 and 1999, some 450 Mexicans lost their lives trying to cross the U.S. border illegally."[33]

Mexico's growing attention to migrants' rights poses a classic tension between national sovereignty and international commitments to human rights for the United States. Transnational advocacy movements, the concentration of Mexican immigrants in state and local municipalities, and international agreements increasingly require U.S. immigration policy-makers to take into account impacts beyond the "national interest." In this sense, consultation with Mexico is a growing necessity for U.S. immigration policy-makers, and both countries may expect their interdependence to deepen with time.

The Mexican government's attention to the protection of migrants' rights dates back to the end of the Bracero Program in 1964. Consular protection of Mexican nationals living in the United States is traditionally a priority in Mexican foreign policy; in fact, with more than forty consulates on U.S. territory, the Mexican government's consular activities in the United States represent the largest network of consulates of any country in the world. Most consular work focuses on the protection of Mexican laborers but also includes assistance with repatriation, hospitalization, and legal trials. The Zedillo administration sought to modernize the consular system by training and updating programs, harmonizing criteria for identifying cases of protection, and improving technical infrastructure.[34]

President Salinas also created the Program for the Mexican Communities Living Abroad (PMCLA) in 1990, the year in which NAFTA negotiations began, making it a priority whose allocation of expenditures—at $1 million annually—exceeded the consular protection program. According to the *Binational Study*, "The establishment of the PMCLA represents the Mexican government's recognition of the potential of Mexican Americans as a source of political support within the United States, and also the potential of the community to develop closer economic ties with Mexico."[35] PMCLA's main activities include programs devoted to community organizing, sports, education and culture, information and communication, health care, business, and fundraising.

In its relationship with the United States, Mexico also pursues the protection of migrants' rights through bilateral institutions such as the Border Liaison Mechanism, the Working Group on Migration and Consular Affairs, the Consulting Mechanism for the Immigration and Naturalization Services Activities and Consular Protection, and the Citizens' Advisory Panel. This formal commitment to the protection of migrants' rights through bilateral institutions is the result of a Memorandum of Understanding signed in May 1996 by Mexican Secretary of Foreign Affairs José Angel Gurría and U.S. Secretary of State Warren Christopher.

Finally, Mexican policy-makers have actively participated in international efforts to protect the rights of migrant workers and their families, regardless of their legal status. Mexico worked in the International Labor Organization and later the United Nations General Assembly to pass the 1990 U.N. International Convention on the Protection of the Rights of All Migrant Workers and Members of Their Families. It also led the development of the Puebla Process, an annual conference of governments of countries in North and Central America (including the United States) devoted to international migration policy. Representatives from ten countries attended the first conference, held in Puebla, Mexico, on March 13 and 14, 1996, where the primary topic was protection of the human rights of migrants.

Aside from formal diplomatic relations, Mexico seeks to protect the rights of its nationals living in the United States by mobilizing and encouraging advocacy within the United States. Relying on strong ties between expatriate Mexicans and their homeland, Mexico encourages the development of Mexican-Americans' political power to advance its policy interests. Mexican immigrants' influence on U.S. policy occurs through lobbying members of Congress, fostering relations with key state governments, and supporting the activities of nongovernmental organizations.

Since they were elected in 2000, presidents Vicente Fox of Mexico and George W. Bush of the United States have reinforced the primacy of migration policy in Mexico-U.S. relations. During Fox's election campaign, a policy memorandum made emigration to the United States a top foreign policy priority for Mexico, saying that "Mexico should consider negotiating a broad new immigration agreement . . . that would commit the U.S. to granting Mexicans many more visas in exchange for what would be unprecedented Mexican cooperation in reducing the northward flow of illegal immigrants."[36] On his first trip to the United States as president, Fox visited California, where he promised migrant farmworkers that he would press for greater rights on their behalf.[37] President Bush also signaled the importance of relations with Mexico when he visited Fox at his home in San Cristobal one month after his inauguration in February 2001. "Mexico is the first foreign country I have visited as president. And I intended it to be that way," said President Bush.[38]

In the days leading up to the presidents' meeting, dozens of advocacy groups called on them to negotiate more humane immigration policies. The U.S.-Mexico Migration Panel, an independent group led by former deputy foreign minister of Mexico Andres Rozental, special envoy to Latin America for the outgoing Clinton administration Mack McLarty, and Bishop Nicholas DiMarzio, urged the presidents to make visas and legal status for Mexican migrants more widely available, cooperatively crack down on criminal smuggling operations to prevent dangerous border crossings, "jointly build[ing] a viable border region," target economic development programs to regions with high rates of emigration, and improve economic conditions throughout Mexico.[39] Known as the "Guanajuato Proposal," the result of the meeting was the formation of a "High Level Working Group on Migration," led by Mexican foreign minister Jorge G. Castenada and interior minister Santiago Creel, and U.S. Secretary of State Colin L. Powell and Attorney General John Ashcroft. In their first meetings in spring 2001, these leaders began to tackle a common, binational agenda, including both short- and long-term goals: "discussion of border safety, the H-2 temporary worker visa program, ideas on regularization of undocumented Mexicans in the United States, alternatives for possible new temporary worker programs, and efforts on regional economic development."[40]

Mexican Migration and Its Effect on Mexico

The immigrants who come to the United States affect not only the communities they arrive in but also those they left behind. In other words, international migration brings change across the spectrum of movement, from the origin to the destination, in both sending and receiving societies. A look at the effects of Mexican immigration to the United States on Mexico illustrates the economic, social, and cultural impacts of migration on home communities.

Remittances—money that immigrants send home from wages earned abroad— constitute the single largest economic impact of U.S. immigration on Mexico. Each year, Mexicans living in the United States send home between $6 billion and $8 billion—making remittances Mexico's third largest source of foreign revenue, behind oil and tourism.[41] However, studies of Mexican remittances show that the impacts of remittances depend heavily on the nature of migrant sending communities, especially the intensity of the sending community's migration experience, the length and frequency of migration, and whether the home community is urban or rural.

First, migrant sending communities are concentrated in a few areas of Mexico, just as receiving communities are concentrated in the United States—a phenomenon that seems to affirm the existence of migrant networks. The concentration of migrant sending communities means that the effect of remittances is also concentrated. Although 62 percent of Mexican municipalities have some experience with migration to the United States, relatively few (only 4.5 percent) have intense levels of migration. Migratory activity is more intense the more community members participate. Roughly half of Mexican municipalities that experience intense migratory activity are found in only three states: Jalisco, Michoacán, and Zacatecas, and remittances to these states account for a large share of the national total.[42] Rodolfo Garcia Zamora, a migration expert at the Autonomous University of Zacatecas, estimated that his state received about $1 million in remittances daily.[43] Because migratory experiences are so concentrated, studies on remittances tend to focus on individual communities, making it difficult to generalize about the national impact of migrant remittances.

Some analysts have suggested that more intense migratory activities lead communities to become economically dependent on remittances. Differences in home communities' consumption and investment behavior, however, mean the evidence for this statement is mixed. According to a study by El Colegio de la Frontera Norte and Pomona University researchers, an estimated 55 percent of remittances are used for consumption and 21 percent for savings and investment.[44] Communities that spend money from remittances on current consumption needs—such as food, clothing, or fiestas—may risk becoming dependent on migrant remittances in order to maintain relative income levels and standards of living. Communities that save or invest money from remittances into productive activities—such as education, urban infrastructure, or agricultural equipment—are perceived to be less dependent on remittances and more likely to progress in economic development. However, some remittance spending behavior is ambiguous. Many families use remittances to expand or improve their homes, adding electricity and plumbing or decorative embellishments. Although some would maintain that home improvement is merely consumption, others would argue that it is actually productive investment that will ultimately contribute to economic development.

Remittance spending behavior is strongly related to the duration and frequency of migratory activity. Many migrants make repeated trips between the United States and Mexico, establishing cycles of income generation through remittances and returns. When remittances occur regularly, home communities may view the money transfers as a secure source of income and therefore can plan to invest in longer-term, productive activities. However, remittances that occur more sporadically constitute less secure sources of income for home communities. In this case, families may be more likely to spend the money on current consumption needs.

Remittance spending behavior is also linked to the urban or rural setting of the home community. The U.S.-Mexico Binational Study reports that, "In the cases of most intense and semi-intense migration, rural municipalities predominate over urban ones, although there is migration from practically all the municipalities that have urban populations."[45] Some argue that urban communities are more likely to spend remittances on imported goods, contributing to the country's foreign debt, while rural communities are more likely to spend remittances on domestic products, contributing to the country's economic growth. In recent years researchers have observed an increase in the number of migrants from urban areas relative to their rural counterparts, which many attribute to unemployment in cities caused by the peso devaluation and subsequent economic problems during the mid-1990s.

Remittances are likely to decline in both size and frequency from the time a Mexican becomes a permanent U.S. resident. The U.S. government's policy of tightening border controls during the 1990s made return migration to Mexico more difficult, upsetting regular flows of remittances and giving Mexicans already living in the United States greater incentive to become permanent residents. More recently, Mexican President Fox has tried to facilitate money transfers from the United States. In response to complaints about the costs of sending money through remittance companies by Mexicans living in the United States, Mexican presidential advisor Juan Hernandez began negotiations with the U.S. National Organization of Credit Unions, saying, "we are considering new technologies offering more security, speed and economy."[46]

In every sending community, migration has a significant impact in areas beyond the economic sector, particularly social and cultural institutions. In communities with a long tradition of migratory activity, migration may become a "rite of passage" for men coming of age. Because migrants are often motivated by potential gains in relative income (many migrants hold jobs before they leave, so unemployment is not a motivating factor in their decision), their absence creates a need to restructure the labor force of the local economy. Sending communities lose young men during their most productive years as laborers, so women often take over traditionally male dominated roles such as running the family business in addition to maintaining their normal activities.

The departure of husbands and fathers may also create friction at the family level, as traditional roles change and cultural expectations are challenged. It is common for this friction to cause families to disintegrate, resulting in new psychological and social disorders. Studies on sending communities have shown that the absence of husbands and fathers lowers birth rates, as well.

The political implications of the demographic changes because of migration are discouraging. Some scholars have suggested that "because some communities are closely linked to international migration processes, there are perceptions and expectations of another kind that have little to do with local living conditions in the communities." They note further that, in sending communities, "It is common for the young people with the most initiative to leave, with the result that communities

Root Causes of International Migration

Why do people migrate from one country to another? Scholars point to changes in the world economy, as well as to "push factors" such as low wages and "pull factors" such as the demand for skilled labor. They also look at a range of individual incentives, including both personal and household economic welfare. As described below, their work makes clear that U.S. immigration policy is only one part of a complex story: potential immigrants respond not only to changes in American policy, but also to changes in their countries of origin and in the world economy.

Economic Theories on Why Migration Begins

Neoclassical economic theory suggests that migration between countries "is caused by geographic differences in the supply of and demand for labor."[1] For example, imagine two countries, A and B. Country A has a relatively abundant supply of labor, so wages are low. Meanwhile Country B has less labor but a relatively abundant supply of capital (raw materials, factories, equipment, or other material resources). In order to make use of this capital, Country B requires more labor than it is able to supply domestically, which results in relatively high wages. Workers from Country A, seeking to maximize their income, will move to Country B, where they can earn a higher wage. As workers leave Country A, the supply of labor there decreases and wages rise. At the same time, the demand for labor in Country B falls as workers from Country A enter the market, causing wages in Country B to stop rising. International migration, therefore, equalizes wages between countries, until they reflect only the costs of movement (such as transportation or psychological hardship).

Of course, not everyone in Country A is equally likely to move, even if wages are higher in Country B. Neoclassical economic theory expects that individual cost-benefit calculations help to regulate migration flows. People consider how they might benefit from higher wages, skills training, or education in the new country, or from keeping up ties with family members who have already migrated. They weigh these expected benefits against expected costs, including the costs of traveling and finding a new job, learning a new language and culture, and cutting ties with the home community. Presumably, individuals whose calculations yield a net benefit will decide to migrate. In this way, microlevel migration decisions affect macro-level migration patterns: the more individuals expect to benefit from migration, the larger the flow will be between countries.

Although neoclassical theory has strong economic arguments, it exhibits two major weaknesses when applied to real migration situations. First, given the large disparities in income, wages, and general welfare that exist between countries, neoclassical theory predicts much larger migration flows than actually occur. Second, neoclassical economic theory excludes political considerations, which, in reality, are major determinants of restrictive admissions policies and other constraints on mobility.[2] For instance, governments in receiving countries may choose to tailor immigration policies that encourage some types of migrants—highly skilled migrants, for instance—while discouraging others. Governments in sending countries may also try to keep migrants at home, by raising wages through economic development or other kinds of programs.

In response to these weaknesses in neoclassical economic theory, the "new economics of migration" looks not at individuals but at groups of people—usually families or households. As they calculate the expected benefits and costs of migration, these households consider not only labor market indicators, such as wages and unemployment rates, but also insurance, futures, and capital markets that may minimize the risk of economic failure. As one study describes: "In developed countries, risks to household income are generally minimized through private insurance markets or governmental programs, but in developing countries these institutional mechanisms for managing risk are imperfect, absent, or inaccessible to poor families, giving them incentives to diversify risks through migration."[3] For example, in developed countries, families who rely on agriculture for income insure their crops against risks of drought, flooding, or other events that would destroy the harvest. But "if crop insurance is not available, families have an incentive to self-insure by sending one or more workers abroad to remit earnings home, thereby guaranteeing family income even if the harvest fails."[4]

This theory also argues that income inequality motivates migration. A household may seek to improve its income not only in absolute terms, but also in relation to the incomes of other households in the community, by sending a worker abroad. For this reason, economic development within sending countries does not necessarily reduce pressures for international migration. In places where the income of middle-class households increases because of economic development, the relative deprivation of poor households increases, creating a greater propensity for poor households to migrate.

The "new economics of migration" theory thus offers two significant policy prescriptions. First, government policies and programs that affect insurance, futures, and capital markets—particularly unemployment insurance—can influence migration rates. Second, governments can alter households' incentives to migrate through policies that shape income distribution, especially by reducing inequality.[5]

Another way of understanding migration is to look, not at the immigrants' decisions to migrate, but at the receiving country's reasons for encouraging immigration. The segmented or dual labor market theory argues that advanced industrial economies are divided between a highly productive capital-intensive primary sector and a less productive labor-intensive secondary sector. In simpler terms, these economies exhibit a stark divide between primary white-collar office jobs and secondary blue-collar jobs. These jobs differ not only in wages, but also in social status. Those who have higher status jobs expect their wages to reflect that status. Thus, "wages must be increased proportionately throughout the job hierarchy in order to keep them in line with social expectations."[6] Even if there is high demand for unskilled laborers, such as farmworkers, in an advanced industrial economy, their position at the bottom of the job hierarchy prevents them from earning significantly higher wages.

Because workers are motivated not only by wages but also by social status, few are willing to work at the bottom of the job hierarchy, where there is little opportunity for advancement.[7] These jobs are also undesirable because they demand fewer skills and less training: workers in these jobs are more interchangeable, so they are the first to be laid off in tough economic times. Native workers, therefore, will try to avoid working in the secondary labor market. This creates opportunities for immigrants: they view jobs simply as a way to earn income, and, as foreigners, have fewer choices and are less concerned with social status or prestige.

Changes in the demographics of domestic workers have also created a structural demand for foreign workers in developed countries. Women and teenagers formerly supplied most labor for low-wage, low-status, unstable jobs. Historically, women's principal social identity was not tied to employment but to the family. Consequently, women "were willing to put up with low wages and instability because they viewed the work as transient and the earnings as supplemental."[8] Likewise, teenagers tended to view jobs in the secondary sector not as their permanent social identity but as the means to gain experience or earn extra money. However, in advanced industrial societies, women now pursue careers for social status as well as income. Birth rates are lower, and fewer teenagers enter the workforce because they spend more years earning a formal education. These changes reduce the domestic supply of labor in the secondary sector, and therefore add to the structural demand for immigrants in advanced industrial economies.

Countries might also attract immigration, not just to fulfill the labor needs of the secondary market, but as an outgrowth of global market trends. World systems theory describes the world market as made up of concentric circles, including core industrialized countries and less developed, "peripheral" countries. Core industrialized countries are those with the most economic power, power that was often acquired by colonization or military superiority. Peripheral countries are those that have been slower to develop, and thus are dependent on the raw materials they can export to core countries. As capitalism expands outward from core countries, it draws increasingly on resources in the periphery, incorporating less-developed countries into the global market. This results in changes in the economy of peripheral countries that generates a flow of migrants, first to cities, and then abroad. In this way, world systems theory views migration not as an equalizing force between countries with labor market imbalances but as a reinforcement of inequality between core and peripheral countries.

These four theories—neoclassical economics, the "new economics of migration," segmented or dual labor market theory, and world systems theory—explain how international migration begins or how the process is initiated. How they play themselves out, however, depends on how government policy interacts with these economic processes. A comparison of immigration policy in the United States and Canada can illustrate this idea. In the United States, the emphasis on family reunification leads to an immigration process shaped much more by "push" factors—the economic calculations of potential immigrants, based on the extent to which their individual or family welfare might be improved by immigrants. By contrast, in Canada, the emphasis on skilled labor migration leads to an immigration process shaped more by "pull" factors: by government attempts to select among potential immigrants to address specific shortages in the Canadian labor market.

Social Theories on Why Migration Continues

Three additional theories explain how certain conditions perpetuate international migration patterns over time: network theory, the theory of cumulative causation, and migration systems theory. As defined by sociologist Joaquìn Arango, migration networks are "sets of interpersonal relations that link migrants or returned migrants with relatives, friends or fellow countrymen at home."[9] Each migrant that communicates with his or her home community conveys information about the country of destination—such as employment opportunities, housing options, transportation, and cultural dynamics—that reduces the costs and uncertainty of migrating for those at home. This increases the likelihood that they will follow a similar path. Migrant networks help explain the concentration of immigrants in particular regions.

Links between individual migrants create a multiplier effect. These personal connections function as social capital, so that as migrant networks grow the costs of migration decline and, by comparison, the benefits increase. Social capital may even generate institutions that further facilitate international movement, institutions that can range from smuggling rings to humanitarian or immigrant advocacy organizations. Eventually, a migration network may become so elaborate and institutionalized that it becomes "progressively independent of the factors that originally caused it, be they structural or individual."[10] In this sense, migration networks are often self-sustaining.

The theory of cumulative causation also addresses this phenomenon of self-sustaining migration. This theory holds that each act of migration makes additional movement more likely over time by changing the socioeconomic context of communities of origin and destination. When migrants leave their home community, they change the job market, social connections, and other factors that influence potential migrants' decisions. Likewise, when migrants arrive in a new community, they alter the socioeconomic context that will influence their own, and others', decisions.

International migration can create changes in six kinds of socioeconomic factors that cause migration flows. These are income distribution or relative deprivation, land distribution, the displacement of labor through mechanization or improvements in technology, unequal education and skill levels, the development of a culture of migration, and the stigmatization of jobs usually performed by immigrants. For instance, those who have migrated and returned home are very likely to migrate again, and they reduce the costs and uncertainty of migrating for others in their community. As more members of the community migrate, the values associated with migration become ingrained in the culture of the community, and "migration becomes a rite of passage."[11]

Migration systems theory combines and elaborates explanations offered by world systems theory, network theory, and the theory of cumulative causation. It states that, as migration trends accumulate, form institutions, and stabilize over time, a migration system develops in which a core receiving region is linked to a set of specific countries that send exceptionally large flows of immigrants.[12] The United States can be characterized as a core receiving region linked through relatively intense exchanges of goods, capital, and people with specific countries in Latin America and the Caribbean. Western Europe also can be characterized as a core receiving region for large immigration flows from specific countries in eastern Europe and Africa.

In general these theories depict migration as a dynamic process, one that it is strongly related to inequality, whether in wages, income, insurance markets, job hierarchies, or global economic power. The theories provide a variety of ways of thinking about migration and its causes, many of which build on or reinforce one another. However, they do not always result in compatible policy implications. For example, a government seeking to deter immigration might infer from the "new economics of migration" theory that it should support economic development in sending countries by increasing foreign aid packages and promoting investment by U.S. firms. But the world systems theory implies that capital investment strengthens ties between core and peripheral countries that actually encourages immigration.

Because it is so difficult to discern the true cause of international migration, governments place less emphasis on policies that influence the volume or direction of migration flows and instead focus on managing what seem to be inevitable, unpredictable migration flows. This approach makes admissions policies the primary tools for managing immigration. The U.S. government's emphasis on border controls and visa quotas in its immigration policy is a prime example of such management techniques. Although this approach appears to be largely in reaction to immigration trends, government leaders must consider that admissions policies also shape future migration flows.[13] Policy-makers around the world must recognize that, "Statements about the impact of immigration on an economy are necessarily based on studies of the experience of the economy with immigration in the past. Yet the set of immigrants observed in the economy were selected according to former immigration policy." [14]

1. Douglas S. Massey et al., "Theories of International Migration: A Review and Appraisal," *Population and Development Review* 19(3), September 1993, 433.
2. Joaquìn Arango, "Explaining Migration: A Critical View," *International Social Science Journal,* September 2000, 286.
3. Massey et al., "Theories of International Migration," 436.
4. Ibid., 437.
5. Ibid., 440.
6. Ibid., 441.
7. Ibid.
8. Ibid., 443.
9. Arango, "Explaining Migration," 291.
10. Massey et al., "Theories of International Migration," 450.
11. Ibid., 453.
12. Ibid., 454.
13. Arango, "Explaining Migration," 293.
14. Alan G. Green and David A. Green, "Canadian Immigration Policy: The Effectiveness of the Point System and Other Instruments," *Canadian Journal of Economics,* November 1995, 1007.

lose their current and potential leaders, and their capacity for interaction with the exterior is also weakened." [47]

Again, recent U.S. policies to tighten border controls have exacerbated the social costs of migration for sending communities. With *coyotes* demanding higher fees, the likelihood of successful crossing diminished, and the increasing availability of legal residency permits, the cyclical nature of migration has slowed. Migration to the United States has become more permanent, and returns to home communities in Mexico less frequent. The level of participation has also expanded from single men to women and sometimes entire families, leaving some sending communities largely vacant. In the village of Casa Blanca in the state of Zacatecas, for example, freshly painted houses and restored churches (improvements funded by migrant remittances) stand empty since nearly 1,800 of the village's 2,200 residents have migrated to the United States during the last ten years. [48]

Still, the Mexican government's enthusiastic welcome of returning migrants has helped to keep local politics alive. Stopping at a border checkpoint in Arizona just after taking office in December 2000, President Fox called Mexican migrants "heroes."[49] By emphasizing that Mexican society values the contributions of its migrant workers, Mexican policy-makers encourage nationals living abroad to remain active participants in their home communities. The government recently guaranteed dual citizenship for Mexican nationals living abroad, encouraging them to maintain their political participation by voting with absentee ballots. As a result of this policy, many Mexican politicians campaign in the United States. "Governor Ricardo Monreal of Zacatecas says he takes at least 14 trips each year to the United States, principally to California and Chicago, which have the largest Zacatecas migrant communities," according to a *New York Times* report. In one instance a Mexican who had lived in the United States for twenty-five years and become a successful tomato grower decided to run for mayor in his native town of Jerez, which receives an estimated $150,000 per day in remittances. Andres Bermudez would be the first U.S. resident to serve as mayor of a Mexican municipality if elected. "I was able to make it, but I know so many people who go to the United States and never get anywhere," said the candidate. "I want to bring jobs here so that people will stop leaving."[50]

Converging Policy Models: A Comparative Analysis of U.S. and European Immigration Policies

Among the developed or industrialized countries, immigration policies share broad similarities despite variation in the type and volume of immigration to each country. The OECD reports that the immigration policies of its member countries exhibit five common features: "acceptance of foreigners to visit for a short period of time for business or tourism purposes (sometimes requiring a visa); rules that allow spouses and close relatives of citizens to enter the country on a permanent basis (family reunion); the possibility for individuals who claim social and political persecution in their country to apply for asylum (asylum seekers); mechanisms for individuals to enter largely for the purpose of employment and business ('skill-based' migration); and naturalisation rules that enable foreign citizens to acquire national citizenship."[51]

The fundamental distinction between the immigration policies of European Union (EU) member states and those of the United States is the traditional belief among EU members that they are *not* countries of immigration. While the United States, Canada, and Australia embrace immigration as an essential part of their nations' founding and economic development, national identities in Europe are based more on common ethnic heritage to which immigrants (outsiders) do not belong. Indeed, much of Europe's economic development occurred during a long period of emigration that began in the eighteenth century, peaked with the Industrial Revolution, and tapered off in the 1960s: from 1840 to 1930, roughly 60 million Europeans emigrated, mostly to the United States.[52] Most of Europe's modern history was characterized by net emigration; it was only after the 1950s that this trend reversed so that by the 1990s all EU countries were experiencing net immigration.[53]

This migration transition occurred during Europe's reconstruction following World War II as immigrants from the South—particularly Turkey and former African colonies—filled the labor shortages of Western industrialized countries that had lost much of their workforce to the war. These immigrants were admitted under temporary worker programs (usually to fill low-skill, low-wage, low-status jobs), which denied them the rights to apply for full citizenship or bring family members from home. When the oil crisis of 1973–1974 ended Europe's recruitment of third-country nationals,[54] governments had difficulty sending "temporary" migrants home and suddenly confronted the problem of integrating substantial immigrant communities into fairly insular societies. One Swiss official bluntly exclaimed, "We asked for workers—and we got people instead."[55] At the same time, immigrants continued to arrive under generous family reunification and humanitarian policies, or—as legal venues closed—illegally.

By the 1990s the collapse of the Soviet bloc led many Europeans to fear uncontrollable mass influxes of immigrants (mostly religious and ethnic minorities) from eastern Europe and the former Soviet Union. In this way, Europe seemed to face migration pressures from both the East and South: "Worries began to be voiced over the apparent threat of 'mass' east-west migration, worries which only added to what was already a growing sense of anxiety over rising numbers of asylum-seekers and illegal immigrants from the 'South.'"[56] Combined with anxiety over Europe's economic integration, the threat of influxes of foreigners fueled xenophobic nationalism and anti-immigrant rhetoric in right-wing politics. Most notably, Jean-Marie Le Pen, leader of France's National Front Party *(le Front*

National), warned that France was becoming an "Islamic nation" and the "international power and influence of world Jewry,"[57] and proposed that foreigners should be segregated from natives within the same territory by creating separate school systems, social security systems, and other "ghettoizing" programs.[58] With an agenda decidedly against immigrant integration, Le Pen won 17 percent of the votes cast in the first round of the 2002 presidential election, displacing Prime Minister Lionel Jospin to face but eventually lose to incumbent President Jacques Chirac in the final round.

In the early 1990s this anti-immigrant climate in Europe roughly matched sentiments in the United States. The rhetoric of the extreme right, though in the minority, pushed more moderate politicians to call for lower admissions levels, stronger enforcement against illegal immigration, and improved integration of legal immigrants. According to one analyst, most EU member states pursued a dual-track approach: "on the one hand working with member states to curb both authorized and unauthorized entry into EC/EU territory and, on the other, promoting the integration of non-EU foreign population already legally resident."[59]

However, immigration policy in Europe also took on a dimension entirely distinct from what was happening in the United States: regional cooperation in the formation of the European Union. The Treaty of Rome had established the European Economic Community[60] in 1957 (the predecessor to the EU), creating a common market that ensured the free movement of goods, services, persons, and capital among member states. As a result of this customs union, citizens of member states could migrate freely within the EEC by 1970. The Single European Act (SEA), which took effect in 1987, further developed the common market and reinforced the freedom of movement among member states in Article 8a, defining an "internal market" as "an area without internal frontiers." By defining this internal market, the Europeans had implied the existence of external frontiers. In fact, during discussions of the SEA, member states also began deliberating the Schengen Agreement, which "envisaged the removal of intra-EC borders in exchange for strengthening the region's external borders."[61]

Loosened controls on internal migration, however, fortified Europe's borders against immigration by third-country nationals. "The coincidence in timing of the wish to remove the common physical borders in Western Europe with that to reduce the rapidly growing flow of immigration has meant that the first moves taken to coordinate the immigration policies of the EU member states came across as the first steps on the road to building 'Fortress Europe,' " wrote one economist.[62] Un-

der the pretext of eliminating internal frontiers and harmonizing migration policies, the series of conventions that took effect during the 1990s required third-
country nationals to meet the criteria of all signatory countries in order to obtain
entry. Before, immigrants who were denied entry in France, for example, could still
seek admission in Germany. Now, however, if denied at the country of arrival, immigrants may not enter through any other signatory country.

The Maastrict Treaty, deemed "the most important building block in the European structure since the Treaty of Rome,"[63] brought European politics into line
with economics at the supranational level, including immigration policy. Adopted
in 1991 and entered into force in 1993, the Maastrict Treaty—also known as the
Treaty on European Union (TEU)—provided for a common visa policy at the European Community level. Article 100c of the TEU stipulated that the executive and
legislative bodies of the European Union, acting in consultation with each other,
"shall determine the third countries whose nationals must be in possession of a
visa when crossing the external borders of the Member States."[64] All other immigration and related matters remained at the intergovernmental level, including (1)
asylum policy, (2) external border crossings, (3) conditions of immigrants' entry
and residence, including family reunion and illegal residence, (4) combating drug
addiction, (5) combating fraud on an international scale, (6) judicial cooperation in
civil matters, (7) judicial cooperation in criminal matters, (8) customs cooperation,
and (9) police cooperation.[65] Perhaps more important than the treaty's actual provisions was the opening it created for increasing coordination and work toward
common immigration policies in the future.

The Schengen Convention (a supplemented version of the 1985 Agreement)
covers many of these areas of "common interest" by providing for: "dismantling
internal border controls on the movement of goods and persons (irrespective of
nationality) between contracting parties; establishment of common external borders; adoption of a common visa policy for short- and long-term stays by nationals of third countries; stronger internal controls (including procedures for the issuance of residence permits, a reporting mechanism for inadmissible aliens, and
mutual cooperation and enforcement in criminal matters); and the creation of a
common *Schengen Information System* (SIS) [a central shared database on entrants
into any member state. . . ."[66] Implemented beginning in 1995, the Schengen
Convention's major impact has been to limit the opportunities for third-country
nationals to enter Europe by creating a common external border and coordinating
admissions criteria.

Taken in conjunction with the Dublin Convention coordinating asylum procedures, the Schengen Convention also tightens asylum seekers' access to protection in Europe. The Dublin Convention, which took effect in 1997, sought to prevent a phenomenon known as "refugees in orbit," where asylum seekers either submitted applications for protection in multiple European countries, or were bounced around from one European state to the next as each government denied responsibility for handling the case. By designing a set of common criteria to determine which state is responsible for processing an individual's claim of refugee status, the Dublin Convention complements the Schengen restriction that "[r]efusal in one country means refusal in all the countries who have signed either of the two conventions."[67] Like the Schengen Convention, the Dublin Convention allowed each nation to maintain its own system of adjudications but created a regional mechanism to "regulate relations between the member-states by designating their mutual obligations."[68] The criteria for determining state responsibility, in order of priority, generally include: the presence of close family members, issuance of a residence permit or entry visa, the state of first entry in cases of illegal entry, or the state where the asylum application is first lodged.[69]

Ironically, the strongest instrument to coordinate EU immigration and asylum policy entered into force in the midst of the NATO bombing campaign in Kosovo on May 1, 1999. The Amsterdam Treaty brought the provisions of the Schengen and Dublin conventions in line with the Maastrict Treaty, elevating previously intergovernmental issues of "common interest"—asylum policy, the crossing of external borders, conditions of immigrants' entry and residence, judicial cooperation, and customs cooperation—to the supranational level of governance. The treaty aims to bring immigration and asylum policy into the scope of community activity by 2004, creating a common immigration and asylum policy for the twelve participating EU states.

While these conventions were being negotiated, events on the ground posed a grave challenge to the EU's spirit of cooperation on immigration and asylum issues. "The lack of a common approach forced EU member states to take unilateral action while embarking on a new phase of activity which is said to be intended to lead to collective policy-making".[70] First in the Yugoslav province of Bosnia and then in the province of Kosovo, civil conflict gave way to mass atrocities, "ethnic cleansing," acts of genocide, and other human rights abuses. Millions of people from these provinces were displaced as a result, fleeing to neighboring countries such as Macedonia and Hungary, and beyond to EU member states and the United States.

When war erupted in Bosnia-Herzegovina in 1992, the disintegration of the Federal Republic of Yugoslavia had already attracted United Nations (UN) peacekeeping forces, European and U.S. mediators, and human rights monitors to Slovenia and Croatia. As news of serious human rights abuses reached Western governments, the most "immediate concern for Europeans . . . was the direct effect the war was beginning to have on them through the flow of refugees."[71] The war produced the largest flow of refugees in Europe since World War II; between July 1992 and April 1994 roughly 700,000 refugees from Yugoslavia were reported across western and eastern Europe, as well as Russia, with nearly half in Germany alone.

Uneasy with the notion of intervening in an internal conflict to defend human rights, and reluctant to host large numbers of refugees, Europeans balked at requests to stop the violence with military force and evaded German demands to set quotas for accepting refugees. Instead, EU leaders focused on sending human rights monitors, humanitarian relief organizations, and UN peacekeepers to create "safe havens" within the region. It was only after the fall of one such "safe haven," Srebrenica, and the massacre of an estimated 6,000 Bosnian Muslims, that U.S. officials urged the North Atlantic Treaty Organization (NATO) to conduct air strikes against Bosnian Serb forces. Serb leaders finally ended the war after peace talks in Dayton, Ohio, in 1995.[72]

The Bosnian experience left Western powers on the alert for ethnic conflict, human rights abuses, and other causes of forced migration in the former Yugoslavia. Drawing from "lessons learned" in Bosnia, European and American officials vowed to prevent such atrocities in the future. Yet by 1998, the media and human rights organizations were reporting grave abuses in fighting between the Kosovo Liberation Army and Serb soldiers. The failure of the Rambouillet peace talks in March 1999 was followed by reports of genocide and massive internal displacement in Kosovo. Television footage of ethnic Albanians packed into trains recalled images of Nazi brutality during the Holocaust. Again, NATO became the venue for European cooperation. On March 24, 1999, NATO began a series of air strikes against Serb forces in Kosovo, targeting military bunkers, weapons stockpiles, and communication infrastructure. The level of displacement in the region soared following the NATO bombings. By one estimate, almost the entire Kosovar Albanian population—about 1.8 million people—was displaced, with at least half crossing international borders in search of refuge while the remainder sought protection inside the province or was unable to flee across Kosovo's border.[73]

The EU states maintained that the reception of the refugees close to home was the optimal solution—a position supported by the United Nations High Commissioner for Refugees (UNHCR). As the crisis unfolded, nongovernmental organizations aided by NATO transport operated large refugee camps just inside the borders of Macedonia and Albania. Outside the camps, refugees joined relatives in neighboring countries, particularly Albania and Macedonia. Twelve days after the NATO bombing campaign began, at least 262,000 Kosovar refugees had arrived in Albania and at least 120,000 had arrived in Macedonia.[74] As the influx continued, the governments of both countries expressed concern that they did not have the resources to provide adequate protection and assistance to the refugee population.

The EU member states pledged financial assistance to Kosovo's neighboring states but insisted that "they could collectively accept only up to 100,000 of the 1,000,000 or more displaced persons."[75] For example, France pledged $40 million in aid to Kosovo's neighboring states and agreed to admit between 5,000 and 10,000 Kosovo refugees under the UNHCR's Humanitarian Evacuation Programme. The United Kingdom, after considerable pressure from UNHCR, agreed to take in 1,000 Kosovo refugees a week. The United States first considered accepting 20,000 refugees on the condition that they be sheltered at the U.S. naval base in Guantanamo, Cuba, where they would not be eligible to apply for asylum. However, after strong opposition from UNHCR, academics, and NGOs, the government agreed to airlift several thousand Kosovo refugees to Fort Dix, New Jersey, where they would remain under temporary protection unless they could identify relatives already living legally in the country. Ultimately, the United State resettled more than 14,000 Kosovo refugees in 1999.[76]

The United States' leading role in ending conflicts in both Bosnia and Kosovo illustrates the importance of migration abroad to American interests in global security and respect for human rights. European responses to refugee crises in the former Yugoslavia were critical factors in the U.S. decision to intervene, and military cooperation through NATO tested the strength of the alliance. After NATO air strikes ended with Serbia's surrender, Europeans and Americans continued to cooperate to aid Kosovar Albanians' repatriation and to build institutions that would prevent future conflict in the region through the UN mission in Kosovo.

The U.S. Role in International Refugee Law and Policy

The United States has been a global superpower since the inception of the international refugee regime in the aftermath of World War II. It played a key role in drafting the human rights documents that formed the backdrop to the 1951 Convention Relating to the Status of Refugees and has continued to be an important figure in the UN Security Council, regional alliances, military operations, and other foreign policy–making activities relating to refugees. Throughout this history, the United States has shown a greater commitment to political and humanitarian approaches to refugee issues than to international law—a dynamic attributed most often to decisions in Congress—which has been perpetuated over the last decade, and which has often frustrated proponents of international law.

A minor case in point is the fact that the United States has "never acceded to the 1951 UN Refugee Convention, although in 1968 it acceded to its 1967 Protocol, thereby agreeing to accept most of the obligations in the 1951 Convention."[77] On the other hand, the United States is the perennial top donor to the UNHCR (the primary international agency for refugee protection and humanitarian relief), and accepted more refugees for resettlement between 1975 and 1999 than the rest of the world put together. In 1999 the United States donated $387.1 million to international refugee aid agencies, compared to $121.8 million given by Japan and $83.1 million by the European Commission.[78] Still, some analysts assert that the United States can afford to accept larger numbers of refugees and make greater donations, given the country's size and wealth. Although the U.S. contribution is largest in absolute terms, it ranks ninth in contributions per capita at $1.40 in 1999. By contrast, Norwegians contributed the most per capita to refugee aid at $12.55, followed by Denmark ($9.36) and Sweden ($7.19) in the same year. Likewise, the United States accepted far more refugees and asylum seekers between 1990 and 1999 than any other country: 1,088,700. Germany, the country with the most asylum applicants, accepted only 269,800 refugees and asylum seekers during this period, while Canada, which is considered to have a fairly generous refugee admissions policy, took in 314,800.[79]

The question of generosity is often framed as one of responsibility and, ultimately, a question of sovereignty. As the number of refugees worldwide soared in the mid-1990s, it became clear that the vast majority were concentrated in poor, developing countries.[80] By the end of 2000, the ratio of refugees to the host country population was highest in countries such as Jordan (1 to 3) and Guinea (1 to 19), whereas in the United States there was only one refugee per 572 American residents. Ratios similar to that of the United States are found in Canada, Germany, and the United Kingdom.[81] High concentrations of refugees have been shown to strain public services and social integration in host countries—a particularly heavy burden for already poor governments. Some analysts claim that the strain on host countries' resources detracts from their ability to provide adequate protection to refugee populations. In some cases, the strain is so great that it may set back the country's economic development, jeopardize its political stability, or even lead to civil or regional conflict.

Is the world's richest nation obliged to share greater responsibility for refugee populations? Is financial contribution enough, or should responsibility include receiving the refugees themselves? If so, how much? From where? And who should decide? The United States does not face these questions alone. The controversy over "burden sharing," sometimes euphemistically referred to as "responsibility sharing," touches all industrialized countries as they balance humanitarian goals against domestic interests. The refugee crisis in Kosovo in 1999 illustrated the challenge of "responsibility sharing": the bulk of the refugees remained in the poorer countries of southeast Europe, while the industrialized NATO countries contributed financial and logistical support and later airlifted selected groups of refugees for temporary protection. The United States justified the comparatively small number of Kosovar refugees that it accepted by arguing that refugees would want to remain in the Balkans, so that they could return home more easily once security was restored. In this spirit, the U.S. State Department's Bureau of Population, Refugees and Migration made an unprecedented decision to pay for transportation costs for any refugee who volunteered to return home.

This emphasis on refugee returns was not unique to the United States. It sparked controversy in the international refugee community during the 1990s. As refugees increasingly fled armed internal conflict rather than the political oppression of the cold war, the United States participated in decisions by the UN Security Council to send peacekeeping missions to quell violence and restore security, thus addressing the "root causes" of refugee flows. In theory, the enormous costs of employing thousands of personnel and supplying infrastructure and resources for each mission are less than the cost of war and refugee resettlement in host countries for the war's duration. The United Nations launched twenty-one new peacekeeping operations between 1988 and 1994, compared to only thirteen in the previous forty years.[82] Major peacekeeping operations in the 1990s occurred in Namibia, Central

America, Cambodia, Mozambique, Iraq-Kuwait, Bosnia-Hercegovina, Rwanda, Kosovo, Sierra Leone, and East Timor, among other nations. In most cases, international military or police forces, human rights monitors, and civilian administrators assisted the country's transition from war to peace, while humanitarian relief providers under the coordination of UNHCR facilitated refugees' repatriation.

However, in practice, the United States does not always support peacekeeping missions. In a 1991 UN peacekeeping mission to Somalia, several U.S. soldiers were killed by rebel factions, and television cameras recorded the body of one of the soldiers being dragged through the streets of Mogadishu. Since this incident, American political leaders recognized the public's low tolerance for U.S. casualties in humanitarian operations abroad, and U.S. troops have been noticeably absent from most international peacekeeping forces. The U.S. experience in Somalia heavily influenced its policy toward Rwanda as genocide unfolded there in 1994. As the crisis broke, the Clinton administration announced Presidential Decision Directive 25, which conditioned U.S. support of UN peacekeeping operations on whether the mission served U.S. national interests and enjoyed domestic support.[83]

This new policy delayed U.S. engagement in Rwanda. According to Kathleen Newland of the Migration Policy Institute, "The Security Council, with the United States in a leading role, repeatedly deflected calls from Secretary-General Boutros-Ghali to increase the UN presence in Rwanda in order to shield civilians from the ongoing massacres. . . . The policy of noninvolvement changed only in response to the refugee crisis that developed in July 1994." With more than one million refugees flooding camps just inside Zaire's border with Rwanda, President Bill Clinton, along with the vice president, chairman of the Joint Chiefs of Staff, national security advisor, and deputy secretary of defense announced on July 29th a commitment of nearly $500 million in relief aid and equipment, plus 2,000 U.S. soldiers to deliver it.[84]

The United States has faced criticism for this type of response to refugee crises in Rwanda and elsewhere. Many refugee advocates assert that providing humanitarian relief in complex emergencies is a Band-Aid solution that does not address the "root causes" of forced migration, namely human rights abuses and economic deprivation. Efforts to address "root causes" are aimed at preventing refugee flows, or stopping them once they have started, by enforcing international human rights standards, building or strengthening democratic governance structures, and aiding poor countries' economic development. The United States pursues democracy and economic development objectives primarily through the U.S. Agency for Interna-

International Aid for Afghanistan

When the U.S. military began a bombing campaign in Afghanistan on October 7, 2001, there were already more than 3.5 million Afghan refugees dispersed among neighboring countries and nearly one million people uprooted from their homes (called internally displaced persons, or IDPs) within Afghan borders. The former number alone made Afghans the single largest refugee group in the world, constituting 30 percent of the global refugee population. U.S. bombing raids and special forces operations in Afghanistan were just the latest events in more than two decades of tribal turmoil, civil strife, proxy wars, and drought. Before the U.S. attack, refugees fled the 1979 Soviet invasion of Afghanistan, the civil war that erupted in 1989 when the Soviets withdrew, the 1996 Taliban takeover, and persistent drought beginning in 1998, producing "generations of exodus"[1] in Afghan communities around the world. In each instance, the vast majority of Afghan refugees fled to neighbors Pakistan and Iran, so that each wave of flight put additional pressure on these nations that had already accepted so many. For much of this period, the United States "led the international community's response to the suffering of the Afghan people," contributing more than $1 billion in humanitarian assistance to Afghanistan since 1979.[2]

In the wake of the September 11 terrorist attacks, U.S. policies toward Afghanistan sought to balance military action against Al Qaeda and Taliban leaders with humanitarian relief to Afghan refugees and IDPs. Aid for displaced Afghans played a key role for three major reasons, in addition to purely altruistic considerations. First, as President George W. Bush and other administration officials repeatedly stated, U.S. attacks on Afghanistan were aimed at agents of terror and not the Afghan people or Muslims. By providing humanitarian assistance to Afghan civilians, the United States could defend its policies against accusations by some countries that it was conducting a war on Islam. Second, humanitarian assistance played a palliative role in relations with countries hosting large numbers of Afghan refugees, particularly Pakistan, whose cooperation was critical to U.S. success in the region. Relief aid to IDPs in Afghanistan may have averted large outflows into neighboring countries, while assistance to international and nongovernmental organizations contributed to the management of refugee populations in camps and other facilities, lessening the burden on host countries. Finally, humanitarian assistance was the first step in the reconstruction of a stable Afghanistan. By alleviating Afghans' suffering and managing refugees' movement in neighboring countries, the United States and other international actors could help create favorable conditions for repatriation and the rebuilding of a society free from terrorist ideology.

Not surprisingly, refugee flows followed the flight from battle during the U.S. assault on Afghanistan. By late November 2001 the conflict had generated an estimated 200,000 new IDPs and at least 135,000 new refugees to Pakistan.

At the same time, once the U.S.-backed Northern Alliance and American forces established control of Afghan territory, region by region, many refugees returned from their host countries. While thousands of refugees fled Kandahar for Pakistan, thousands returned to western Afghanistan from Iran. Repatriation from Iran surpassed expectations so much that some refugee advocates feared the Iranian government was forcibly returning Afghans in violation of international law.[3]

As mass population movements and military operations continued, the United States, in cooperation with the World Food Program, began emergency food distribution activities in an effort to avert starvation among the displaced during the harsh Afghan winter. While some food shipments could be distributed by land, the lack of security throughout most of the country prevented many aid agencies from operating effectively inside Afghanistan. As a short-term solution, the U.S. Department of Defense conducted a series of airdrops of humanitarian daily rations, dropping nearly two million packages in targeted locations by late November 2001.

However, the longer-term questions about providing aid for Afghanistan's reconstruction and development were less easily resolved. Specifically, questions arose about who should fund Afghanistan's reconstruction effort, whether an international peacekeeping force was needed to ensure security or whether funding for Afghan security forces was sufficient, and, if an international peacekeeping force was agreed upon, which nations should lead it.

At the outset of the crisis (on October 4, 2001), President Bush announced that the United States would contribute $320 million in humanitarian assistance for Afghanistan and neighboring states. This package included $25 million to assist Pakistan, Iran, Tajikistan, Uzbekistan, and Turkmenistan in receiving potentially large numbers of Afghan refugees, with the remaining $295 million going to aid providers such as the United Nations High Commissioner for Refugees, International Committee of the Red Cross, and nongovernmental organizations.[4] When international donors gathered for a two-day conference in January 2002 to raise the estimated $10 billion needed to rebuild Afghanistan over the next five years, U.S. Secretary of State Colin L. Powell pledged $296 million, including $111 million leftover from the October package. This amount fell below levels of funding typically offered by the United States, signaling the Bush administration's reluctance to engage in nation-building.[5] According to the *New York Times*, "administration officials have repeatedly emphasized that because Washington has borne the bulk of the cost of the war against the Taliban, it expects other nations to play a greater role in peacekeeping and rebuilding."[6]

This stance meant that the Bush administration opposed U.S. troops leading any peacekeeping force. In testimony before the Senate Foreign Relations Committee, Richard N. Haass, who coordinated the State Department's efforts on peacekeeping in Afghanistan, depicted the multinational force operating there in December 2001 as a "gap filler" confined to Kabul until an Afghan security force could be trained. He and other analysts feared that U.S. peacekeepers and U.S. troops searching for Al Qaeda members may be indistinguishable and become targets of unreconciled Afghans. "Americans would be exposed to a disproportionate amount of animosity," said Gary Dempsey, a foreign policy analyst at the Cato Institute.[7]

Despite this political aversion to nation-building and peacekeeping responsibilities in Afghanistan, U.S. policy analysts recognize that "the United States has a vital interest and an essential role to play in Afghanistan's future." Most believe that stable economic, political, and security conditions will prevent the growth of terrorist groups. As Teresita Schaffer, director of South Asia programs at the Center for Strategic and International Studies and a former State Department official, explained: "If we're at all serious about Afghanistan not becoming again a haven for terrorists, there has to be some kind of orderly government there—because it was the lack of order that made it an attractive place for bin Laden in the first place."[8]

---

1. Peter Maass, "How a Camp Becomes a City," *New York Times Magazine*, November 18, 2001, 6.

2. U.S. Department of State, "U.S. Assistance to the Afghan People," *Fact Sheet*, October 4, 2001. See http://www.state.gov/p/sa/rls/fs/5254.htm

3. Peter Baker and Alan Sipress, "Concern Grows Over Refugees; Aid Groups Protest Forced Returns, Lack of Foreign Security," *Washington Post*, December 1, 2001, A16.

4. U.S. Department of State, "U.S. Assistance to the Afghan People."

5. Kenneth Jost, "Rebuilding Afghanistan," *CQ Researcher*, December 21, 2001, 1049.

6. Todd S. Purdum and Howard W. French, "A Nation Challenged: Donors; U.S. Makes Pledge for $300 Million in Aid to Afghans," *New York Times*, January 21, 2002, A1.

7. Jost, "Rebuilding Afghanistan," 1047, 1159.

8. Ibid, 1050.

tional Development (USAID), as well as by supporting the World Bank and United Nations Development Program (UNDP).

The U.S. commitment to enforcing human rights standards remains tied to political considerations. This pleases protectors of sovereignty but frustrates proponents of international law. This policy of enforcing human rights only when the situation affects national interests explains the United States' very different responses to the human rights violations that caused massive refugee flows out of Kosovo and Sierra Leone. Citing the potential for refugee flows to destabilize parts of Europe, including U.S. allies, policy-makers announced that swift and firm intervention in Kosovo was in the U.S. national interest. As a result, American military and diplomatic corps were able to seek a political solution to end human rights violations in the region. During the same period, human rights abuses in Sierra Leone produced shocking images of refugees with severed limbs and mutilated faces. Yet the crisis was deemed not to threaten U.S. national interests and received only minor attention from U.S. policy-makers.

For these reasons, the U.S. role in international refugee law and policy remains ambiguous. On one hand, the United States has consistently donated the most aid to refugee agencies and admitted the largest numbers of refugees for resettlement and asylum. On the other hand, U.S. foreign policies on intervention, international law, and human rights have not always served the best interests of refugees.

Notes

1. David M. Reimers and Harold Troper, "Canadian and American Immigration Policy since 1945," in Barry R. Chiswick, ed., *Immigration, Language, and Ethnicity: Canada and the United States* (Washington, D.C.: AEI Press, 1992), 15.

2. Organization for Economic Cooperation and Development (OECD), *Trends in International Migration*, 2000, 161.

3. See http://www.census.gov/population/estimates/nation/nativity/fbtab001.txt

4. OECD, *Trends in International Migration*, 157.

5. Nathan Glazer, ed., *Clamor at the Gates: The New American Immigration* (San Francisco: IES Press, 1985).

6. OECD, *Trends in International Migration*, 157.

7. Ibid.

8. Alan G. Green and David A. Green, "Canadian Immigration Policy: The Effectiveness of the Point System and Other Instruments," *Canadian Journal of Economics*, 28(4), November 1995, 1009.

9. Ibid.

10. Ibid., 1008.

11. Mary Agnes Welch, "Migrants Chase the $7 Dream," *Windsor Star*, November 2, 2000, A1.

12. OECD, *Trends in International Migration*, 160.

13. U.S. Committee for Refugees, *World Refugee Survey 1998* (Washington, D.C.: Immigration and Refugee Services of America, 1998), 224.

14. Michael Grunwald, "Economic Crossroads on the Line; Security Fears Have U.S. and Canada Rethinking Life at 49th Parallel," *Washington Post*, December 26, 2001, A1.

15. John Kifner, "Arrest at the U.S. Border Points to a Terrorist Ring," *New York Times*, December 26, 1999. See also John Kifner and William K. Rashbaum, "Brooklyn Man Is Charged with Aiding in Bomb Plot," *New York Times*, December 31, 1999.

16. James Brooke, "Canada's Haven: For Notorious Fugitives, Too?" *New York Times*, December 29, 2000, A14.

17. Colin Nickerson, "Fighting Terror/Security, Roundup Border Patrol; U.S., Canada OK Historic Pact Partners in Trade to Tighten Security, Tackle Terrorism," *Boston Globe*, December 4, 2001, A24.

18. Ibid.

19. Martin, "Mexican-U.S. Migration," 59.

20. Weintraub et al., "Responses to Migration Issues," 455–456.

21. Ibid., 448–449, 462.

22. Ibid., 496.

23. Ibid., 497.

24. Cornelius and Martin, "The Uncertain Connection," 485.

25. Martin, "Mexican-U.S. Migration," 58.

26. OECD, *Trends in International Migration*, 223.

27. Martin, "Mexican-U.S. Migration," 60.

28. Cornelius and Martin, "The Uncertain Connection," 497.

29. Smith, *Inevitable Partnership*, 77–85.

30. Martin, "Mexican-U.S. Migration," 61.

31. Weintraub et al., "Responses to Migration Issues," 466.

32. Ibid., 462.

33. OECD, *Trends in International Migration*, 223.

34. Weintraub et al., "Responses to Migration Issues," 456–457.

35. Ibid., 457.

36. José de Cordoba and Joel Millman, "Mexico Charts Shifts in Relations with U.S.—Mexico's Fox Plans for Broader Policy on U.S. Immigration," *Wall Street Journal*, July 7, 2000, A8.

37. Ginger Thompson, "Fox, on Tour, Stresses Mexico's Economic Importance for California," *New York Times*, March 23, 2001, A3.

38. "Press Conference with President George W. Bush and Mexican President Vicente Fox," *Federal News Service*, February 16, 2001.

39. U.S.-Mexico Migration Panel, *Mexico-U.S. Migration: A Shared Responsibility*, 34.

40. U.S. Department of State, Office of the Spokesman, "Joint Communique: U.S.-Mexico Migration Talks and Plan of Action for Cooperation on Border Safety," Washington, D.C., June 22, 2001. See http://www.state.gov/r/pa/prs/ps/2001/index.htm

41. Ginger Thompson, "U.S. and Mexico to Open Talks on Freer Migration for Workers," *New York Times*, February 16, 2001, A1.

42. Gustavo Verduzco and Kurt Unger, "Impacts of Migration in Mexico," in Mexican Ministry of Foreign Affairs and U.S. Commission on Immigration Reform, *Migration Between Mexico and the United States: Binational Study*, Vol. 1 (Austin, Texas: Morgan, 1998), 402–404.

43. Ginger Thompson, "An Exodus of Migrant Families Is Bleeding Mexico's Heartland," *New York Times*, June 17, 2001, A1.

44. Germán A Zárate-Hoyos, "A New View of Financial Flows from Labor Migration: A Social Accounting Matrix Perspective," *Estudios Interdisciplinarios de America Latina y el Caribe* 10(2), July–December 1999.

45. Gustavo Verduzco and Kurt Unger, "Impacts of Migration in Mexico," in Mexican Ministry of Foreign Affairs and U.S. Commission on Immigration Reform, *Migration Between Mexico and the United States: Binational Study*, Vol. 1 (Austin, Texas: Morgan, 1998), 410.

46. "US-Mexico Fox Wants Lower Costs for Remittances from Mexicans," *EFE News Services*, January 26, 2001.

47. Ibid., 428, 430.

48. Thompson, "An Exodus of Migrant Families," A1.

49. "Mexican President Praises Migrant 'Heroes,'" *New York Times*, December 13, 2000, A13.

50. Ginger Thompson, "Jerez Journal; Candidate Lives in U.S., but so Does Half the State," *New York Times*, June 19, 2001, A4.

51. Jonathan Coppel, Jean-Christophe Dumont, and Ignazio Visco, "Trends in Immigration and Economic Consequences," *Economics Department Working Papers No. 284*, Organization for Economic Cooperation and Development, February 1, 2001, 5.

52. Hans Kornø Rasmussen, *No Entry: Immigration Policy in Europe*, (Denmark: Copenhagen Business School Press, 1997), 80.

53. Demetrios G. Papademetriou, *Coming Together or Pulling Apart? The European Union's Struggle with Immigration and Asylum* (Washington, D.C.: Carnegie Endowment for International Peace, 1996), 13.

54. The term "third-country national" refers to a person whose country of origin is outside Europe. Presumably, a "first-country national" would be a citizen of the country of resi-

dence, and a "second-country national" would be a citizen of an EU member state residing in another EU member state, though these latter terms are seldom used.

55. Rasmussen, *No Entry*, 96.

56. Sarah Collinson, *Europe and International Migration* (London: Pinter, 1993), 126.

57. Rasmussen, *No Entry*, 40.

58. Robert Miles and Dietrich Thränhardt, eds., *Migration and European Integration: The Dynamics of Inclusion and Exclusion* (London: Pinter, 1995), 62.

59. Papademetriou, *Coming Together or Pulling Apart*, 4.

60. The Treaty of Rome was signed by six western European states: France, Germany, Italy, Belgium, Luxembourg, and the Netherlands.

61. Papademetriou, *Coming Together or Pulling Apart*, 16, 23, 24.

62. Rasmussen, *No Entry*, 157.

63. Grete Brochmann, *European Integration and Immigration from Third Countries* (Boston: Scandinavian University Press, 1996), 88.

64. Treaty on European Union, Article 100c.1.

65. Rasmussen, *No Entry*, 160.

66. Papademetriou, *Coming Together or Pulling Apart*, 26–27.

67. Rasmussen, *No Entry*, 162.

68. Brochmann, *European Integration*, 84.

69. Papademetriou, *Coming Together or Pulling Apart*, 41.

70. Joanne van Selm, ed., *Kosovo's Refugees in the European Union* (New York: Pinter, 2000), 9.

71. Susan Woodward, *Balkan Tragedy: Chaos and Dissolution After the Cold War* (Washington, D.C.: Brookings Institution, 1995), 295.

72. Stephen Engelberg and Tim Weiner, "Massacre in Bosnia; Srebrenica: The Days of Slaughter," *New York Times*, October 29, 1995, A1.

73. Joanne van Selm, ed., *Kosovo's Refugees in the European Union* (New York: Pinter, 2000), 6.

74. Ibid., 210–212.

75. Ibid., 6.

76. U.S. Committee for Refugees, *World Refugee Survey 2000*, Washington, D.C., 2000, 315.

77. UNHCR, *The State of the World's Refugees* (New York: Oxford University Press, 2000), 173.

78. These figures include funding to three international agencies: UNHCR, the International Organization for Migration, and the U.N. Relief and Works Agency for Palestinian Relief in the Near East (UNRWA). See U.S. Committee for Refugees, "2000 Contributions

to International Refugee Aid Agencies: Top 20 Countries," *Worldwide Refugee Information*, http://www.refugees.org/world/statistics/wrs01_table7.htm

79. UNHCR, *The State of the World's Refugees* (New York: Oxford University Press, 2000), 321–324.

80. James C. Hathaway, *Reconceiving International Refugee Law* (Boston: Martinus Nijhoff, 1997), xxi.

81. U.S. Committee for Refugees, "Ratio of Refugees to Host Country Population in Selected Countries," *Worldwide Refugee Information*. See http://www.refugees.org/world/statistics/wrs01_table8.htm

82. UNHCR, *The State of the World's Refugees* (New York: Oxford University Press, 2000), 133.

83. Kathleen Newland, "The Impact of U.S. Refugee Policies on U.S. Foreign Policy: A Case of the Tail Wagging the Dog?" in Michael S. Teitelbaum and Myron Weiner, eds., *Threatened Peoples, Threatened Borders* (New York: Norton, 1995), 194–195.

84. Ibid., 195, 196.

Appendix

Further Research and Chronology   201

    Bibliography of Book Sources   201

    Bibliography of Journal and Report Sources   203

    Bibliography of News Sources   206

    Bibliography of Internet Sources   210

    Chronology   212

Primary Documents   216

    Convention Relating to the Status of Refugees (1951)   216

    Protocol Relating to the Status of Refugees (1967)   230

    Immigration and Nationality Act of 1952   234

    Illegal Immigration Reform and Immigrant Responsibility Act of 1996
        (Public Law 104-208)   242

    Treaty on European Union (1993)   247

    California Proposition 187 (1994)   250

    North American Free Trade Agreement (1994)   255

    AFL-CIO Executive Council Actions (2000)   260

    U.S.-Mexico Migration: Joint Communiqué (2001)   263

    Supreme Court Decision in *Zadvydas v. Davis* (2001)   268

    Smart Border Declaration and Action Plan (2001)   272

Further Research and Chronology

Bibliography of Book Sources

Aleinikoff, T. Alexander, David A. Martin, and Hiroshi Motomura. *Immigration and Citizenship: Process and Policy.* 4th ed. St. Paul, Minn.: West Group, 1998.

Aleinikoff, T. Alexander, Deborah Waller Meyers, and Demetrios G. Papademetriou. *Reorganizing the U.S. Immigration Function: Toward a New Framework for Accountability.* Washington, D.C.: Carnegie Endowment for International Peace, 1998.

Anker, Deborah E. *Law of Asylum in the United States.* 3rd ed. Boston: Refugee Law Center, 1999.

Auerswald, Phillip. *The Kosovo Conflict: A Diplomatic History Through Documents.* Cambridge, Mass: Kluwer Law International, 2000.

Brochmann, Grete. *European Integration and Immigration from Third Countries.* Stockholm, Sweden: Scandinavian University Press, 1996.

Buckley, William. *Kosovo: Contending Voices on Balkan Interventions.* Grand Rapids, Mich.: Eerdmans, 2000.

Chiswick, Barry R., ed. *Immigration, Language and Ethnicity: Canada and the United States.* Washington, D.C.: AEI Press, 1992.

Collinson, Sarah. *Europe and International Migration.* London: Royal Institute of International Affairs, 1994.

Gimpel, James G., and James R. Edwards, Jr. *The Congressional Politics of Immigration Reform.* Boston: Allyn and Bacon, 1999.

Halli, Shiva. *Immigrant Canada: Demographic, Economic, and Social Challenges.* Toronto: University of Toronto Press, 1999.

Hamilton, Kimberly. *Migration and the New Europe.* Washington, D.C.: Center for Strategic and International Studies, 1994.

Hathaway, James C. *The Law of Refugee Status.* Toronto: Butterworths, 1991.

———. *Reconceiving International Refugee Law.* Boston: Nijhoff, 1997.

Hawkins, Freda. *Critical Years in Immigration: Canada and Australia Compared.* Quebec, Canada: McGill-Queen's University Press, 1989.

Independent International Commission on Kosovo. *The Kosovo Report: Conflict, International Response, Lessons Learned.* Oxford, England: Oxford University Press, 2000.

Kelly, Ninette, and Michael Trebilcock. *The Making of a Mosaic.* Toronto: University of Toronto Press, 1998.

Lowell, B. Lindsay, ed. *Foreign Temporary Workers in America: Policies that Benefit the U.S. Economy.* Westport, Conn.: Quorum Books, 1999.

Luciani, Giacomo. *Migration Policies in Europe and the United States.* Dodrecht, Netherlands: Kluwer Academic Publishers, 1993.

Massey, Douglas S. et al. *Worlds in Motion: Understanding International Migration at the End of the Millennium.* New York: Oxford University Press, 1998.

Meissner, Doris. *International Migration Challenges in a New Era.* New York: Trilateral Commission, 1993.

Mexican Ministry of Foreign Affairs and U.S. Commission on Immigration Reform. *Binational Study: Migration Between Mexico and the United States.* Vols. 1–3. Austin, Texas: Morgan Printing, 1998.

Miles, Robert, and Dietrich Thränhardt, eds. *Migration and European Integration: The Dynamics of Inclusion and Exclusion.* London: Pinter, 1995.

Newland, Kathleen. *U.S. Refugee Policy: Dilemmas and Directions.* Washington, D.C.: Carnegie Endowment for International Peace, 1995.

Organization for Economic Cooperation and Development (SOPEMI). *Trends in International Migration, 2000.*

Papademetriou, Demetrios G. *Coming Together or Pulling Apart? The European Union's Struggle with Immigration and Asylum.* Washington, D.C.: Carnegie Endowment for International Peace, 1996.

———, and Deborah Waller Meyers. *Caught in the Middle: Border Communities in an Era of Globalization.* Washington, D.C.: Carnegie Endowment for International Peace, 2001.

———, and Monica L. Heppel. *Balancing Acts: Toward a Fair Bargain on Seasonal Agricultural Workers.* Washington, D.C.: Carnegie Endowment for International Peace, 1999.

———, and Stephen Yale-Loehr. *Balancing Interests: Rethinking U.S. Selection of Skilled Immigrants.* Washington, D.C.: Carnegie Endowment for International Peace, 1996.

Portes, Alejandro, ed. *The New Second Generation.* New York: Russell Sage, 1996.

Rasmussen, Hans Korno. *No Entry: Immigration Policy in Europe.* Denmark: Copenhagen Business School Press, 1997.

Rothenberg, Daniel. *With These Hands: The Hidden World of Migrant Farmworkers Today.* New York: Harcourt Brace, 1998.

Simon, Julian L. *The Economic Consequences of Immigration.* Ann Arbor: University of Michigan Press, 1999.

Smith, Clint E. *Inevitable Partnership: Understanding Mexico-U.S. Relations.* Boulder, Colo.: Lynne Rienner, 2000.

Smith, James P., and Barry Edmonston, eds. *The New Americans: Economic, Demographic, and Fiscal Effects of Immigration.* Washington, D.C.: National Academy Press, 1997.

———, eds. *The Immigration Debate: Studies on the Economic, Demographic, and Fiscal Effects of Immigration.* Washington, D.C.: National Academy Press, 1998.

Teitelbaum, Michael S., and Myron Weiner, eds. *Threatened Peoples, Threatened Borders.* New York: Norton, 1995.

United Nations High Commissioner for Refugees. *The State of the World's Refugees.* New York: Oxford University Press, 2000.

U.S. Committee for Refugees. *World Refugee Survey 2001.* Washington, D.C.: U.S. Committee for Refugees, 2001.

U.S. Immigration and Naturalization Service. *Statistical Yearbook of the Immigration and Naturalization Service, 1998.* Washington, D.C.: Government Printing Office, 2000.

Van Selm, Joanne. *Kosovo's Refugees in the European Union.* London: Continuum Imprint, 2000.

Woodward, Susan L. *Balkan Tragedy: Chaos and Dissolution After the Cold War.* Washington, D.C.: Brookings Institution, 1995.

Bibliography of Journal and Report Sources

"A Bold Proposal on Immigration." *Atlantic Monthly,* June 1994.

Aleinikoff, T. Alexander. "The Green Card Solution." *The American Prospect,* December 20, 1999.

Arango, Joaquìn. "Explaining Migration: A Critical View." *International Social Science Journal,* September 2000.

Barnett, Pamela. "Congress Finally Clears High-Tech Visa Bill." *National Journal,* October 7, 2000.

Bass, Loretta E., and Lynne M. Casper. "Are There Differences in Registration and Voting Behavior Between Naturalized and Native-Born Americans?" *Population Division Working Paper No. 28.* Washington, D.C.: U.S. Bureau of the Census, February 1999.

Borjas, George. "The Economic Benefits from Immigration." *Journal of Economic Perspectives,* Spring 1995.

———. "The New Economics of Immigration." *Atlantic Monthly,* November 1996.

Bush, George W. "Joint Statement Between the United States of America and the United Mexican States." *Weekly Compilation of Presidential Documents,* September 10, 2001.

Carnegie Endowment for International Peace. "New American Co-Ethnic Voting." *Research Perspectives on Migration* 1(3), March/April 1997.

Carney, Dan. "GOP Casts a Kinder Eye on 'Huddled Masses.' " *CQ Weekly*, May 15, 1999.

———. "Immigration Bill's Fine Print Sends Industry into High-Tech Turmoil." *CQ Weekly*, May 2, 1998.

———. "Republicans Feeling the Heat as Policy Becomes Reality." *CQ Weekly*, May 17, 1997.

———. "Restructuring the INS." *CQ Weekly*, April 4, 1998.

———. "Special Report—Presidential Issues: Can the U.S. Regain Control of Its Borders?" *CQ Weekly*, October 5, 1996.

Clark, Rebecca L., and Scott A. Anderson. "Illegal Aliens in Federal, State, and Local Criminal Justice Systems: Summary." Washington, D.C.: Urban Institute.

Clinton, William J. "Protecting U.S. Borders Against Illegal Immigration." U.S. Department of State Dispatch, August 9, 1993.

———. "Message to the Congress Transmitting the Immigration Enforcement Improvements Act of 1995." *Weekly Compilation of Presidential Documents*, May 8, 1995.

———. "U.S. Efforts to Expand and Strengthen the Fight Against Illegal Immigration." U.S. Department of State Dispatch, February 13, 1995.

"Clinton Offers Justification for Invasion of Haiti." *CQ Weekly*, September 17, 1994, 2605.

Coppel, Jonathan, Jean-Christophe Dumont, and Ignazio Visco. "Trends in Immigration and Economic Consequences." *Economics Department Working Papers No. 284*, Organization for Economic Cooperation and Development, ECO/WKP(2001)10, February 1, 2001.

Cooper, Mary H. "Global Refugee Crisis." *CQ Researcher*, July 9, 1999.

Cornelius, Wayne A., and Philip L. Martin. "The Uncertain Connection: Free Trade and Rural Mexican Migration to the United States." *International Migration Review* 27(3), Fall 1993.

"Cracking Down on Immigration." *CQ Researcher*, February 3, 1995.

"Debate Over Immigration." *CQ Researcher*, July 14, 2000.

Donegan, Craig. "Debate Over Bilingualism." *CQ Researcher*, January 19, 1996.

Emery, Margaret, Hiram Ruiz, and Jeff Drumtra. "Aid Drops in Afghanistan." U.S. Committee for Refugees Web site, October 11, 2001. Available at http://www.refugees.org/news/press_releases/2001/Afghan101101.cfm

Fessler, Pamela. "Foreign Policy: Members Decry Haiti Policy, Vow to Seek Changes." *CQ Weekly*, May 30, 1992, 1547.

Flynn, Stephen E. "Beyond Border Control." *Foreign Affairs*, November/December 2000.

Foerstel, Karen. "House Panel Approves INS Breakup." *CQ Weekly*, November 6, 1999.

Fragomen, Augustin T., Jr. "The Illegal Immigration Reform and Immigrant Responsibility Act of 1996: An Overview." *International Migration Review*, Summer 1997.

Frey, William. "Immigration, Domestic Migration, and Demographic Balkanization in America: New Evidence for the 1990s." *Population and Development Review,* December 1996.

Green, Alan G., and David A. Green. "Canadian Immigration Policy: The Effectiveness of the Point System and Other Instruments." *Canadian Journal of Economics,* 28(4), November 1995.

Griffin, Rodman D. "Illegal Immigration." *CQ Researcher,* April 24, 1992.

Idelson, Holly. "Proposals Would Crack Down on Illegals and Tighten Rules for Legal Immigrants." *CQ Weekly,* April 15, 1995.

———. "Supreme Court: Haitian Policy Sanctioned; Refugee Groups Object." *CQ Weekly,* June 26, 1993, 1666.

"INS: Border, 245, Asylum, Detention." *Migration News,* May 2001.

Jost, Kenneth. "Rebuilding Afghanistan." *CQ Researcher,* December 21, 2001.

Judis, John B. "Temporary Help." *New Republic,* June 19, 2000.

Kennedy, David M. "Can We Still Afford to Be a Nation of Immigrants?" *Atlantic Monthly,* November 1996.

Koch, Kathy. "High-Tech Labor Shortage." *CQ Researcher,* April 24, 1998.

Lollock, Lisa. "The Foreign-Born Population in the United States: March 2000." *Current Population Reports.* Washington, D.C.: U.S. Census Bureau, 2000, 520–534.

Martin, Philip. "Mexican-U.S. Migration: Policies and Economic Impacts." *Challenge* 38(2), March 1995.

Masci, David. "Assisting Refugees." *CQ Researcher,* February 7, 1997.

———. "Hispanic Americans' New Clout." *CQ Researcher,* September 18, 1998.

———. "U.S.-Mexico Relations." *CQ Researcher,* November 9, 2001.

———. "War on Terrorism." *CQ Researcher,* October 12, 2001.

Massey, Douglas S. et al. "Theories of International Migration: A Review and Appraisal." *Population and Development Review* 19(3), September 1993.

Meissner, Doris. "After the Attacks: Protecting Borders and Liberties." *Policy Brief No. 8,* Carnegie Endowment for International Peace, November 2001.

Newberg, Paula R. "Politics at the Heart: The Architecture of Humanitarian Assistance to Afghanistan." *Working Paper No. 2,* Carnegie Endowment for International Peace, 1999.

Office of the United States Trade Representative, "Fact Sheet: Summary of Principal Provisions of NAFTA." U.S. Department of State Dispatch, 4(35), August 30, 1993.

O'Neill, Robert. "INS Reform Sends Panel to the Barricades." *National Journal,* March 25, 2000.

Palmer, Elizabeth A. "Immigration Liberalization: Delayed but Not Abandoned." *CQ Weekly,* November 17, 2001.

"Panel Approves Bill to Weaken Immigration Law." *CQ Weekly,* April 25, 1998.

Pomper, Miles A. "Cuban-American Agenda Marked by New Diversity." *CQ Weekly,* February 27, 1999.

Rumbaut, Rubén G. "Coming of Age in Immigrant America." *Research Perspectives on Migration* 1(6) Jan/Feb 1998.

Schuck, Peter H. "Removing Criminal Aliens: The pitfalls and promises of federalism." *Harvard Journal of Law and Public Policy,* Spring 1999.

Schwartz, Wendy. "Immigrants and Their Educational Attainment: Some Facts and Findings." *ERIC Digest,* New York: ERIC Clearinghouse on Urban Education, November 1996.

Singer, Audrey, and Douglas S. Massey. "The Social Process of Undocumented Border Crossing Among Mexican Migrants." *International Migration Review* 32(3), Fall 1998, 561–592.

Tell, David. "Republicans and Immigration." *Weekly Standard,* February 26, 1996.

U.S. Department of Justice, Immigration and Naturalization Service. *INS Communiqué* 20(5), May 1997.

U.S. Department of Labor, Office of the Assistant Secretary for Policy, Office of Program Economics. "Findings of the National Agricultural Workers Survey (NAWS) 1997-98." Research Report No. 8, March 2000.

U.S. Department of State, Office of the Spokesman. "Joint Communique: U.S.-Mexico Migration Talks and Plan of Action for Cooperation on Border Safety." Washington, D.C., June 22, 2001.

U.S. Department of State. "Summary of U.S. Assistance to the Afghan People Since Oct. 1, 2001." *Fact Sheet.* Washington, D.C., November 23, 2001.

———. "U.S. Assistance to the Afghan People." *Fact Sheet.* Washington, D.C., October 4, 2001.

"U.S. Policy on Haitian Refugees." *U.S. Department of State Dispatch,* Washington, D.C., June 15, 1992.

Vaida, Bara. "Wanted! U.S. Citizens for High-Tech Jobs." *National Journal,* November 18, 2000.

Vargas, Arturo. "Latino Voters: The New Political Landscape." *Vital Speeches of the Day,* New York, January 1, 2000.

Zárate-Hoyos, Germán A. "A New View of Financial Flows from Labor Migration: A Social Accounting Matrix Perspective." *Estudios Interdisciplinarios De America Latina Y El Caribe* 10(2), July-December 1999.

Bibliography of News Sources

Alvarez, Lizette. "Lawyers for Boy's Miami Relatives Rule Out Directly Releasing Him to His Father." *New York Times,* April 1, 2000, A9.

Ayres, B. Drummon, Jr. "Accepting a Dare to Debate, Perot Retakes the Spotlight." *New York Times*, November 6, 1993, A10.

Baker, Peter, and Alan Sipress. "Concern Grows Over Refugees; Aid Groups Protest Forced Returns, Lack of Foreign Security." *Washington Post*, December 1, 2001, A16.

Branigin, William. "Immigrants Question Idea of Assimilation." *Washington Post*, May 25, 1998, A1.

Broder, David S., and Eric Pianin, "Border Agencies May Be Merged, Ridge Says." *Washington Post*, November 14, 2001, A31.

Bronner, Ethan. "Bilingual Education Is Facing Push Toward Abandonment." *New York Times*, May 30, 1998, A1.

Brooke, James. "Canada's Haven: For Notorious Fugitives, Too?" *New York Times*, December 29, 2000, A14.

Cordoba, José de, and Joel Millman, "Mexico Charts Shifts in Relations with U.S.—Mexico's Fox Plans for Broader Policy on U.S. Immigration." *Wall Street Journal*, July 7, 2000, A8.

Clymer, Adam. "A Nation Challenged: Immigration Law; Bills Require C.I.A. to Share Its Information on Foreigners." *New York Times*, November 2, 2001, B7.

Crabtree, Susan. "Clinton Says 'Me Too' as GOP Blasts Immigration." *Insight on the News*, March 18, 1996, 11.

Cummings, Jeanne, and Neil King Jr. "Mexico's Fox Gets Commitment from Bush to Reshape Ties, Even if Congress Balks." *Wall Street Journal*, September 7, 2001, A16.

"D'Amato Proposes Bill for Criminal Aliens." *New York Times*, January 13, 1992, A5.

Dao, James. "Immigrant Diversity Slows Traditional Political Climb." *New York Times*, December 28, 1999.

Dusky, Lorraine. "Emma Lazarus Would Be Crying." *Newsday*, March 26, 1996, A37.

Eggen, Dan. "Delays Cited in Charging Detainees; with Legal Latitude, INS Sometimes Took Weeks." *Washington Post*, January 15, 2002, A1.

Engelberg, Stephen, and Tim Weiner. "Massacre in Bosnia; Srebrenica: The Days of Slaughter." *New York Times*, October 29, 1995, A1.

English, Merle. "In Queens, Push to Get Amnesty for Illegal Immigrants." *Newsday*, February 11, 1998, A41.

Firestone, David. "Al Qaeda Link Seen in Only a Handful of 1,200 Detainees." *New York Times*, November 29, 2001, A1.

———. "U.S. Makes It Easier to Detain Foreigners." *New York Times*, November 28, 2001, B7.

Gall, Carlotta. "Refugees; as Afghans Return Home, Need for Food Intensifies." *New York Times*, December 26, 2001, B3.

Greenhouse, Linda. "The Supreme Court: Supreme Court Roundup; Justices Permit Immigrants to Challenge Deportations." *New York Times*, June 26, 2001, A1.

———. "The Supreme Court: The Issue of Confinement; Supreme Court Limits Detention in Cases of Deportable Immigrants." *New York Times,* June 29, 2001, A1.

Greenhouse, Steven. "Coalition Urges Easing of Immigration Laws." *New York Times,* May 16, 2000, A16.

———. "Labor Urges Amnesty for Illegal Immigrants." *New York Times,* February 17, 2000, A26.

———. "U.S. to Expand Anti-Discrimination Rights for Illegal Immigrants Working in This Country." *New York Times,* October 28, 1999.

———. "U.S. Will Return Refugees to Cuba in Policy Switch." *New York Times,* May 3, 1995, A1.

Grunwald, Michael. "Economic Crossroads on the Line; Security Fears Have U.S. and Canada Rethinking Life at 49th Parallel." *Washington Post,* December 26, 2001, A1.

Hammer, Joshua. "Death in the Desert Heat." *Newsweek,* August 24, 1998.

Janofsky, Michael. "Undocumented Immigrants Scramble to Get Through a Small Window of Opportunity." *New York Times,* May 1, 2001, A12.

Keefe, Bob. "Hispanic's Bid for L.A. Mayor Could Mark a National Trend." *Cox News Service,* June 1, 2001.

Kifner, John. "Arrest at the U.S. Border Points to a Terrorist Ring." *New York Times,* December 26, 1999.

———, and William K. Rashbaum. "Brooklyn Man Is Charged with Aiding in Bomb Plot." *New York Times,* December 31, 1999.

Leavitt, Paul. "INS Deploying Agents to Target Smuggling." *USA Today,* March 31, 1999.

Maass, Peter. "How a Camp Becomes a City." *New York Times Magazine,* November 18, 2001.

Mapes, Lynda V. " 'I Need the Work, They Need the Work Done,' Northwest Farmworker Says." *Seattle Times,* June 19, 2000.

Mittelstadt, Michelle. "INS Changes Its Mandatory Detention Policy for Criminal Aliens." *Associated Press State & Local Wire,* July 13, 1999.

Nickerson, Colin. "Access Via the North Next Steps Roots of Terrorism; Some See Canada as a Staging Area for Terrorists." *Boston Globe,* September 17, 2001, A13.

———. "Fighting Terror/Security, Roundup Border Patrol; U.S., Canada OK Historic Pact Partners in Trade to Tighten Security, Tackle Terrorism." *Boston Globe,* December 4, 2001, A24.

Nieves, Evelyn. "California Calls Off Effort to Carry Out Immigrant Measure." *New York Times,* July 30, 1999.

Pear, Robert. "G.O.P. and White House Are Near Accord on Immigrants." *New York Times,* December 13, 2000, A33.

Pearl, Daniel. "For Afghan Refugees, No Return in Sight—With or Without the Taliban, Poverty at Home Keeps Millions Stranded Abroad." *Wall Street Journal,* November 20, 2001, A14.

Perlez, Jane. "Refugee Agency Officials Play Down Mass Exodus." *New York Times,* October 23, 2001, B3.

Perlman, Shirley E. "Deported/the No. 1 Priority for State, INS: Criminal Aliens." *Newsday,* May 11, 1997, A5.

"Press Conference with President George W. Bush and Mexican President Vicente Fox." *Federal News Service,* February 16, 2001.

Puente, Maria. "At the Border, Preventive Policing." *USA Today,* February 18, 1997.

Purdum, Todd S., and Howard W. French, "A Nation Challenged: Donors; U.S. Makes Pledge for $300 Million in Aid to Afghans." *New York Times,* January 21, 2002, A1.

Roberts, Steven V., and Anne Kates Smith. "Uncle Sam, Bar the Door." *U.S. News & World Report,* April 29, 1996.

Rodriguez, Gregory. "A Look at . . . Assimilation; It Only Takes a Generation or Three." *Washington Post,* July 4, 1999, B3.

Rogers, John. "L.A. Mayor Election Offers Two Liberals; One Could Make History." *Associated Press State & Local Wire,* June 4, 2001.

Sachs, Susan. "A Hue, and a Cry, in the Heartland." *New York Times,* April 8, 2001, WK5.

———. "Give Me Your Tired, Your Poor, Your Vote." *New York Times,* April 8, 2001, A37.

Salins, Peter D. "From Many, One Nation; America Must Again Assimilate Its Immigrants." *Washington Post,* February 9, 1997, C1.

Sanger, David E. "Mexico's President Rewrites the Rules." *New York Times,* September 8, 2001, A1.

Schemo, Diana Jean. "A Nation Challenged: Immigration; Senate Bill Would Stiffen Some Controls Over Visas." *New York Times,* December 6, 2001, B7.

Schmitt, Eric. "Americans (a)Love (b)Hate Immigrants." *New York Times,* January 14, 2001.

———. "Vote in House Strongly Backs an End to INS." *New York Times,* April 26, 2002.

Seelye, Katharine Q. "Gore Supporting Residency for Cuban Child." *New York Times,* March 31, 2000, A1.

Shepardson, David. "New Law Opens Citizenship: Metro Immigrants Apply as April 30 Deadline Nears." *Detroit News,* April 30, 2001, A1.

———. "U.S. Northern Border Gets 200 More Agents." *Detroit News,* January 9, 2002.

Smith, Elliot Blair. "INS Cracks Down on Meatpackers." *USA Today,* April 13, 1999.

Smith, James F. "Mexico Weighs Ideas to Reduce Migrant Deaths." *Los Angeles Times,* May 25, 2001, A5.

Solomon, Melissa. "H-1B Refugees." *Computer World,* December 3, 2001.

Stein, Dan. "Amnesty for Illegal Aliens Undermines the Law." *Record* (Bergen County, N.J.), November 26, 1999, L7.

Sullivan, Kevin. "U.S., Mexico Set New Border Effort." *Washington Post,* June 23, 2001, A21.

"The Supreme Court; Excerpts from Opinions in Ruling on the Detention of Immigrants-Criminals." *New York Times,* June 29, 2001, A20.

Thomas, Paulette. "In the Land of Bratwurst, a New Hispanic Boom—In a Big Population Shift, Latino Immigrants Flock to Towns in the Midwest." *Wall Street Journal,* March 16, 2000, B1.

Thompson, Ginger. "An Exodus of Migrant Families Is Bleeding Mexico's Heartland." *New York Times,* June 17, 2001, A1.

———. "Fox, on Tour, Stresses Mexico's Economic Importance for California." *New York Times,* March 23, 2001, A3.

———. "Fox Urges Congress to Grant Rights to Mexican Immigrants in U.S." *New York Times,* September 7, 2001, A6.

———. "Jerez Journal; Candidate Lives in U.S., but so Does Half the State." *New York Times,* June 19, 2001, A4.

———. "U.S. and Mexico to Open Talks on Freer Migration for Workers." *New York Times,* February 16, 2001.

———, and Steven Greenhouse. "Mexican 'Guest Workers': A Project Worth a Try?" *New York Times,* April 3, 2001.

Tobar, Hector, Nancy Cleeland, and Patrick McDonnell. "Election 2001: In the End, It Was a Crusade for Latinos and for the Future." *Los Angeles Times,* June 6, 2001, A19.

Uchitelle, Louis. "I.N.S. Is Looking the Other Way as Illegal Immigrants Fill Jobs." *New York Times,* March 9, 2000, A1.

"U.S.-Mexico Fox Wants Lower Costs for Remittances from Mexicans." *EFE News Services,* January 26, 2001.

Valbrun, Marjorie. "Beefed-up Border Patrol Encounters Growing Pains." *Wall Street Journal,* October 15, 1998.

———. "Clamor for U.S. Citizenship Spurs Debate on Its Cause." *Wall Street Journal,* February 25, 1999, A20.

Verhovek, Sam Howe. "Illegal Immigrant Workers Being Fired in I.N.S. Tactic." *New York Times,* April 2, 1999.

———. "The Northern Border; Vast U.S.-Canada Border Suddenly Poses a Problem to Patrol Agents." *New York Times,* October 4, 2001, B1.

Welch, Mary Agnes. "Migrants Chase the $7 Dream." *Windsor Star* (Canada), November 2, 2000, A1.

Bibliography of Internet Sources

Alexis de Tocqueville Institution   http://www.adti.net
American Immigration Lawyers' Association   http://www.aila.org

Carnegie Endowment for International Peace   http://www.ceip.org

Cato Institute   http://www.cato.org

Center for Immigration Studies   http://www.cis.org

Citizenship and Immigration Canada   http://www.cic.gc.ca

Federation for American Immigration Reform   http://www.fairus.org

Immigration and Refugee Services of America   http://www.irsa-uscr.org

InterAction   http://www.interaction.org

International Organization for Migration   http://www.iom.int

International Rescue Committee   http://www.theirc.org

Lawyers' Committee for Human Rights   http://www.lchr.org

Mexican American Legal Defense and Education Fund   http://www.maldef.org

Migration Policy Institute   http://www.migrationpolicy.org

National Association of Latino Elected and Appointed Officials
    http://www.naleo.org

National Council of La Raza   http://www.nclr.org

National Immigration Forum   http://www.immigrationforum.org

National Network for Immigrant and Refugee Rights   http://www.nnirr.org

Organization for Economic Cooperation and Development   http://www.oecd.org

United Nations High Commissioner for Refugees   http://www.unhcr.ch

University of California at Davis, Migration Dialogue   http://migration.ucdavis.edu

University of Michigan Law School Refugee Caselaw Site
    http://www.refugeecaselaw.org

Urban Institute, Population Studies Center   http://www.urban.org

U.S. Census Bureau   http://www.census.gov

U.S. Commission on Immigration Reform   http://www.utexas.edu/lbj/uscir

U.S. Committee for Refugees   http://www.refugees.org

U.S. Department of Health and Human Services, Office of Refugee Resettlement
    http://www.acf.dhhs.gov/programs/orr

U.S. Department of Justice, Executive Office for Immigration Review
    http://www.usdoj.gov/eoir

U.S. Department of Labor, Bureau of International Labor Affairs, Division of Immigra-
    tion Policy and Research   http://www.dol.gov/dol/ilab

U.S. Department of State, Bureau of Population, Refugees, and Migration
    http://www.state.gov/g/prm

U.S. House of Representatives, Committee on the Judiciary, Subcommittee on Immigra-
    tion and Claims   http://www.house.gov/judiciary/immigration.htm

U.S. Immigration and Naturalization Service   http://www.ins.gov

U.S. Senate, Committee on the Judiciary, Subcommittee on Immigration   http://judiciary.senate.gov/subcommittees/immigration.cfm

U.S. Supreme Court   http://www.supremecourtus.gov

White House   http://www.whitehouse.gov

Chronology

1845–1849   Ireland's potato famine sends more than a million Irish immigrants to the United States. Later in the century, masses of immigrants fled poverty in southern Europe and found work in the rapid industrial expansion occurring in the United States.

1882   The Immigration Act of 1882, which levied a head tax of fifty cents on each immigrant, leads to the creation of the first corps of U.S. immigration inspectors within the Department of Treasury in 1891.

1886   President Grover Cleveland dedicates the Statue of Liberty, a gift from France.

1898   Supreme Court rules in *United States v. Wong Kim Ark* that a man born in California to Chinese parents is a U.S. citizen.

1910   The census shows 13.5 million Americans out of a total population of 92 million are foreign-born (more than 14 percent).

1913   Recognizing the need for consistency in the nation's naturalization procedures, Congress creates the Bureau of Immigration and Naturalization within what was then the Department of Commerce and Labor.

1921   Congress passes the Quota Act, which establishes a new system of national-origin quotas favoring northern Europeans over immigrants from southern Europe and elsewhere.

1924   Congress passes the Johnson-Reed Act, which stiffens the national-origin quotas established three years earlier. The law also creates the U.S. Border Patrol to combat illegal immigration.

1930   The coming decade will see immigration drop to roughly 500,000, down substantially from the more than 8 million who emigrated to the United States during the first decade of the twentieth century.

1942   Workers from Mexico and other nations are admitted to work temporarily in the United States, mainly in California's agricultural industry, under an initiative later called the Bracero Program.

1951   The Convention Relating to the Status of Refugees is adopted by the United Nations in Geneva, Switzerland.

1952   The McCarran-Walter Act retains the system of national-origin quotas.

1954   The U.S. government institutes "Operation Wetback" to stem the increase in illegal immigration. The program is successful.

1964   The Bracero Program ends.

1965   Congress passes the Immigration and Nationality Act Amendments, which remove racial quotas and substantially increase the number of immigrants allowed entry into the United States each year.

1967   The United Nations adopts the Protocol Relating to the Status of Refugees, which amends the 1951 Refugee Convention. The U.S. Congress ratifies the protocol on November 1, 1968, making it party to the 1951 convention, as well.

1968   Immigrants from the Western Hemisphere, previously admitted freely into the United States, are subjected to quotas, largely in response to a surge in illegal immigration after the 1964 expiration of the Bracero Program.

1980   The annual number of legal immigrants entering the country surpasses a half-million. Congress passes the Refugee Act, which sets refugees apart as a class distinct from other immigrants and establishes systems to regulate their entry and provide social services.

1986   The Immigration Reform and Control Act makes many illegal aliens eligible for permanent residence and establishes sanctions against employers who hire illegal workers.

1990   Congress passes the Immigration Act, which raises the immigration ceiling to 700,000 a year and grants preferences to relatives of U.S. residents or citizens and to aliens with high-demand work skills. The law also includes a provision for "temporary protected status" (TPS) and the Lautenberg Amendment, which identifies specific groups vulnerable to persecution in the former Soviet Union for resettlement in the United States.

1992   The Bush administration orders the Coast Guard to interdict and return thousands of boat people fleeing Haiti's military dictators. Television commentator Patrick J. Buchanan makes curtailing legal and illegal immigration one of the cornerstones of his unsuccessful bid for the Republican presidential nomination.

1993   President Bill Clinton, Vice President Al Gore, and Attorney General Janet Reno announce plans to crack down on illegal immigration, particularly smuggling operations. The

INS launches Operation Hold the Line as a pilot program along the Mexican border in El Paso, Texas.

1994   Congress ratifies the North American Free Trade Agreement (NAFTA). The Commission on Immigration Reform recommends reducing the number of immigrants. Californians pass Proposition 187, which denies social services to illegal aliens. The initiative is later struck down in the courts.

1995   The INS launches the Citizenship USA drive. President Clinton and Canadian Prime Minister Jean Chrétien sign the Canada-United States Accord on Our Shared Border.

1996   Congress passes the Illegal Immigration and Immigrant Responsibility Act, which toughens border enforcement and streamlines deportation procedures.

1998   The INS carries out Operation Seek and Keep, an investigation that dismantles the largest smuggling cartel to date. Congress passes legislation to increase the number of temporary visas available for highly skilled workers, particularly in the technology and science industries. California voters approve Proposition 227, eliminating most bilingual education programs in the state.

1999   The United States leads NATO in a bombing campaign against Serb forces in Kosovo (a province of the former Yugoslavia) and accepts more than 14,000 refugees from Kosovo for temporary protection. The Equal Employment Opportunity Commission extends antidiscrimination rights to illegal immigrants for the first time. A Miami fisherman rescues six-year-old Cuban boy, Elián González from an inner tube off the Florida coast. Elián becomes a pawn for politicians debating his asylum status and attracts months of national media attention.

2000   The census shows that 28.4 million people, or 10.4 percent of the U.S. population, are foreign-born. The American Federation of Labor-Congress of Industrial Organizations (AFL-CIO) announces an historic shift in its policy to support immigrant workers and begins a campaign to grant amnesty to undocumented workers. GOP presidential candidate George W. Bush proposes splitting the INS into two separate agencies—one to guard the border and the other to process legal immigrants.

February 2001   President Bush visits Mexican President Vicente Fox; they agree to form a "high-level working group on migration."

June 2001   The Supreme Court rules in favor of immigrants' rights in two separate cases. Its decision in *Zadvydas v. Davis et al.* bars the government from detaining deportable immigrants indefinitely. In *INS v. St. Cyr*, the justices determined that the government may allow judicial review of a criminal alien's request for a waiver of deportation, and that the government may not apply 1996 provisions in the Antiterrorism and Effective Death Penalty Act (AEDPA) and Illegal Immigration Reform and Immigration Responsibility Act (IIRIRA) retroactively.

September 2001   Nineteen terrorists from Middle Eastern countries hijack four commercial jets and steer them into the World Trade Center towers in New York City and the Pentagon in Arlington, Virginia. The crashes lead to the collapse of the towers, and the largest number of casualties on American soil since the attack on Pearl Harbor during World War II. All nineteen terrorists had obtained temporary visas—some fraudulently but others legally, and only three were in the country illegally, having overstayed their visas. The attacks profoundly alter U.S. immigration policy, shifting the focus from deterring unauthorized economic migrants to protecting homeland security. Proposals for a guest worker program with Mexico and amnesty for certain illegal immigrants are tabled, while programs to fortify the borders, track foreign students, and improve immigration intelligence take priority.

December 2001   The United States and Canada sign the Smart Border Declaration, including a thirty-point action plan to improve security along the countries' shared border.

March 2002   A Florida flight school receives notices from INS that the visa applications of two of the now-dead September 11th hijackers have been approved. The news report outrages leaders in the Bush administration and Congress, who demand urgent reform of INS. President Bush and Mexican President Fox meet in Washington to sign a smart border plan similar to the one signed between the United States and Canada in 2001.

April 2002   The U.S. House of Representatives votes overwhelmingly in favor of the Barbara Jordan Immigration Reform and Accountability Act (HR 3231), which would abolish the INS by separating enforcement and service functions in two new bureaus within the Department of Justice. Similar legislation, with the endorsement of the Bush administration, is before the Senate.

Primary Documents

Each of the following legal and policy documents played an important role in U.S. immigration policy during the past decade. The section begins with selected U.S. immigration laws and policies and then provides the text of international agreements and treaties to which the United States is party.

Convention Relating to the Status of Refugees (1951)

This binding international treaty is the primary source of refugee law and is considered part of the body of international human rights law. The Refugee Convention, as it is often called, provides a definition of the term 'refugee' and defines refugees' rights to protection in host countries. Signed in 1951, the Refugee Convention originally dealt solely with refugees from European nations who had been displaced by events during World War II. The 1967 Protocol Relating to the Status of Refugees amended the 1951 Convention. The United States is party to the Refugee Convention since it ratified the 1967 Protocol in November 1968.

United Nations Conference of Plenipotentiaries on the Status of Refugees and Stateless Persons, Geneva, 2-25 July 1951.

Entry into force:	22 April 1954, in accordance with article 43.
Registration:	22 April 1954, No. 2545.
Text:	United Nations, Treaty Series, vol. 189, p. 137.
Status as at 17 May 2001:	Signatories: 19. Parties: 137.

Notes: The Convention was adopted by the United Nations Conference of Plenipotentiaries on the Status of Refugees and Stateless Persons, held at Geneva from 2 to 25 July 1951. The Conference was convened pursuant to resolution 429 (V).[1] adopted by the General Assembly of the United Nations on 14 December 1950. All references to chapters refer to the United Nations publication, *Multilateral Treaties Deposited with the Secretary-General* (MTDSG).

Preamble

The High Contracting Parties,

Considering that the Charter of the United Nations and the Universal Declaration of Human Rights approved on 10 December 1948 by the General Assembly have affirmed the principle that human beings shall enjoy fundamental rights and freedoms without discrimination,

Considering that the United Nations has, on various occasions, manifested its profound concern for refugees and endeavoured to assure refugees the widest possible exercise of these fundamental rights and freedoms,

Considering that it is desirable to revise and consolidate previous international agreements relating to the status of refugees and to extend the scope of and protection accorded by such instruments by means of a new agreement,

Considering that the grant of asylum may place unduly heavy burdens on certain countries, and that a satisfactory solution of a problem of which the United Nations has recognized the international scope and nature cannot therefore be achieved without international co-operation,

Expressing the wish that all States, recognizing the social and humanitarian nature of the problem of refugees will do everything within their power to prevent this problem from becoming a cause of tension between States,

Noting that the United Nations High Commissioner for Refugees is charged with the task of supervising international conventions providing for the protection of refugees, and recognizing that the effective co-ordination of measures taken to deal with this problem will depend upon the co-operation of States with the High Commissioner,

Have agreed as follows:

Chapter I: General Provisions

Article 1 Definition of the term "Refugee"

A. For the purposes of the present Convention, the term "refugee" shall apply to any person who:

1. Has been considered a refugee under the Arrangements of 12 May 1926 and 30 June 1928 or under the Conventions of 28 October 1933 and 10 February 1938, the Protocol of 14 September 1939 or the Constitution of the International Refugee Organization; Decisions of non-eligibility taken by the International Refugee Organization during the period of its activities shall not prevent the status of refugee being accorded to persons who fulfill the conditions of paragraph 2 of this section;

2. As a result of events occurring before 1 January 1951 and owing to well-founded fear of being persecuted for reasons of race, religion, nationality, membership of a particular social group or political opinion, is outside the country of his nationality and is unable or, owing to such fear, is unwilling to avail himself of the protection of that coun-

try; or who, not having a nationality and being outside the country of his former habitual residence as a result of such events, is unable or, owing to such fear, is unwilling to return to it.

In the case of a person who has more than one nationality, the term "the country of his nationality" shall mean each of the countries of which he is a national, and a person shall not be deemed to be lacking the protection of the country of his nationality if, without any valid reason based on well-founded fear, he has not availed himself of the protection of one of the countries of which he is a national.

B. (1) For the purposes of this Convention, the words "events occurring before 1 January 1951" in Article 1, Section A, shall be understood to mean either

    (a) "events occurring in Europe before 1 January 1951"; or

    (b) "events occurring in Europe or elsewhere before 1 January 1951", and each Contracting State shall make a declaration at the time of signature, ratification or accession, specifying which of these meanings it applies for the purpose of its obligations under this Convention.

(2) Any Contracting State which has adopted alternative

    (a) may at any time extend its obligations by adopting alternative

    (b) by means of a notification addressed to the Secretary-General of the United Nations.

C. This Convention shall cease to apply to any person falling under the terms of Section A if:

(1) He has voluntarily re-availed himself of the protection of the country of his nationality; or

(2) Having lost his nationality, he has voluntarily re-acquired it, or

(3) He has acquired a new nationality, and enjoys the protection of the country of his new nationality; or

(4) He has voluntarily re-established himself in the country which he left or outside which he remained owing to fear of persecution; or

(5) He can no longer, because the circumstances in connection with which he has been recognized as a refugee have ceased to exist, continue to refuse to avail himself of the protection of the country of his nationality;

Provided that this paragraph shall not apply to a refugee falling under Section A(1) of this Article who is able to invoke compelling reasons arising out of previous persecution for refusing to avail himself of the protection of the country of nationality;

(6) Being a person who has no nationality he is, because of the circumstances in connection with which he has been recognized as a refugee have ceased to exist, able to return to the country of his former habitual residence;

Provided that this paragraph shall not apply to a refugee falling under section A(1) of this Article who is able to invoke compelling reasons arising out of previous persecution for refusing to return to the country of his former habitual residence.

D. This Convention shall not apply to persons who are at present receiving from organs or agencies of the United Nations other than the United Nations High Commissioner for Refugees protection or assistance.

   When such protection or assistance has ceased for any reason, without the position of such persons being definitively settled in accordance with the relevant resolutions adopted by the General Assembly of the United Nations, these persons shall *ipso facto* be entitled to the benefits of this Convention.

E. This Convention shall not apply to a person who is recognized by the competent authorities of the country in which he has taken residence as having the rights and obligations which are attached to the possession of the nationality of that country.

F. The provisions of this Convention shall not apply to any person with respect to whom there are serious reasons for considering that:

   (a) he has committed a crime against peace, a war crime, or a crime against humanity, as defined in the international instruments drawn up to make provision in respect of such crimes;

   (b) he has committed a serious non-political crime outside the country of refuge prior to his admission to that country as a refugee;

   (c) he has been guilty of acts contrary to the purposes and principles of the United Nations.

Article 2 General obligations

Every refugee has duties to the country in which he finds himself, which require in particular that he conform to its laws and regulations as well as to measures taken for the maintenance of public order.

Article 3 Non-discrimination

The Contracting States shall apply the provisions of this Convention to refugees without discrimination as to race, religion or country of origin.

Article 4 Religion

The Contracting States shall accord to refugees within their territories treatment at least as favourable as that accorded to their nationals with respect to freedom to practice their religion and freedom as regards the religious education of their children.

Article 5 Rights granted apart from this Convention

Nothing in this Convention shall be deemed to impair any rights and benefits granted by a Contracting State to refugees apart from this Convention.

Article 6 The term "in the same circumstances"

For the purposes of this Convention, the term "in the same circumstances" implies that any requirements (including requirements as to length and conditions of sojourn or residence) which the particular individual would have to fulfil for the enjoyment of the right in question, if he were not a refugee, must be fulfilled by him, with the exception of requirements which by their nature a refugee is incapable of fulfilling.

Article 7 Exemption from reciprocity

(1) Except where this Convention contains more favourable provisions, a Contracting State shall accord to refugees the same treatment as is accorded to aliens generally.

(2) After a period of three years' residence, all refugees shall enjoy exemption from legislative reciprocity in the territory of the Contracting States.

(3) Each Contracting State shall continue to accord to refugees the rights and benefits to which they were already entitled, in the absence of reciprocity, at the date of entry into force of this Convention for that State.

(4) The Contracting States shall consider favourably the possibility of according to refugees, in the absence of reciprocity, rights and benefits beyond those to which they are entitled according to paragraphs 2 and 3, and to extending exemption from reciprocity to refugees who do not fulfil the conditions provided for in paragraphs 2 and 3.

(5) The provisions of paragraphs 2 and 3 apply both to the rights and benefits referred to in Articles 13, 18, 19, 21 and 22 of this Convention and to rights and benefits for which this Convention does not provide

Article 8 Exemption from exceptional measures

With regard to exceptional measures which may be taken against the person, property or interests of nationals of a foreign State, the Contracting States shall not apply such measures to a refugee who is formally a national of the said State solely on account of such nationality. Contracting States which, under their legislation, are prevented from applying the general principle expressed in this Article, shall, in appropriate cases, grant exemptions in favour of such refugees.

Article 9 Provisional measures

Nothing in this Convention shall prevent a Contracting State, in time of war or other grave and exceptional circumstances, from taking provisionally measures which it considers to be essential to the national security in the case of a particular person, pending a determination by the Contracting State that that person is in fact a refugee and that the continuance of such measures is necessary in his case in the interests of national security.

Article 10 Continuity of residence

(1) Where a refugee has been forcibly displaced during the Second World War and removed to the territory of a Contracting State, and is resident there, the period of such enforced sojourn shall be considered to have been lawful residence within that territory.

(2) Where a refugee has been forcibly displaced during the Second World War from the territory of a Contracting State and has, prior to the date of entry into force of this

Convention, returned there for the purpose of taking up residence, the period of residence before and after such enforced displacement shall be regarded as one uninterrupted period for any purposes for which uninterrupted residence is required.

Article 11 Refugee Seamen

In the case of refugees regularly serving as crew members on board a ship flying the flag of a Contracting State, that State shall give sympathetic consideration to their establishment on its territory and the issue of travel documents to them or their temporary admission to its territory particularly with a view to facilitating their establishment in another country.

Chapter II: Juridical Status

Article 12 Personal status

(1) The personal status of a refugee shall be governed by the law of the country of his domicile or, if he has no domicile, by the law of the country of his residence.

(2) Rights previously acquired by a refugee and dependent on personal status, more particularly rights attaching to marriage, shall be respected by a Contracting State, subject to compliance, if this be necessary, with the formalities required by the law of that State, provided that the right in question is one which would have been recognized by the law of that State had he not become a refugee.

Article 13 Movable and immovable property

The Contracting States shall accord to a refugee treatment as favourable as possible and, in any event, not less favourable than that accorded to aliens generally in the same circumstances, as regards the acquisition of movable and immovable property and other rights pertaining thereto, and to leases and other contracts relating to movable and immovable property.

Article 14 Artistic rights and industrial property

In respect of the protection of industrial property, such as inventions, designs or models, trade marks, trade names, and of rights in literary, artistic, and scientific works, a refugee shall be accorded in the country in which he has his habitual residence the same protection as is accorded to nationals of that country. In the territory of any other Contracting State, he shall be accorded the same protection as is accorded in that territory to nationals of the country in which he has his habitual residence.

Article 15 Right of association

As regards non-political and non-profit making associations and trade unions the Contracting States shall accord to refugees lawfully staying in their territory the most-favourable treatment accorded to nationals of a foreign country, in the same circumstances.

Article 16 Access to courts

(1) A refugee shall have free access to the courts of law on the territory of all Contracting States.

(2) A refugee shall enjoy in the Contracting State in which he has his habitual residence the same treatment as a national in matters pertaining to access to the Courts, including legal assistance and exemption from *cautio judicatem solvi*.

(3) A refugee shall be accorded in the matters referred to in paragraph 2 in countries other than that in which he has his habitual residence the treatment granted to a national of the country of his habitual residence.

Chapter III: Gainful Employment

Article 17 Wage-earning employment

(1) The Contracting State shall accord to refugees lawfully staying in their territory the most favourable treatment accorded to nationals of a foreign country in the same circumstances, as regards the right to engage in wage-earning employment.

(2) In any case, restrictive measures imposed on aliens or the employment of aliens for the protection of the national labour market shall not be applied to a refugee who was already exempt from them at the date of entry into force of this Convention for the Contracting State concerned, or who fulfils one of the following conditions: (a) He has completed three years' residence in the country, (b) He has a spouse possessing the nationality of the country of residence. A refugee may not invoke the benefits of this provision if he has abandoned his spouse, (c) He has one or more children possessing the nationality of the country of residence.

(3) The Contracting States shall give sympathetic consideration to assimilating the rights of all refugees with regard to wage-earning employment to those of nationals, and in particular of those refugees who have entered their territory pursuant to programmes of labour recruitment or under immigration schemes.

Article 18 Self-employment

The Contracting States shall accord to a refugee lawfully in their territory treatment as favourable as possible and, in any event, not less favourable that that accorded to aliens generally in the same circumstances, as regards the right to engage on his own account in agriculture, industry, handicrafts and commerce and to establish commercial and industrial companies.

Article 19 Liberal professions

(1) Each Contracting State shall accord to refugees lawfully staying in their territory who hold diplomas recognized by the competent authorities of that State, and who are desirous of practicing a liberal profession, treatment as favourable as possible and, in any event, not less favourable than that accorded to aliens generally in the same circumstances.

(2) The Contracting States shall use their best endeavours consistently with their laws and constitutions to secure the settlement of such refugees in the territories, other than the metropolitan territory, for whose international relations they are responsible.

Chapter IV: Welfare

Article 20 Rationing

Where a rationing system exists, which applies to the population at large and regulates the general distribution of products in short supply, refugees shall be accorded the same treatment as nationals.

Article 21 Housing

As regards housing, the Contracting States, in so far as the matter is regulated by laws or regulations or is subject to the control of public authorities, shall accord to refugees lawfully staying in their territory treatment as favourable as possible and, in any event, not less favourable than that accorded to aliens generally in the same circumstances.

Article 22 Public education

(1) The Contracting States shall accord to refugees the same treatment as is accorded to nationals with respect to elementary education.

(2) The Contracting States shall accord to refugees treatment as favourable as possible, and, in any event, not less favourable than that accorded to aliens generally in the same circumstances, with respect to education other than elementary education and, in particular, as regards access to studies, the recognition of foreign school certificates, diplomas and degrees, the remission of fees and charges and the award of scholarships.

Article 23 Public relief

The Contracting States shall accord to refugees lawfully staying in their territory the same treatment with respect to public relief and assistance as is accorded to their nationals.

Article 24 Labour legislation and social security

(1) The Contracting States shall accord to refugees lawfully staying in their territory the same treatment as is accorded to nationals in respect of the following matters:

(a) In so far as such matters are governed by laws or regulations or are subject to the control of administrative authorities: remuneration, including family allowances where these form part of remuneration, hours of work, overtime arrangements, holidays with pay, restrictions on home work, minimum age of employment, apprenticeship and training, women's work and the work of young persons, and the enjoyment of the benefits of collective bargaining;

(b) Social security (legal provisions in respect of employment injury, occupational diseases, maternity, sickness, disability, old age, death, unemployment, family responsibilities and any other contingency which, according to national laws or regulations, is covered by a social security scheme), subject to the following limitations:

(i) There may be appropriate arrangements for the maintenance of acquired rights and rights in course of acquisition;

(ii) National laws or regulations of the country of residence may prescribe special arrangements concerning benefits or portions of benefits which are payable wholly out of public funds, and concerning allowances paid to persons who do not fulfil the contribution conditions prescribed for the award of a normal pension.

(2) The right to compensation for the death of a refugee resulting from employment injury or from occupational disease shall not be affected by the fact that the residence of the beneficiary is outside the territory of the Contracting State.

(3) The Contracting States shall extend to refugees the benefits of agreements concluded between them, or which may be concluded between them in the future, concerning the maintenance of acquired rights and rights in the process of acquisition in regard to social security, subject only to the conditions which apply to nationals of the States signatory to the agreements in question.

(4) The Contracting States will give sympathetic consideration to extending to refugees so far as possible the benefits of similar agreements which may at any time be in force between such Contracting States and non-contracting States.

Chapter V: Administrative Measures

Article 25 Administrative assistance

(1) When the exercise of a right by a refugee would normally require the assistance of authorities of a foreign country to whom he cannot have recourse, the Contracting States in whose territory he is residing shall arrange that such assistance be afforded to him by their own authorities or by an international authority.

(2) The authority or authorities mentioned in paragraph 1 shall deliver or cause to be delivered under their supervision to refugees such documents or certifications as would normally be delivered to aliens by or through their national authorities.

(3) Documents or certifications so delivered shall stand in the stead of the official instruments delivered to aliens by or through their national authorities, and shall be given credence in the absence of proof to the contrary.

(4) Subject to such exceptional treatment as may be granted to indigent persons, fees may be charged for the services mentioned herein, but such fees shall be moderate and commensurate with those charged to nationals for similar services.

(5) The provisions of this Article shall be without prejudice to Articles 27 and 28.

Article 26 Freedom of movement

Each Contracting State shall accord to refugees lawfully in its territory the right to choose their place of residence to move freely within its territory, subject to any regulations applicable to aliens generally in the same circumstances.

Article 27 Identity papers

The Contracting States shall issue identity papers to any refugee in their territory who does not possess a valid travel document.

Article 28 Travel documents

(1) The Contracting States shall issue to refugees lawfully staying in their territory travel documents for the purpose of travel outside their territory unless compelling reasons of national security or public order otherwise require, and the provisions of the Schedule to this Convention shall apply with respect to such documents. The Contracting States may issue such a travel document to any other refugee in their territory; they shall in particular give sympathetic consideration to the issue of such a travel document to refugees in their territory who are unable to obtain a travel document from the country of their lawful residence.

(2) Travel documents issued to refugees under previous international agreements by parties thereto shall be recognized and treated by the Contracting States in the same way as if they had been issued pursuant to this article.

Article 29 Fiscal charges

(1) The Contracting States shall not impose upon refugee duties, charges or taxes, of any description whatsoever, other or higher than those which are or may be levied on their nationals in similar situations.

(2) Nothing in the above paragraph shall prevent the application to refugees of the laws and regulations concerning charges in respect of the issue to aliens of administrative documents including identity papers.

Article 30 Transfer of assets

(1) A Contracting State shall, in conformity with its laws and regulations, permit refugees to transfer assets which they have brought into its territory, to another country where they have been admitted for the purposes of resettlement.

(2) A Contracting State shall give sympathetic consideration to the application of refugees for permission to transfer assets wherever they may be and which are necessary for their resettlement in another country to which they have been admitted.

Article 31 Refugees unlawfully in the country of refuge

(1) The Contracting States shall not impose penalties, on account of their illegal entry or presence, on refugees who, coming directly from a territory where their life or

freedom was threatened in the sense of Article 1, enter or are present in their territory without authorization, provided they present themselves without delay to the authorities and show good cause for their illegal entry or presence.

(2) The Contracting States shall not apply to the movements of such refugees restrictions other than those which are necessary and such restrictions shall only be applied until their status in the country is regularized or they obtain admission into another country. The Contracting States shall allow such refugees a reasonable period and all the necessary facilities to obtain admission into another country.

Article 32 Expulsion

(1) The Contracting States shall not expel a refugee lawfully in their territory save on grounds of national security or public order.

(2) The expulsion of such a refugee shall be only in pursuance of a decision reached in accordance with due process of law. Except where compelling reasons of national security otherwise require, the refugee shall be allowed to submit evidence to clear himself, and to appeal to and be represented for the purpose before competent authority or a person or persons specially designated by the competent authority.

(3) The Contracting States shall allow such a refugee a reasonable period within which to seek legal admission into another country. The Contracting States reserve the right to apply during that period such internal measures as they may deem necessary.

Article 33 Prohibition of expulsion or return ("refoulement")

(1) No Contracting State shall expel or return ("refouler") a refugee in any manner whatsoever to the frontiers of territories where his life or freedom would be threatened on account of his race, religion, nationality, membership of a particular social group or political opinion.

(2) The benefit of the present provision may not, however, be claimed by a refugee whom there are reasonable grounds for regarding as a danger to the security of the country in which he is, or who, having been convicted by a final judgment of a particularly serious crime, constitutes a danger to the community of that country.

Article 34 Naturalization

The Contracting States shall as far as possible facilitate the assimilation and naturalization of refugees. They shall in particular make every effort to expedite naturalization proceedings and to reduce as far as possible the charges and costs of such proceedings.

Chapter VI: Executory and Transitory Provisions

Article 35 Co-operation of the national authorities with the United Nations

(1) The Contracting States undertake to co-operate with the Office of the United Nations High Commissioner for Refugees, or any other agency of the United Nations

which may succeed it, in the exercise of its functions, and shall in particular facilitate its duty of supervising the application of the provisions of this Convention.

(2) In order to enable the Office of the High Commissioner or any other agency of the United Nations which may succeed it, to make reports to the competent organs of the United Nations, the Contracting States undertake to provide them in the appropriate form with information and statistical data requested concerning:

(a) the condition of refugees,

(b) the implementation of this Convention, and

(c) laws, regulations and decrees which are, or may hereafter be, in force relating to refugees.

Article 36 Information on national legislation

The Contracting States shall communicate to the Secretary-General of the United Nations the laws and regulations which they may adopt to ensure the application of this Convention.

Article 37 Relation to previous Conventions

Without prejudice to Article 28, paragraph 2, of this Convention, this Convention replaces, as between parties to it, the Arrangements of 5 July 1922, 31 May 1924, 12 May 1926, 30 June 1928 and 30 July 1935, the Conventions of 28 October 1933 and 10 February 1938, the Protocol of 14 September 1939 and the Agreement of 15 October 1946.

Chapter VII: Final Clauses

Article 38 Settlement of disputes

Any dispute between parties to this Convention relating to its interpretation or application, which cannot be settled by other means, shall be referred to the International Court of Justice at the request of any one of the parties to the dispute.

Article 39 Signature, ratification and accession

(1) This Convention shall be opened for signature at Geneva on 28 July 1951 and shall hereafter be deposited with the Secretary-General of the United Nations. It shall be open for signature at the European Office of the United Nations from 28 July to 31 August 1951 and shall be re-opened for signature at the Headquarters of the United Nations from 17 September 1951 to 31 December 1952.

(2) This Convention shall be open for signature on behalf of all States Members of the United Nations, and also on behalf of any other State invited to attend the Conference of Plenipotentiaries on the Status of Refugees and Stateless Persons or to which an invitation to sign will have been addressed by the General Assembly. It shall be ratified and the instruments of ratification shall be deposited with the Secretary-General of the United Nations.

(3) This Convention shall be open from 28 July 1951 for accession by the States referred to in paragraph 2 of this Article. Accession shall be effected by the deposit of an instrument of accession with the Secretary-General of the United Nations.

Article 40 Territorial application clause

(1) Any state may, at the time of signature, ratification or accession, declare that this Convention shall extend to all or any of the territories for the international relations of which it is responsible. Such a declaration shall take effect when the Convention enters into force for the State concerned.

(2) At any time thereafter any such extension shall be made by notification addressed to the Secretary-General of the United Nations and shall take effect as from the ninetieth day after the day of receipt by the Secretary-General of the United Nations of this notification, or as from the date of entry into force of the Convention for the State concerned, whichever is the later.

(3) With respect to those territories to which this Convention is not extended at the time of signature, ratification or accession, each State concerned shall consider the possibility of taking the necessary steps in order to extend the application of this Convention to such territories, subject, where necessary for constitutional reasons, to the consent of the governments of such territories.

Article 41 Federal clause

In the case of a Federal or non-unitary State, the following provisions shall apply:

(a) With respect to those Articles of this Convention that come within the legislative jurisdiction of the federal legislative authority, the obligations of the Federal Government shall to this extent be the same as those of Parties which are not Federal States,

(b) With respect to those Articles of this Convention that come within the legislative jurisdiction of constituent States, provinces or cantons which are not, under the constitutional system of the federation, bound to take legislative action, the Federal Government shall bring such Articles with a favourable recommendation to the notice of the appropriate authorities of States, provinces or cantons at the earliest possible moment.

(c) A Federal State Party to this Convention shall, at the request of any other Contracting State transmitted through the Secretary-General of the United Nations, supply a statement of the law and practice of the Federation and its constituent units in regard to any particular provision of the Convention showing the extent to which effect has been given to that provision by legislative or other action.

Article 42 Reservations

(1) At the time of signature, ratification or accession, any State may make reservations to articles of the Convention other than to Articles 1, 3, 4, 16(1), 33, 36–46 inclusive.

(2) Any State making a reservation in accordance with paragraph 1 of this article may at any time withdraw the reservation by a communication to that effect addressed to the Secretary-General of the United Nations.

Article 43 Entry into force

(1) This Convention shall come into force on the ninetieth day following the day of deposit of the sixth instrument of ratification or accession.

(2) For each State ratifying or acceding to the Convention after the deposit of the sixth instrument of ratification or accession, the Convention shall enter into force on the ninetieth day following the date of deposit by such State of its instrument or ratification or accession.

Article 44 Denunciation

(1) Any Contracting State may denounce this Convention at any time by a notification addressed to the Secretary-General of the United Nations.

(2) Such denunciation shall take effect for the Contracting State concerned one year from the date upon which it is received by the Secretary-General of the United Nations.

(3) Any State which has made a declaration or notification under Article 40 may, at any time thereafter, by a notification to the Secretary-General of the United Nations, declare that the Convention shall cease to extent to such territory one year after the date of receipt of the notification by the Secretary-General.

Article 45 Revision

(1) Any Contracting State may request revision of this Convention at any time by a notification addressed to the Secretary-General of the United Nations.

(2) The General Assembly of the United Nations shall recommend the steps, if any, to be taken in respect of such request.

Article 46 Notifications by the Secretary-General of the United Nations

The Secretary-General of the United Nations shall inform all Members of the United Nations and non-member States referred to in Article 39:

   (a) of declarations and notifications in accordance with Section B of Article 1;

   (b) of signatures, ratifications and accessions in accordance with Article 39;

   (c) of declarations and notifications in accordance with Article 40;

   (d) of reservations and withdrawals in accordance with Article 42;

   (e) of the date on which this Convention will come into force in accordance with Article 43;

   (f) of denunciations and notifications in accordance with Article 44;

   (g) of requests for revision in accordance with Article 45.

IN FAITH WHEREOF the undersigned, duly authorized, have signed this Convention on behalf of their respective Governments,

DONE at GENEVA, this twenty-eighth day of July, one thousand nine hundred and fifty-one, in a single copy, of which the English and French texts are equally authentic and which shall remain deposited in the archives of the United Nations, and certified true copies of which shall be delivered to all Members of the United Nations and to the non-member States referred to in Article 39.

---

1. *Official Records of the General Assembly, Fifth Session, Supplement No. 20* (A/1775), 48.

Protocol Relating to the Status of Refugees (1967)

The 1967 Protocol Relating to the Status of Refugees amended the 1951 Convention to respond to more universal refugee situations.

United Nations General Assembly, 16 December 1966.

Entry into force:	4 October 1967, in accordance with article VIII.
Registration:	4 October 1967, No. 8791.
Text:	United Nations, Treaty Series, vol. 606, p. 267.
Status as at 15 February 2001:	Parties: 136

Note: On the recommendation of the Executive Committee of the Programme of the United Nations High Commissioner for Refugees, the High Commissioner submitted the draft of the above-mentioned Protocol to the General Assembly of the United Nations, through the Economic and Social Council, in the addendum to his report concerning measures to extend the personal scope of the Convention relating to the Status of Refugees. The Economic and Social Council, in resolution 1186 (XLI)[1] of 18 November 1966, took note with approval of the draft Protocol and transmitted the said addendum to the General Assembly. The General Assembly, in resolution 2198 (XXI)[2] of 16 December 1966, took note of the Protocol and requested the Secretary-General "to transmit the text of the Protocol to the States mentioned in article V thereof, with a view to enabling them to accede to the Protocol."

Note: All references to chapters refer to the United Nations publication, Multilateral treaties deposited with the Secretary General (MTDSG).

Preamble

The States Parties to the present Protocol,

Considering that the Convention relating to the Status of Refugees done at Geneva on 28 July 1951 (hereinafter referred to as the Convention) covers only those persons who have become refugees as a result of events occurring before 1 January, 1951,

Considering that new refugee situations have arisen since the Convention was adopted and that the refugees concerned may therefore not fall within the scope of the Convention,

Considering that it is desirable that equal status should be enjoyed by all refugees covered by the definition in the Convention irrespective of the dateline 1 January 1951,

Have agreed as follows:

Article I General provision

(1) The States Parties to the present Protocol undertake to apply Articles 2 to 34 inclusive of the Convention to refugees as hereinafter defined.

(2) For the purpose of the present Protocol, the term "refugee" shall, except as regards the application of paragraph 3 of this Article, mean any person within the definition of Article 1 of the Convention as if the words "As a result of events occurring before 1 January 1951 and . . . "and the words". . . a result of such events," in Article 1 A (2) were omitted.

(3) The present Protocol shall be applied by the States Parties hereto without any geographic limitation, save that existing declarations made by States already Parties to the Convention in accordance with Article 1 B (1)(a) of the Convention, shall, unless extended under Article 1 B (2) thereof, apply also under the present Protocol.

Article II Co-operation of the national authorities with the United Nations

(1) The States Parties to the present Protocol undertake to co-operate with the Office of the United Nations High Commissioner for Refugees, or any other agency of the United Nations which may succeed it, in the exercise of its functions, and shall in particular facilitate its duty of supervising the application of the provisions of the present Protocol.

(2) In order to enable the Office of the High Commissioner, or any other agency of the United Nations which may succeed it, to make reports to the competent organs of the United Nations, the States Parties to the present Protocol undertake to provide them with the information and statistical data requested, in the appropriate form, concerning:

  (a) The condition of refugees;

  (b) The implementation of the present Protocol;

  (c) Laws, regulations and decrees which are, or may hereafter be, in force relating to refugees.

Article III Information on national legislation

The States Parties to the present Protocol shall communicate to the Secretary-General of the United Nations the laws and regulations which they may adopt to ensure the application of the present Protocol.

Article IV Settlement of disputes

Any dispute between States Parties to the present Protocol which relates to its interpretation or application and which cannot be settled by other means shall be referred to the International Court of Justice at the request of any one of the parties to the dispute.

Article V Accession

The present Protocol shall be open for accession on behalf of all States Parties to the Convention and of any other State Member of the United Nations or member of any of the specialized agencies or to which an invitation to accede may have been addressed by the General Assembly of the United Nations. Accession shall be effected by the deposit of an instrument of accession with the Secretary-General of the United Nations.

Article VI Federal clause

In the case of a Federal or non-unitary State, the following provisions shall apply:
  (a) With respect to those articles of the Convention to be applied in accordance with Article I, paragraph 1, of the present Protocol that come within the legislative jurisdiction of the federal legislative authority, the obligations of the Federal Government shall to this extent be the same as those of States Parties which are not Federal States;
  (b) With respect to those articles of the Convention to be applied in accordance with Article I, paragraph 1, of the present Protocol that come within the legislative jurisdiction of constituent States, provinces or cantons which are not, under the constitutional system of the federation, bound to take legislative action, the Federal Government shall bring such articles with a favourable recommendation to the notice of the appropriate authorities of States, provinces or cantons at the earliest possible moment;
  (c) A Federal State Party to the present Protocol shall, at the request of any other State Party hereto transmitted through the Secretary-General of the United Nations, supply a statement of the law and practice of the Federation and its constituent units in regard to any particular provision of the Convention to be applied in accordance with Article I, paragraph 1, of the present Protocol, showing the extent to which effect has been given to that provision by legislative or other action.

Article VII Reservations and declarations

1. At the time of accession, any State may make reservations in respect of Article IV of the present Protocol and in respect of the application in accordance with Article I of the present Protocol of any provisions of the Convention other than those contained in Articles 1, 3, 4, 16 (1) and 33 thereof, provided that in the case of a State Party to the Convention reservations made under this Article shall not extend to refugees in respect of whom the Convention applies.

2. Reservations made by States Parties to the Convention in accordance with Article 42 thereof shall, unless withdrawn, be applicable in relation to their obligations under the present Protocol.

3. Any State making a reservation in accordance with paragraph 1 of this Article may at any time withdraw such reservation by a communication to that effect addressed to the Secretary-General of the United Nations.

4. Declarations made under Article 40, paragraphs 1 and 2, of the Convention by a State Party thereto which accedes to the present Protocol shall be deemed to apply in respect of the present Protocol, unless upon accession a notification to the contrary is addressed by the State Party concerned to the Secretary-General of the United Nations. The provisions of Article 40, paragraphs 2 and 3, and of Article 44, paragraph 3, of the Convention shall be deemed to apply *mutatis mutandis* to the present Protocol.

Article VIII Entry into force

1. The present Protocol shall come into force on the day of deposit of the sixth instrument of accession.

2. For each State acceding to the Protocol after the deposit of the sixth instrument of accession, the Protocol shall come into force on the date of deposit by such State of its instrument of accession.

Article IX Denunciation

1. Any State Party hereto may denounce this Protocol at any time by a notification addressed to the Secretary-General of the United Nations.

2. Such denunciation shall take effect for the State Party concerned one year from the date on which it is received by the Secretary-General of the United Nations.

Article X Notifications by the Secretary-General of the United Nations

The Secretary-General of the United Nations shall inform the States referred to in Article V above of the date of entry into force, accessions, reservations and withdrawals of reservations to and denunciations of the present Protocol, and of declarations and notifications relating hereto.

Article XI Deposit in the archives of the Secretariat

A copy of the present Protocol, of which the Chinese, English, French, Russian and Spanish texts are equally authentic, signed by the President of the General Assembly and by the Secretary-General of the United Nations, shall be deposited in the archives of the Secretariat of the United Nations. The Secretary-General will transmit certified copies thereof to all States Members of the United Nations and to the other States referred to in Article V above.

Declarations and Reservations to the Protocol relating to the Status of Refugees

(Unless otherwise indicated, the declarations and reservations were made upon accession or succession. For objections thereto and territorial applications, see hereinafter.)

United States of America

With the following reservations in respect of the application, in accordance with article I of the Protocol, of the Convention relating to the Status of Refugees, done at New York on 28 July 1951:

"The United States of America construes Article 29 of the Convention as applying only to refugees who are resident in the United States and reserves the right to tax refugees who are not residents of the United States in accordance with its general rules relating to non-resident aliens.

"The United States of America accepts the obligation of paragraph 1 (b) of Article 24 of the Convention except insofar as that paragraph may conflict in certain instances with any provisions of title II (old age, survivors' and disability insurance) or title XVIII (hospital and medical insurance for the aged) of the Social Security Act. As to any such provision, the United States will accord to refugees lawfully staying in its territory treatment no less favorable than is accorded aliens generally in the same circumstances."

---

1. *Official Records of the Economic and Social Council, Forty-first Session, Supplement No. 1A* (E/4264/Add.1), 1.

2. *Official Records of the General Assembly, Twenty-first Session, Supplement No. 16* (A/6316), 48.

Immigration and Nationality Act of 1952

The Immigration and Nationality Act (INA), originally created in 1952, organized immigration law in one, primary location. The INA underwent two significant revisions during the 1990s. First, the Immigration Act of 1990 included significant amendments to temporary foreign worker provisions, particularly highly skilled workers and farmworkers. Second, the Illegal Immigration Reform and Immigrant Responsibility Act of 1996 (IIRIRA) included significant amendments to restrict immigrants' access to benefits, expedite the removal of deportable immigrants, and remove criminal aliens, among other provisions. The laws excerpted below are amended versions of the INA, which include congressional actions up to 2001. Section 214 is excerpted to focus on the admission of highly skilled temporary foreign workers—specifically, the H-1B visa category. Section 218 is presented in its entirety because it exclusively addresses migrant farmworker employment.

Section 214 - Admission of Nonimmigrants

. . .

(g)(1)   The total number of aliens who may be issued visas or otherwise provided nonimmigrant status during any fiscal year (beginning with fiscal year 1992)-

   (A) Under section 101(a)(15)(H)(i)(b), may not exceed

      (i)   65,000 in each fiscal year before fiscal year 1999;

      (ii)   115,000 in fiscal year 1999;

      (iii)   115,000 in fiscal year 2000;

      (iv)   195,000 in fiscal year 2001;

      (v)   195,000 in fiscal year 2002;

      (vi)   195,000 in fiscal year 2003 and

      (vii) 65,000 in each succeeding fiscal year; or

   (B) under section 101(a)(15)(H)(ii)(b) may not exceed 66,000.

   (C) [was repealed by Sec. 202(a)(3) of the Miscellaneous and Technical Immigration and Naturalization Amendments of 1991 (P.L. 102-232, Dec. 12, 1991, 105 Stat. 1737), effective April 1, 1992.]

(2) The numerical limitations of paragraph (1) shall only apply to principal aliens and not to the spouses or children of such aliens.

(3) Aliens who are subject to the numerical limitations of paragraph (1) shall be issued visas (or otherwise provided nonimmigrant status) in the order in which petitions are filed for such visas or status. If an alien who was issued a visa or otherwise provided nonimmigrant status and counted against the numerical limitations of paragraph (1) is found to have been issued such visa or otherwise provided such status by fraud or willfully misrepresenting a material fact and such visa or nonimmigrant status is revoked, then one number shall be restored to the total number of aliens who may be issued visas or otherwise provided such status under the numerical limitations of paragraph (1) in the fiscal year in which the petition is revoked, regardless of the fiscal year in which the petition was approved.

(4) In the case of a nonimmigrant described in section 101(a)(15)(H)(i)(b), the period of authorized admission as such a nonimmigrant may not exceed 6 years.

(5) The numerical limitations contained in paragraph (1)(A) shall not apply to any nonimmigrant alien issued a visa or otherwise provided status under section 101(a)(15)(H)(i)(b) who is employed (or has received an offer of employment) at—

   (A) an institution of higher education (as defined in section 101(a) of the Higher Education Act of 1965 (20 U.S.C. 1001(a))), or a related or affiliated nonprofit entity; or

   (B) a nonprofit research organization or a governmental research organization.

(6) Any alien who ceases to be employed by an employer described in paragraph (5)(A)shall, if employed as a nonimmigrant alien described in section 101(a)(15)(H)(i)(b), who has not previously been counted toward the numerical limitations contained in paragraph(1)(A), be counted toward those limitations the first time the alien is employed by an employer other than one described in paragraph (5).

(7) Any alien who has already been counted within the 6 years prior to the approval of a petition described in subsection (c), toward the numerical limitations of paragraph (1)(A)shall not again be counted toward those limitations unless the alien

would be eligible for a full 6 years of authorized admission at the time the petition is filed. Where multiple petitions are approved for 1 alien, that alien shall be counted only once.

(h) The fact that an alien is the beneficiary of an application for a preference status filed under section 204 or has otherwise sought permanent residence in the United States shall not constitute evidence of an intention to abandon a foreign residence for purposes of obtaining a visa as a nonimmigrant described in subparagraph 10/ (H)(i), (L), or (V) of section 101(a)(15) or otherwise obtaining or maintaining the status of a nonimmigrant described in such subparagraph, if the alien had obtained a change of status under section 248 to a classification as such a nonimmigrant before the alien's most recent departure from the United States.

(i)(1) For purposes of section 101(a)(15)(H)(i)(b) and paragraph (2), the term "specialty occupation" means an occupation that requires-

(A) theoretical and practical application of a body of highly specialized knowledge, and

(B) attainment of a bachelor's or higher degree in the specific specialty (or its equivalent) as a minimum for entry into the occupation in the United States.

(2) For purposes of section 101(a)(15)(H)(i)(b), the requirements of this paragraph, with respect to a specialty occupation, are-

(A) full state licensure to practice in the occupation, if such licensure is required to practice in the occupation,

(B) completion of the degree described in paragraph (1)(B) for the occupation, or

(C)(i) experience in the specialty equivalent to the completion of such degree, and

(ii) recognition of expertise in the specialty through progressively responsible positions relating to the specialty.

. . .

Section 218 - Admission of Temporary H-2A Workers

(a) Conditions for Approval of H-2A Petitions.-

(1) A petition to import an alien as an H-2A worker (as defined in subsection (i)(2)) may not be approved by the Attorney General unless the petitioner has applied to the Secretary of Labor for a certification that-

(A) there are not sufficient workers who are able, willing, and qualified, and who will be available at the time and place needed, to perform the labor or services involved in the petition, and

(B) the employment of the alien in such labor or services will not adversely affect the wages and working conditions of workers in the United States similarly employed.

(2) The Secretary of Labor may require by regulation, as a condition of issuing the certification, the payment of a fee to recover the reasonable costs of processing applications for certification.

(b) Conditions for Denial of Labor Certification.-The Secretary of Labor may not issue a certification under subsection (a) with respect to an employer if the conditions described in that subsection are not met or if any of the following conditions are met:

(1) There is a strike or lockout in the course of a labor dispute which, under the regulations, precludes such certification.

(2)(A) The employer during the previous two-year period employed H-2A workers and the Secretary of Labor has determined, after notice and opportunity for a hearing, that the employer at any time during that period substantially violated a material term or condition of the labor certification with respect to the employment of domestic or nonimmigrant workers.

(B) No employer may be denied certification under subparagraph (A) for more than three years for any violation described in such subparagraph.

(3) The employer has not provided the Secretary with satisfactory assurances that if the employment for which the certification is sought is not covered by State workers' compensation law, the employer will provide, at no cost to the worker, insurance covering injury and disease arising out of and in the course of the worker's employment which will provide benefits at least equal to those provided under the State workers' compensation law for comparable employment.

(4) The Secretary determines that the employer has not made positive recruitment efforts within a multi- state region of traditional or expected labor supply where the Secretary finds that there are a significant number of qualified United States workers who, if recruited, would be willing to make themselves available for work at the time and place needed. Positive recruitment under this paragraph is in addition to, and shall be conducted within the same time period as, the circulation through the interstate employment service system of the employer's job offer. The obligation to engage in positive recruitment under this paragraph shall terminate on the date the H-2A workers depart for the employer's place of employment.

(c) Special Rules for Consideration of Applications.-The following rules shall apply in the case of the filing and consideration of an application for a labor certification under this section:

(1) Deadline for filing applications.-The Secretary of Labor may not require that the application be filed more than 45 days 1/ before the first date the employer requires the labor or services of the H-2A worker.

(2) Notice within seven days of deficiencies.-

(A) The employer shall be notified in writing within seven days of the date of filing if the application does not meet the standards (other than that described in subsection (a)(1)(A)) for approval.

(B) If the application does not meet such standards, the notice shall include the reasons therefor and the Secretary shall provide an opportunity for the prompt resubmission of a modified application.

(3) Issuance of certification.-

(A) The Secretary of Labor shall make, not later than 30 days 1/ before the date such labor or services are first required to be performed, the certification described in subsection (a)(1) if-

(i)   the employer has complied with the criteria for certification (including criteria for the recruitment of eligible individuals as prescribed by the Secretary), and

(ii) the employer does not actually have, or has not been provided with referrals of, qualified eligible individuals who have indicated their availability to perform such labor or services on the terms and conditions of a job offer which meets the requirements of the Secretary.

In considering the question of whether a specific qualification is appropriate in a job offer, the Secretary shall apply the normal and accepted qualifications required by non-H-2A-employers in the same or comparable occupations and crops.

(B)(i) For a period of 3 years subsequent to the effective date of this section, labor certifications shall remain effective only if, from the time the foreign worker departs for the employer's place of employment, the employer will provide employment to any qualified United States worker who applies to the employer until 50 percent of the period of the work contract, under which the foreign worker who is in the job was hired, has elapsed. In addition, the employer will offer to provide benefits, wages and working conditions required pursuant to this section and regulations.

(ii) The requirement of clause (i) shall not apply to any employer who-

(I)   did not, during any calendar quarter during the preceding calendar year, use more than 500 man-days of agricultural labor, as defined in section 3(u) of the Fair Labor Standards Act of 1938 (29 U.S.C. 203(u)),

(II) is not a member of an association which has petitioned for certification under this section for its members, and

(III) has not otherwise associated with other employers who are petitioning for temporary foreign workers under this section.

(iii) Six months before the end of the 3-year period described in clause (i), the Secretary of Labor shall consider the findings of the report mandated by section 403(a)(4)(D) of the Immigration Reform and Control Act of 1986 as well as other relevant materials, including evidence of benefits to United States workers and costs to employers, addressing the advisability of continuing a policy which requires an employer, as a condition for certification under this section, to continue to accept qualified, eligible United States workers for employment after the date the H-2A workers depart for work with the employer. The Secretary's review of such findings and materials shall lead to the issuance of findings in furtherance of the Congressional policy that aliens not be admitted under this section unless there are not sufficient workers in the

United States who are able, willing, and qualified to perform the labor or service needed and that the employment of the aliens in such labor or services will not adversely affect the wages and working conditions of workers in the United States similarly employed. In the absence of the enactment of Federal legislation prior to three months before the end of the 3-year period described in clause (i) which addresses the subject matter of this subparagraph, the Secretary shall immediately publish the findings required by this clause, and shall promulgate, on an interim or final basis, regulations based on his findings which shall be effective no later than three years from the effective date of this section.

(iv) In complying with clause (i) of this subparagraph, an association shall be allowed to refer or transfer workers among its members: Provided, That for purposes of this section an association acting as an agent for its members shall not be considered a joint employer merely because of such referral or transfer.

(v) United States workers referred or transferred pursuant to clause (iv) of this subparagraph shall not be treated disparately.

(vi) An employer shall not be liable for payments under section 655.202(b)(6) of title 20, Code of Federal Regulations (or any successor regulation) with respect to an H-2A worker who is displaced due to compliance with the requirement of this subparagraph, if the Secretary of Labor certifies that the H- 2A worker was displaced because of the employer's compliance with clause (i) of this subparagraph.

(vii)(I) No person or entity shall willfully and knowingly withhold domestic workers prior to the arrival of H-2A workers in order to force the hiring of domestic workers under clause (I).

(II) Upon the receipt of a complaint by an employer that a violation of subclause (I) has occurred the Secretary shall immediately investigate. He shall within 36 hours of the receipt of the complaint issue findings concerning the alleged violation. Where the Secretary finds that a violation has occurred, he shall immediately suspend the application of clause (i) of this subparagraph with respect to that certification for that date of need.

(4) Housing.-Employers shall furnish housing in accordance with regulations. The employer shall be permitted at the employer's option to provide housing meeting applicable Federal standards for temporary labor camps or to secure housing which meets the local standards for rental and/or public accommodations or other substantially similar class of habitation: Provided, That in the absence of applicable local standards, State standards for rental and/or public accommodations or other substantially similar class of habitation shall be met: Provided further, That in the absence of applicable local or State standards, Federal temporary labor camp standards shall apply: Provided further, That the Secretary of Labor shall is-

sue regulations which address the specific requirements of housing for employees principally engaged in the range production of livestock: Provided further, That when it is the prevailing practice in the area and occupation of intended employment to provide family housing, family housing shall be provided to workers with families who request it: And provided further, That nothing in this paragraph shall require an employer to provide or secure housing for workers who are not entitled to it under the temporary labor certification regulations in effect on June 1, 1986.

(d) Roles of Agricultural Associations.-

   (1) Permitting filing by agricultural associations.-A petition to import an alien as a temporary agricultural worker, and an application for a labor certification with respect to such a worker, may be filed by an association of agricultural producers which use agricultural services.

   (2) Treatment of associations acting as employers.-If an association is a joint or sole employer of temporary agricultural workers, the certifications granted under this section to the association may be used for the certified job opportunities of any of its producer members and such workers may be transferred among its producer members to perform agricultural services of a temporary or seasonal nature for which the certifications were granted.

   (3) Treatment of violations.-

      (A) Member's violation does not necessarily disqualify association or other members.-If an individual producer member of a joint employer association is determined to have committed an act that under subsection (b)(2) results in the denial of certification with respect to the member, the denial shall apply only to that member of the association unless the Secretary determines that the association or other member participated in, had knowledge of, or reason to know of, the violation.

      (B) Association's violation does not necessarily disqualify members.-

         (i)   If an association representing agricultural producers as a joint employer is determined to have committed an act that under subsection (b)(2) results in the denial of certification with respect to the association, the denial shall apply only to the association and does not apply to any individual producer member of the association unless the Secretary determines that the member participated in, had knowledge of, or reason to know of, the violation.

         (ii) If an association of agricultural producers certified as a sole employer is determined to have committed an act that under subsection (b)(2) results in the denial of certification with respect to the association, no individual producer member of such association may be the beneficiary of the services of temporary alien agricultural workers admitted under this section in the commodity and occupation in which such aliens were employed by the association which was denied certification during the period such denial is in force, unless such producer member employs such aliens in the commodity and occupation in question directly or through an association which is a joint employer of such workers with the producer member.

(e) Expedited Administrative Appeals of Certain Determinations.-

    (1) Regulations shall provide for an expedited procedure for the review of a denial of certification under subsection (a)(1) or a revocation of such a certification or, at the applicant's request, for a de novo administrative hearing respecting the denial or revocation.

    (2) The Secretary of Labor shall expeditiously, but in no case later than 72 hours after the time a new determination is requested, make a new determination on the request for certification in the case of an H-2A worker if able, willing, and qualified eligible individuals are not actually available at the time such labor or services are required and a certification was denied in whole or in part because of the availability of qualified workers. If the employer asserts that any eligible individual who has been referred is not able, willing, or qualified, the burden of proof is on the employer to establish that the individual referred is not able, willing, or qualified because of employment- related reasons.

(f) Violators Disqualified for 5 Years.-An alien may not be admitted to the United States as a temporary agricultural worker if the alien was admitted to the United States as such a worker within the previous five-year period and the alien during that period violated a term or condition of such previous admission.

(g) Authorizations of Appropriations.-

    (1) There are authorized to be appropriated for each fiscal year, beginning with fiscal year 1987, $10,000,000 for the purposes-

        (A) of recruiting domestic workers for temporary labor and services which might otherwise be performed by nonimmigrants described in section 101(a)(15)(H)(ii)(a), and

        (B) of monitoring terms and conditions under which such nonimmigrants (and domestic workers employed by the same employers) are employed in the United States.

    (2) The Secretary of Labor is authorized to take such actions, including imposing appropriate penalties and seeking appropriate injunctive relief and specific performance of contractual obligations, as may be necessary to assure employer compliance with terms and conditions of employment under this section.

    (3) There are authorized to be appropriated for each fiscal year, beginning with fiscal year 1987, such sums as may be necessary for the purpose of enabling the Secretary of Labor to make determinations and certifications under this section and under section 212(a)(5)(A)(i).

    (4) There are authorized to be appropriated for each fiscal year, beginning with fiscal year 1987, such sums as may be necessary for the purposes of enabling the Secretary of Agriculture to carry out the Secretary's duties and responsibilities under this section.

(h) Miscellaneous Provisions.-
   (1) The Attorney General shall provide for such endorsement of entry and exit documents of nonimmigrants described in section 101(a)(15)(H)(ii) as may be necessary to carry out this section and to provide notice for purposes of section 274A.
   (2) The provisions of subsections (a) and (c) of section 214 and the provisions of this section preempt any State or local law regulating admissibility of nonimmigrant workers.
(i) Definitions.-For purposes of this section:
   (1) The term "eligible individual" means, with respect to employment, an individual who is not an unauthorized alien (as defined in section 274A(h)(3) with respect to that employment.
   (2) The term "H-2A worker" means a nonimmigrant described in section 101(a)(15)(H)(ii)(a).

Illegal Immigration Reform and Immigrant Responsibility Act of 1996 (Public Law 104-208)

This law is the second major revision of the Immigration and Nationality Act to occur during the past decade. Its amendments have been incorporated into the INA. The sections excerpted below cover controversial new provisions authorizing the expedited removal of inadmissible aliens arriving at U.S. borders and ports of entry.

104th Congress
Sept. 30, 1996
110 Stat. 3009

SEC. 302. INSPECTION OF ALIENS; EXPEDITED REMOVAL OF INADMISSIBLE ARRIVING ALIENS; REFERRAL FOR HEARING (REVISED SECTION 235).

(a) IN GENERAL.-Section 235 (8 U.S.C. 1225) is amended to read as follows:

INSPECTION BY IMMIGRATION OFFICERS; EXPEDITED REMOVAL OF INADMISSIBLE ARRIVING ALIENS; REFERRAL FOR HEARING
"SEC. 235. (a) INSPECTION.-
   "(1) ALIENS TREATED AS APPLICANTS FOR ADMISSION.-An alien present in the United States who has not been admitted or who arrives in the United States (whether or not at a designated port of arrival and including an alien who is brought to the United States after having been interdicted in international or United States waters) shall be deemed for purposes of this Act an applicant for admission.
   "(2) STOWAWAYS.-An arriving alien who is a stowaway is not eligible to apply for admission or to be admitted and shall be ordered removed upon inspection by an immigration officer. Upon such inspection if the alien indicates an intention to apply for asylum under section 208 or a fear of persecution, the officer shall refer the alien

for an interview under subsection (b)(1)(B). A stowaway may apply for asylum only if the stowaway is found to have a credible fear of persecution under subsection (b)(1)(B). In no case may a stowaway be considered an applicant for admission or eligible for a hearing under section 240.

"(3) INSPECTION.-All aliens (including alien crewmen) who are applicants for admission or otherwise seeking admission or readmission to or transit through the United States shall be inspected by immigration officers.

"(4) WITHDRAWAL OF APPLICATION FOR ADMISSION.-An alien applying for admission may, in the discretion of the Attorney General and at any time, be permitted to withdraw the application for admission and depart immediately from the United States.

"(5) STATEMENTS.-An applicant for admission may be required to state under oath any information sought by an immigration officer regarding the purposes and intentions of the applicant in seeking admission to the United States, including the applicant's intended length of stay and whether the applicant intends to remain permanently or become a United States citizen, and whether the applicant is inadmissible.

"(b) INSPECTION OF APPLICANTS FOR ADMISSION.-

"(1) INSPECTION OF ALIENS ARRIVING IN THE UNITED STATES AND CERTAIN OTHER ALIENS WHO HAVE NOT BEEN ADMITTED OR PAROLED.-

"(A) SCREENING.-

"(i) IN GENERAL.-If an immigration officer determines that an alien (other than an alien described in subparagraph (F)) who is arriving in the United States or is described in clause

"(ii) CLAIMS FOR ASYLUM.-If an immigration officer determines that an alien (other than an alien described in subparagraph (F)) who is arriving in the United States or is described in clause (iii) is inadmissible under section 212(a)(6)(C) or 212(a)(7) and the alien indicates either an intention to apply for asylum under section 208 or a fear of persecution, the officer shall refer the alien for an interview by an asylum officer under subparagraph (B).

"(iii) APPLICATION TO CERTAIN OTHER ALIENS.-

"(I) IN GENERAL.-The Attorney General may apply clauses (i) and (ii) of this subparagraph to any or all aliens described in subclause (II) as designated by the Attorney General. Such designation shall be in the sole and unreviewable discretion of the Attorney General and may be modified at any time.

"(II) ALIENS DESCRIBED.-An alien described in this clause is an alien who is not described in subparagraph (F), who has not been admitted or paroled into the United States, and who has not affirmatively shown, to the satisfaction of an immigration officer, that the alien has been physically present in the United States continuously for the 2-year period immediately prior to the date of the determination of inadmissibility under this subparagraph.

"(B) ASYLUM INTERVIEWS.-

"(i)   CONDUCT BY ASYLUM OFFICERS.-An asylum officer shall conduct interviews of aliens referred under subparagraph (A)(ii), either at a port of entry or at such other place designated by the Attorney General.

"(ii) REFERRAL OF CERTAIN ALIENS.-If the officer determines at the time of the interview that an alien has a credible fear of persecution (within the meaning of clause (v)), the alien shall be detained for further consideration of the application for asylum.

"(iii) REMOVAL WITHOUT FURTHER REVIEW IF NO CREDIBLE FEAR OF PERSECUTION.-

"(I)   IN GENERAL.-Subject to subclause (III), if the officer determines that an alien does not have a credible fear of persecution, the officer shall order the alien removed from the United States without further hearing or review.

"(II) RECORD OF DETERMINATION.-The officer shall prepare a written record of a determination under subclause (I). Such record shall include a summary of the material facts as stated by the applicant, such additional facts (if any) relied upon by the officer, and the officer's analysis of why, in the light of such facts, the alien has not established a credible fear of persecution. A copy of the officer's interview notes shall be attached to the written summary.

"(III) REVIEW OF DETERMINATION.-The Attorney General shall provide by regulation and upon the alien's request for prompt review by an immigration judge of a determination under subclause (I) that the alien does not have a credible fear of persecution. Such review shall include an opportunity for the alien to be heard and questioned by the immigration judge, either in person or by telephonic or video connection. Review shall be concluded as expeditiously as possible, to the maximum extent practicable within 24 hours, but in no case later than 7 days after the date of the determination under subclause (I).

"(IV) MANDATORY DETENTION.-Any alien subject to the procedures under this clause shall be detained pending a final determination of credible fear of persecution and, if found not to have such a fear, until removed.

"(iv) INFORMATION ABOUT INTERVIEWS.-The Attorney General shall provide information concerning the asylum interview described in this subparagraph to aliens who may be eligible. An alien who is eligible for such interview may consult with a person or persons of the alien's choosing prior to the interview or any review thereof, according to regulations prescribed by the Attorney General. Such consultation shall be at no expense to the Government and shall not unreasonably delay the process.

"(v)   CREDIBLE FEAR OF PERSECUTION DEFINED.-For purposes of this subparagraph, the term 'credible fear of persecution' means that there is a significant possibility, taking into account the credibility of the statements made by the alien in support of the alien's claim and such other facts as are known to the officer, that the alien could establish eligibility for asylum under section 208.

"(C) LIMITATION ON ADMINISTRATIVE REVIEW.-Except as provided in subparagraph (B)(iii)(III), a removal order entered in accordance with subparagraph (A)(i) or (B)(iii)(I) is not subject to administrative appeal, except that the Attorney General shall provide by regulation for prompt review of such an order under subparagraph (A)(i) against an alien who claims under oath, or as permitted under penalty of perjury under section 1746 of title 28, United States Code, after having been warned of the penalties for falsely making such claim under such conditions, to have been lawfully admitted for permanent residence, to have been admitted as a refugee under section 207, or to have been granted asylum under section 208.

"(D) LIMIT ON COLLATERAL ATTACKS.-In any action brought against an alien under section 275(a) or section 276, the court shall not have jurisdiction to hear any claim attacking the validity of an order of removal entered under subparagraph (A)(i) or (B)(iii).

"(E) ASYLUM OFFICER DEFINED.-As used in this paragraph, the term 'asylum officer' means an immigration officer who-

  "(i) has had professional training in country conditions, asylum law, and interview techniques comparable to that provided to full-time adjudicators of applications under section 208, and

  "(ii) is supervised by an officer who meets the condition described in clause (i) and has had substantial experience adjudicating asylum applications.

"(F) EXCEPTION.-Subparagraph (A) shall not apply to an alien who is a native or citizen of a country in the Western Hemisphere with whose government the United States does not have full diplomatic relations and who arrives by aircraft at a port of entry.

"(2) INSPECTION OF OTHER ALIENS.-

  "(A) IN GENERAL.-Subject to subparagraphs (B) and (C), in the case of an alien who is an applicant for admission, if the examining immigration officer determines that an alien seeking admission is not clearly and beyond a doubt entitled to be admitted, the alien shall be detained for a proceeding under section 240.

  "(B) EXCEPTION.-Subparagraph (A) shall not apply to an alien-

    "(i) who is a crewman,

    "(ii) to whom paragraph (1) applies, or

    "(iii) who is a stowaway.

  "(C) TREATMENT OF ALIENS ARRIVING FROM CONTIGUOUS TERRITORY.-In the case of an alien described in subparagraph (A) who is arriving on land (whether or not at a designated port of arrival) from a foreign territory contiguous to the United States, the Attorney General may return the alien to that territory pending a proceeding under section 240.

"(3) CHALLENGE OF DECISION.-The decision of the examining immigration officer, if favorable to the admission of any alien, shall be subject to challenge by any other immigration officer and such challenge shall operate to take the alien whose privilege to be admitted is so challenged, before an immigration judge for a proceeding under section 240.

"(c) REMOVAL OF ALIENS INADMISSIBLE ON SECURITY AND RELATED GROUNDS.-

"(1) REMOVAL WITHOUT FURTHER HEARING.-If an immigration officer or an immigration judge suspects that an arriving alien may be inadmissible under subparagraph (A) (other than clause (ii)), (B), or (C) of section 212(a)(3), the officer or judge shall-

"(A) order the alien removed, subject to review under paragraph (2);

"(B) report the order of removal to the Attorney General; and

"(C) not conduct any further inquiry or hearing until ordered by the Attorney General.

"(2) REVIEW OF ORDER.-(A) The Attorney General shall review orders issued under paragraph (1).

"(B) If the Attorney General-

"(i)   is satisfied on the basis of confidential information that the alien is inadmissible under subparagraph (A) (other than clause (ii)), (B), or (C) of section 212(a)(3), and

"(ii) after consulting with appropriate security agencies of the United States Government, concludes that disclosure of the information would be prejudicial to the public interest, safety, or security, the Attorney General may order the alien removed without further inquiry or hearing by an immigration judge.

"(C) If the Attorney General does not order the removal of the alien under subparagraph (B), the Attorney General shall specify the further inquiry or hearing that shall be conducted in the case.

"(3) SUBMISSION OF STATEMENT AND INFORMATION.-The alien or the alien's representative may submit a written statement and additional information for consideration by the Attorney General.

"(d) AUTHORITY RELATING TO INSPECTIONS.-

"(1) AUTHORITY TO SEARCH CONVEYANCES.-Immigration officers are authorized to board and search any vessel, aircraft, railway car, or other conveyance or vehicle in which they believe aliens are being brought into the United States.

"(2) AUTHORITY TO ORDER DETENTION AND DELIVERY OF ARRIVING ALIENS.- Immigration officers are authorized to order an owner, agent, master, commanding officer, person in charge, purser, or consignee of a vessel or aircraft bringing an alien (except an alien crewmember) to the United States-

"(A) to detain the alien on the vessel or at the airport of arrival, and

"(B) to deliver the alien to an immigration officer for inspection or to a medical officer for examination.

"(3) ADMINISTRATION OF OATH AND CONSIDERATION OF EVIDENCE.-The Attorney General and any immigration officer shall have power to administer oaths and to take and consider evidence of or from any person touching the privilege of any alien or person he believes or suspects to be an alien to enter, reenter, transit through, or reside in the United States or concerning any matter which is material and relevant to the enforcement of this Act and the administration of the Service.

"(4) SUBPOENA AUTHORITY.-(A) The Attorney General and any immigration officer shall have power to require by subpoena the attendance and testimony of witnesses before immigration officers and the production of books, papers, and documents relating to the privilege of any person to enter, reenter, reside in, or pass through the United States or concerning any matter which is material and relevant to the enforcement of this Act and the administration of the Service, and to that end may invoke the aid of any court of the United States.

"(B) Any United States district court within the jurisdiction of which investigations or inquiries are being conducted by an immigration officer may, in the event of neglect or refusal to respond to a subpoena issued under this paragraph or refusal to testify before an immigration officer, issue an order requiring such persons to appear before an immigration officer, produce books, papers, and documents if demanded, and testify, and any failure to obey such order of the court may be punished by the court as a contempt thereof.".

(b) GAO STUDY ON OPERATION OF EXPEDITED REMOVAL PROCEDURES.-

(1) STUDY.-The Comptroller General shall conduct a study on the implementation of the expedited removal procedures under section 235(b)(1) of the Immigration and Nationality Act, as amended by subsection (a). The study shall examine-

(A) the effectiveness of such procedures in deterring illegal entry,

(B) the detention and adjudication resources saved as a result of the procedures,

(C) the administrative and other costs expended to comply with the provision,

(D) the effectiveness of such procedures in processing asylum claims by undocumented aliens who assert a fear of persecution, including the accuracy of credible fear determinations, and

(E) the cooperation of other countries and air carriers in accepting and returning aliens removed under such procedures.

(2) REPORT.-By not later than 18 months after the date of the enactment of this Act, the Comptroller General shall submit to the Committees on the Judiciary of the House of Representatives and the Senate a report on the study conducted under paragraph (1).

Treaty on European Union (1993)

The Treaty on European Union (TEU), also known as the Maastrict Treaty, signified a major step in European integration when it entered into force in 1993. The following excerpt contains the treaty's preamble and highlights its discussion of the free movement of people—immigration and refugee issues—as an area of "common interest" for members of the European Union.

I Text of the Treaty

His Majesty the King of the Belgians, Her Majesty the Queen of Denmark, the President of the Federal Republic of Germany, the President of the Hellenic Republic, His Majesty the King of Spain, the President of the French Republic, the President of Ireland, the President of the Italian Republic, His Royal Highness the Grand Duke of Luxembourg, Her Majesty the Queen of the Netherlands, the President of the Portuguese Republic, Her Majesty the Queen of the United Kingdom of Great Britain and Northern Ireland,

RESOLVED to mark a new stage in the process of European integration undertaken with the establishment of the European Communities,

RECALLING the historic importance of the ending of the division of the European continent and the need to create firm bases for the construction of the future Europe,

CONFIRMING their attachment to the principles of liberty, democracy and respect for human rights and fundamental freedoms and of the rule of law,

DESIRING to deepen the solidarity between their peoples while respecting their history, their culture and their traditions,

DESIRING to enhance further the democratic and efficient functioning of the institutions so as to enable them better to carry out, within a single institutional framework, the tasks entrusted to them,

RESOLVED to achieve the strengthening and the convergence of their economies and to establish an economic and monetary union including, in accordance with the provisions of this Treaty, a single and stable currency,

DETERMINED to promote economic and social progress for their peoples, within the context of the accomplishment of the internal market and of reinforced cohesion and environmental protection, and to implement policies ensuring that advances in economic integration are accompanied by parallel progress in other fields,

RESOLVED to establish a citizenship common to nationals of their countries,

RESOLVED to implement a common foreign and security policy including the eventual framing of a common defence policy, which might in time lead to a common defence, thereby reinforcing the European identity and its independence in order to promote peace, security and progress in Europe and in the world,

REAFFIRMING their objective to facilitate the free movement of persons, while ensuring the safety and security of their peoples, by including provisions on justice and home affairs in this Treaty,

RESOLVED to continue the process of creating an ever closer union among the peoples of Europe, in which decisions are taken as closely as possible to the citizen in accordance with the principle of subsidiarity,

IN VIEW of further steps to be taken in order to advance European integration,

HAVE DECIDED to establish a European Union and to this end have designated as their Plenipotentiaries. . . .

TITLE VI

Provisions on cooperation in the fields of justice and home affairs.

Article K

Cooperation in the fields of justice and home affairs shall be governed by the following provisions.

Article K.1

For the purposes of achieving the objectives of the Union, in particular the free movement of persons, and without prejudice to the powers of the European Community, Member States shall regard the following areas as matters of common interest:

1. asylum policy;
2. rules governing the crossing by persons of the external borders of the Member States and the exercise of controls thereon;
3. immigration policy and policy regarding nationals of third countries:
    a. conditions of entry and movement by nationals of third countries on the territory of Member States;
    b. conditions of residence by nationals of third countries on the territory of Member States, including family reunion and access to employment;
    c. combating unauthorized immigration, residence and work by nationals of third countries on the territory of Member States;
4. combating drug addiction in so far as this is not covered by (7) to (9);
5. combating fraud on an international scale in so far as this is not covered by (7) to (9);
6. judicial cooperation in civil matters;
7. judicial cooperation in criminal matters;
8. customs cooperation;
9. police cooperation for the purposes of preventing and combating terrorism, unlawful drug-trafficking and other serious forms of international crime, including if necessary certain aspects of customs cooperation, in connection with the organization of a Union-wide system for exchanging information within a European Police Office (Europol).

DECLARATION (No. 31) on asylum

1. The Conference agrees that, in the context of the proceedings provided for in Articles K.1 and K.3 of the provisions on cooperation in the fields of justice and home affairs, the Council will consider as a matter of priority questions concerning Member States'

asylum policies, with the aim of adopting, by the beginning of 1993, common action to harmonize aspects of them, in the light of the work programme and timetable contained in the report on asylum drawn up at the request of the European Council meeting in Luxembourg on 28 and 29 June 1991.

2. In this connection, the Council will also consider, by the end of 1993, on the basis of a report, the possibility of applying Article K.9 to such matters.

California Proposition 187 (1994)

California voters approved this state initiative in 1994, significantly restricting immigrants and signaling a broader crackdown on illegal immigration. California's Proposition 187 received national attention and drew strong opposition from immigrant advocates. It was ultimately overturned by a federal court.

Text of Proposition

Proposition: #187
Title: Illegal Aliens. Ineligibility for Public Services. Verification and Reporting.
Year: 1994
Proposition type: Initiative Statute
Popular vote: Yes (58.8%); No (41.2%)
Pass/Fail: Pass
Text of Prop.   Proposition 187: Text of Proposed Law

This initiative measure is submitted to the people in accordance with the provisions of Article II, Section 8 of the Constitution.

This initiative measure adds sections to various codes; therefore, new provisions proposed to be added are printed in italic type to indicate that they are new.

Proposed Law

SECTION 1. Findings and Declaration.

The People of California find and declare as follows:

That they have suffered and are suffering economic hardship caused by the presence of illegal aliens in this state.

That they have suffered and are suffering personal injury and damage caused by the criminal conduct of illegal aliens in this state.

That they have a right to the protection of their government from any person or persons entering this country unlawfully.

Therefore, the People of California declare their intention to provide for cooperation between their agencies of state and local government with the federal government, and to establish a system of required notification by and between such agencies to prevent illegal aliens in the United States from receiving benefits or public services in the State of California.

SECTION 2. Manufacture, Distribution or Sale of False Citizenship or Resident Alien Documents:

Crime and Punishment.

Section 113 is added to the Penal Code, to read:

113. Any person who manufactures, distributes or sells false documents to conceal the true citizenship or resident alien status of another person is guilty of a felony, and shall be punished by imprisonment in the state prison for five years or by a fine of seventy-five thousand dollars ($75,000).

SECTION 3. Use of False Citizenship or Resident Alien Documents: Crime and Punishment.

Section 114 is added to the Penal Code, to read:

114. Any person who uses false documents to conceal his or her true citizenship or resident alien status is guilty of a felony, and shall be punished by imprisonment in the state prison for five years or by a fine of twenty-five thousand dollars ($25,000).

SECTION 4. Law Enforcement Cooperation with INS.

Section 834b is added to the Penal Code, to read:

834b. (a) Every law enforcement agency in California shall fully cooperate with the United States Immigration and Naturalization Service regarding any person who is arrested if he or she is suspected of being present in the United States in violation of federal immigration laws.

(b) With respect to any such person who is arrested, and suspected of being present in the United States in violation of federal immigration laws, every law enforcement agency shall do the following:

  (1) Attempt to verify the legal status of such person as a citizen of the United States, an alien lawfully admitted as a permanent resident, an alien lawfully admitted for a temporary period of time or as an alien who is present in the United States in violation of immigration laws. The verification process may include, but shall not be limited to, questioning the person regarding his or her date and place of birth, and entry into the United States, and demanding documentation to indicate his or her legal status.

  (2) Notify the person of his or her apparent status as an alien who is present in the United States in violation of federal immigration laws and inform him or her that, apart from any criminal justice proceedings, he or she must either obtain legal status or leave the United States.

  (3) Notify the Attorney General of California and the United States Immigration and Naturalization Service of the apparent illegal status and provide any additional information that may be requested by any other public entity.

(c) Any legislative, administrative, or other action by a city, county, or other legally authorized local governmental entity with jurisdictional boundaries, or by a law enforcement agency, to prevent or limit the cooperation required by subdivision (a) is expressly prohibited.

SECTION 5. Exclusion of Illegal Aliens from Public Social Services.

Section 10001.5 is added to the Welfare and Institutions Code, to read:

10001.5. (a) In order to carry out the intention of the People of California that only citizens of the United States and aliens lawfully admitted to the United States may receive the benefits of public social services and to ensure that all persons employed in the providing of those services shall diligently protect public funds from misuse, the provisions of this section are adopted.

(b) A person shall not receive any public social services to which he or she may be otherwise entitled until the legal status of that person has been verified as one of the following:

(1) A citizen of the United States.

(2   An alien lawfully admitted as a permanent resident.

(3) An alien lawfully admitted for a temporary period of time.

(c) If any public entity in this state to whom a person has applied for public social services determines or reasonably suspects, based upon the information provided to it, that the person is an alien in the United States in violation of federal law, the following procedures shall be followed by the public entity:

(1) The entity shall not provide the person with benefits or services.

(2) The entity shall, in writing, notify the person of his or her apparent illegal immigration status, and that the person must either obtain legal status or leave the United States.

(3) The entity shall also notify the State Director of Social Services, the Attorney General of California, and the United States Immigration and Naturalization Service of the apparent illegal status, and shall provide any additional information that may be requested by any other public entity.

SECTION 6. Exclusion of Illegal Aliens from Publicly Funded Health Care.

Chapter 1.3 (commencing with Section 130) is added to Part 1 of Division 1 of the Health and Safety Code, to read:

Chapter 1.3. Publicly-Funded Health Care Services

130. (a) In order to carry out the intention of the People of California that, excepting emergency medical care as required by federal law, only citizens of the United States and aliens lawfully admitted to the United States may receive the benefits of publicly-funded health care, and to ensure that all persons employed in the providing of those services shall diligently protect public funds from misuse, the provisions of this section are adopted.

(b) A person shall not receive any health care services from a publicly-funded health care facility, to which he or she is otherwise entitled until the legal status of that person has been verified as one of the following:

(1) A citizen of the United States.

(2) An alien lawfully admitted as a permanent resident.

(3) An alien lawfully admitted for a temporary period of time.

(c) *If any publicly-funded health care facility in this state from whom a person seeks health care services, other than emergency medical care as required by federal law, determines or reasonably suspects, based upon the information provided to it, that the person is an alien in the United States in violation of federal law, the following procedures shall be followed by the facility:*

(1) *The facility shall not provide the person with services.*

(2) *The facility shall, in writing, notify the person of his or her apparent illegal immigration status, and that the person must either obtain legal status or leave the United States.*

(3) *The facility shall also notify the State Director of Health Services, the Attorney General of California, and the United States Immigration and Naturalization Service of the apparent illegal status, and shall provide any additional information that may be requested by any other public entity.*

(d) *For purposes of this section "publicly-funded health care facility" shall be defined as specified in Sections 1200 and 1250 of this code as of January 1, 1993.*

SECTION 7. Exclusion of Illegal Aliens from Public Elementary and Secondary Schools.

Section 48215 is added to the Education Code, to read:

48215. (a) No public elementary or secondary school shall admit, or permit the attendance of, any child who is not a citizen of the United States, an alien lawfully admitted as a permanent resident, or a person who is otherwise authorized under federal law to be present in the United States.

(b) Commencing January 1, 1995, each school district shall verify the legal status of each child enrolling in the school district for the first time in order to ensure the enrollment or attendance only of citizens, aliens lawfully admitted as permanent residents, or persons who are otherwise authorized to be present in the United States.

(c) By January 1, 1996, each school district shall have verified the legal status of each child already enrolled and in attendance in the school district in order to ensure the enrollment or attendance only of citizens, aliens lawfully admitted as permanent residents, or persons who are otherwise authorized under federal law to be present in the United States.

(d) By January 1, 1996, each school district shall also have verified the legal status of each parent or guardian of each child referred to in subdivisions (b) and (c), to determine whether such parent or guardian is one of the following:

(1) *A citizen of the United States.*

(2) *An alien lawfully admitted as a permanent resident.*

(3) *An alien admitted lawfully for a temporary period of time.*

(e) *Each school district shall provide information to the State Superintendent of Public Instruction, the Attorney General of California, and the United States Immigration and Naturalization Service regarding any enrollee or pupil, or parent or guardian, attending a public elementary or secondary school in the school district determined or reasonably suspected to be in violation of federal immigration laws within forty-five days after becoming aware of an apparent violation. The notice shall also be provided to the parent or legal guardian of the enrollee or pupil, and shall state that an existing pupil may not continue to attend the school after ninety calendar days from the date of the notice, unless legal status is established.*

(f) For each child who cannot establish legal status in the United States, each school district shall continue to provide education for a period of ninety days from the date of the notice. Such ninety day period shall be utilized to accomplish an orderly transition to a school in the child's country of origin. Each school district shall fully cooperate in this transition effort to ensure that the educational needs of the child are best served for that period of time.

SECTION 8. Exclusion of Illegal Aliens from Public Postsecondary Educational Institutions.

Section 66010.8 is added to the Education Code, to read:

66010.8. (a) No public institution of postsecondary education shall admit, enroll, or permit the attendance of any person who is not a citizen of the United States, an alien lawfully admitted as a permanent resident in the United States, or a person who is otherwise authorized under federal law to be present in the United States.

(b) Commencing with the first term or semester that begins after January 1, 1995, and at the commencement of each term or semester thereafter, each public postsecondary educational institution shall verify the status of each person enrolled or in attendance at that institution in order to ensure the enrollment or attendance only of United States citizens, aliens lawfully admitted as permanent residents in the United States, and persons who are otherwise authorized under federal law to be present in the United States.

(c) No later than 45 days after the admissions officer of a public postsecondary educational institution becomes aware of the application, enrollment, or attendance of a person determined to be, or who is under reasonable suspicion of being, in the United States in violation of federal immigration laws, that officer shall provide that information to the State Superintendent of Public Instruction, the Attorney General of California, and the United States Immigration and Naturalization Service. The information shall also be provided to the applicant, enrollee, or person admitted.

SECTION 9. Attorney General Cooperation with the INS.

Section 53069.65 is added to the Government Code, to read:

53069.65. Whenever the state or a city, or a county, or any other legally authorized local governmental entity with jurisdictional boundaries reports the presence of a person who is suspected of being present in the United States in violation of federal immigration laws to the Attorney General of California, that report shall be transmitted to the United States Immigration and Naturalization Service. The Attorney General shall be responsible for maintaining on-going and accurate records of such reports, and shall provide any additional information that may be requested by any other government entity.

SECTION 10. Amendment and Severability.

The statutory provisions contained in this measure may not be amended by the Legislature except to further its purposes by statute passed in each house by roll call vote entered in the journal, two-thirds of the membership concurring, or by a statute that becomes effective only when approved by the voters.

In the event that any portion of this act or the application thereof to any person or circumstance is held invalid, that invalidity shall not affect any other provision or application of the act, which can be given effect without the invalid provision or application, and to that end the provisions of this act are severable.

North American Free Trade Agreement (1994)

The North American Free Trade Agreement (NAFTA) between the United States, Canada, and Mexico has had a significant impact on immigration throughout the region since it was ratified by Congress in 1994. The treaty's primary function was economic; however, with the free movement of goods has come increasing movement of people (labor) across international borders. The following excerpt includes the treaty's provisions regarding the movement of people.

Chapter Sixteen: Temporary Entry for Business Persons

Article 1601: General Principles

Further to Article 102 (Objectives), this Chapter reflects the preferential trading relationship between the Parties, the desirability of facilitating temporary entry on a reciprocal basis and of establishing transparent criteria and procedures for temporary entry, and the need to ensure border security and to protect the domestic labor force and permanent employment in their respective territories.

Article 1602: General Obligations

1. Each Party shall apply its measures relating to the provisions of this Chapter in accordance with Article 1601 and, in particular, shall apply expeditiously those measures so as to avoid unduly impairing or delaying trade in goods or services or conduct of investment activities under this Agreement.
2. The Parties shall endeavor to develop and adopt common criteria, definitions and interpretations for the implementation of this Chapter.

Article 1603: Grant of Temporary Entry

1. Each Party shall grant temporary entry to business persons who are otherwise qualified for entry under applicable measures relating to public health and safety and national security, in accordance with this Chapter, including the provisions of Annex 1603.
2. A Party may refuse to issue an immigration document authorizing employment to a business person where the temporary entry of that person might affect adversely:

(a) the settlement of any labor dispute that is in progress at the place or intended place of employment; or

(b) the employment of any person who is involved in such dispute.

3. When a Party refuses pursuant to paragraph 2 to issue an immigration document authorizing employment, it shall:

(a) inform in writing the business person of the reasons for the refusal; and

(b) promptly notify in writing the Party whose business person has been refused entry of the reasons for the refusal.

4. Each Party shall limit any fees for processing applications for temporary entry of business persons to the approximate cost of services rendered.

Article 1604: Provision of Information

1. Further to Article 1802 (Publication), each Party shall:

(a) provide to the other Parties such materials as will enable them to become acquainted with its measures relating to this Chapter; and

(b) no later than one year after the date of entry into force of this Agreement, prepare, publish and make available in its own territory, and in the territories of the other Parties, explanatory material in a consolidated document regarding the requirements for temporary entry under this Chapter in such a manner as will enable business persons of the other Parties to become acquainted with them.

2. Subject to Annex 1604.2, each Party shall collect and maintain, and make available to the other Parties in accordance with its domestic law, data respecting the granting of temporary entry under this Chapter to business persons of the other Parties who have been issued immigration documentation, including data specific to each occupation, profession or activity.

Article 1605: Working Group

1. The Parties hereby establish a Temporary Entry Working Group, comprising representatives of each Party, including immigration officials.

2. The Working Group shall meet at least once each year to consider:

(a) the implementation and administration of this Chapter;

(b) the development of measures to further facilitate temporary entry of business persons on a reciprocal basis;

(c) the waiving of labor certification tests or procedures of similar effect for spouses of business persons who have been granted temporary entry for more than one year under Section B, C or D of Annex 1603; and

(d) proposed modifications of or additions to this Chapter.

Article 1606: Dispute Settlement

1. A Party may not initiate proceedings under Article 2007 (Commission Good Offices, Conciliation and Mediation) regarding a refusal to grant temporary entry under this Chapter or a particular case arising under Article 1602(1) unless:

(a) the matter involves a pattern of practice; and

(b) the business person has exhausted the available administrative remedies regarding the particular matter.

2. The remedies referred to in paragraph (1)(b) shall be deemed to be exhausted if a final determination in the matter has not been issued by the competent authority within one year of the institution of an administrative proceeding, and the failure to issue a determination is not attributable to delay caused by the business person.

Article 1607: Relation to Other Chapters

Except for this Chapter, Chapters One (Objectives), Two (General Definitions), Twenty (Institutional Arrangements and Dispute Settlement Procedures) and Twenty Two (Final Provisions) and Articles 1801 (Contacts Points), 1802 (Publication), 1803 (Notification and Provision of Information) and 1804 (Administrative Proceedings), no provision of this Agreement shall impose any obligation on a Party regarding its immigration measures.

Article 1608: Definitions

For purposes of this Chapter:

business person means a citizen of a Party who is engaged in trade in goods, the provision of services or the conduct of investment activities;

citizen means "citizen" as defined in Annex 1608 for the Parties specified in that Annex;

existing means "existing" as defined in Annex 1608 for the Parties specified in that Annex; and

temporary entry means entry into the territory of a Party by a business person of another Party without the intent to establish permanent residence.

Annex 1603: Temporary Entry for Business Persons

Section A - Business Visitors

1. Each Party shall grant temporary entry to a business person seeking to engage in a business activity set out in Appendix 1603.A.1, without requiring that person to obtain an employment authorization, provided that the business person otherwise complies with existing immigration measures applicable to temporary entry, on presentation of:

(a) proof of citizenship of a Party;

(b) documentation demonstrating that the business person will be so engaged and describing the purpose of entry; and

(c) evidence demonstrating that the proposed business activity is international in scope and that the business person is not seeking to enter the local labor market.

2. Each Party shall provide that a business person may satisfy the requirements of paragraph 1(c) by demonstrating that:

(a) the primary source of remuneration for the proposed business activity is outside the territory of the Party granting temporary entry; and

(b) the business person's principal place of business and the actual place of accrual of profits, at least predominantly, remain outside such territory.

A Party shall normally accept an oral declaration as to the principal place of business and the actual place of accrual of profits. Where the Party requires further proof, it shall normally consider a letter from the employer attesting to these matters as sufficient proof.

3. Each Party shall grant temporary entry to a business person seeking to engage in a business activity other than those set out in Appendix 1603.A.1, without requiring that person to obtain an employment authorization, on a basis no less favorable than that provided under the existing provisions of the measures set out in Appendix 1603.A.3, provided that the business person otherwise complies with existing immigration measures applicable to temporary entry.

4. No Party may:
    (a) as a condition for temporary entry under paragraph 1 or 3, require prior approval procedures, petitions, labor certification tests or other procedures of similar effect; or
    (b) impose or maintain any numerical restriction relating to temporary entry under paragraph 1 or 3.

5. Notwithstanding paragraph 4, a Party may require a business person seeking temporary entry under this Section to obtain a visa or its equivalent prior to entry. Before imposing a visa requirement, the Party shall consult, on request, with a Party whose business persons would be affected with a view to avoiding the imposition of the requirement. With respect to an existing visa requirement, a Party shall consult, on request, with a Party whose business persons are subject to the requirement with a view to its removal.

Section B - Traders and Investors

1. Each Party shall grant temporary entry and provide confirming documentation to a business person seeking to:
    (a) carry on substantial trade in goods or services principally between the territory of the Party of which the business person is a citizen and the territory of the Party into which entry is sought, or
    (b) establish, develop, administer or provide advice or key technical services to the operation of an investment to which the business person or the business person's enterprise has committed, or is in the process of committing, a substantial amount of capital, in a capacity that is supervisory, executive or involves essential skills, provided that the business person otherwise complies with existing immigration measures applicable to temporary entry.

2. No Party may:
    (a) as a condition for temporary entry under paragraph 1, require labor certification tests or other procedures of similar effect; or

    (b) impose or maintain any numerical restriction relating to temporary entry under paragraph 1.

3. Notwithstanding paragraph 2, a Party may require a business person seeking temporary entry under this Section to obtain a visa or its equivalent prior to entry.

Section C - Intra-Company Transferees

1. Each Party shall grant temporary entry and provide confirming documentation to a business person employed by an enterprise who seeks to render services to that enterprise or a subsidiary or affiliate thereof, in a capacity that is managerial, executive or involves specialized knowledge, provided that the business person otherwise complies with existing immigration measures applicable to temporary entry. A Party may require the business person to have been employed continuously by the enterprise for one year within the three-year period immediately preceding the date of the application for admission.

2. No Party may:

    (a) as a condition for temporary entry under paragraph 1, require labor certification tests or other procedures of similar effect; or

    (b) impose or maintain any numerical restriction relating to temporary entry under paragraph 1.

3 Notwithstanding paragraph 2, a Party may require a business person seeking temporary entry under this Section to obtain a visa or its equivalent prior to entry. Before imposing a visa requirement, the Party shall consult with a Party whose business persons would be affected with a view to avoiding the imposition of the requirement. With respect to an existing visa requirement, a Party shall consult, on request, with a Party whose business persons are subject to the requirement with a view to its removal.

Section D - Professionals

1. Each Party shall grant temporary entry and provide confirming documentation to a business person seeking to engage in a business activity at a professional level in a profession set out in Appendix 1603.D.1, if the business person otherwise complies with existing immigration measures applicable to temporary entry, on presentation of:

    (a) proof of citizenship of a Party; and

    (b) documentation demonstrating that the business person will be so engaged and describing the purpose of entry.

2. No Party may:

    (a) as a condition for temporary entry under paragraph 1, require prior approval procedures, petitions, labor certification tests or other procedures of similar effect; or

    (b) impose or maintain any numerical restriction relating to temporary entry under paragraph 1.

3. Notwithstanding paragraph 2, a Party may require a business person seeking temporary entry under this Section to obtain a visa or its equivalent prior to entry. Before

imposing a visa requirement, the Party shall consult with a Party whose business persons would be affected with a view to avoiding the imposition of the requirement. With respect to an existing visa requirement, a Party shall consult, on request, with a Party whose business persons are subject to the requirement with a view to its removal.

4. Notwithstanding paragraphs 1 and 2, a Party may establish an annual numerical limit, which shall be set out in Appendix 1603.D.4, regarding temporary entry of business persons of another Party seeking to engage in business activities at a professional level in a profession set out in Appendix 1603.D.1, if the Parties concerned have not agreed otherwise prior to the date of entry into force of this Agreement for those Parties. In establishing such a limit, the Party shall consult with the other Party concerned.

5. A Party establishing a numerical limit pursuant to paragraph 4, unless the Parties concerned agree otherwise:

   (a) shall, for each year after the first year after the date of entry into force of this Agreement, consider increasing the numerical limit set out in Appendix 1603.D.4 by an amount to be established in consultation with the other Party concerned, taking into account the demand for temporary entry under this Section;

   (b) shall not apply its procedures established pursuant to paragraph 1 to the temporary entry of a business person subject to the numerical limit, but may require the business person to comply with its other procedures applicable to the temporary entry of professionals; and

   (c) may, in consultation with the other Party concerned, grant temporary entry under paragraph 1 to a business person who practices in a profession where accreditation, licensing, and certification requirements are mutually recognized by those Parties.

6. Nothing in paragraph 4 or 5 shall be construed to limit the ability of a business person to seek temporary entry under a Party's applicable immigration measures relating to the entry of professionals other than those adopted or maintained pursuant to paragraph 1.

7. Three years after a Party establishes a numerical limit pursuant to paragraph 4, it shall consult with the other Party concerned with a view to determining a date after which the limit shall cease to apply.

AFL-CIO Executive Council Actions (2000)

Until 2000, organized labor generally opposed immigration with the argument that immigrants provided cheap labor that competed with—or even took away jobs from—American workers. With this historic policy statement, the American Federation of Labor-Congress of Industrial Organizations (AFL-CIO) reversed its position, arguing in favor of amnesty for undocumented immigrant workers.

February 16, 2000
New Orleans, LA
Immigration

The AFL-CIO proudly stands on the side of immigrant workers. Throughout the history of this country, immigrants have played an important role in building our nation and its democratic institutions. New arrivals from every continent have contributed their energy, talent, and commitment to making the United States richer and stronger. Likewise, the American union movement has been enriched by the contributions and courage of immigrant workers. Newly arriving workers continue to make indispensable contributions to the strength and growth of our unions. These efforts have created new unions and strengthened and revived others, benefiting all workers, immigrant and native-born alike. It is increasingly clear that if the United States is to have an immigration system that really works, it must be simultaneously orderly, responsible and fair. The policies of both the AFL-CIO and our country must reflect those goals.

The United States is a nation of laws. This means that the federal government has the sovereign authority and constitutional responsibility to set and enforce limits on immigration. It also means that our government has the obligation to enact and enforce laws in ways that respect due process and civil liberties, safeguard public health and safety, and protect the rights and opportunities of workers.

The AFL-CIO believes the current system of immigration enforcement in the United States is broken and needs to be fixed. Our starting points are simple:

- Undocumented workers and their families make enormous contributions to their communities and workplaces and should be provided permanent legal status through a new amnesty program.
- Regulated legal immigration is better than unregulated illegal immigration.
- Immigrant workers should have full workplace rights in order to protect their own interests as well as the labor rights of all American workers.
- Labor and business should work together to design cooperative mechanisms that allow law-abiding employers to satisfy legitimate needs for new workers in a timely manner without compromising the rights and opportunities of workers already here.
- Labor and business should cooperate to undertake expanded efforts to educate and train American workers in order to upgrade their skill levels in ways that enhance our shared economic prosperity.
- Criminal penalties should be established to punish employers who recruit undocumented workers from abroad for the purpose of exploiting workers for economic gain.

Current efforts to improve immigration enforcement, while failing to stop the flow of undocumented people into the United States, have resulted in a system that causes discrimination and leaves unpunished unscrupulous employers who exploit undocumented workers, thus denying labor rights for all workers.

The combination of a poorly constructed and ineffectively enforced system that results in penalties for only a few of the employers who violate immigration laws has had especially detrimental impacts on efforts to organize and adequately represent workers. Unscrupulous employers have systematically used the I-9 process in their efforts to retaliate against workers who seek to join unions, improve their working conditions, and otherwise assert their rights.

Therefore, the AFL-CIO calls for replacing the current I-9 system as a tool of workplace immigration enforcement. We should substitute a system of immigration enforcement strategies that focuses on the criminalization of employer behavior, targeting those employers who recruit undocumented workers from abroad, either directly or indirectly. It should be supplemented with strong penalties against employers who abuse workers' immigration status to suppress their rights and labor protections. The federal government should aggressively investigate, and criminally prosecute, those employers who knowingly exploit a worker's undocumented status in order to prevent enforcement of workplace protection laws.

We strongly believe employer sanctions, as a nationwide policy applied to all workplaces, has failed and should be eliminated. It should be replaced with an alternative policy to reduce undocumented immigration and prevent employer abuse. Any new policy must meet the following principles: 1) it must seek to prevent employer discrimination against people who look or sound foreign; 2) it must allow workers to pursue legal remedies, including supporting a union, regardless of immigration status; and 3) it must avoid unfairly targeting immigrant workers of a particular nationality.

There is a long tradition in the United States of protecting those who risk their financial and physical well-being to come forward to report violations of laws that were enacted for the public good. Courageous undocumented workers who come forward to assert their rights should not be faced with deportation as a result of their actions. The recent situation at the Holiday Inn Express in Minneapolis highlights the perversity of the current situation. Therefore, the AFL-CIO calls for the enactment of whistleblower protections providing protected immigration status for undocumented workers who report violations of worker protection laws or cooperate with federal agencies during investigations of employment, labor and discrimination violations. Such workers should be accorded full remedies, including reinstatement and back pay. Further, undocumented workers who exercise their rights to organize and bargain collectively should also be provided protected immigration status.

Millions of hard-working people who make enormous contributions to their communities and workplace are denied basic human rights because of their undocumented status. Many of these men and women are the parents of children who are birthright U.S. citizens. The AFL-CIO supports a new amnesty program that would allow these members of local communities to adjust their status to permanent resident and become eligible for naturalization. The AFL-CIO also calls on the Immigration and Naturalization Service to address the shameful delays facing those seeking to adjust their status as a result of the Immigration Reform and Control Act.

Immediate steps should include legalization for three distinct groups of established residents: 1) approximately half-a-million Salvadorans, Guatemalans, Hondurans, and Haitians, who fled civil war and civil strife during the 1980s and early 1990s and were unfairly denied refugee status, and have lived under various forms of temporary legal status; 2) approximately 350,000 long-resident immigrants who were unfairly denied legalization due to illegal behavior by the INS during the amnesty program enacted in the late 1980s; and 3) approximately 10,000 Liberians who fled their homeland's brutal civil war and have lived in the United States for years under temporary legal status.

Guestworker programs too often are used to discriminate against U.S. workers, depress wages and distort labor markets. For these reasons, the AFL-CIO has long been troubled by the operation of such programs. The proliferation of guestworker programs has resulted in the creation of a class of easily exploited workers, who find themselves in a situation very similar to that faced by undocumented workers. The AFL-CIO renews our call for the halt to the expansion of guestworker programs. Moreover, these programs should be reformed to include more rigorous labor market tests and the involvement of labor unions in the labor certification process. All temporary guestworkers should be afforded the same workplace protections available to all workers.

The rights and dignity of all workers can best be ensured when immigrant and non-immigrant workers are fully informed about the contributions of immigrants to our society and our unions, and about the rights of immigrants under current labor, discrimination, naturalization and other laws. Labor unions have led the way in developing model programs that should be widely emulated. The AFL-CIO therefore supports the creation of education programs and centers to educate workers about immigration issues and to assist workers in exercising their rights.

Far too many workers lack access to training programs. Like all other workers, new immigrants want to improve their lives and those of their families by participating in job training. The AFL-CIO supports the expansion of job training programs to better serve immigrant populations. These programs are essential to the ability of immigrants to seize opportunities to compete in the new economy.

Immigrant workers make enormous contributions to our economy and society, and deserve the basic safety net protections that all other workers enjoy. The AFL-CIO continues to support the full restoration of benefits that were unfairly taken away through Federal legislation in 1996, causing tremendous harm to immigrant families.

U.S.–Mexico Migration: Joint Communiqué (2001)

Shortly after each took office, U.S. President George W. Bush and Mexican President Vicente Fox made improving immigration between their countries a priority for their administrations. Their efforts signaled unprecedented cooperation in U.S.-Mexico relations. The following document provides a framework (the "Guanajuato Proposal") for continued cooperation on migration issues.

U.S. Department of State
Joint Communique
Office of the Spokesman
Washington, DC
June 22, 2001

U.S.–Mexico Migration Talks and Plan of Action for Cooperation on Border Safety

Presidents Vicente Fox and George W. Bush, in the "Guanajuato Proposal" issued following their meeting in February, characterized migration as one of the major ties that bind Mexico and the United States. Accordingly, our respective policies should work to create a process of orderly migration that guarantees humane treatment of migrants, provides protection of their legal rights, ensures acceptable work conditions for migrants and also recognizes the right of nations to control the flow of people across their borders.

For this purpose, the two Presidents directed the Secretary of State and the Attorney General of the United States, and the Secretaries of Foreign Relations and of the Interior of Mexico, to engage in formal high-level discussions to reach short and long-term agreements on migration and labor issues between Mexico and the United States. Both governments recognize that migration and its relationship with border safety are a shared responsibility.

The initial meeting of the High Level Working Group on Migration occurred in Washington, DC on April 4. The two sides began talks aimed at achieving the goal of safe, legal, orderly and humane migration as set forth by our Presidents in Guanajuato. The binational agenda includes discussion of border safety, the H-2 temporary worker visa program, ideas on regularization of undocumented Mexicans in the United States, alternatives for possible new temporary worker programs, and efforts on regional economic development.

The tragic deaths of fourteen Mexican migrants in the Arizona desert in May highlighted the pressing need for coordinated efforts to ensure safe and legal movement between Mexico and the U.S., and for considering and evaluating the potentials and consequences of expanded avenues for legal entries of Mexican nationals to the U.S.

A binational working group met June 6 in San Antonio, Texas, to address border cooperation and safety. A second meeting took place on June 8 in Washington to continue our discussions of all migration-related issues on the binational agenda and to establish a timeframe for future action. As a result of these meetings, we agreed to increase immediately existing efforts to ensure safety on the border and to review our respective border policies in order to develop ways to accomplish our common goal of reducing risks and eliminating deaths of migrants along the border.

These unprecedented cooperative efforts will be guided by a plan of action whose progress and implementation will be subject to regular review and evaluation. We have instructed our respective border authorities to implement immediately the following actions:

- Strengthen public safety campaigns to alert potential migrants of the dangers of crossing the border in high-risk areas;

- Reinforce operational plans for the protection, search and rescue of migrants along the border, including the increased aerial surveillance of desert areas on the U.S. side and increased presence of Grupo Beta elements on the Mexican side;
- Implement a cooperative, comprehensive and aggressive plan to combat and dismantle human smuggling and trafficking organizations; and
- Initiate a pilot-program on use of non-lethal weapons by Border Patrol agents.

In order to coordinate special bilateral efforts to protect lives during the summer season, Mexican and U.S. officials held meetings in Tucson, Arizona, on June 14 and will hold additional meetings in the next several weeks in high-risk areas of California (San Diego and Calexico) and Texas (El Paso and Laredo).

We are committed to making progress in preparing a comprehensive package of possible alternatives to address all migration-related issues on the binational agenda for consideration by our two Presidents when they meet in Washington in September.

Plan of Action for Cooperation on Border Safety

1. Both governments agree to coordinate their efforts toward addressing border safety concerns in order to reduce risks to migrants, law enforcement authorities and border communities. Such coordination is the only way effectively to achieve our common goal of enhancing public safety in the U.S.-Mexico border region.
2. Both governments agreed that combating human smugglers, traffickers and criminal organizations should be given the utmost priority. Only cooperation in this regard can ensure the full success of this new comprehensive plan. To that end, Mexican and U.S. law enforcement agencies will be instructed to embark on an unprecedented joint effort to dismantle and penalize with all the weight of the law these criminal organizations.
3. The Mexican Government commits to intensify immediately comprehensive actions in its territory designed to accomplish the following: reinforce border safety programs; consider actions to prevent access to crossing in high-risk areas; alert potential migrants of the dangers associated with non-authorized entries into the U.S; and underscore the serious consequences for migrants when they engage smugglers and criminals who only exploit their vulnerability.
4. The U.S. Government commits to review immediately existing border control operations such as Gatekeeper, Hold the Line, Safeguard and Rio Grande, and to consider appropriate adjustments or alternatives to promote safety for migrants, law enforcement authorities and border communities and to prevent migrant deaths in the border region.

In addition to the above-mentioned agreements, the Plan of Action for Cooperation on Border Safety includes the following:

I. National and Binational Programs for Migrant Safety

- Develop a comprehensive set of binational programs and actions in areas of immediate concern to eliminate extreme risks to migrants. The deserts in Western Arizona, the All American Canal and the Rio Grande should be a priority in this regard.
- Strengthen public safety campaigns in Mexico to alert potential migrants of the imminent dangers of crossing the border through high-risk areas.
- Develop and implement specific operational plans for the search and rescue of migrants in dangerous areas along the border.
- Reinforce training programs on safety and migrant search and rescue operations.
- Map high-risk areas along the border to have an accurate portrait of new routes and implement preventive actions to reduce migrant risks.
- Activate additional cooperative binational actions on both sides of the border, like operations "Sky Watch II"—a programs of aerial surveillance in the Arizona desert—along with the reinforced presence of Beta Group elements in the Mexican side.
- Schedule periodic meetings, as needed, with Mexican and U.S. border consulates and law enforcement authorities to review regularly the results and the progress of local coordination efforts on border safety.

II. Targeting Alien Trafficking

- Strengthen binational coordination among law enforcement agencies to fight human smugglers and traffickers on both sides of the border.
- Expedite and reinforce the exchange of bilateral information that targets migrant smugglers and traffickers.
- Review operations to that end (Denial, Crossroads, and Mexican operations).
- Embark on an unprecedented binational effort to combat and dismantle alien smuggling, trafficking and criminal organizations.
- Oversee and evaluate the outcomes of the implementation of such bilateral programs by holding periodic meetings.

III. Border Violence

- Implement the U.S.-Mexico Memorandum of Understanding on Cooperation against Border Violence (Mérida, February 15, 1999) and corresponding Guidelines (Washington, June 8, 2000) for cooperation between Mexican consuls and U.S. Attorneys in the border region. These memoranda facilitate the investigation of diverse violent incidents occurring at the border.
- Initiate a pilot program on use of non-lethal weapons by Border Patrol agents.
- Strengthen bilateral cooperation on preventive actions in order to:
  - Reduce incidents of aggression against Border Patrol agents;
  - Prevent assaults against migrants and border authorities;
  - Deter migrant detentions by civilians.

IV. Incursions

- Agree on an immediate plan of action that reduces incursions and incidents on both sides of the border
- Develop a binational program for demarcation at isolated areas to avoid incursions

V. Cooperative Responses to Border Region Emergencies

- Agree on a Rapid Response Program that guarantees early alert and information exchanges between authorities of both governments for the immediate attention to critical border incidents.
  - Such a program should aim to coordinate actions between central (Washington-Mexico City) and local authorities (Mexican consul-INS/BP) including measures to ensure that proper investigations are conducted.
- Develop cooperative mechanisms to respond to emergencies at the border, such as Emergency Management and Response Mechanisms:
  - At border crossing points and international bridges in cases of bomb threats or trans-border pursuit of criminals.
  - During weather related and natural disaster emergencies (wild fires, snow storms, rainstorms, heat waves,) for search and rescue coordination, publication of weather advisories, etc.
- Enhance coordination to attend to injured persons during emergencies:
  - Consider installation of dedicated telephone alarm system tied to emergency services

VI. Safe and Orderly Repatriations

- Review, via the Interior Consultative Mechanisms (ICM), the appropriate implementation of the six existing local Safe and Orderly Repatriation Arrangements, including:
  - Coordination of removals from the U.S. interior to the border, and
  - Prevention of the removal to Mexico of non-Mexican nationals.

VII. Repatriation of Ex-Convicts

- Reinforce cooperation and coordination through the appropriate authorities for an orderly, legal and safe return of ex-convicts to Mexico.
- Meet, as needed, in order to review commitments and adjust existing programs.

VIII. Border Liaison Mechanisms

- Enhance the role of the ten Border Liaison Mechanisms as bilateral coordinating entities at the local level.

Supreme Court Decision in *Zadvydas v. Davis* (2001)

The U.S. Supreme Court's landmark decision prohibiting the indefinite detention of removable aliens is excerpted below. In the 5–4 ruling, Justices Sandra Day O'Connor, John Paul Stevens, David H. Souter, and Ruth Bader Ginsburg joined the majority opinion written by Stephen G. Breyer. Justice Anthony M. Kennedy wrote the dissenting opinion, and was joined by Chief Justice William H. Rehnquist and Justices Clarence Thomas and Antonin Scalia.

SUPREME COURT OF THE UNITED STATES

Nos. 99-7791 and 00-38

KESTUTIS ZADVYDAS, PETITIONER

v.

CHRISTINE G. DAVIS AND IMMIGRATION AND
NATURALIZATION SERVICE

ON WRIT OF CERTIORARI TO THE UNITED STATES COURT OF
APPEALS FOR THE FIFTH CIRCUIT

JOHN D. ASHCROFT, ATTORNEY GENERAL, ET AL.,
PETITIONERS

v.

KIM HO MA

ON WRIT OF CERTIORARI TO THE UNITED STATES COURT OF
APPEALS FOR THE NINTH CIRCUIT

[June 28, 2001]

JUSTICE BREYER delivered the opinion of the Court.

When an alien has been found to be unlawfully present in the United States and a final order of removal has been entered, the Government ordinarily secures the alien's removal during a subsequent 90-day statutory "removal period," during which time the alien normally is held in custody.

A special statute authorizes further detention if the Government fails to remove the alien during those 90 days. It says:

"An alien ordered removed who is inadmissible . . . [or] removable [as a result of violations of status requirements or entry conditions, violations of criminal law, or reasons of security or foreign policy] or who has been determined by the Attorney General to be a risk to the community or unlikely to comply with the order of removal, may be detained beyond the removal period and, if released, shall be subject to [certain] terms of supervision. . . ."8 U.S.C. §1231(a)(6)(1994 ed., Supp.V).

In these cases, we must decide whether this post-removal-period statute authorizes the Attorney General to detain a removable alien *indefinitely* beyond the removal period or only for a period *reasonably necessary* to secure the alien's removal. We deal here with aliens who were admitted to the United States but subsequently ordered removed. Aliens who have not yet gained initial admission to this country would present a very different question. Based on our conclusion that indefinite detention of aliens in the former category would raise serious constitutional concerns, we construe the statute to contain an implicit "reasonable time" limitation, the application of which is subject to federal court review. . . .

We consider two separate instances of detention. The first concerns Kestutis Zadvydas, a resident alien who was born, apparently of Lithuanian parents, in a displaced persons camp in Germany in 1948. When he was eight years old, Zadvydas immigrated to the United States with his parents and other family members, and he has lived here ever since.

Zadvydas has a long criminal record, involving drug crimes, attempted robbery, attempted burglary, and theft. He has a history of flight, from both criminal and deportation proceedings. Most recently, he was convicted of possessing, with intent to distribute, cocaine; sentenced to 16 years 'imprisonment; released on parole after two years; taken into INS custody; and, in 1994, ordered deported to Germany. In 1994, Germany told the INS that it would not accept Zadvydas because he was not a German citizen. Shortly thereafter, Lithuania refused to accept Zadvydas because he was neither a Lithuanian citizen nor a permanent resident. In 1996, the INS asked the Dominican Republic (Zadvydas' wife's country) to accept him, but this effort proved unsuccessful. In 1998, Lithuania rejected, as inadequately documented, Zadvydas' effort to obtain Lithuanian citizenship based on his parents' citizenship; Zadvydas' reapplication is apparently still pending....

The second case is that of Kim Ho Ma. Ma was born in Cambodia in 1977. When he was two, his family fled, taking him to refugee camps in Thailand and the Philippines and eventually to the United States, where he has lived as a resident alien since the age of seven. In 1995, at age 17, Ma was involved in a gang-related shooting, convicted of manslaughter, and sentenced to 38 months' imprisonment. He served two years, after which he was released into INS custody.

In light of his conviction of an "aggravated felony," Ma was ordered removed. The 90-day removal period expired in early 1999, but the INS continued to keep Ma in custody, because, in light of his former gang membership, the nature of his crime, and his planned participation in a prison hunger strike, it was "unable to conclude that Mr. Ma would remain nonviolent and not violate the conditions of release."

. . . The post–removal-period detention statute applies to certain categories of aliens who have been ordered removed, namely inadmissible aliens, criminal aliens, aliens who have violated their nonimmigrant status conditions, and aliens removable for certain national security or foreign relations reasons, as well as any alien "who has been determined by the Attorney General to be a risk to the community or unlikely to comply with the order of removal." It says that an alien who falls into one of these categories "may be detained beyond the removal period and, if released, shall be subject to [certain] terms of supervision."

The Government argues that the statute means what it literally says. It sets no "limit on the length of time beyond the removal period that an alien who falls within one of the Section 1231(a)(6)categories may be detained." Hence, "whether to continue to detain such an alien and, if so, in what circumstances and for how long" is up to the Attorney General, not up to the courts.

"[I]t is a cardinal principle" of statutory interpretation, however, that when an Act of Congress raises "a serious doubt" as to its constitutionality, "this Court will first ascertain whether a construction of the statute is fairly possible by which the question may be avoided." We have read significant limitations into other immigration statutes in order to avoid their constitutional invalidation. For similar reasons, we read an implicit limitation into the statute before us. In our view, the statute, read in light of the Constitution's demands, limits an alien's post-removal-period detention to a period reasonably necessary to bring about that alien's removal from the United States. It does not permit indefinite detention.

A statute permitting indefinite detention of an alien would raise a serious constitutional problem. The Fifth Amendment's Due Process Clause forbids the Government to "depriv[e]"any "person . . . of . . . liberty . . . without due process of law." Freedom from imprisonment—from government custody, detention, or other forms of physical restraint— lies at the heart of the liberty that Clause protects. And this Court has said that government detention violates that Clause unless the detention is ordered in a *criminal* proceeding with adequate procedural protections, or, in certain special and "narrow" non-punitive "circumstances," where a special justification, such as harm-threatening mental illness, outweighs the "individual's constitutionally protected interest in avoiding physical restraint."

The proceedings at issue here are civil, not criminal, and we assume that they are non-punitive in purpose and effect. There is no sufficiently strong special justification here for indefinite civil detention—at least as administered under this statute. The statute, says the Government, has two regulatory goals: "ensuring the appearance of aliens at future immigration proceedings" and "[p]reventing danger to the community." But by definition the first justification—preventing flight—is weak or nonexistent where removal seems a remote possibility at best. As this Court said in *Jackson* v. *Indiana* ,406 U.S.715 (1972), where detention's goal is no longer practically attainable, detention no longer "bear[s] [a] reasonable relation to the purpose for which the individual [was] committed."

The second justification—protecting the community—does not necessarily diminish in force over time. But we have upheld preventive detention based on dangerousness only when limited to specially dangerous individuals and subject to strong procedural protections. . . . In cases in which preventive detention is of potentially *indefinite* duration, we have also demanded that the dangerousness rationale be accompanied by some other special circumstance, such as mental illness, that helps to create the danger.

The civil confinement here at issue is not limited, but potentially permanent. The provision authorizing detention does not apply narrowly to "a small segment of particularly dangerous individuals," say suspected terrorists, but broadly to aliens ordered removed for many and various reasons, including tourist visa violations. And, once the flight risk justification evaporates, the only special circumstance present is the alien's removable status itself, which bears no relation to a detainee's dangerousness.

Moreover, the sole procedural protections available to the alien are found in administrative proceedings, where the alien bears the burden of proving he is not dangerous, without (in the Government's view) significant later judicial review. This Court has suggested, however, that the Constitution may well preclude granting "an administrative body the unreviewable authority to make determinations implicating fundamental rights." The serious constitutional problem arising out of a statute that, in these circumstances, permits an indefinite, perhaps permanent, deprivation of human liberty without any such protection is obvious.

The Government argues that, from a constitutional perspective, lien status itself can justify indefinite detention, and points to *Shaughnessy* v. *United States ex rel. Mezei*, 345 U.S. 206 (1953), as support. That case involved a once lawfully admitted alien who left the United States, returned after a trip abroad, was refused admission, and was left on Ellis Island, indefinitely detained there because the Government could not find another country to accept him. The Court held that Mezei's detention did not violate the Constitution.

Although *Mezei*, like the present cases, involves indefinite detention, it differs from the present cases in a critical respect. As the Court emphasized, the alien's extended departure from the United States required him to seek entry into this country once again. His presence on Ellis Island did not count as entry into the United States. Hence, he was "treated," for constitutional purposes, "as if stopped at the border." And that made all the difference.

The distinction between an alien who has effected an entry into the United States and one who has never entered runs throughout immigration law. It is well established that certain constitutional protections available to persons inside the United States are unavailable to aliens outside of our geographic borders. But once an alien enters the country, the legal circumstance changes, for the Due Process Clause applies to all "persons "within the United States, including aliens, whether their presence here is lawful, unlawful, temporary, or permanent. Indeed, this Court has held that the Due Process Clause protects an alien subject to a final order of deportation, see *Wong Wing* v. *United States*, 163 U.S. 228, 238 (1896), though the nature of that protection may vary depending upon status and circumstance, . . .

[T]he Government argues that, whatever liberty interest the aliens possess, it is "greatly diminished" by their lack of a legal right to "liv[e] at large in this country." The choice, however, is not between imprisonment and the alien "living at large." It is between imprisonment and supervision under release conditions that may not be violated. And, for the reasons we have set forth, we believe that an alien's liberty interest is, at the least, strong enough to raise a serious question as to whether, irrespective of the procedures used, the Constitution permits detention that is indefinite and potentially permanent. . . .

In early 1996, Congress explicitly expanded the group of aliens subject to mandatory detention, eliminating provisions that permitted release of criminal aliens who had at one time been lawfully admitted to the United States. Antiterrorism and Effective Death Penalty Act of 1996, §439(c),110 Stat. 1277. And later that year Congress enacted the present law, which liberalizes pre-existing law by shortening the removal period from six months to 90 days, mandates detention of certain criminal aliens during the removal proceedings and for the subsequent 90-day removal period, and adds the post-removal-period provision here at issue. Illegal Immigration Reform and Immigrant Responsibility Act of 1996, Div. C, §§303,305, 110 Stat.3009 -585,3009 -598 to 3009 -599;8 U.S.C. §§1226(c),1231(a)(1994 ed., Supp.V).

We have found nothing in the history of these statutes that clearly demonstrates a congressional intent to authorize indefinite, perhaps permanent, detention. Consequently, interpreting the statute to avoid a serious constitutional threat, we conclude that, once removal is no longer reasonably foreseeable, continued detention is no longer authorized by statute. . . .

The Fifth Circuit held Zadvydas' continued detention lawful as long as "good faith efforts to effectuate . . . deportation continue" and Zadvydas failed to show that deportation will prove "impossible." But this standard would seem to require an alien seeking release to show the absence of *any* prospect of removal—no matter how unlikely or unforeseeable—which demands more than our reading of the statute can bear. The Ninth Circuit held that the Government was required to release Ma from detention because there was no reasonable likelihood of his removal in the foreseeable future. But its conclusion may have rested solely upon the "absence "of an "extant or pending "repatriation agreement without giving due weight to the likelihood of successful future negotiations. Consequently, we vacate the decisions below and remand both cases for further proceedings consistent with this opinion.

It is so ordered.

The Smart Border Declaration and Action Plan (2001)

Following the terrorist attacks on the United States in September 2001, U.S. and Canadian officials sought to address security weaknesses along their shared border. Meeting with Canada's prime minister in Ottawa, U.S. Homeland Security Director Tom Ridge led a delegation including representatives from the Departments of Justice, Transportation, Defense, State, and Treasury, as well as the INS, National Security Council, Customs Service, and Coast Guard. The Smart Border Declaration identifies four joint principles (or "pillars") to guide cooperation on a thirty-point plan of action.

The Smart Border Declaration

Building a Smart Border for the 21st Century on the Foundation of a North American Zone of Confidence

The terrorist actions of September 11 were an attack on our common commitment to democracy, the rule of law and a free and open economy. They highlighted a threat to our public and economic security. They require our governments to develop new approaches to meet these challenges. This declaration commits our governments to work together to address these threats to our people, our institutions and our prosperity.

Public security and economic security are mutually reinforcing. By working together to develop a zone of confidence against terrorist activity, we create a unique opportunity to build a smart border for the 21st century; a border that securely facilitates the free flow of people and commerce; a border that reflects the largest trading relationship in the world.

Our countries have a long history of cooperative border management. This tradition facilitated both countries' immediate responses to the attacks of September 11. It is the foundation on which we continue to base our cooperation, recognizing that our current and future prosperity and security depend on a border that operates efficiently and effectively under all circumstances.

Action Plan

The attached Action Plan for Creating a Secure and Smart Border includes the measures already identified by our colleagues as well as new initiatives. Four pillars support the action plan:

(1) The Secure Flow of People

We will implement systems to collaborate in identifying security risks while expediting the flow of low risk travelers.

We will identify security threats before they arrive in North America through collaborative approaches to reviewing crew and passenger manifests, managing refugees, and visa policy coordination.

We will establish a secure system to allow low risk frequent travelers between our counties to move efficiently across the border.

(2) The Secure Flow of Goods

We will implement a system to collaborate in identifying high risk goods while expediting the flow of low risk goods.

We will identify security threats arriving from abroad by developing common standards for screening cargo before it arrives in North America, while working to clear goods at the first port of entry.

We will adopt compatible security standards at production and distribution facilities to minimize security threats. We will expedite the flow of low risk traffic between our countries by harmonizing commercial processes at the border.

We will expedite the flow of low risk goods between our countries by establishing secure procedures to clear goods away from the border, including at rail yards and at marine ports.

(3) Secure Infrastructure

We will relieve congestion at key crossing points by investing reciprocally in border infrastructure and identifying technological solutions that will help to speed movement across the border.

We will identify and minimize threats to our critical infrastructure, including the airports, ports, bridges, tunnels, pipelines and powerlines that link our countries.

(4) Coordination and Information Sharing in the Enforcement of these Objectives

We will put the necessary tools and legislative framework in place to ensure that information and intelligence is shared in a timely and coherent way within our respective countries as well as between them.

We will strengthen coordination between our enforcement agencies for addressing common threats.

Next Steps

We will meet again early in the new year to review the critical paths that we have asked our officials to develop for realizing each of the objectives set out in the action plan. We will consult regularly to ensure continued progress on this plan to achieve the goals outlines as quickly as possible.

This joint action plan is an important step. Our governments are committed to building on this plan to continually identify and implement measures that can be taken to secure a smart border.

These measures are regarded by both governments as matters of the highest priority.

Action Plan for Creating a Secure and Smart Border

The Secure Flow of People

1. Biometric identifiers

   Jointly develop on an urgent basis common biometric identifiers in documentation such as permanent resident cards, NEXUS, and other travel documents to ensure greater security.

2. Permanent Resident Cards

   Develop and deploy a secure card for permanent residents which includes a biometric identifier.

3. Single Alternative Inspection System

   Resume NEXUS pilot project, with appropriate security measures, for two-way movement of pre-approved travelers at Sarnia-Port Huron, complete pilot project evaluation and expand a single program to other areas along the land border. Discuss expansion to air travel.

4. Refugee/Asylum Processing

   Review refugee/asylum practices and procedures to ensure that applicants are thoroughly screened for security risks and take necessary steps to share information on refugee and asylum claimants.

5. Handling of Refugee/Asylum Claims

   Negotiate a safe third-country agreement to enhance the handling of refugee claims.

6. Visa Policy Coordination

   Initiate joint review of respective visa waiver lists and share look-out lists at visa issuing offices.

7. Air Preclearance

   Finalize plans/authority necessary to implement the Preclearance Agreement signed in January 2001. Resume intransit preclearance at Vancouver and expand to other airports per Annex I of the Agreement.

8. Advance Passenger Information / Passenger Name Record

   Share Advance Passenger Information and agreed-to Passenger Name Records on flights between Canada and the United States, including in-transit flights. Explore means to identify risks posed by passengers on international flights arriving in each other's territory.

9. Joint Passenger Analysis Units

   Establish joint units at key international airports in Canada and the United States.

10. Ferry Terminals

    Review customs and immigration presence and practices at international ferry terminals.

11. Compatible Immigration Databases

    Develop jointly an automated database, such as Canada's Support System for Intelligence, as a platform for information exchange, and enhance sharing of intelligence and trend analysis.

12. Immigration Officers Overseas

    Increase number of Canadian and US immigration officers at airports overseas and enhance joint training of airline personnel.

13. International Cooperation

    Undertake technical assistance to source and transit countries.

The Secure Flow of Goods

14. Harmonized Commercial Processing

    Establish complementary systems for commercial processing, including audit-based programs and partnerships with industry to increase security. Explore the merits of a common program.

15. Clearance away from the border

    Develop an integrated approach to improve security and facilitate trade through away-from-the-border processing for truck/rail cargo (and crews), including inland preclearance/post-clearance, international zones and pre-processing centers at the border, and maritime port intransit preclearance.

16. Joint facilities

    Establish criteria, under current legislation and regulations, for the creation of small, remote joint border facilities. Examine the legal and operational issues associated with the establishment of international zones and joint facilities, including armed protection or the arming of law enforcement officers in such zones and facilities.

17. Customs Data

    Sign the Agreement on Sharing Data Related to Customs Fraud, exchange agreed upon customs data pursuant to NAFTA, and discuss what additional commercial and trade data should be shared for national security purposes.

18. Intransit Container Targeting at Seaports

    Jointly target marine intransit containers arriving in Canada/US by exchanging information and analysts. Work in partnership with the industry to develop advance electronic commercial manifest data for marine containers arriving from overseas.

Secure Infrastructure

19. Infrastructure improvements

    Work to secure resources for joint and coordinated physical and technological improvements to key border points and trade corridors aimed at overcoming traffic management and growth challenges, including dedicated lanes and border modeling exercises.

20. Intelligent Transportation Systems

    Deploy interoperable technologies in support of other initiatives to facilitate the secure movement of goods and people, such as transponder applications and electronic container seals.

21. Critical Infrastructure Protection

    Conduct binational threat assessments on trans-border infrastructure and identify necessary additional protection measures, and initiate assessments for transportation networks and other critical infrastructure.

22. Aviation security

    Finalize Federal Aviation Administration-Transport Canada agreement on comparability/equivalence of security and training standards.

Coordination and Information Sharing in the Enforcement of These Objectives

23. Integrated Border and Marine Enforcement Teams

    Expand IBET/IMET to other areas of the border and enhance communication and coordination.

24. Joint Enforcement Coordination

    Work toward ensuring comprehensive and permanent coordination of law enforcement, anti-terrorism efforts and information sharing, such as by strengthening the Cross-Border Crime Forum and reinvigorating Project Northstar.

25. Integrated Intelligence

    Establish joint teams to analyze and disseminate information and intelligence, and produce threat and intelligence assessments. Initiate discussions regarding a Canadian presence on the U.S. Foreign Terrorist Tracking Task Force.

26. Fingerprints

    Implement the Memorandum of Understanding to supply equipment and training that will enable the RCMP to access FBI fingerprint data directly via real time electronic link.

27. Removal of deportees

    Address legal and operational challenges to joint removals, and coordinate initiatives to encourage uncooperative countries to accept their nationals.

28. Counter-Terrorism Legislation

    Bring into force legislation on terrorism, including measures for the designation of terrorist organizations.

29. Freezing of terrorist assets

    Exchange advance information on designated individuals and organizations in a timely manner.

30. Joint Training and Exercises

    Increase dialogue and commitment for the training and exercise programs needed to implement the joint response to terrorism guidelines. Joint counter-terrorism training and exercises are essential to building and sustaining effective efforts to combat terrorism and to build public confidence.

Ottawa, Canada, December 12, 2001

Index

Note: *t* next to page number refers to tables, and *n* refers to notes.

AAI. *See* Arab-American Institute
ABLI. *See* American Business for Legal Immigration Coalition
Abraham, Spencer, 57, 73
Abu Mezer, 161
ACLU. *See* American Civil Liberties Union
ADC. *See* American Arab Anti-Discrimination Committee
Adler, Tamar, 13, 14
AdTI. *See* Alexis de Tocqueville Institution
Advisory Panel to Assess Domestic Response Capabilities for Terrorism Involving Weapons of Mass Destruction, 102
Advocacy organizations, 128, 129–133
AeA. *See* American Electronics Association
AEA. *See* American Engineering Association
AFB. *See* American Farm Bureau
Afghanistan, 124, 138, 190–192
Africa, 40, 130, 138, 156, 178, 181
African Americans, 5, 92
African Methodist Episcopal Church, 135
AFSC. *See* American Friends Service Committee
Agencies and organizations, 122, 128–153. *See also* Governmental agencies
Agricultural issues. *See also* American Farm Bureau; Visas exports, 52

Guatemalan poultry workers, 32–33
insurance, 175
labor standards, 53
Mexican farms and farming, 166
Mexican migrant workers, 17, 18, 19
migrant workers, 47, 50–51, 60–61
temporary foreign workers, 47–55, 156
undocumented farmworkers, 149
value of production, 52
Agriculture Department, 51
Ahmed Ressam, 161
AILA. *See* American Immigration Lawyers' Association
Albania and Albanians, 74, 185–186
Alexis de Tocqueville Institution (AdTI), 2, 27, 129
Algeria, 161
Alien Nation (Brimelow), 6, 11
Al Qaeda. *See* Terrorism and terrorists
American-Arab Anti-Discrimination Committee (ADC), 110, 140–141
American Business for Legal Immigration Coalition (ABLI), 145
American Civil Liberties Union (ACLU), 60, 110
American Council for Voluntary International Action, 138

American Council on Education, 105
American Electronics Association (AeA), 145–146
American Engineering Association (AEA), 146
American Farm Bureau (AFB), 52, 146–147
American Federation of Labor-Congress of Industrial Organizations (AFL-CIO), 16, 57, 63, 147–148, 163, 260–263
American Friends Service Committee (AFSC), 135
American Immigration Lawyers' Association (AILA), 67, 129–130
American Red Cross, 138
Americans for Tax Reform, 63–64
Amsterdam Treaty, 184
Antiterrorism and Effective Death Penalty Act (1996), 66, 128
Arab-American Institute (AAI), 63–64, 141
Arab American Leadership Council, 141
Arab American Leadership Political Action Committee, 141
Arango, Joaquìn, 177
Archer, Bill, 59
Aristide, Jean-Bertrand, 82, 83
Arizona, 13–14, 45, 71, 72
Arkansas, 74
Armed Islamic Group, 161
Ashcroft, John, 107, 108, 109, 170–171

Asia
    assimilation of emigrants
        from, 91
    educational factors, 42
    emigration to Canada, 158, 159,
        160
    emigration to the U.S., 18, 20,
        40, 156, 160
    fast-growing U.S. minority
        groups, 5
    gangs, 161
    migrant farmworkers, 51
Asian American Legal Defense
    and Education Fund, 132
Asian-Americans, 98, 99–100, 143
Asylum. *See also* Refugees
    applications and approval
        rates, 88*t*
    Canadian applications, 161
    China's one-child policy, 89–90
    Cubans, 82–83
    definitions, 84
    documentation, 87
    European applications, 184
    gender persecution, 35, 88
    global population of, 84–85
    Haitian boat people, 82–83
    hearings for, 132
    human rights protection, 81
    international view of, 161
    numbers of admissions, 87
    policies, 81–88
    political persecution, 36
AT&T, 56
Atlanta, 11
Australia, 40, 156, 181
Auto Pact (U.S.-Canada; 1965),
    162, 164

Bahamas, 74
Baird, Zoë, 43
Barnett, Donald, 13–14
Barnett, Roger, 13–14
Belize, 152
Bergeron, Russell A., 66–67
Berman, Howard L., 54
Bermudez, Andres, 180
Bernstein, Josh, 95
BIA. *See* Board of Immigration
    Appeals

Bilingual Education Act (1968), 93
Board of Immigration Appeals
    (BIA), 35, 88, 89, 108
Boat people, 82–83
Bond, Phil, 58
Border Liaison Mechanism (U.S.-
    Mexico), 166, 169
Border Patrol, U.S.
    assistance to, 13–14
    border security issues,
        102–103
    dangerous border conditions
        and, 168
    detentions, 68
    funding for, 71
    number of apprehensions, 123
    staffing of, 4, 13, 21, 59, 69, 71,
        72, 103
    U.S. border with Canada,
        102–103, 148
    U.S. border with Mexico, 69,
        70, 102–103, 123
Bosnia, 86, 87, 184–185, 188–189
Boutros-Ghali, Boutros, 189
Boyd, Ralph, Jr., 110
Bracero Program (1942), 18, 19, 47,
    49–50, 169
Breyer, Stephen G., 68, 69, 268
Brimelow, Peter, 5–6, 11, 17, 21–22
Brotons, Elizabet, 96
Brownback, Sam, 104, 107
Brownsville, Texas, 71
Buchanan, Patrick J., 19, 59
Bucks County, Pennsylvania, 139
Buffalo, 73
Bureau of International Labor Af-
    fairs (ILAB), 125. *See also* Labor
    Department
Bureau of Population, Refugees,
    and Migration (PRM), 124–125,
    188. *See also* State Department
Burundi, 87
Bureau for Immigration Enforce-
    ment, 106
Bush, George, 89, 165
    administration of, 82
Bush, George W., 19, 54, 96, 99,
    170, 191
    administration of, 107, 123, 141,
        191–192

Business and corporate issues
    business and labor organiza-
        tions, 145–149
    electronic workplace verifica-
        tion systems, 62
    high-technology companies,
        6–7
    immigrant business startups, 2,
        7
    permanent work visas, 22–23
    service sector, 8

California, 40, 45, 47, 60, 80, 94.
    See also Proposition 187; Silicon
    Valley
Camarota, Steven, 101
Cambodia, 68, 128, 188–189
Canada. *See also* North American
    Free Trade Agreement
    admission of refugees, 187
    economic factors, 157, 158
    illegal immigrants, 45
    immigrants and immigration
        policies, 40, 156–164, 177, 181
    Immigration Act of 1976,
        158–159
    point system, 159
    population, 158
    recreational boaters, 72
    Regional Conference on Migra-
        tion, 152
    terrorists in, 161–162
    views of increased border secu-
        rity, 73, 103
Canadian American Border Trade
    Alliance, 148
Cannon, Chris, 143
Caribbean countries, 42, 67, 83, 91,
    156, 178
Carnegie Endowment for Interna-
    tional Peace, 67, 134
Castenada, Jorge G., 170–171
Castro, Fidel, 96. *See also* Cuba
Catholic Church, 139, 168
Cato Institute, 15, 133
Celluci, Paul, 103
Center for Immigration Studies
    (CIS), 3, 27, 101, 133–134
Central America
    educational factors, 42

emigration to the U.S., 17, 24, 34
migrant farmworkers, 51, 61
peacekeeping in, 188–189
Central America Political Asylum
Project, 135
Central Intelligence Agency
(CIA), 103
Charitable organizations, 62–63
Chavez, Cesar, 149
Chavez, Linda, 43, 44
Child Nutrition Act, 62
China, People's Republic of, 56,
74, 89–90
Chirac, Jacques, 182
Christians, Evangelical, 85
Christopher, Warren, 167, 169
Church World Service (CWS),
135–136, 138
CIA. See Central Intelligence
Agency
CIC. See Citizenship and Immi-
gration Canada
CIR. See U.S. Commission on Im-
migration Reform
CIS. See Center for Immigration
Studies
Cisneros, Henry G., 33, 99
Citibank, 56
Citizens' Advisory Panel, 169
Citizenship, 35, 36. See also Natu-
ralization
Citizenship and Immigration
Canada (CIC), 158
Citizenship USA, 97
Civil rights movement, 18, 149. See
also Human and civil rights is-
sues
CJF. See Council of Jewish Federa-
tions
Clinton, Bill, 59, 61, 83, 96, 97–98
Clinton administration
crime policies, 59
Cuban refugees, 142
enforcement of employer sanc-
tions, 75
Haiti, 83
immigration regulations, 32,
33, 34, 62
importation of foreign work-
ers, 57–58

INS restructuring, 106
peacekeeping operations, 189
smuggling of aliens, 90
suggested immigration re-
forms, 127
CMRA. See Committee on Migra-
tion and Refugee Affairs
Coast Guard (U.S.), 82
Cold war, 84
Colombia, 31, 74, 137
Colorado, 74
Colosio, Luis Donaldo, 167
Commerce Department, 73
Commission on Immigration Re-
form, 57, 61
Commission on National Secu-
rity/21st Century, 102
Committee on Migration and
Refugee Affairs (CMRA), 138
Communism, 17
Congress (U.S.), 126. See also Polit-
ical issues
Congressional Black Caucus, 82
Constitutional issues
detention, 105, 108
due process, 68–69, 87
involuntary sterilization, 89
Consulting Mechanism for the
Immigration and Naturalization
Services Activities and Consular
Protection, 169
Convention Relating to the Status
of Refugees and Additional Pro-
tocol (1951, 1967), 81, 83–84, 187,
216–234
Costa Rica, 152
Council of Jewish Federations
(CJF), 136
Council on Foreign Relations, 101
Creel, Santiago, 170–171
Crime. See also Deportation; Detention
border patrols and, 71
Canadian immigration policies
and, 161
criminal aliens, 35, 59, 65–69
document fraud, 74–75
foreign-born prison inmates,
65
hate crimes, 110

indefinite incarceration, 128
judicial review of cases,
127–128, 130
Mexican immigration policies
and, 170–171
penalties, 65
Proposition 187 (California),
60
round up of illegal immigrants,
36
terrorist activity, 108–109
Croatia, 185
Cuba
detainees, 128
emigration to the U.S., 17, 32,
82, 84
González, Elián, 31, 32, 96–97
Haitian boat people, 82
in-country refugee processing
programs, 85
refugees from, 81, 136
refusals of deported aliens, 68
smuggling of aliens through, 74
Cuban American National Foundation (CANF), 142
CWS. See Church World Service

Daley, William H., 56–57
D'Amato, Alfonse, 65
Davis, Gray, 61, 142
Dayton Accords (1995), 185
Defense Department, 56, 191
Deferred Removal Orders Class
(Canada), 161
Democratic Party, 26, 97, 106
Denmark, 187
Deportation
absconders, 110
from Canada, 161
criminals, 35–36, 65–66
economic factors of, 66, 76
illegal aliens, 59
jailing of noncitizens, 35
naturalization and, 95
streamlining of procedures, 21,
66
waivers, 66, 68
Detention and detainees, 66–69,
105, 108, 128, 139, 141
Detroit, 65, 72–73

Detroit Free Press, 141
DHHS. *See* Health and Human
    Services Department
DiMarzio, Nicholas (Bishop), 67,
    170
Dole, Bob, 59
Domenici, Pete, 44
Dominican Republic, 152
Donnelly, Paul, 57
Dublin Convention (1997), 184

East Timor, 188–189
Eavesdropping, 109
Economic issues. *See also* Employ-
    ment issues; Poverty
    benefits and costs of immigra-
        tion, 78–81, 156
    border security, 101–102
    competition and competitive-
        ness, 52, 56, 80
    devaluation of the peso, 167,
        173
    economic development, 175
    economic factors of illegal
        workers, 11, 12, 76
    effects on immigration, 1, 23,
        26, 38, 70, 76–77, 111, 133, 157
    immigrant workers, 2, 7
    income and wage effects, 79–80
    inflation, 56
    money remittances sent home
        by immigrants, 171–173
    recession, 58, 111
    theoretical factors, 156, 174–177,
        178
    U.S.-Canadian trade and econ-
        omy, 156, 162
    U.S.-Mexican trade and econ-
        omy, 166
Ecuador, 74
Educational issues
    bilingual education, 93
    dropout rates, 93
    English as an official language,
        94
    migrant farmworkers, 51, 61
    notification of INS of students,
        104–105
    performance of immigrant's
        children, 94

    student monitoring, 105, 109
    U.S. science education, 55, 56
Education Department, 93–94
EEC. *See* European Economic
    Community
EEOC. *See* Equal Employment
    Opportunity Commission
Einstein, Albert, 138
El Colegio de la Frontera Norte,
    172
El Paso, 70, 139
El Salvador, 31, 34, 45, 51, 61, 86,
    152
Employment issues. *See also* Agri-
    culture; Visas
    Canadian point system, 159
    competition for jobs, 2, 11,
        52–53, 54, 55–56
    dangers of work, 50
    documentation, 75
    dual labor market theory,
        175–176
    economic factors, 76
    employers, 2, 4
    hard-to-fill and low-wage jobs,
        7–8, 34, 176
    high-technology workers, 6–7,
        12, 15, 34, 47, 55–58
    INS interior enforcement,
        69–70, 74
    job contracting, 55
    labor markets, 56–57, 79, 156,
        166–167, 174, 177
    Mexican manufacturing indus-
        try, 166–167
    Mexican migration, 173
    minimum wage and benefits,
        53
    North American Free Trade
        Agreement, 163, 166
    profiling and discrimination,
        75–76
    service industries, 8
    smuggling, 74, 75
    training and education, 8, 15,
        16, 56, 57, 58, 174
    temporary foreign workers,
        46–58, 60–61
    wages and earnings, 8, 15–16,
        25, 50, 53, 79–80, 174, 175, 176

    work ethic of immigrants, 2, 7
Employment issues, and undocu-
    mented workers/illegal immi-
    grants
    agricultural work, 17
    employer hires and sanctions,
        4, 10–12, 19, 63, 64, 75, 147
    general issues, 1
    migratory workers, 51
    monetary sanctions against
        employers, 19
    permanent work visas and,
        22–23
Enforcement. *See* Border Patrol,
    U.S.; Terrorism and terrorists
Entry without inspection (EWI).
    See Immigrants, illegal
Equal Employment Opportunity
    Commission (EEOC), 76
Este Pais, 168
Environmental issues, 8
Ethiopian Community Develop-
    ment Council, 138
Ethnic issues. *See* Racial, ethnic,
    and minority issues
Europe and European Union
    assimilation and acceptance of
        immigrants, 91, 181–182
    asylum seekers, 181, 185–186
    Bosnia and Kosovo atrocities,
        184–186
    common market, 182
    as core receiving region, 178
    donations for refugees, 187
    economic factors, 181
    educational factors, 42
    emigration from, 40, 160, 181
    entrance of third-country na-
        tionals, 183–184
    immigration to, 17, 20, 33, 181
    rebuilding of, 151, 181
    refugees in, 85, 185–186
    return of temporary workers,
        181
    U.S. and European immigra-
        tion policies compared,
        180–186
European Economic Community
    (EEC), 182
Evans, Brentnold, 67

EWI (entry without inspection). *See* Immigrants, illegal

Executive Office of the President, 102

48 Hours, 55

FAA. *See* Federal Aviation Administration

FAIR. *See* Federation for American Immigration Reform

Family issues. *See* Immigration

Farfan, Jimmy, 97

FBI. *See* Federal Bureau of Investigation

Federal Aviation Administration (FAA), 56

Federal Bureau of Investigation (FBI), 100, 103, 104, 105, 109

Federation for American Immigration Reform (FAIR), 2, 27, 56, 130

Feinstein, Dianne, 57, 104

Filipinos for Affirmative Action, 132

Fischer, Thomas, 11

Florida, 40, 45

Flushing. *See* New York City

Flynn, Stephen, 101

"Forgotten Refugees Campaign," 139

Forror, Mark, 32

"Fortress Europe," 182–183

Fox, Vicente, 54–55, 170, 173, 180

France, 186

Franklin, Benjamin, 2

Frey, William, 92

GAO. *See* General Accounting Office

Gekas, George, 107

General Accounting Office (GAO), 106

Geneva Conventions, 130–131, 150

Georgetown, Delaware, 32–33

Georgia, 45, 74

Gephardt, Richard A., 107

Germany, 185, 187

Gilmore Commission. *See* Advisory Panel to Assess Domestic

Response Capabilities for Terrorism Involving Weapons of Mass Destruction

Gilmore, James, III, 102

Ginsburg, Ruth Bader, 68

González, Elián, 31, 32, 96–97

Gore, Al, 96

Governmental agencies, 122–128. *See also* Immigration and Naturalization Service; *individual agencies*

Great Britain, 156, 186

Great Depression, 17, 47, 156

Greek Orthodox Archdiocese of North and South America, 135

Green cards. *See* Visas

Greenspan, Alan, 2

Gregorio T. v. Wilson, 142

Guanajuato Proposal, 170–171, 263–267

Guantanamo Bay (Cuba), 82, 96, 130–131, 186

Guatemala, 31–33, 34, 45, 51, 61, 152

Guatemale Support Project, 132

Guinea, 187

Guinea-Bissau, 87

Gurría, José Angel, 169

H-1B visas, *See* Visas, H-1B

H-2A visas, *See* Visas, H-2A

Haass, Richard N., 191–192

Hahn, James, 98, 99, 100

Haiti, 24, 45, 51, 82–83, 136, 144

Haitian Constituency USA Inc., 63

Hanjour, Hani, 104

Hart, Gary, 102

Hart-Rudman Commission. *See* Commission on National Security/21st Century

Hatch, Orrin, 75

Health and Human Services Department (DHHS), 81, 124

Health issues, 50, 62, 89–90

Hebrew Immigrant Aid Society (HIAS), 136–137, 138

Hernandez, Juan, 173

HIAS. *See* Hebrew Immigrant Aid Society

High Level Working Group on Migration, 170–171

Hijackers and hijackings. *See* Terrorism and terrorists

Hispanics and Latinos. *See also* Mexican American Legal Defense and Education Fund; National Association of Latino Elected and Appointed Officials; National Council of La Raza
assimilation of, 10
bilingual education, 94
high school dropout rate, 93
as largest U.S. minority, 5, 34
political issues, 98–99
Proposition 187 (California), 60

Hitler, Adolf, 138

Homeownership, 88, 90–91

Honduras, 86–87, 152

Houston, 13

Hudson Institute, 55

Human and civil rights issues. *See also* Interest groups
American-Arab-Discrimination Committee, 140–141
Bosnia-Herzegovina, 184–185
China's one-child policy, 89–90
political issues of, 192–193
rights of Mexican migrants, 167–171
Universal Declaration of Human Rights, 149
U.S. Committee for Refugees, 132
U.S. immigration policy, 129–130

Hurricane Mitch, 86–87

ICRC. *See* International Committee for the Red Cross

IEEE. *See* Institute of Electronics and Electrical Engineers

ILAB. *See* Bureau of International Labor Affairs

Illegal Immigration Reform and Immigrant Responsibility Act (IIRIRA; 1996)
asylum provision, 87

automated tracking system, 73

benefits provision, 62

criminal aliens, 65–69

felony provision, 136

INS v. St. Cyr, 128

passage of, 19

refugees, 90

restrictive measures of, 38, 59

student monitoring, 104

text of, 242–247

Illinois, 40, 45

Immigrant Rights Project, 135

Immigrants. *See also* Economic is-sues; Immigrants, illegal; Immi-gration; Marriage

assimilation of, 3–4, 9–10, 47, 77, 88–94

background and historical overview, 17–23, 41

benefits for, 62, 95, 131

birth rate of, 10

debate over, 2, 17

definition of, 39

demographics of, 5, 41, 42, 43

educational factors with, 41–42, 51

effects on culture and society, 77–78

employment factors with, 42, 47. *See also* Employment is-sues

geographic concentration, 40–41, 98

illegal immigrants. *See* Immi-grants, illegal

legal permanent residents, 40–43

migrant farmworkers, 50–51

numbers of, 1, 2, 3, 5, 7–11, 13, 17, 18–20, 37, 39, 44

opposition to, 8

political issues of, 94–100

rights of, 66–67

socioeconomic factors with, 42

sponsorship, 39, 55, 56, 64–65

temporary foreign workers, 46–58

top countries of origin, 20*t*

Immigrants, illegal, 43–46

amnesty for, 19, 24–25, 34, 52, 54, 63–65

benefits for, 62

characteristics of, 43–46

costs of, 25

criminal aliens, 35

dangers facing, 14, 71–72, 167–168

deportation of, 23, 25

deterrence of, 14

employment factors, 4, 43

entry without inspection (EWI), 45

farmworkers, 51

forged documents, 35

geographic concentration, 45

nonimmigrant overstays, 45

numbers of, 4, 9, 23, 25, 33, 34, 45–46, 123

public view of, 43–44

smuggling of aliens, 59, 71–72, 74, 102, 167, 168

Immigration. *See also* Deporta-tion; Detention; Immigrants; Naturalization

admissions by type, 157

causes of international migra-tion, 174–179

changes in U.S. immigration from Mexico, 179–180

cumulative effects of, 37

economic benefits and costs, 78–81, 157

enforcement, 58–62, 69–76

family factors, 17, 22–23, 33, 38, 41, 64, 65, 77, 81, 99, 158–159, 177

grants of permanent residence, 36

impact on the U.S., 76–78

intelligence, 103–105

lotteries, 22, 32, 38

quotas, 17, 25, 38, 58

recent developments and in-formation, 31–36

rules and legislation, 21–22

suggested reforms, 127, 178–179

U.S. and Canadian policies compared, 156–164, 177

U.S. and European policies compared, 180–186

U.S. and Mexican policies compared, 165–173, 179–180

Immigration Act of 1965, 38

Immigration Act of 1990, 3, 19–20, 46, 51–52, 57, 85, 86

Immigration Act of 1996, 143

Immigration and Nationality Act (1965), 18, 83–84, 90, 104, 234–242

Immigration and Naturalization Service (INS). *See also* Justice Department; Visas

asylum officers, 87

backlog of, 95, 97, 136, 147, 158

Border Patrol. *See* Border Pa-trol, U.S.

Bush administration reform, 99

citizenship applications, 36

commissioners, 123–124

crack down on employers, 10–12, 74–76

directory information, 27

effectiveness of, 9, 12, 13, 14

enforcement by, 4, 11, 12, 14, 19, 36, 69–76

expedited removal, 87

general information, 123

González, Elián, and, 31, 32

in-country refugee processing programs, 85

interior enforcement, 69–70, 73–76

lottery, 22, 32, 38

notification of, 104–105

profiling by, 69, 110

reforms, 99, 100, 106–107, 123, 124

role and responsibilities, 38–39, 69, 73–74, 123

Immigration and Naturalization Ser-vice v. St. Cyr (2001), 68, 127–128

Immigration and Refugee Pro-gram, 135–136

Immigration and Refugee Ser-vices of America (IRSA), 132, 137

Immigration Enforcement Im-provement Act of 1995, 71

Immigration Law Enforcement
  Monitoring Project, 135
Immigration Reform and Control
  Act (IRCA; 1986)
    amnesty, 24, 34, 63
    deportation, 65
    employer sanctions, 4, 19, 75
    enforcement of, 10
    NNIRR and, 132
    passage of, 19
Immigration Reform Coalition, 57
Imperial Beach, California, 71
Imperial Valley, California, 71–72
India, 56
Indochina, 17
Industrial Revolution, 156, 181
Information resources and tech-
  nology, 27, 56
Information Technology Associa-
  tion of America (ITAA), 6, 56,
  148
INS. *See* Immigration and Natu-
  ralization Service
INS v. St. Cyr. See Immigration and
  Naturalization Service v. St. Cyr
Institute of Electronics and Elec-
  trical Engineers (IEEE), 57
Insurance, 175
Integrated Entry and Exit Data
  System Task Force, 73
Intelligence. *See* Terrorism and
  terrorists; *individual agencies*
InterAction, 138
Interest groups
    consumer groups, 54
    ethnic advocacy groups, 95,
      140–145
    human rights, 71
    immigrant political interest
      groups, 94–95
    for/against legal immigration,
      58–59
Intergovernmental Committee for
  European Migration, 151
Intergovernmental Committee for
  Migration, 151
International Bill of Human
  Rights, 130
International Committee for the
  Red Cross (ICRC), 149, 150

International Federation of Red
  Cross/Red Crescent Societies,
  150
International Labor Organization,
  169
International Migration Policy
  Program, 134
International Organization for
  Migration (IOM), 149, 151, 152
International organizations,
  149–153
International Rescue Committee
  (IRC), 138
IOM. *See* International Organiza-
  tion for Migration
Iowa, 74
Iran, 190, 191
Iraq, 188–189
IRC. *See* International Rescue
  Committee
Ireland, 56
IRSA. *See* Immigration and
  Refugee Services of America
ITAA. *See* Information Technol-
  ogy Association of America
Italy, 85

Jamaica, 51
Japan, 187
Jeffe, Sherry Bebitch, 98–99
Jesuit Refugee Service (JRS),
  139
Jews, 85, 136–137
Johnson-Reed Act (1924), 18
Joint voluntary agencies (JVAs),
  85
Jordan, 187
Jordan, Barbara, 61–62, 70, 126
Jospin, Lionel, 182
JRS. *See* Jesuit Refugee Service
Judiciary Committee, 126
Justice Department, 73, 90, 105,
  108–110. *See also* Board of Immi-
  gration Appeals; Immigration
  and Naturalization Service
JVAs. *See* Joint voluntary agencies

Keeley, Charles, 86
Kemp, Jack, 33, 63–64
Kennedy, Anthony M., 68

Kennedy, Edward M., 57, 75, 104,
  107, 111
Kentucky, 74
Khokha, Sasha, 95
Kim Ho Ma, 68
Kosovo
    Bureau of Population,
      Refugees, and Migration, 124
    European Union and, 184–185
    Lawyer's Committee for Hu-
      man Rights, 130
    NATO and, 185–186
    numbers of refugees and dis-
      placed, 185–186
    temporary protection status,
      87
    U.S. and, 81, 86, 186, 192–193
Krikorian, Mark, 3, 4, 10, 11, 13,
  14, 26, 86
Kuwait, 188–189
Kuwata, Kam, 100
Kyl, Jon, 104

Labor Department, 47, 51, 52, 55,
  125, 148
Labor unions, 63, 76, 79, 145–149
Labor laws. *See* Employment is-
  sues; Laws and policy
Laforst, Raynald, 63
Lance, Bronwyn, 2, 7, 10, 12, 26
Laos, 51, 128
Laredo, Texas, 71, 73
Latin America
    assimilation of emigrants
      from, 91
    educational factors, 42
    emigration to Canada, 160
    emigration to the U.S., 17, 18,
      20, 40, 156, 158, 160, 178
Latinos. *See* Hispanics and Lati-
  nos
Lautenberg, Frank, 85
Lautenberg Amendment, 85–86,
  136
Laws and policy
    forging documents, 35
    fraud and abuse, 57
    investigation of terrorist at-
      tacks, 105, 108–111
    labor laws, 53

lack of enforcement, 11
opposition to 11–12
proposed legislation, 24, 31–32, 33, 34, 35–36
"sticking it to foreigners," 26
Lawyers' Committee for Human Rights (LCHR), 130–131
League of United Latin American Citizens (LULAC), 142
Legal Immigration Family Equity (LIFE) Act (1994), 49, 64
Leopold, David W., 108
Le Pen, Jean-Marie, 181–182
Lieberman, Joseph I., 102
LIFE Act. *See* Legal Immigration Family Equity Act
LIRS. *See* Lutheran Immigration and Refugee Services
Los Angeles
    detention assistance, 139
    document warehouse, 75
    immigrants in, 6, 41, 65, 98
    political factors, 98–99
Los Angeles Times, 98
Lott, Trent, 124
LULAC. *See* League of United Latin American Citizens
Lutheran Immigration and Refugee Services (LIRS), 139–140

Maastrict Treaty. *See* Treaty on European Union
MacAulay, Laurence, 164
Macedonia, 186
MALDEF. *See* Mexican American Legal Defense and Educational Fund
Marriage, 5, 65, 91
Marshall Plan, 151
Martinez, Virginia, 94
Mastech, 55
Matloff, Norman, 6–7, 15, 16, 56
Matter of Chang (1989), 89, 90
McCarran-Walter Act (1952), 18
McKenna, Tom, 8–9
McLarty, Mack, 170
McNary v. Haitian Centers Council (1993), 83
Meeder, Hans, 56

Meissner, Doris
    background of, 123–124
    dangers at the borders, 14
    deportations, 66
    INS backlog, 95, 97
    National Border Patrol Strategy, 70
    restructuring of INS, 106–107
    views of Mexico, 167
    worksite enforcement, 75–76
Memorandum of Understanding (U.S.-Mexico; 1996), 169
Mexican American Legal Defense and Educational Fund (MALDEF), 60–61, 142–143
Mexican-American War, 165
Mexico. *See also* North American Free Trade Agreement
    citizenship and emigration, 180
    crackdown on illegal U.S. immigration, 9, 13, 72
    dangers to undocumented migrants, 168
    economic factors, 165, 166–167
    effects of Mexican migration, 171–173, 179–180
    emigration to Canada, 159
    emigration to the U.S., 17, 19, 20, 40, 130, 163, 164–180
    illegal U.S. immigration, 45, 70–71, 74, 111
    in-country refugee processing programs, 85
    instability in, 167
    migrant farmworkers, 51, 61
    migrant sending and receiving communities, 171–173
    naturalization of, 95
    North American Free Trade Agreement, 163–167
    protection of migrant rights, 167–171
    Regional Conference on Migration, 152
    relations with the U.S., 164–171
    views of migrant workers, 180
    World War II farmworkers, 47
Mexico-U.S. Binational Study on Migration, 165, 169

Michigan, 110
Michigan Farm Bureau, 52
Microsoft, 15
Migration Policy Institute (MPI), 134
Military issues, 13, 55. *See also* Defense Department
Miller, Harris N., 6, 12, 15, 56
Minority issues. *See* Racial, ethnic, and minority issues
Missouri, 74
Mogadishu. *See* Somalia
Monreal, Ricardo, 180
Montgomery, Maryland, 65
Montserrat, 87
Moore, Steven, 1, 4, 7–8, 12, 23
Mozambique, 188–189
MPI. *See* Migration Policy Institute
Muñoz, Cecilia, 4, 8, 10, 12, 22, 53

NAALC. *See* North American Agreement on Labor Cooperation
NAFTA. *See* North American Free Trade Agreement
NALEO. *See* National Association of Latino Elected and Appointed Officials
NAM. *See* National Association of Manufacturers
Namibia, 188–189
NAPALC. *See* National Asian Pacific American Legal Consortium
National Academy of Sciences, 58
National Agricultural Workers Survey (NAWS), 51, 53
National Asian Pacific American Legal Consortium (NAPALC), 63–64, 143
National Association of Latino Elected and Appointed Officials (NALEO), 61, 97, 143–144
National Association of Manufacturers (NAM), 145
National Baptist Convention of America, 135
National Border Patrol Strategy, 70–71

National Center for Educational Statistics, 93

National Coalition for Haitian Refugees, 144

National Coalition for Haitian Rights (NCHR), 63–64, 144

National Council of Agricultural Employers, 52

National Council of La Raza (NCLR), 4, 27, 54, 142, 144–145

National Crime Information Center, 104

National Front Party (France), 181–182

National Guard, 103

National Immigration Forum, 5, 11, 27, 131

National Immigration Law Center (NILC), 95, 131–132

National Network for Immigrant and Refugee Rights (NNIRR), 95, 132

National Office for Combating Terrorism, 102

National Retail Federation, 63–64

National Review, 4

National School Lunch Act, 62

National Science Foundation (NSF), 55

National security, 100, 105, 108, 109, 110–111, 120*n*155. *See also* Terrorism and terrorists

NATO. *See* North Atlantic Treaty Organization

Naturalization. *See also* Immigrants; Immigration
immigrant aid groups, 63
numbers of immigrants naturalizing, 95, 97
political factors, 95, 96, 97
Proposition 187 and, 61

NAWS. *See* National Agricultural Workers Survey

NCHR. *See* National Coalition for Haitian Rights

NCLR. *See* National Council of La Raza

Nebraska, 74

Nevada, 41

New America Foundation, 13

New Jersey, 40, 45, 80

Newland, Kathleen, 189

New York City, 41, 98, 99–100, 161

New York state, 40, 45

New York Times, 70, 180, 191

Nicaragua, 86–87, 152

Nigeria, 74

NILC. *See* National Immigration Law Center

NNIRR. *See* National Network for Immigrant and Refugee Rights

Nogales, Arizona, 71

North, David S., 55

North American Agreement on Labor Cooperation (NAALC), 125

North American Free Trade Agreement (NAFTA; 1994), 125, 162, 163–164–166, 255–260

North Atlantic Treaty Organization (NATO), 184, 185–186

North Carolina, 41, 74

Northern Manhattan Coalition for Immigrant Rights, 63

Norway, 187

NSF. *See* National Science Foundation

Nuvation Labs, 12, 15

OARS. *See* Outlying Area Reporting System

OAS. *See* Organization of American States

OECD. *See* Organization for Economic Cooperation and Development

Office of Bilingual Education and Minority Language Affairs, 93–94

Office of Homeland Security, 73, 102

Office of Refugee Resettlement (ORR), 81, 125–126. *See also* Health and Human Services Department

Open door policy, 58–76. *See also* Policies and policymaking

Operation Gatekeeper, 9, 71–72, 168

Operation Hold the Line, 70, 71

Operation Rio Grande, 71

Operation Safeguard, 71

Operation Seek and Keep, 74

Operation Wetback, 18

Organization for Economic Cooperation and Development (OECD), 149, 151–152, 168, 180

Organization for European Economic Co-Operation, 151

Organization of American States (OAS), 149

ORR. *See* Office of Refugee Resettlement

Orthodox Church in America, 135

O'Sullivan, John, 4, 9–10, 16, 26

Outlying Area Reporting System (OARS), 72

Pachon, Harry, 99

Pakistan, 138, 190, 191

Panama, 74, 152

Papademetriou, Demetrois, G., 46

Partido Revolucionario Institucional (Mexico), 167

Passel, Jeff, 5

Perot, H. Ross, 163

Personal Responsibility and Work Opportunity Act (1996), 62

Philippines, 45, 51

PMCLA. *See* Program for the Mexican Communities Living Abroad

Poland, 45

Policies and policymaking, 38
airport security, 110–111
assumptions concerning immigration, 100
comparison of U.S. and Canadian policies, 177
failures of immigration policy, 11
Mexican immigration policies, 168–169
migration rates and, 175, 177
terrorism and terrorists, 100
U.S. and Canadian policies compared, 156–164, 177
U.S. and European policies compared, 180–186

U.S. and Mexican policies compared, 165–173, 179–180
U.S. role in international policy, 187–189, 192–193
weaknesses of, 100–101, 178–179
Political issues. *See also* Proposition 187
amnesty, 63–64
assimilation of immigrants, 92, 181–182
bilingual education, 93
criminal aliens, 65, 67–68
cultural assimilation, 88
employment factors, 75
European immigration, 181–182
expansion of U.S. Border Patrol, 71
Haiti, 82–83
immigration, 59–62, 63, 71, 77–78, 97, 127, 156
interest groups and, 58–59
investigation of terrorist attacks, 105
Mexican Americans, 169, 170
Mexican migration, 173, 179, 180
migrant farmworkers, 52–55
national identification system, 73
North American Free Trade Agreement, 163
partisanship, 98t
peacekeeping, 189
power of the vote for immigrants, 61
preservation of immigration status quo, 26
profiling, 69, 75–76, 110, 141
public views of legal and illegal immigration, 46, 81
regional refugee allotments, 85–86
restructuring of the INS, 106–107
role of immigrants in politics, 94–100
student monitoring, 104–105
temporary foreign workers, 46, 55, 55–58

U.S. role in international law and policy, 187
Pomona University, 172
Population-Environment Balance, 8
Population Studies Center, 134–135
Port Passenger Accelerated Service System (PortPASS), 72
Poverty, 50, 53
Powell, Colin L., 170–171, 191
Presidential Decision Directive 25, 189
President's Commission on Migratory Labor, 49, 51
PRI. *See* Partido Revolucionario Institucional
PRM. *See* Bureau of Population, Refugees, and Migration
Prince, Ron, 60
Profiling. *See* Political issues
Program for the Mexican Communities Living Abroad (PMCLA), 169
Proposition 187 (California)
effects of, 95
issues of, 60–61
Mexican American Legal Defense and Education Fund and, 142
passage of, 19, 26
political issues of, 59, 60–61, 167–168
text of, 250–255
Proposition 227 (California), 94
Protocol Relating to the Status of Refugees (1967), 187, 230–234
"Puebla Process." *See* Regional Conference on Migration

Quota Act (1921), 18
Quotas. *See* Immigration

Racial, ethnic, and minority issues
assimilation, 92–93
category changes, 5
discrimination, 91–92
ethnic advocacy groups, 140–145
ethnic cleansing, 184–185

ethnic heritage in European countries, 181
green cards, 22
groups for special consideration, 85–86
multiracial societies, 6
political hostility, 97
profiling, 69, 75–76, 110
white flight, 93
Rambouillet peace talks (1999), 185
RCM. *See* Regional Conference on Migration
Reagan, Ronald, 24
Red Cross/Red Crescent Societies, 150
Refugee Act of 1980, 84
Refugee assistance and resettlement organizations, 135–140
Refugee Convention. *See* Convention Relating to the Status of Refugees and Additional Protocol
Refugees. *See also* Bureau of Population, Refugees, and Migration; U.S. Committee for Refugees
admitted to Canada, 157, 159, 161, 187
admitted to Europe, 184, 187
admitted to the U.S., 187
Afghan, 190–191
assistance to, 125, 135–140, 149
benefits and costs of, 81, 125, 188
burden-sharing, 188
during the cold war, 84
definition of, 83–84, 89, 90
ethnic cleaning and, 186
global population of, 84–85, 187–188
immigrants to the U.S., 23
numbers of, 125
policies, 77, 81–88
"refugees in orbit," 184
resettlement of, 136–140, 149, 153
return of, 188
rights of, 81
from specific countries, 81
temporary protected status, 86, 137, 186

U.S. allocations, 85t
U.S. role in international law and policy, 187–189, 192–193
vulnerable special groups, 85–86
Regional Conference on Migration (RCM), 124, 152–153, 169–170
Regional Network of Civic Organizations for Migration (RNCOM), 152
Reich, Robert, 55, 57
Reimers, David M., 157
Remote Video Inspection Service (RVIS), 72
Reno, Janet, 10, 31, 59, 70, 96, 167
Reno v. Kim Ho Ma, 68
Republican Party, 26, 97, 99, 106
Ridge, Tom, 102
Rio Grande Valley, 71
RNCOM. *See* Regional Network of Civic Organizations for Migration
Rodriguez, Arturo, 63
Rodriguez, Gregory, 13
Rogers, Harold, 106
Roll Call, 57
Rozental, Andrés, 165, 170
Rudman, Warren, 102
Russia, 74, 85, 185
RVIS. *See* Remote Video Inspection Service
Rwanda, 188–189

60 Minutes, 55
Saenz, Thomas, 60–61
Salinas, Carlos, 165, 166
administration of, 168
"Save Our State" initiative. *See* Proposition 187
Schengen Agreement (1985), 182
Schengen Convention (1995), 183, 184
Schengen Information System (SIS), 183
Scotland, 56
SEA. *See* Single European Act
Seattle, 73
Secure Electronic Network for Travelers Rapid Inspection (SENTRI), 72

Sensenbrenner, James, 107
SENTRI. *See* Secure Electronic Network for Travelers Rapid Inspection
Serbia, 185–186
Service Employees International Union (SEIU), 132, 147
Shared Border Accord (U.S.-Canada; 1995), 162, 164
Sharry, Frank, 6, 11–12, 22–23, 24, 26–27, 44
Sierra Leone, 87, 188–189, 192, 193
Silicon Valley, 7, 12
Simpson, Alan K., 57
Single European Act (SEA; 1987), 182
SIS. *See Schengen Information System*
Slovenia, 185
Smart Border Declaration (U.S.-Canada, 2001), 103, 162, 164, 272–277
Smith, Christopher, 90
Smith, David A., 15–16
Smith, Gordon H., 54
Smith, Lamar, 11, 15, 66
Social Security system, 62, 79, 127
Social services, 25
Sociocultural issues, 173, 177–179
Somalia, 87, 189
Souter, David H., 68
South America, 42, 74
South Carolina, 74
Soviet Union and Soviet bloc, 20, 55, 84, 85, 86, 136, 181, 190
Sponsors and sponsorship. *See* Immigrants
St. Cyr, Enrico, 68
State Department, 73, 85, 103, 104, 124, 148. *See also* Bureau of Population, Refugees and Migration
Stein, Dan, 2, 7, 8, 11, 23, 25, 64
Stevens, John Paul, 68
Strassberger, William, 65
Student Adjustment Act, 143
Students, 104
Sudan, 87
Supreme Court (U.S.)
González, Elián, 97
indefinite detention, 108

interpretation of immigration laws, 127
laws regarding criminal aliens, 68
ruling on refugees, 83
Sweden, 187

21st Century Workforce Commission, 56
Tajikistan, 191
Taliban. *See* Afghanistan
Taxation issues, 80
Taylor, Ed, 167
Technology, 70
Temporary protected status (TPS). *See* Refugees
Tennessee, 74
Terrorism and terrorists
in Afghanistan, 190
Canada as terrorist haven, 161–162
effects on immigration policy, 55, 70, 73, 100–103
intelligence, 103–105
investigation of, 105, 108–111
terrorist organizations, 108–109
Texas, 40, 45
TEU. *See* Treaty on European Union
Thailand, 85
Theoretical issues
dual labor market theory, 175–176, 177
migration systems theory, 178
neoclassical economic theory, 156, 174–175, 177
new economics of migration theory, 175, 177, 178
theory of cumulative causation, 177–178
world systems theory, 176–177, 178
Think tanks, 133–135
Third International Mathematics and Science Study (TIMSS), 56
Tomas Rivera Policy Institute, 99
Torvalds, Linus, 57
TPS (Temporary protected status). *See* Refugees
Treasury Department, 73

Treaty of Rome, 182
Treaty on European Union (1993), 183, 184, 247–250
Troper, Harold, 157
Turkey, 181
Turkmenistan, 191

UFW. *See* United Farm Workers
Ukrainian Catholic and Orthodox Churches, 85
U.N. *See* United Nations
UNHCR. *See* United Nations, High Commissioner for Refugees
Union of Soviet Socialist Republics (USSR). *See* Soviet Union
United Church of Christ, 135
United Farm Workers (UFW), 53, 63, 149
United Jewish Communities, 136
United Kingdom. *See* Great Britain
United Methodist Church, 135–136
United Methodist Committee on Relief, 132
United Nations
    Development Program, 192
    High Commissioner for Refugees, 82, 85, 86, 138, 149, 152, 153, 186, 187, 189, 191
    Humanitarian Evacuation Programme, 186
    International Convention on the Protection of the Rights of All Migrant Workers and Members of Their Families, 169
    migration issues, 149
    peacekeeping, 185, 188–189
    Refugee Convention (1951), 187
    sanctions on Haiti, 83
    Security Council, 187, 188, 189
United States
    advantages of immigration, 80
    aid to Afghanistan, 190–192
    approval of requests for asylum/refuge, 87, 186, 188

assimilation and Americanization, 91–92
border security, 101–103
changing demographics, 5–6
as core receiving region, 178
donations for refugees, 187
educational factors, 42
ethnic issues, 6, 186
farmworkers, 51
foreign-born citizens, 37
freedoms of, 4
global security and, 186
international view of, 81
limitations on admissions, 39
migration issues, 92–93, 152
as a nation of immigrants, 1, 92–93
overseas resettlement programs, 84
population, 3, 8–9, 21, 45, 50, 158
repatriation agreements, 128
role in international law, policy, and politics, 122, 187–189, 192–193
spending on food, 54
terrorist attacks on, 100–111
United States Catholic Conference (USCC), 63–64, 139, 140
Universal Declaration of Human Rights, 149
University of Texas at Austin, 13
Unz, Ronald K., 94
Urban areas, 172–173
Urban Institute, 5, 41, 134–135
U.S. Agency for International Development (USAID), 124, 189, 192
USA Patriot Act of 2001, 73, 103, 104, 108–109
U.S. Border Patrol. *See* Border Patrol, U.S.
U.S.-Canada Free Trade Agreement (1989), 162
USCC. *See* United States Catholic Conference
U.S. Census and Census Bureau, 5, 46

U.S. Commission for the Study of International Migration and Economic Development, 166
U.S. Commission on Immigration Reform (CIR), 38, 106, 126–127
U.S. Committee for Refugees (USCR), 132–133, 137
USCR. *See* U.S. Committee for Refugees
U.S.-Cuban Migration Agreement (1994), 96
U.S.-Mexico Bilateral Framework Agreement on Trade and Investment, 166
U.S.-Mexico Binational Study, 172
U.S.-Mexico Joint Communiqué (2001), 263–267
U.S.-Mexico Migration Panel, 170
U.S. National Organization of Credit Unions, 173
U.S. Sentencing Commission, 64–65
USSR (Union of Soviet Socialist Republics). *See* Soviet Union
U.S. trade representative, 125
Utah, 74
Uzbekistan, 191

Vargas, Arturo, 61, 97
Vidalia, Georgia, 10
Vietnam, 51, 68, 81, 84, 85, 86, 128
Villaraigosa, Antonio, 98, 99
Visas. *See also* Immigration and Naturalization Service (INS)
    abuse of the system, 16
    amnesty and, 64
    application for permanent status and, 39
    background checks for, 104
    for Canadian immigration, 163
    for Cuban immigration, 96
    employment-related visas (green cards), 22, 36, 39, 52, 57, 95
    in Europe, 180, 183
    family reunification and, 22, 32, 81

H-1B (temporary skilled), 6, 12,
 15–16, 31, 33, 34, 55–58, 133,
 145, 146, 148
H-2A (temporary agricultural),
 47–55, 147
 under Immigration Act of
 1990, 20
 limitations, 39
 for Mexican immigration,
 163
 nonimmigrant categories,
 48–49t
 S ("snitch")-visas, 109
 student visas, 104
 temporary, 39, 46, 163
 temporary protection status,
 86
 of terrorists, 70, 100, 104
 overstays, 12, 45, 70, 73

Wages. *See* Employment issues
War, 150. *See also individual wars*
Ward, David, 105
Washington Post, 92
Washington state, 53
Welfare, 62, 79, 80
West Virginia, 45
Wilson, Pete, 59, 60
Windsor (Ontario, Canada),
 72–73
Women's issues, 176
"Workforce 2000" report (Hud-
 son Institute), 55
Working Group on Migration and
 Consular Affairs, 166, 169
World Bank, 192
World Food Program, 191
World systems theory. *See* Theo-
 retical issues

World War II, 17, 47, 149, 153, 185
Worry, Michael, 12, 15
Wozniack, Steven, 57
Wunsch, Jon, 52

Yugoslavia, 20, 86, 184–185,
 186

Zadvydas, Kestutis, 68–69
Zadvydas v. Davis (2001), 68–69,
 128, 268–272
Zaire, 189
Zamora, Rodolfo Garcia, 171
Zedillo, Ernesto, 169
 administration of, 168,
 169
Zigler, James, 107, 124
Zimbabwe, 32
Zogby, James, 141